Brave New Bass

Edited by Chris Jisi

INTERVIEWS
& LESSONS
WITH THE
INNOVATORS,
TRENDSETTERS
& VISIONARIES

Backbeat
Books
San Francisco

Published by Backbeat Books
600 Harrison Street, San Francisco, CA 94107
www.backbeatbooks.com
email: books@musicplayer.com

An imprint of the Music Player Network
Publishers of *Guitar Player*, *Bass Player*, *Keyboard*, and other magazines
United Entertainment Media, Inc.
A CMP Information company

CMP
United Business Media

Distributed to the book trade in the US and Canada by
Publishers Group West, 1700 Fourth Street, Berkeley, CA 94710

Distributed to the music trade in the US and Canada by
Hal Leonard Publishing, P.O. Box 13819, Milwaukee, WI 53213

Text design and composition by Chris Ledgerwood
Music engraving by Elizabeth Ledgerwood
Cover design and back cover photo by Paul Haggard
Front cover photo by Jeroen Bos

Library of Congress Cataloging-in-Publication Data

Brave new bass : interviews & lessons with the innovators, trendsetters
& visionaries / [compiled] by Chris Jisi.
      p. cm.
Includes bibliographical and discographical references and index.
  ISBN 0-87930-763-3 (alk. paper)
1. Bass guitarists—Interviews. 2. Bass guitar. 3. Bass guitar—Instruction and study.
I. Jisi, Chris, 1959–

ML399.B67 2003
787.87'092'2—dc22

                                                                    2003052392

Printed in the United States of America

03 04 05 06 07   5 4 3 2 1

Table of Contents

Dedication

To James Jamerson and Jaco Pastorius for boldly pursuing
their visions and in the process giving the bass guitar
a heart, soul, and mind.

And to Joan Walker,
whose love, support, and inspiration
makes being a bass player the greatest job in the world.

Foreword
An Appreciation

"We'd like to do an interview."

THESE WORDS, spoken for the first time, are likely a major event for the majority of players. No matter how numerous such calls eventually become, the first one represents a conspicuous graduation; an elevation of stature: Your mates may respect you, audiences may be showing more and more attention, but now "the world wants to know." What will "the world" ask? What if the questions get too personal? Too technical?

My personal experience being interviewed—by now extensive—has always been and remains stressful. I always feel, after the fact, that at least some of the questions were poorly conceived, that the information to be elicited was irrelevant or perfunctory.

Hence this appreciation for Chris Jisi. His double interview of me in the first and second issues of *Bass Player* remain, in my mind, a revelation. Only my interviews for Japan's *Bass Magazine* have been of comparable quality, and for the same reasons—the skill, sensitivity, and intelligence of the interviewer. These characteristics alone, however, do not go far enough to explain Chris's skills.

The *Bass Player* interview in question took many hours over more than two days and wandered over a great many biographical- and career-related areas. The good interviewer is able to manage the subject's often stream-of-consciousness outbursts, rephrasings, on-the-fly corrections, and outright ramblings. Needless to say, asking the right questions is crucial and, sadly, many have a formulaic, even banal approach. ("This is a bass player. I ask these questions of bass players.") But Chris emphatically directed me with I'm-glad-you-asked-that questions. (And there was much rambling/chopping later on, let me tell you.)

A final point that explains the skill of Mr. Jisi is his status as a working bass player of considerable experience. Better trained than many of those he interviews, he brings an understanding and camaraderie to the process, and thereby offers a resource to the subject.

This appreciation is clearly personal, and I do not claim that anyone else agrees with my thoughts on Chris or the exigencies of the interview process. But since this is my dime—and also since Chris will never say anything about himself—I am grateful for the chance to put something in the record for him.

Thank you for your support and encouragement all these years, my friend.

— *Anthony Jackson*

Introduction

THERE ARE THOSE WHO MAINTAIN that the revolutionary musical concepts set forth in the '60s didn't fully flourish until the '70s and beyond. Likewise, electric bass guitar concepts simmered with the input of '60s pioneers and '70s radicals before finally boiling over in a bountiful wave of well-informed interpreters during the '80s and '90s. This book is about the players in that movement—a talented lot who forever dispelled the notion that the electric bass is a second-class instrument. As Stanley Clarke, bass's most eminent emancipator, told me in his March 2003 *Bass Player* cover story, "The work is finished; I feel like renting a billboard announcing THE BASS HAS BEEN LIBERATED!" In addition to securing their instrument's status, these players collectively spread their artistry into all corners of contemporary music, from the top of the charts to the underground fringe, in almost every conceivable style and genre.

The eight chapters herein provide an in-depth look at 30 of the important post-Jaco/Stanley pluckers (several of whom are peers of that dynamic duo). Drawn from *Bass Player* interviews, each profile provides detailed background information, insights into each player's artistry, private-lesson-style analysis with music notation and tablature, and a roundup of relevant equipment. In all, it's just about everything you young, eight-hour-a-day woodshedders could ask for. But what about you average working-Joe and -Jane bass players, to whom the skills of this chops-laden, solo-ready, low-end elite may seem out of reach? Don't be misled by the title; each player profiled is a fanatic about laying down the groove and serving the song. Their early experiences as developing musicians will ring with familiarity and bring a smile to your face, and their seemingly stratospheric technical advances, when broken down and examined step-by-step, will make musical sense and allow you to apply similar concepts to your own style.

Of course, there are numerous "brave new bassists" who aren't included in this book, due mostly to space limitations: from session vets Lee Sklar and Jimmy Johnson to fusion figureheads like Mark Egan, Gerald Veasley, and Alain Caron to slap-and-tap terrors such as Stu Hamm, T.M. Stevens, and Bill Dickens. Not to mention the global bass forces of Latin, African, and other descents. The good news is that there are enough forward-thinking thumpers—both established and emerging—to fill several more editions. In the meantime, putting this tome together confirmed for me how fortunate I feel to have helped chronicle the history of what Marcus Miller calls "the coolest instrument in the band," and in the process, perhaps help inspire the next round of innovators, trendsetters, and visionaries. Bottom's up!

CHAPTER 1

Millennium Masters
MARCUS MILLER • ANTHONY JACKSON
JOHN PATITUCCI • VICTOR WOOTEN

In the final two decades of the 20th century, four dominant bass guitarists elevated the instrument and their own artistry to the level of such pioneering giants as James Jamerson, Larry Graham, Stanley Clarke, and Jaco Pastorius. And as the third millennium was beginning, the latter-day quartet showed no signs of letting up.

MARCUS MILLER
Blueprint Bassist

Interviewed by Chris Jisi, October 1992, September/October 1995, April 1998, and June 2001.

AT THE DAWN OF THE '80s, Marcus Miller—then a 21-year-old studio-bass phenom—told an interviewer: "I know there are a lot of people who would love to be studio bassists, and I'm very fortunate. But for it to happen so fast lets me know there must be some place further to go." Prophetic words.

Since then, Miller's career has been a blueprint for bassists. As a player, he parlayed his session-gained versatility into a deep mastery of the pocket. Fans dubbed him "The Thumbslinger" for his cutting-edge slap style, while music critics—impressed with his expressive vocal-like melodies and solos—hailed his "trademark talking bass." After honing his playing and composing skills throughout the '80s, most significantly with David Sanborn, Luther Vandross, and especially Miles Davis, in the '90s Miller began to focus on his solo-artist side. Through five subsequent albums — including 2001's

Marcus Miller

Grammy-winning *M2*—his instantly recognizable playing *and* writing voices have firmly established him as the most important bassist-composer-leader since Jaco Pastorius.

Equally crucial to Miller's role-model status is his longstanding commitment to becoming a complete musician. As a result, his much-sought-after skills as a composer, producer, arranger, and multi-instrumentalist in the pop, R&B, funk, jazz, and film-scoring fields have earned him studio moguldom comparisons to Prince and Quincy Jones.

Marcus Miller was born in Brooklyn, New York, on June 14, 1959, and raised in Rochdale Village, in the Jamaica section of Queens. His initial enchantment with music began in church, where his father, an organist, performed everything from classical music to gospel. Marcus acquired a taste for jazz after hearing pianist Wynton Kelly, a second cousin best known for his work with Miles Davis. Inspired by what he heard, Marcus began singing and at age ten took up the clarinet. Soon after, the pop sounds of such artists as Kool & the Gang, Stevie Wonder, the Jackson 5, and Isaac Hayes started to draw his attention. With little chance of getting into a local band as a clarinetist, he tried saxophone and organ before latching onto the bass at age 13. With help from his parents, he bought a semi-hollowbody Univox bass before moving on to his first Fender Jazz Bass.

While Miller's aptitude on clarinet gained him entry into New York City's prestigious High School of Music & Art and then Queens College, his attitude on bass landed him his first pro gigs with such local talent as Harlem River Drive and keyboardist Lonnie Liston Smith. Still a teenager, he made his first recording with flutist Bobbi Humphrey (*Individuals*) and went on the road with a fellow "Jamaica boy," drummer Lenny White. When Marcus returned, drummer Buddy Williams (his section-mate in Humphrey's band), got him an audition for the *Saturday Night Live* band. There he met Sanborn, who integrated the bassist into his *Voyeur* album and subsequent tours. Miller soon began to get calls for jingle and record dates, and he joined Roberta Flack's band, where he met a backup singer named Luther Vandross. By the time Miles Davis called in 1981, the music world seemed to be unanimously acknowledging that it was, indeed, Miller Time.

Your first two solo albums were in 1983 and 1984. Why did you wait eight years to do another one?

I wanted to make a bass album all along, but I didn't have the compositional skills early on. Soundwise, it's hard to put things under a bass, and the material has to be very strong to make the whole concept work. My first two albums were basically vocal-oriented R&B on which I got to co-produce and play all of the instruments myself. That was invaluable because it helped to launch my producing career, but after the second one I realized I hadn't found my own identity. Gradually, through working with Miles, Luther Vandross, and David Sanborn, I developed confidence. Finally, around 1990, I started thinking of compositions for a bass project, and the ideas came pretty fast. Then it was a matter of finding time and waiting for people to be available. The actual recording took about six months.

Why did you call it The Sun Don't Lie?

The message to listeners is that this album exposes the *real* me and my true musical direction. The message to myself is that I've finally reached a point as a writer and artist where I can let the sun shine on *me* without having to hide behind someone else's project. Right after I started recording, I was asked to put together a group for the Live Under the Sky concert series in Japan. That allowed me to work on material and solidify ideas for the album with a band that included Joe Sample, [vocalist] Lalah Hathaway, [drummer] Poogie Bell, [guitarist] Dean Brown, and [saxophonist] Everette Harp, all of whom appear on various tracks.

How did you get your start as a composer?

I used to watch my cousin, Denzil Miller, write for a local band we were in, Harlem River Drive, and I just assumed you weren't a complete musician unless you wrote your own material. Later, when I met

Sanborn in the *SNL* Band, I gave him a demo of some fusion tunes I'd written, and he asked to record them. Shortly afterward, I began writing vocal demos with Luther Vandross; he's so talented I was able to gain a lot of insight. What I always try to do when I write for another artist is see his face in my mind. If I can envision him moving to the music, then I know it's appropriate. It was difficult trying to use that method for my songs on this album [*The Sun Don't Lie*], though, since it's hard to get an objective view of yourself.

The melody on the opening track, "Panther," reminds me of Stanley Clarke.

I tried playing it with my thumb, and when I switched to my fingers for a bit more articulation and speed, the sound paled in comparison. I knew the only way to combine both approaches was to move my fingers closer to the neck and pluck very hard to get that popping sound. I wasn't trying to sound like Stanley, but he was certainly an important influence. At the time, to hear a young black musician come out of nowhere with such amazing technique and that aggressive bass-in-your-face sound was an inspiration.

What other bassists had an impact on you?

Robert "Kool" Bell, James Jamerson, Rocco Prestia, and all the Jacksons—Jermaine, Paul, and Anthony. I got into slapping through Larry Graham during his Graham Central Station period. In my neighborhood, if you couldn't play like Larry, you might as well put the bass down. We used to have slap competitions on a little cafeteria stage in high school to attract girls. When fusion hit and piqued my interest, I was fortunate to have a friend, [drummer] Kenny Washington, who sat me down and played me the history of jazz, which put things in perspective. That got me into upright players like Paul Chambers, Sam Jones, Ron Carter, and Eddie Gomez. Then Jaco came out and blew my mind. He had it all covered; I left his first album [*Jaco Pastorius*] on my turntable for two years and learned every solo note for note. But without a true knowledge of harmony, I had no idea what the notes meant. Jaco's playing and writing were like a wake-up call; it led me to study bebop, which really got my harmony together.

The MARCUS MILLER Sound

Over 25 years after he first plucked it, Marcus Miller's 1977 Fender Jazz Bass has become as celebrated as McCartney's Hofner Beatle Bass, Jamerson's "Funk Machine" P-Bass, or Jaco's "Bass of Doom" J-Bass. It's the key to the Marcus Miller sound. The instrument features a natural finish, ash body, maple neck, stock pickups, a Badass II bridge, and Sadowsky-modified onboard preamps (originally a Stars Guitar preamp that was destroyed by a direct box surge at Media Sound Studios in 1983. At that time Sadowsky replaced it with a Bartolini TCT preamp). In 1992 Marcus noted, "People describe my sound as being very bright, but what they don't realize is that they're also hearing clarity and punch over the full tone range." Other basses Miller has strapped on include his signature 4- and 5-string Fender Jazz Basses, a fretless Fodera Emperor 5-string, Sadowsky fretted and fretless 4- and 5-strings, a '66 Jazz Bass, a 5-string F Bass, and a Modulus 6-string. His main upright is a '30s Kay, his backup a German-made Morelli. For strings he prefers either DR Marcus Miller Signature Fat Beams (which, he says, have a more pronounced midrange) or DR Hi-Beams (both gauged .045, .065, .080, .105, .130).

After choosing SWR amps for years (including SM-900 heads, 4x10 Goliath cabinets, and Redhead combos), Miller switched to EBS gear around 2000, employing two EBS HD350 heads and two EBS-410 cabinets. His effects, which are run through Custom Audio Electronics controllers, include an EBS Octabass, an Ernie Ball stereo volume pedal, a Dunlop GCB-535Q Cry Baby Multi-Wah pedal, a Vintage Mu-Tron III+, a Boss FZ-3 Fuzz, a Boss BF-2 Flanger, an Empirical Labs Distressor EL8 compressor/limiter, a Lexicon MPX-1 multi-effect, an MXR Phase 90, and a Boss TU-2 Tuner. His studio gear includes a Demeter VTDB-2 tube DI and Aguilar DB680 and DB924 preamps.

"Steveland" is a moving, melodic tribute to Stevie Wonder, again featuring a plucked bass melody. Are you also tapping in the introduction?

Yes. I used my right index finger and two left-hand fingers to tap and hammer a little passage up on the G string of my Jazz Bass. That's a technique I picked up from [guitarist] Hiram Bullock. There's also a Stevie-ish Wurlitzer bass line on the bottom; he's such a huge influence on anyone who writes, plays, or sings. I think the more you listen to the melodies and the mood of the solos played by Wayne Shorter, Jonathan Butler, and David Sanborn, the more Stevie comes across on the track.

On "Juju," you combined sequenced bass with real bass, which is something you've often done with Luther Vandross and on other commercial projects. What's your take on synth bass?

It doesn't really bother me; I view it as a separate sound from electric bass, which is why I combine the two a lot. It's the same with drums: I like to program whatever feels good into a drum machine and then combine that with a real drummer. The two together are interesting and reflect what's happening these days. But everything goes in cycles, and the trend toward real bass will come back. I've been trying to create keyboard-bass sounds with my basses; that's what I was going for when I overdubbed the 5-string F Bass, played with a pick, on "Funny."

"Funny" and your cover of "Ain't No Sunshine" feature your lead vocals. As a producer who has worked with so many singers, do you find yourself monitoring your own voice as you sing, or do you just go for it?

I just go for a take; then I listen back and maybe fix something. I wrote "Funny" with Boz Scaggs for his album *Other Roads*; after I performed it in Japan, I decided to record it. "Ain't No Sunshine" was the first song I ever played on bass in front of an audience. I used to sing it at the end of the Jamaica Boys concerts, and I also sang it in Japan. It's really just an excuse for drum and bass solos.

You used to play Jaco's "Teen Town" slap-style as a lead-in to the commercial breaks on David Sanborn's Night Music *show. Were you aware of the buzz you were creating among bassists?*

Yes, and that's why I included "Teen Town" on the album. I wanted to cut it live, since the focus is on the energy and musicianship. You should have seen the studio that day: There were drums everywhere for Omar Hakim, Steve Ferrone, Andy Narrell, Don Alias, and Paulinho Da Costa. We stuck to the original arrangement, except we opened it up in the middle for Hiram Bullock's solo, which is where I switched to fingers.

As a slapper, you've developed a reputation for having a clear sound and for using mostly your thumb with only the occasional pop.

I strike the strings right in front of the chrome neck-pickup cover, not at the bottom of the neck where you get all the overtones. A lot of times I don't pluck [pop] at all. That developed during my jingle days, because I found that using my thumb was the best way to hear the bass coming out of a tiny TV speaker. Plus, if you use two alternating fingers, as I do when I play fingerstyle, there's always a strong note followed by a weak one; with the thumb, every note is strong. That became really important when I started doubling sequenced keyboard-bass parts. Then I began challenging myself to see if I could develop the speed to play entire charts using only my thumb. I still add plucks whenever they're necessary, as they were on "Teen Town." But I think a lot of players tend to overuse them. The plucks are just accents, afterthoughts—the funk is in the thumb.

Your muting technique surfaces throughout The Sun Don't Lie *and figures prominently on David Sanborn's latest disc,* Upfront.

That started when I was 21 and playing in Ralph MacDonald's rhythm section with Steve Gadd, Richard Tee, and Eric Gale, doing jingles and backing people like Grover Washington Jr. and Sadao Watanabe. Eric doubled on electric bass before me, and one day Ralph put on a track they'd done and said, "C'mere kid. Here's what a bass should sound like." I imitated it and he was thrilled. The way I do it is by muting the strings with my right palm near the bridge and plucking with my thumb. Sometimes I'll use a pick if I want more speed. You can also get a decent upright sound with muting.

Tell me about your left-hand technique, especially with regard to intonation on the fretless.

Playing a 4-string requires a lot of hand-position changes; fortunately, studying bebop helped me to get up and down the neck. I'm basically a one-finger-per-fret guy. As far as the fretless goes, it's important to stick with one instrument and find where the pressure points on your fingers are in relation to the notes on the neck. Beyond that, you just have to keep putting in time, really using your ears. I'll check myself with open strings, but it's always a battle—especially when you play with other instruments that use tempered tunings, like keyboards.

On the bebop middle section of your tribute to Miles, "The King Is Gone," you play the first chorus of your fretless solo muted, almost as if you're paying tribute to Paul Chambers as well.

That's right. For me, *the* bass player with Miles was Paul Chambers, especially at a tempo like the one on this tune. People think of him mainly as a groovemaster, but check out his bowed solo on "Moment's Notice" [on John Coltrane's *Blue Train*]. Coltrane handed him the changes and they recorded it! He's *the* cat as far as I'm concerned. He doesn't get his due.

How would you sum up your relationship with Miles?

Miles was like a musical father to me. In 1980 I was booked to play on a session for him, but he never showed up. A year later, during a country date, I got a note saying, "Call Miles." He answered the phone and asked me to meet him at CBS Studios in an hour. I went in and introduced myself and played with everybody for a while without much being said. When we were finished, he asked me to join his band. Early on he occasionally gave me a hard time, but he was always very supportive and proud of my session career. He used to tell his girlfriend, "This is Marcus Miller. He drives a BMW." Eventually, as we grew together musically, he placed entire projects in my hands, which was incredibly scary yet extremely encouraging. In retrospect, I would say that my bass style solidified on *The Man with the Horn,* and my composing took giant strides beginning with *Tutu.*

When you talk to young players, do you stress the importance of playing grooves?

No. Telling young players they have to play grooves is like telling painters they have to use blue. You have to encourage beginners to do whatever turns them on, because that's what they're going to do best. When they get a bit older, you can tell them the realities of the music business—that there are more opportunities to work if they learn to function as a bass player. The important thing is to listen to as much music as possible. The young ear is naturally drawn to the high frequencies played by solo bassists, but if you listen to a lot of groove players, you'll get caught up in that as well. Ultimately, you should be able to lay down the baddest groove *and* blow the hottest solo.

When I spoke to Marcus three years later, the solo side of his career was well established, culminating in the release of Tales. *Filled with spoken-word interludes, the disc drew its cohesiveness from the use of Miller's road band throughout, and fewer (but potent) guests such as Joshua Redman and Me'Shell NdegéOcello.*

How did you come up with the storytelling concept?

I knew I wanted to incorporate some elements of rap, including the beat, but I wanted to keep the disc's focus instrumental. So I thought, How else can I use words, and what voices are important to me? Then I realized that what I remember most are the stories older musicians have told me through the years—between sets, or between takes in the studio, or on tour buses. A lot of players would tune them out, but I was always very interested because there's so much to learn by hearing about the lives these musicians led.

In addition to the voices, I was struck by the '70s R&B/soul flavor throughout.

In many ways the '70s, of which I'm a product, were the transition period between what's happening today and the music of the '40s and '50s—so it seemed to be a natural ingredient. Also, because that's the sound I grew up on, I felt very comfortable using it. I didn't want to stay in an area I wasn't totally familiar with, like jazz or rap. I even broke out my old Minimoog synthesizer.

You've credited much of your writing influence to Herbie Hancock's Speak Like a Child.

Yes—that one and his other '60s albums, as well as *Head Hunters* from the '70s. They all have intriguing harmonies and colors, with intangible chords you can't really name. For me, harmony is the most interesting part of composing, because of the many different ways you can make people feel with it. It gives the music dimension. I've been working with Wayne Shorter on a project that includes orchestral instruments, and he's opened up a whole other harmonic sensibility to me.

Both "The Blues" and "Tales" confirm the album's stylistic ties to The Sun Don't Lie.

That's intentional, up to a point. For instance, [trumpeter] Patches Stewart and I talked about moving away from the Miles-style muted-trumpet sound eventually, but we weren't ready yet [*laughs*]. The trick is not to deny your roots or your musical identity, yet continue to grow each time out.

Your relationship with Miles is warmly reflected on the fretless ballad "True Geminis," which features a spoken intro and outro by Miles himself.

Marcus Miller Selected Discography

Solo albums: *The Ozell Tapes*, www.marcusmiller.com; *M2*, 3 Deuces; *Live & More*, PRA/GRP; *Tales*, PRA; *The Sun Don't Lie*, PRA; *Marcus Miller*, Warner Bros.; *Suddenly*, Warner Bros. **With the Jaco Pastorius Big Band:** *Word of Mouth Revisited*, Heads Up. **With Jamaica Boys:** (both on Reprise) *J Boys*; *The Jamaica Boys*. **With Miles Davis:** (on Warner Bros.) *Amandla*; *Music from Siesta*; *Tutu*; (on Columbia) *Star People*; *Man with the Horn*; *We Want Miles*. **With David Sanborn:** (on Elektra) *Inside*, *Hearsay*, *Upfront*, *Close-up*, Reprise; (on Warner Bros.) *A Change of Heart*; *Straight to the Heart*; *As We Speak*; *Voyeur*. **With Luther Vandross:** (all on Epic, except where noted) *Dance with My Father*, J-Records; *I Know*, Virgin; *Never Let Me Go*; *Power of Love*; *The Night I Fell in Love*, *Never Too Much*. **With Donald Fagen:** *The Nightfly*, Warner Bros. **With Wayne Shorter:** *High Life*, Verve. **With Grover Washington Jr.:** *Winelight*, Elektra. **With Jason Miles:** (both on Telarc) *Love Affair: The Music of Ivan Lins*; *Celebrating the Music of Weather Report*. **With Lenny White:** *Streamline*, Elektra. **With Joe Sample:** *Ashes to Ashes*, Warner Bros. **With the** Brecker Brothers: *Straphangin'*, Arista. **With Don Grolnick:** *Hearts and Numbers*, Windham Hill. **With Aretha Franklin:** *Jump to It*, Arista. **With Roberta Flack & Peabo Bryson:** *Born to Love*, Capitol. **With Paul Simon:** *Hearts and Bones*, Warner Bros. **With Bryan Ferry:** *Boys and Girls*, Warner Bros. **With Scritti Politti:** *Cupid & Psyche '85*, Warner Bros. **With Take 6:** *Beautiful World*, Warner Bros. **With Al Jarreau:** *Tenderness*, Warner Bros. **With Dean Brown:** *Here*, ESC. **With McCoy Tyner and Jackie McLean:** *It's About Time*, Blue Note. **With Was (Not Was):** *What Up, Dog?*, Chrysalis. **With Frank Sinatra:** *L.A. Is My Lady*, Qwest. **With Whitney Houston:** *Whitney*, Arista. **With Mariah Carey:** *Mariah Carey*, Sony. **With Chaka Khan:** *The Woman I Am*, Warner Bros. **With Kenny Garrett:** *Happy People*, Warner Bros. **With Urszula Dudziak:** *Future Talk*, Inner City. **With various artists:** *Who Loves You/Tribute to Jaco Pastorius*, Concord. **Soundtracks:** *Serving Sara*; *The Brothers*; *Two Can Play That Game*; *Trumpet of the Swan*; *Ladies Man*; *An American Love Story* (for PBS); *The Sixth Man*; *Great White Hype*; *Above the Rim*; *Low Down Dirty Shame*; *Boomerang*; *House Party*; *Siesta*.

That was a melody I'd had in my head for a while; the title comes from Miles's quote at the end, where he says he's a true Gemini because he can't remember something after playing it. He says, "When I hear it, it's like I'm another person."

How did you hook up with Me'Shell NdegéOcello for "Rush Over"?

I prefer hip-hop music that has some depth, which is why I love Me'Shell's work. I called her and asked her to finish some ideas I had put on tape, and it worked out well. I told her to bring her bass, but she brought a clavinet [keyboard] instead and played the solo on it. She also wrote and sang the lyrics and found a melody that allowed the bass to come through.

What's the origin of the short tapped piece, "Running Through My Dreams (Interlude)"?

I was trying to tap through some harmonies you don't usually hear in tapped-bass pieces. We ended up recording it and using it as a lead-in to "Ethiopia."

What effects did you use during the unison bass/vocal solos on "Infatuation"?

I used both a talk box, which has a tube [connected to a speaker] you put in your mouth, as well as some other effects to simulate that sound. The song was put together much like "Rush Over": I gave Lalah Hathaway the basic track, and she added the lyrics and vocals.

How does your commitment to being a solo artist affect your schedule?

For me it's all about balance. I love being in the studio making records, but that wouldn't be enough. I love being onstage playing, but that wouldn't be enough. And I love scoring movies, but *that* wouldn't be enough. I try to maintain a balance, because each situation helps all the others. The precision of the studio helps me when I play live; then I'll come off the road with a lot of inspiration to take into the studio—or I'll come out of a movie score with new colors I otherwise wouldn't have found. The cool thing about having a solo career is that I have a place to experiment and apply everything.

Do you ever worry about spreading yourself too thin?

Never. For me, the main purpose of any art is to reflect what's going on in the artist's life. If it's done honestly, people are able to contrast their own lives with it, sort of like a mirror. I believe music should capture the world in which it was created. Years from now, I want my music to reflect what's happening now, while also capturing the history that came before it. A lot of people worry about their creativity running dry, but to me, as long as you're living and observing and experiencing life, you'll always have music coming out of you.

Three years later Marcus released the live album Live & More. *In his interview he offered tips on live sound.*

What made you decide to release a live CD?

I was really happy with how we were sounding. Over the course of several tours I realized I should document the music before the inevitable happened and everyone decided to go their separate ways.

What was your live setup?

I played my '77 Jazz Bass on the entire album, although I picked up my fretless Sadowsky 5-string during "Funny." I changed my strings, which are DR H-Beams, every five days or so. My rig was an SWR SM-350—which served as the preamp—and an SWR SM-400 for the power. They sat on two stacked Goliath 4x10 cabinets. I also used a Boss OC-2 octave pedal, a Mu-Tron III+, and a DigiTech RP10 multi-effects for reverb, delay, and distortion. It's really a guitar processor and it took a toll on my bass sound, but at the time I was too lazy to check out bass processors.

How were your basses recorded on the live tracks?

Direct into the ADATs via an ADL tube direct box. My fretted and fretless went into separately EQ'd modules. I didn't mic my rig because I didn't want to have to worry about it. I knew I could EQ the bass later or run the signal through an amp to make it beefier, although we didn't end up doing that. The sound from my amp was picked up by the horn mics, so I turned up those at various points while we were mixing because I dug what it added to the bass sound. We also added some compression later in the mix. I was most concerned with capturing the band sound and vibe as a whole, and focusing on things like feel and performance.

How do you make sure you're hearing the right bass sound onstage?

It comes down to the monitor system, because I'm usually standing up front at the center of the stage. My amp, which is offstage right, is there to add volume and presence and to fill out the low end the monitors lack. If I turn it up too loud, though, the band complains that they can't hear anything *but* bass. The best sound I've gotten is when I've had first-rate monitors in front of me—then I feel good. With great monitors I can also put the whole band in my mix. When the monitors are less than great, I'll just put in whatever I can't hear onstage: usually kick and hi-hat and maybe some keyboards. For my solos I have the soundman ride my bass in the monitor mix, because if I can't clearly hear what I'm playing I start hitting too hard. A lot of times I'll walk back in front of my amp so I can really hear and feel what I'm doing.

In your liner notes you mention how much the music changed and evolved on the road.

That was the main reason I wanted to record the band. I've been in groups where the music evolved, and then it got worse because the musicians had played it so often they started to become self-indulgent and ignore important aspects of the original compositions. Everyone in this group is very sensitive to and respectful of the music, which enabled them to express themselves within the context of the band sound. We continually found new ways to interpret and explore these songs. Each night a different band member would have something new to say. It became like a game of hoops: When someone was hot, we would go to him. And because we were doing as much refining and improving as stretching, we often didn't realize how much the music was growing until we listened back to a tape from one of the previous year's tours.

That would explain how "Funny," originally a vocal pop tune you wrote with Boz Scaggs, is transformed into a 13-minute epic with whole new sections and fretted and fretless bass solos.

Yeah, that track really typifies the concept of the band and the album. "Funny" turned into a whole other song on tour. In fact, the take on the album was still going when we faded it. That was one of those nights when we pretty much played one tune for the entire set! Even though I had already taken a solo, I went back and picked up the fretless after being inspired by Patches Stewart's beautiful trumpet solo.

In your first solo you break out all of your techniques: plucking, slapping, muting, tapping, and perhaps even your overhand slapping. How did that technique come about?

Actually, I think all of those techniques are in there *except* the overhand slapping, although there's a photo of me doing it on the CD jacket. That started back when I was playing R&B clubs in the '70s. The people there weren't really into the music, so I figured I'd give them something to look at. When I got my band together I started finding musical ways to apply it. My original concept was to use both thumbs, but the left thumb is just too far from the pickups. To compensate I brought my left hand over the top of the neck; I found I could get more power and create a sound that's more balanced with my right-hand attack. Now when I use it either I'll bring both arms over the neck and pat the strings like a drum, or I'll use my left fingers overhand in conjunction with right-hand slaps. In both cases the bottom knuckles of my left-hand fingers are striking the *E* string, while the rest of my fingers hit and mute the top three strings.

You sing lead on "Funny"; how do you approach singing while playing bass?

The best way to develop your singing and playing skills is just to do it a lot. You need to learn one part by heart so you don't have to think about it; that's usually the bass part. Once you get that going, the top-and-bottom relationship will feel very natural. That is, until you try singing behind the beat; that can really screw things up!

Your original version of "Panther" from The Sun Don't Lie *has multiple bass, keyboard, and guitar parts. How did you recreate it live?*

The key is to not worry about making it sound like the album as much as taking the essence and recreating that. For example, when the groove begins on "Panther," Bernard Wright was covering the bass on keyboard, and Hiram was playing the rhythm guitar part. So I grabbed the guitar countermelody. One thing I never worry about is the bottom, because Bernard plays seriously heavy keyboard bass. We grew up together, so even though I try not to play the same thing every night, there's really not anything I can do that he doesn't anticipate. Often I'll come to the end of a phrase and he'll complete it for me! [Drummer] Poogie Bell has that mind-lock with me, too.

Your muting approach differs slightly when you use it in an acoustic jazz, R&B, or hip-hop context. Is that something you're conscious of?

I never really think about varying my technique, but subconsciously I do play the notes differently. Essentially, a note on the electric bass lasts too long, so it doesn't have any thump. If you can get it to die out, either by slapping or muting, you give it a whole new character. I mute the strings with my palm and pluck with my thumb. Over the years I've been able to incorporate my first two fingers in order to play faster, but I like muting because it prevents you from moving *too* quickly. You have to play more simple and solid and choose better notes.

"Sophie" exemplifies the way you write in minor keys without sounding overly dark or melancholy.

I write a lot in minor, but the melodies usually hang out in the relative major. Another way to look at it is writing in major keys with the bass a minor 3rd below. The minor bottom adds a little darkness and a bit more depth and keeps things from sounding too damn happy. Lately, though, I've been getting into using more major triads; when you contrast them with complex chords, the added colors are really welcome.

On "Strange Fruit"—which features your bass clarinet—and "Maputo" you don't play bass at all.

I wanted to give a sense of one of our shows, and that usually includes me picking up the bass clarinet at some point. For me, hearing bass guitar all night is kind of hard to take—no matter how well it's played.

In keeping with what seems to have become a three-year cycle, I spoke to Marcus in 2001 about M2—*at that point, his first studio album in seven years. It featured such guests as Herbie Hancock, Wayne Shorter, Chaka Khan, Raphael Saadiq, Branford Marsalis, and the JB Horns' Maceo Parker and Fred Wesley:*

The opener, "Power," and "Cousin John" stand out as potential bass anthems. Are you slapping or hard-plucking?

I slapped both. "Power" is built around the opening bass lick. Someone told me recently, "Whenever you play, you sound hungry." I always think of that when I play this tune because it has that hungry, New York–rooted sound. The "Cousin John" bass line came out of jamming with Poogie, who played an interesting Latin/go-go kind of beat. The chord changes recall what we were doing with Miles in the mid-'80s *Amandla* period.

You subdivide your grooves and solos with percussive 16ths and triplets. What's your intent?

I think of them as almost an accompaniment to the main note. I don't really hear those fast notes as part of the bass line; it's more like filling lighter ones in between the strong notes or accents, so you get a sort of sub-conversation going on. It's similar to a rhythm guitar's offbeat strums or a drummer's hi-hat. When tempos slowed down in the '90s with hip-hop and rap, it really opened up those rhythmic possibilities for me.

Can you trace the influence of those in-between rhythms?

A key influence was Lenny White's snare drum, when I first started playing with him in the late '70s. He'd play the backbeat, and while I was waiting for the next backbeat he'd do all this dancing on the snare, kind of keeping the time in the spaces. Another early factor was having to solo in an environment where you could come to blows with a cat for messing with the groove! For my solo spots I tried to develop a way to play something fast and impressive—that showed I spent a lot of time with my instrument—yet not kill the groove. Something that would make people appreciate the solo and at the same time *feel* it. I was heavily into Stanley and Jaco, but if I was going to try playing all those notes and melodies I had to find a way to keep the pocket at the same time.

Your increased use of up-and-down thumb plucks, often called double-thumbing, seems to be a key to your hyper-rhythms.

I started messing with that in the '80s, but because I was mainly doing sessions everyone wanted uniformity of attack, and thumbing up and down is inherently uneven—with a stronger downbeat and a weaker, softer beat when you come back up. I got into it again when I heard Victor Wooten and some of the newer guys doing it. Like slapping, it's all in the wrist twist. I strike the strings with the fleshy top side of my thumb going down and a bit of the nail coming up. I use it more for soloing, because when you're trying to hold down a band it's not as effective as a heavy, full-thumb slap—although it can add a nice balance.

On "Power" and several other tracks, the rhythm-section groove drops out briefly.

Those are like hip-hop drops. The only way DJs can affect the music is to drop the whole beat out, since they can't stop just a hi-hat or a bass line. I'm simulating that. It works well because you really feel a lift when the beat comes back in.

A prominent color on M2 is your use of real stringed instruments, often playing sparse, open voicings.

I've been getting into strings lately from the movie scores I've done—particularly the warmer, lower strings like viola and cello. I thought about the strings on the CTI records I grew up with, from arrangers like Don Sebesky and Claus Ogerman. I tried to incorporate that sound but on a smaller scale—more like a string quartet, where you hear the rosin and the grain of individuals. I experimented with voicings on my sequencer and then brought in the real strings. Fortunately, I was able to find three very hip players. When we did "Red Baron" one of them said, "Oh, Billy Cobham, right?" They really got into playing the music, and that made a big difference.

For this album you use your Jazz Bass for many of the low-end parts you would normally assign to synth bass.

I've kind of come full circle. Lately I've preferred the tone and punch of the bass guitar down there. Synth bass still plays a role, like the burping sound on "Cousin John," which is from a Korg Triton. I've also been doubling my bass melodies at certain points, using a cello or my bass clarinet or just an effect such as vocoder. I like to find other colors to give the melody a unique sound.

You cover two jazz standards, "Lonnie's Lament" and "Goodbye Pork Pie Hat."

Coltrane wrote some really spiritual-sounding songs in the period between *Giant Steps* and *A Love Supreme*, and "Lonnie's Lament" is one of my favorites. I tried to give it a contemporary rhythmic flavor, mixed with a bit of organ-trio sound. As for Mingus, I never got to dig into his music as deeply as I should have, so I checked out some compilation CDs. "Pork Pie Hat," which he wrote about Lester Young, is a melody you just want to play. And since I wear that style of hat I liked the connection. What made this special for me was having one of my idols, Herbie Hancock, play piano to the backing tracks while I laid down the melody with my fretless Fodera. Toward the end of the take Herbie answers something I play, and we start trading ideas.

Your tune "3 Deuces" mines the same bop-meets-hip-hop vein.

I got the title from the famous club on 52nd Street in the '40s, and it's also the name of my new label. I told saxophonist James Carter to play as if he were at that club. The changes have a "Night in Tunisia" flavor, and he alludes to several bop heads in his solo. For the bass line/melody I palm-mute the strings while plucking with my thumb. Later, I contrast that with straight plucking, with the neck pickup backed off slightly to get some growly bite.

What's the story behind "Boomerang"?

After I did the score for the Eddie Murphy movie of the same name in '92, I received a lot of letters from people asking about the 20-second cue during the opening title credits. So I figured I'd take the opportunity to develop it into a whole tune, with lyrics and additional sections. I called Raphael Saadiq to sing it with me, having been a fan of his unique voice and his bass playing. There's an eight-bar loop that's a sample of my bass line on the original cue, which I played on a borrowed upright. Later in the track I introduce a groove on my Jazz Bass with some phase shifter added. The lead Jazz Bass track was most fun for me, because in addition to playing some of the melody and soloing, I got to comment and fill between the vocals.

What's the concept behind the three "Ozell" interludes?

CDs don't have sides like records or cassettes, which have a natural break in the material. To compensate, I added these interludes as "set changes" between songs. I used my fretless Fodera 5 with a lot of board reverb to get a swamp-bass kind of sound that's introduced in Part 1. In Part 2 I add the melody on tenor and bass clarinet, and in Part 3 Wayne Shorter improvises around the theme and brings it home.

The album's most ambitious tracks are "Burning Down the House" and "Red Baron."

We developed both of those on the road and then cut them live with my full band in the studio, plus Fred Wesley and Maceo Parker. I always liked the Talking Heads' "Burning," so I fleshed out some of the chords, which are very subtle on the original, and I hard-plucked the melody in unison with Hiram Bullock. When we got to the end of the track I put down my bass and went into the control room, and the band had been grooving so hard they wouldn't stop! I went back in and resumed playing. The take ended up being over ten minutes long. Once I saw how strong the foundation was, I figured it could sustain some offbeat ideas, so I added my harmonics solo and the eerie string breakdown that had everyone looking at me sideways. [*Laughs*].

"Red Baron" has a similarly striking brass breakdown.

As a teen I wore out Billy Cobham's classic album *Spectrum*. It occurred to me to cover "Red Baron" because it lends itself to my harmonic style. I wanted to capture how the song struck me as a kid, so I arranged it from memory rather than listening to it first. I slapped the melody but hard-plucked my solos.

You close with the traditional "Your Amazing Grace."

We've been playing it live for a while now, and people of all ages really respond. One reason is to be able to tell people how much I appreciate that they come to hear what I have to say with my instrument. Also, one of Christianity's most powerful concepts is that nobody is really good enough, no matter how good they are. The only way for you to be accepted by God is basically for Him to give you a break, and that's what grace is: God giving you a break and saying, "You're not perfect, but I love you anyway." It's something we can all use in dealing with each other.

How do you feel you've grown in your career, both as a bassist and an artist?

As a bass player I don't think I shoot as many blanks. In the '80s I was so busy playing on session after session that I was basically just reacting the whole time and playing from the bass instead of from the music. But that was how I found my sound. Now, I try to make sure whatever I play is appropriate and has meaning and emotion. Artist-wise, the ideas come quicker and easier than before. I feel more comfortable with who I am, which enables me to put myself in different situations that keep me moving forward.

Web site

www.marcusmiller.com

The Thumb Don't Lie

MARCUS MILLER'S POST-'90S SOLO ALBUMS best show his superhero range in groove, melody, and solo mode. Examples 1a and 1b are inspired by "Jazz in the House," one of two studio tracks on Miller's 1998 disc, *Live & More*. **Example 1a** recalls the entrance of Marcus's slapped melody (on his '77 Jazz): "I just wanted the melody to be funky and I tried to be vocal-like in my attention to articulation and phrasing." Also note his interesting harmonic motion over the *C* pedal-tone. **Example 1b** occurs at the start of what appears to be a tasty eight-bar slap solo: "Actually I'm pre-viewing and expanding on a melodic section that's played by bass clarinet and trumpet at the end of the song." After playing subtly different variations on the thematic material in each measure of the first four-bar phrase, Miller continues the trend in the second four-bar phrase that begins at bar 5. In bars 6 and 8 his "solo" builds to a high point as he adds colorful upper extensions and rhythmic density.

Ex. 1a

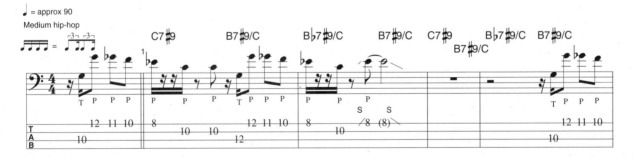

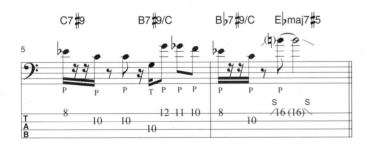

Ex. 1b

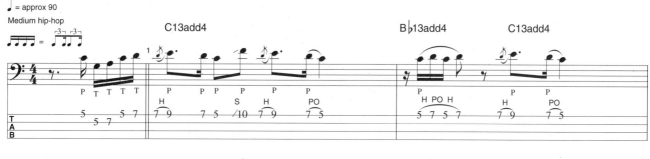

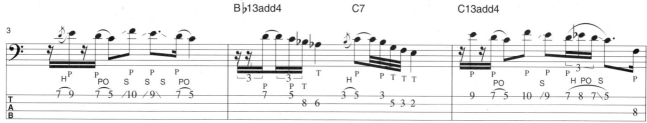

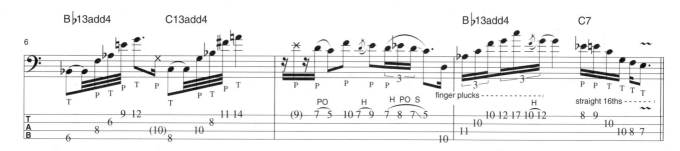

Examples 2–6 are inspired by Miller's Grammy-winning *M2*. Example 2 recalls two bars of the opening groove figure from "Power." Note the three-finger popped chord on beat *one*, the double-thumbed 32nd-note figure in beat *two*, and the accentuated, Larry Graham–style slides and walk-up at the end of bar 2: "I was looking for a key signature that would give me a different slap sound than the usual *E* or *A*, and B worked out well—especially being able to drop down for the octave walk-ups." Example 3 illustrates Miller's hard-plucked bebop lick in "Lonnie's Lament." Note the "outside"-sounding arpeggio movement in beats *two* and *three*: "That was inspired by saxophonist Kenny Garrett, who likes to run triads in his solos. When you want to leave the tonality of a tune, triad arpeggios are great because they have their own built-in tonality, so whatever you play is sort of self-supported. Then the trick is finding your way back home."

Ex. 2

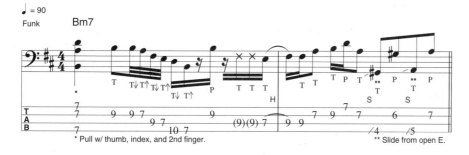

Examples 4a and 4b show "Nikki's Groove." Ex. 4a contains a slapped breakdown melody rife with expressive inflections. When the rhythm section returns (Ex. 4b), Miller turns up the rhythmic juice in his solo. He uses a cool, descending double-thumb run in bar 1 and brisk, board-scaling double-triplets in bar 3. Marcus switches to his fretless Fodera 5 in Ex. 5, which recalls the fetching Brazilian bridge melody of "It's Me Again." Mind the half-time feel, lay back, and listen to the vocals of Djavan, who doubles the melody. Miller's Jazz Bass returns in Ex. 6, the opening groove of "Cousin John," the disc's most wicked slap track. He tuned his *E* string down a half-step to *Eb*. "In bar 1 I play the last 16th of beats *two*, *three*, and *four* on a different string than the three preceding 16ths, so you have to hammer them strongly with your left hand to get the note to sound."

Ex. 3

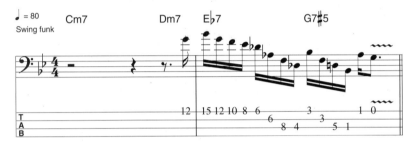

Ex. 4a

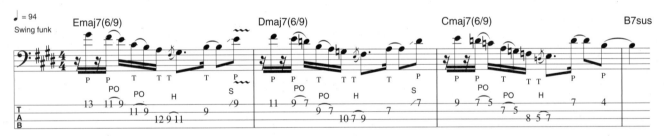

Ex. 4b

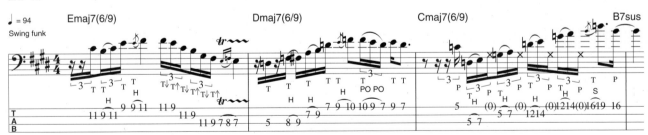

Ex. 5

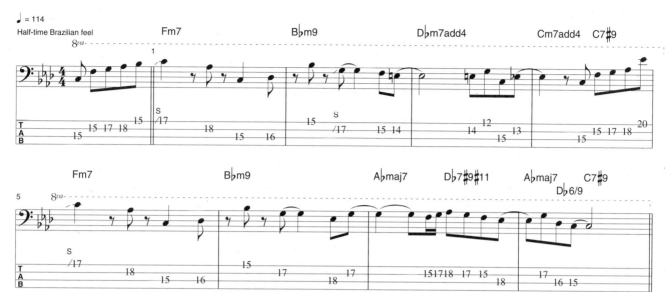

Ex. 6

ANTHONY JACKSON
Defining Bass Artistry

Interviewed by Chris Jisi, Spring 1990/Summer 1990, December 1994, December 1998, and May 2002.

THE ELECTRIC BASS GUITAR HAS NOT DONE BADLY IN MODERN MUSIC. Practitioners such as Paul McCartney, Jack Bruce, John Entwistle, Stanley Clarke, Jaco, Geddy Lee, Flea, and Sting have achieved household-name status, while pioneers like James Jamerson, Larry Graham, and Rocco Prestia are receiving due recognition. Like Jamerson, one of the most innovative and important bassists of our time has functioned primarily as a sideman, remaining largely unknown to contemporary audiences. His name is Anthony Jackson.

Driven by an unshakeable love for, and dedication to, music, Jackson has consistently broken down musical barriers. His mastery of various pick and fingerstyle techniques and his startling ability to instantly restructure the melodic, harmonic, and rhythmic direction of a piece of music mark him as an innovator of the highest order. Jackson has also conducted exhaustive research into the instrument's design and sonic reproduction, and his idea for a "contrabass guitar" predated the current boom in extended-range basses by nearly 20 years. Most important, as an artist, his refusal to compromise his integrity for popular trends has enabled him to retain his individuality in all musical situations. Indeed, among the many bassists awed by his sheer genius he is referred to by one reverently spoken word: "Anthony."

Anthony Jackson was born in New York City on June 23, 1952—approximately one year after Leo Fender introduced his Precision Bass. By age 12 Anthony's voracious listening habits, combined with a few years of "poking" at the piano, evolved into a desire to play the guitar. He started out on a standard 6-string but soon began to play bass guitar as well. By the time he was 16 he had moved to bass full-time, drawing from a diverse collection of musical influences, principally James Jamerson, the Jefferson Airplane's Jack Casady, and French modernist composer Olivier Messiaen.

Jackson began to perform locally in 1966 and played on his first recording session in 1970. Two years later, he joined Billy Paul's band, receiving his first gold record for the hit "Me and Mrs. Jones." As a result, he started working regularly with the Philadelphia production team of Gamble and Huff. In 1973 he earned a writer's credit as well as an immediate reputation for his unforgettable bass line on the O'Jays' hit "For the Love of Money." Shortly after, an informal New York City demo session for arranger Leon Pendarvis led to a session with Roberta Flack, and word of Jackson's sophisticated style spread quickly through the Big Apple's studio scene.

A 13-month stint with Buddy Rich's sextet at the drummer's East Side club gave Jackson additional exposure. He then toured with both Flack and violinist Michael Urbaniak before the demands of session work kept him in town. Always one to disdain categorization, he nevertheless became known as a "studio musician," despite his seminal work with fusion artists such as Chick Corea, Al Di Meola, and John Scofield. (He also received an offer to join Weather Report in 1975.)

In 1975 Jackson "terrorized" luthier Carl Thompson into building his first contrabass guitar—a 6-string bass tuned (low to high) *BEADGC*—an idea Jackson conceived while in his teens. Working with successive guitar makers to improve design and playability, he finally began playing the instrument exclusively in 1982. Jackson spent 1977 in Los Angeles recording with Lee Ritenour, Dave Grusin, Tom Scott, and others. Upon his return to New York in 1978, Anthony entered a pivotal period that led to new technical and creative developments captured on albums by such artists as Chaka Khan, Paul Simon, Al Di Meola, Steely Dan, and pianist Michel Camilo. In 1989 he fulfilled a lifelong goal by paying homage to his mentor James Jamerson, contributing three transcriptions and a thoughtful analysis to Alan "Dr. Licks" Slutsky's book *Standing in the Shadows of Motown: The Life and Music of Legendary Bassist James Jamerson* (Hal Leonard). He also performed one of his transcriptions on the accompanying recording.

Although his uncompromising commitment to the contrabass guitar, his refusal to "mindlessly" slap and pop, and the increasing mechanization of music have led to unpredictable career turns, Jackson has remained on course. Observes guitarist Steve Khan, who founded Eyewitness in 1980: "People are impressed by Anthony's technique, his sound, his incredible time and feel, and his innovative work in developing the 6-string contrabass guitar. But on our recordings, the quality that shines through is his unique sense of spontaneous reharmonization. He's willing to step into places where other bassists would not dare to go."

What was your inspiration to play bass guitar?
I first became aware of it on an album called *Mr. Twelve String Guitar* by a then-unknown Glen Campbell and a studio band performing some generally awful pop hits. Let's just say that one particular instrument reached out of the stereo and bit me on the ass. The love affair with the bass guitar dates roughly from that

moment. The jacket listed a credit for "Fender Bass," and while the player's name has long escaped me, the memory of how the sound of the instrument affected me is still strong. In June of 1965 my mother took me to Ben's Music on West 48th Street and bought my first bass guitar—a nameless cherry-sunburst medium-scale, single-pickup instrument—for $43. I continued playing standard as well as bass guitar until 1968, when I was forced to admit that my standard guitar playing should be quietly put to death.

When did you discover James Jamerson, and what kind of impact did he have on you?

I heard him with the Four Tops on "Baby, I Need Your Lovin'" [1964], on which he played upright. Much of Jamerson's earliest Motown output is on the upright, but his character was nevertheless distinctive enough to catch my ear. The beginning of a lifetime of being knocked to the floor and stomped on came in the summer of 1966 when "Road Runner" by Jr. Walker and the All Stars was released. The song opens with a classic fill by [drummer] Benny Benjamin followed by eight bars of Jamerson at his best. At that point, I knew I had my mentor, although I didn't know his name.

Was there something specific about his playing?

I could point to his tone or his rhythmic feel or

Anthony Jackson

his use of passing tones to redefine harmonic structures, but it was more the mentor relationship. He simply turned the key in the lock, in a very big way. A while later, in 1972, I discovered a 1968 Diana Ross and the Supremes album called *Love Child*, containing several major Jamerson performances and a consummate one—"How Long Has That Evening Train Been Gone?"—and was in a position to spend virtually every waking hour for several months playing along with and studying them. It was probably then that one of the foundations of my style took root.

Having Jack Casady as your other main influence seems like such a striking contrast, much like the vast difference between your pick performances and the way you play when using your fingers.

I was fortunate in having two very individualistic and diverse bass guitar talents as mentors. Casady, whom I'd first heard on the Jefferson Airplane's *Surrealistic Pillow* album in late 1966, had a big, rich, metallic sound with a full bottom, and a curious guitaristic way of playing that I was immediately drawn to. When I saw him perform live, I was struck by his dignity and serious mien. Both he and Jamerson were preoccupied with performance, not hype. I had doubled with a pick since the very beginning and had always been aware of the tendency for English players to use it, in particular John Entwistle—go back and listen to the Who's "Happy Jack" for a first-class pick outing, still very difficult to duplicate even after more than two decades— but it was Casady's sound that kept me exploring the expressive possibilities of using the pick. To this day, when I use one and a flanger, Casady's influence emerges and can be clearly detected by an aficionado.

I am always intrigued by the drastic shift in direction my style takes when I use the pick. A whole new set of solutions to creative problems comes forth. Richard Tee is a perfect example of this: He sounds completely different when playing the acoustic piano than he does on the Fender Rhodes, and the two disparate styles remain separate and clearly defined, yet there is enough carryover between them to ensure that they can be identified with only one man. People often express a fear that drastically changing either instrument or approach is going to affect their identity or caliber of performance, especially as perceived by an employer. However, I feel the possession of an alternative to an already developed style is a positive, and allows a uniquely panoramic perspective on any creative situation. The belief that this is a hindrance or obstacle has probably arrested the maturation of countless individual styles.

What was your introduction to the music of Olivier Messiaen, and why is he a pivotal figure for you?

Most of my exposure to organ music traditionally centered around Bach, but in 1967 I came across an obscure recording that featured, along with works by Franck and Bach, a piece by Messiaen, whose name and works were unknown to me. The piece was entitled "Dieu Parmi Nous (God Among Us)"—described as part of a nine-piece suite. I found it curious, even compelling, but somewhat unsettling, which criticism I soon traced to problems I perceived in Virgil Fox's interpretation. I decided to look for another interpreter, and was stunned to quickly find an extensive collection of Messiaen organ works performed by the composer, including the complete *La Nativite du Seigneur*, the suite from which "Dieu Parmi Nous" was drawn. I bought that album, and as I was on my way home, I had a peculiar feeling that something spectacular was about to occur.

That night I listened to the album, and in the space of two hours my life had changed completely and irrevocably. *La Nativite* totally and instantly changed the way I heard and played music. The effect was so shattering, so ecstatic, that all of my other sensual perceptions were subtly altered as well. Although there are many other composers whose music inspires in me sensations that can only be directly associated with the divine, Olivier Messiaen, alone among them, persists in having a voice, along with Jamerson and Casady, in every intuitively creative decision I make.

Upright jazz bassists such as Scott LaFaro and Ron Carter are masters of improvisational accompaniment, a concept you apply in many musical situations. Was jazz an influence?

Yes. I was very fortunate to discover jazz when I was about 16 through the album *The John Coltrane Quartet Plays*, with McCoy Tyner, Elvin Jones, and Jimmy Garrison. Coltrane had died only a year before, and his influence was still fresh and dominant. Making the rounds of the New York jazz clubs, most of which are now gone, I slipped quickly and deliriously under the spell of the music, feeling at home with it alongside my other creative areas. The album *Ornette* [by saxophonist Ornette Coleman], which was recorded shortly before Scott LaFaro's death in 1961, made a terrific impact on me as well. LaFaro had an uncanny ability to suggest key centers without elaborating them, forcing them to exist as what we could call subsidiary tonal islands in a larger sea of chromaticism. His approach differed from that of Ron Carter, who seemed to me a less angular inventor, no doubt due not only to his being a separate personality from Scott, but to the very different improvisational environment of the Miles Davis group compared to the Ornette Coleman ensemble. I am still astonished at how very different and unique LaFaro and Carter are, and how room remains for several more chromatically oriented upright players, including Garrison and Charlie Haden. Each is a master at supporting and pointing out directions to their respective ensembles without playing in a fixed key. Ron Carter was an early influence of mine. In my formative years, I learned to play largely by practicing along with records; beginning about 1969, two that became essential were [Miles Davis's] *Miles Smiles* and *Filles de Kilimanjaro*.

There has been some criticism leveled at the 6-string bass guitar. Some players call it a marketing gimmick while others feel they should master the "standard" 4-string before concerning themselves with a 6-string.

My feeling is: Why is 4 the standard and not 6? As the lowest-pitched member of the guitar family, the instrument should have had six strings from the beginning. The only reason it had four was because Leo Fender was thinking in application terms of an upright bass, but he built it along guitar lines because that was his training. The logical conception for the bass guitar encompasses six strings. As regards the issue of "mastering the 4-string" before moving on to the 6, consider that inasmuch as there is no point where one can be said to have "mastered" anything, to make this inane suggestion reveals the speakers to be idiots. As long as we remain seekers, never truly achieving our ultimate goals, we may as well start with the full basic blueprint and enjoy the expanded expressive possibilities of the extended range of the instrument. Of course, the undoubtedly famous-name superstars who utter this nonsense probably regard themselves as masters in their own right. So be it. For the rest of us, their attitude reveals them to be jealous, angry, and frustrated. Too damn bad.

When did the idea occur to you?

As a beginner, I observed proper tuning sequence (4ths), but often brought the entire sequence down a

6-String Saga

Before his first 6-string contrabass (built by Carl Thompson in 1975), Anthony Jackson picked a '73 Fender Precision on the O'Jays hit "For the Love of Money," and he played Gibsons—including and EB-2D —with Buddy Rich. Many a hit was cut with his Fender "Career Girl," a hybrid consisting of a '73 Jazz Bass body and a '75 Precision neck. Following his early '80s Vinnie Fodera–built Ken Smith 6-strings, Jackson and Fodera joined forces for a series of 36"-scale prototypes, beginning with the first signature model in 1984. In 1989 Fodera presented Anthony with his first single-cutaway signature model. He has been playing prototype No. 10 (also a single-cutaway) since 1998.

Having long favored high-end audio equipment for live performances, Anthony has been playing through a Millennia Media H3VB mic preamp, an API 550b EQ, and Turbosound TQ440SP and Meyer Sound USW1P self-powered speakers. His cables are a Nordost Quatro Fil and AudioQuest Lapis for his bass, and Monster Pro Link cables running between the pre-amp and powered speakers.

half- or whole-step in order to put certain important bass notes in the lowest possible octave. A typical example would be a song in $E\flat$: Sometimes, especially when playing with bands, I found myself willing to take chances with switching octaves that I might feel too intimidated to attempt when practicing to records. As I progressed, I began consistently observing normal tuning discipline, but I continued feeling constrained when practicing to a particular record whose bass part would drop below low *E*. The numerous recordings of organist Jimmy Smith were important to me because practicing with them helped give me a firm foundation in swing, but there was one piece, now forgotten, that had an altogether different effect: I heard a significant note, one I simply had to play, that was below my range. I realized by this point that tuning down, while it allowed the note to be played, caused a loss of sonority.

For one reason or another, I decided I'd had enough of this very unfortunate need to compromise, and an idea that had been hovering just outside of awareness popped forward. That idea was a special instrument with an extra string on the bottom. This was probably 1970. At the time, I did not possess the slightest idea about how to carry this idea further, so I bandied it about for several months, passing up a possible variation in which a low *B* would be the fourth string while the high *G* would be eliminated, thus producing a 4-string tuned down a 4th. This meant, however, that I would lose my upper range. Sometime during this period, the idea of simply putting an extra string on the bottom along with an extra string on the top began to sound logical. By the time I began traveling extensively, in 1972, the 6-string extended-range bass guitar had become, for me, an inevitability. Just a few more pieces of the puzzle had to fall into place before the dream could take shape. The most important was the discovery that there were people in the business of building electric guitars to order. I had no idea whether or not they would be amenable to building odd or unusual instruments, but I knew it would do no harm to ask. Other points to be cleared up included finding strings, determining specialized means of amplification and reproduction and, of course, the accumulation of lots of money, along with a backbone stiff enough to be willing to expend this money on an instrument that just might wind up a failure. By 1974 I was ready to search for a builder and begin the unending odyssey with the "big 6."

Along with Stanley Clarke, Alphonso Johnson, and Jaco Pastorius, you are one of the original voices of the bass revolution of the early '70s. What was the atmosphere that existed then?

There was more of a sense of adventure. Miles Davis's *Bitches Brew* was relatively new and had gotten a lot of people buzzing about new ideas and new avenues to try with rhythm sections. Even before that album came out, my best friend in high school, [guitarist/producer] Reggie Lucas, myself, and many of our friends were experimenting with the concept of putting jazz ideas on top of funk rhythms. We'd all grown up on the Beatles, James Brown, and John Coltrane, and there were endless clubs and loft spaces to play and experiment in. In 1972 I joined Billy Paul's band, Stanley was playing with Chick Corea, Alphonso had left Billy Paul's band and was with Woody Herman en route to Weather Report, and Jaco was down in Florida—a sensation, but not yet having attained international recognition.

When did you first meet Stanley Clarke?

Reggie had told me about him, and I saw him play for the first time at Max's Kansas City with Return to Forever. Our second meeting took place at his West Side apartment in 1973. Reggie and I had finished a project and he had to stop by Stanley's to get something, so I went along. We had a mutual respect for each other's playing, and when we met it was really quite funny. I tried his upright bass, which had the lowest action I'd ever felt, enabling me to get around on it fairly well, to which he commented, "Man, you should play upright." I said, "If I had one with this action I probably would," although in retrospect, even though I've had the opportunities, I realize the instrument has never captivated me. Anyway, inevitably he said, "Let me see your axe." I had my Gibson EB-2D with me, and I picked up his bass guitar, which was also a Gibson, I think. There was no amp in the apartment, so we sat opposite each other, one thing led to another, and we wound up dueling acoustically. It was good-natured, but because we were still young and mindful of our growing reputations, there was a serious undertone, rather like two big cats circling each other. I would lay down a *moderato* chordal passage, and Stanley would play everything he knew as fast as he could, and then we would switch roles. This went on, back and forth, for 15 or 20 minutes, after which we shook hands and had a real good laugh.

Who were some of the other important fusion bass guitarists?

"Slim" [Alphonso] Johnson. When we met in 1972, he struck me as the first player to show the same neurotic love for the instrument as I did. Steve Swallow is a very special case. He switched from the upright to the bass guitar because he also had a genuine love for the instrument. He went on to develop his own voice on it, despite blood-chilling cries of horror from the "jazz" community. John Lee, who played with McCoy Tyner and Larry Coryell, was a great composer in addition to being a fine player. Percy Jones is a first-rate innovator and is wrongfully labeled a Jaco clone by a large and very ignorant faction. One often overlooked but extremely important bassist was Michael Henderson, who played with Miles Davis and was one of James Jamerson's understudies at Motown. He was primarily an R&B/funk player, but with the unusual combination of big ears and a fearless ego, which enabled him to take a basic funk formula and try—successfully—to make it work in the context of Miles's music.

Anthony Jackson Selected Discography

With Chaka Khan: (all on Warner Bros.) *What Cha' Gonna Do for Me?*; *Naughty*; *Chaka*. **With Michel Camilo:** *Triangulo*, Telarc; *Calle 54: Music from the Motion Picture*, Blue Note. *Thru My Eyes*, RMM; *One More Once*, Sony; *Rendezvous*, Columbia; *Suntan*, Evidence (also released as *In Trio* on Electric Bird); *Why Not?*, Evidence. **With Steely Dan:** *Gaucho*, MCA. **With Donald Fagen:** *Nightfly*, Warner Bros. **With Al Di Meola:** (all on Columbia, except where noted) *Flesh on Flesh*, Telarc; *Kiss My Axe*, Rhino; *Tour De Force: Live*; *Electric Rendezvous*; *Splendido Hotel*; *Casino*; *Elegant Gypsy*; *Land of the Midnight Sun*. **With Steve Khan:** *Crossings*, Polygram; *Headline*, Blue Moon; *Public Access*, GRP; *Casa Loco*, Polygram; *Blades*, Passport; *Eyewitness*, Polygram. **With The O'Jays:** *Ship Ahoy*, Philadelphia International. **With Buddy Rich:** *Very Live at Buddy's Place*, Groove Merchant; *Tough Dude*, LRC; **With Michel Petrucciani:** *Trio in Tokyo*, Dreyfus; *Both Worlds*, Dreyfus; *Playground*, Blue Note. **With Paul Simon:** *Greatest Hits, Etc.*, Columbia. **With Simon & Garfunkel:** *Concert in Central Park*, Warner Bros. **With Lee Ritenour:** *Captain Fingers*, Epic; *Festival*, GRP; **With Roberta Flack:** *Blue Lights in the Basement*, Atlantic; *Feel Like Makin' Love*, Atlantic. **With John Scofield:** *Who's Who?*, Arista/Novus. **With Chick Corea:** *Leprechaun*, Polygram. **With Wayne Krantz:** *Signals*, Enja. **With Jim Beard:** *Song of the Sun*, CTI. **With Mike Stern:** *Odds or Evens*, Atlantic. **With Quincy Jones:** *Sounds . . . And Stuff Like That!*, A&M; *The Wiz*, Atlantic. **With Madonna:** *Madonna*, Warner Bros. **With Anita Baker:** *Rhythm of Love*, Elektra. **With Billy Paul:** *360 Degrees of Billy Paul*, Philadelphia International. **With Patti Austin:** *Very Best of Patti Austin*, Rhino. **With Pat Metheny:** *Secret Story*, Geffen. **With Luther Van Dross:** *Never Too Much*, Epic. **With Dave Grusin:** *Dave Grusin & the L.A.-N.Y. Dream Band*, GRP. **With Al Jarreau:** *L Is for Lover*, Warner Bros. **With Easy Pieces:** *Easy Pieces*, A&M. **With Tania Maria:** *Made in New York*, Manhattan. **With David Sanborn:** *Change of Heart*, Warner Bros. **With Akiko Yano:** *Love Is Here*, Epic. **With Hiromi:** *Another Mind*, Telarc. **With Grover Washington Jr.:** *A Secret Place*, Motown. **With Michael Urbaniak:** *Fusion III*, Columbia. **With Wlodek Gulgowovski:** *Time Check*, Polydor International. **With Steve Smith:** *Buddy's Buddies*, Tone Center. **With Milton Nascimento:** *Angelus*, Warner Bros. **With Roland Vasquez:** *Further Dance*, RVCD. **With The Writers:** *The Writers*, Columbia; *All in Fun*, CBS. **With Harvey Mason:** *Funk in a Mason Jar*, Arista. **With French Toast:** *French Toast*, Electric Bird. **With Simon Phillips:** *Another World*, Lipstick. **With Bass Extremes:** *Just Add Water*, Tone Center. **On DVD:** *Calle 54*, Miramax.

Some of your peers in the fusion world were critical of fellow players who became studio musicians. How did you enter the session scene and how did you feel about the criticism?

I didn't set out to be a "studio," "stage," or any other "type" of musician. Understand that I was a child when I started playing and my only motivation, reflecting a child's innocent idealism, was to find the greatest music to play and the greatest musicians to play it with. My first major recording experiences were very intense, beginning with Gamble and Huff in Philadelphia in 1972, and later as a freelancer in New York in 1974. One of the first people I came across in New York was L. Leon Pendarvis Jr., a very great composer and arranger who managed to get me on a Roberta Flack recording project he was producing. That led me to one of his other sessions, which is where I first met the great Steve Gadd. And as far as I'm concerned, there isn't anything that any fusion artist has done that exceeds the quality of work produced by what we can call the Pendarvis rhythm section, consisting of "The Darvis" on keyboards, Gadd on drums, Ralph MacDonald or Crusher Bennett on percussion, David Spinozza, Hugh McCracken, and Jeff Mironov—any two out of three—on guitars, and myself. We recorded hundreds of tracks, most of which were never released, but for sheer quality of composition and performance, the music is as good as anything I or anyone else has experienced. "The Darvis" is one the few composers who knows how to write for the rhythm section. He writes for the basic unit—guitar, bass guitar, keyboards, drums, and percussion—with the proficiency of a composer of string quartets. Working with that unit was significant because it stimulated major personal growth. Steve Gadd decisively influenced the way I hear music and is really the only drummer I've worked with who has. He is one of the important talents of the 20th century.

You also recorded three albums and did a 13-month stint with Buddy Rich's sextet at his East Side club around that time.

That was an equally rewarding, though totally different, situation. My first experience with Buddy was with the big band in 1973. I came in cold without a rehearsal and got sent home in shame after one show because I didn't read well enough. I boned up and about a year later I managed to get an audition with his sextet and was hired. I would say that Buddy is the only bona fide genius I've worked with. His importance to his instrument equals that of Heifitz and Horowitz to theirs. He's the ultimate example of an individual who allowed the warpage of personality to occur in exchange for the development and expression of a transcendental gift. He took a lot of flack for his apparently dated style, four-on-the-floor bass drumming in particular, but let me tell you, it swung, and it swung hard.

By all accounts, it was one thing to play your part while he guided the band, but quite another to initiate something and have him react or follow. Were you able to do that?

Astonishingly, yes. I never got over my fear of him, because he was such an intimidating figure, but onstage I was soon able to communicate with him and persuade him to "dialogue" with me. By sheer coincidence, my emerging Jamerson-based funk conception fit very well with Buddy's busy, polyrhythmically based conception, which was only a modern variation on the way he'd always played. It often sounded cluttered, but I believe this was only because few risked trying to interact with him. I took a chance and tried, and his total mastery of all things musical allowed him to fit his style around mine like a glove. Of course, he didn't have to like it—I had heard endless warnings about how one could never presume to engage in a back-and-forth with Buddy Rich onstage—but I think Buddy realized that he finally had a player in the bass chair who genuinely knew and loved the so-called "New Music" while also satisfying his demand for a genuine jazz player. By the way, the great guitarist Jack Wilkins [in Rich's band], who always played sitting down without a strap, explained that this was the logical way to play the guitar, convinced me to do the same. I've been playing that way ever since.

Many of your concepts seemed to come together on the O'Jays' "For the Love of Money" in 1973: the tone of roundwound strings, the rhythmic and sonic possibilities of playing with a pick, and the use of time-delay effects. How did everything fall into place?

To me, the ideal bass guitar sound has always seemed to be the sound of a standard guitar dropped an octave or more in pitch. My acceptance of this principle predates my first experiences as a bass guitarist and can possibly be traced to experiments involving records played at half-speed. Sometime back in the very beginning, I can recall commenting to a school friend on the shimmering, exquisite beauty of a now-forgotten performer's bronze-stringed flat-top guitar heard on a record played at 16 RPM. At the time, I simply could not accept not being able to achieve this sound, even if my intention was not to use it all the time. A few people—Jack Casady, John Entwistle, and the Dead's Phil Lesh—achieved a sound that at least seemed to be on the right track.

I decided to try roundwound strings in 1972, when they were still a novelty and people were saying, "Don't be a fool. They're noisy, they'll eat your frets, and they make the bass sound too much like a guitar." They were a revelation. Combined with the flatpick, which I had been using since the beginning as well as fingerstyle, my instrument assumed an identity completely removed from my Jamerson self, accentuating Casady's influence.

Around the same time, the Maestro company released a phase shifter. I knew the theory behind the device, and I heard it demonstrated by a guitarist one day at Manny's Music in New York City. Henry Aldrich, the owner, insisted that the box simply would not work for me: "It's for guitar, not for bass." I bought it anyway, and when I plugged it in at home, the world changed. I was completely flabbergasted. Here was a sound I had never heard—it was beautiful and just plain *right*. After a few weeks, I took the unit apart and located the intensity adjustment. I did some careful tweaking and was able to subtly enhance the effect.

That particular unit and my recently purchased Fender Precision were used on "For the Love of Money." That was, as far as I know, the first time a recording was made with a phased bass guitar. Kudos to Gamble and Huff for taking a chance on the sound—I loved it desperately, but it was still alien to the marketplace, as was the right-hand technique I was using with it. It would have been understandable had they elected to follow a more conservative approach, as was their norm. The success of the record clearly vindicated my decision to incorporate the pure guitar-consciousness brought forth by the roundwound string-and-pick endeavors. I continued experimenting until I met Al Di Meola in 1975, when he saw the possibilities and thereafter provided a powerful developmental stimulus.

One increasingly prominent aspect of your playing is a muting technique involving your right-hand palm and either a pick or your thumb.

There are several aspects to right-hand muting. The use of what I call the "palm mute with pick" dates back to my early association with Di Meola. Al is quite simply a virtuoso in just about any technique involving the flatpick, and his use of mute-and-pick was, when I first saw and heard it, a revelation. I spent some time trying to cultivate it for myself and had many opportunities to apply it because of his propensity for writing parallel lines for guitar and bass guitar. I recall some mute-and-pick duets on *Elegant Gypsy*, and I gave it major prominence on *Splendido Hotel*.

As for the "palm mute with thumb," that seems to be much older. Around 1972 I began falling heavily under the sway of Latin music, and I became enamored of the old Ampeg Baby Bass. Although it sounded pretty awful in nearly every other context, in Latin music no other bass sound could touch it, and I wanted it. I wasn't comfortable with the idea of playing an instrument with such a stylistically limited range—or perhaps I should just be honest and say that I was determined to force my instrument to give me the sound of the Baby Bass. One way or the other, thumb-and-palm emerged as a personal technique giving me what I hoped was a compatible and effective sound for Latin music. Over the years I've gotten comfortable with it, and I feel confident using it in non-Latin situations as well, although the peculiar problems of coordination due to the non-standard right-hand position have taken a lot of effort to overcome.

I'll sometimes use thumb-and-palm for the majority of a particular recording project, often surprising my associates, who can't figure out why such an unusual approach works so well. It doesn't always work, of course, but it's great to have it available as a creative alternative. There was also a period when, in an attempt to acquire something resembling Jamerson's sound, I would carry a piece of foam to insert under the strings just ahead of the bridge. The resulting sound is similar to that achieved by the thumb-and-palm, with the advantage of full mobility for the fingers of the right hand. Lost, however, is the ability to switch quickly from muted to open strings and back, and the subtle gradations of muting, whether from string-to-string or note-to-note on a single string. The desire to use muting as an expressive stylistic device, as opposed to a simple technique, has prompted me to attempt to cultivate a more elaborate version of the thumb-and-palm method. I'm trying to integrate my right-hand fingers into the operation of picking along with the thumb, while maintaining the palm as an increasingly mobile and sensitive mute.

On Chaka Khan's Naughty *and* What Cha' Gonna Do for Me *you were able to express highly creative ideas while not only supporting the songs but kicking the hell out of the grooves. Is that the most freedom you've ever been given as a sideman?*

Certainly those recordings are among the best examples of blatant commerciality infused with high art that I've been involved with. The basic tracks went down quickly and easily. They probably could have been left untouched, ready for overdubs and sweetening, were it not for my inability to find anything good to say about my own performances. They were competent, but I was absolutely not thrilled, and this was unacceptable. This situation has generally prevailed throughout my career, and in most cases I have had no recourse but to stuff a sock in my mouth and go quietly home. Those who know me, of course, know that often the sock came out and I let everyone know that if they had any sense they would let me redo my parts until I felt they were right. For the most part, this got me nowhere, though I did make many close enemies.

I will probably never know what could have been going through the minds of Chaka and her producer, Arif Mardin, in allowing me to redo every single note of every single track I played on. To make a fascinating but long story short, *Naughty*, which was recorded in New York in 1979, went on without concern for the bass tracks. I was given absolute artistic license, with one exception, and an unheard-of amount of time—three months—to recompose the bass parts, whereupon I notified Arif of my readiness to record. I was then given all the studio time that I required. I never found out how much my indulgence cost Chaka, but the end result is as pure an example as exists, in my own case, of the ends justifying the means.

The performances represent, with only scattered exceptions, the peak of my creative abilities at the time and in that genre. They are, hopefully, only elemental today, but I recall listening to the final mixes just before release and realizing that I was able, for the first time, to hear evidence of a defined, mature, and effective style coming through my playing. This was a revelation, a coming-of-age, and, I hoped, proof that my stubbornness in playing what I heard despite intense pressure to "conform or else" was paying off. The succeeding album, *What Cha' Gonna Do for Me*, recorded in Montreux in 1980, was made along similar "highbrow" lines, but with the first signs of an end of an era in sight—the budget was down and the time restricted—although the end result remains impressive.

Unfortunately, reality closed in around us after that album, and the crucial prerequisites to recordmaking of this quality are difficult to come by today. Producers are no longer inclined to grant sidemen, however esteemed, unlimited control of anything, and certainly time is more tightly rationed than anything else. The right combination of players is now highly unlikely, inasmuch as a full rhythm section is seldom seen. Machine augmentation is the rule. Most important of all, few artists of major stature have ever possessed the patience, supportiveness, musicality, and virtuosity of Chaka Khan. I've worked with countless singers, from divas to bicycle pumps, and none has been able to gather and harness such powerful creative forces as Chaka.

Many people think that you used a 5- or 6-string bass on those recordings.

I've never used a 5-string, period. Around the time of Chaka's first solo album [*Chaka*, 1978], I resumed the search for an effective 6-string. Remember that the first two instruments had not been successful, despite my using Number One [the Carl Thompson contrabass built in 1975] for some recording and touring. In pursuing Number Three, I began discussions with Ken Smith and later Ken Parker, but these went exceedingly slowly, so I did what I could to tide myself over and secure, however awkwardly, a sub-bass range for recording. A little common sense, combined with a willingness to experiment, led me to modify my Fender [the "Career Girl"] accordingly. I raised the nut, readjusted the trussrod, and did much bridge-fiddling until the instrument felt manageable when tuned down two whole-steps.

I remember feeling rather light-headed, sitting at home the night before the third or fourth session for *Naughty*, modifying the only instrument I was playing at the time, rendering it unsuitable for any standard project. The rashness of my actions strengthened my resolve to keep on pushing for a true contrabass guitar, confirmed by each minute spent hearing this awesome, thundering sound from my poor, abused 4-string come roaring out of the giant Altec monitors in Atlantic's Studio A.

Was working with Walter Becker and Donald Fagen of Steely Dan, reportedly among the most demanding of artists, comparable to working with Chaka Khan?

Becker and Fagen—and also Paul Simon—approach their goals a bit differently than Chaka, but all parties, at the end of the day, want all asses to have been thoroughly kicked. Fagen, in particular, is a stickler for detail, but no more so than I am, so the only important issue is whether my detailing as interpreter coincides with his as composer. Once a stylistic approach to a song has been decided—such approach, of course, having been determined almost entirely by Fagen—the actual recording of the performance begins, and this is where the legend of cruelty to musicians originates. It's true that Becker, Fagen, and Simon split more hairs than most and never hype players: no high-fives, no reverential cursing. You've played well? Good; next song. Or more likely: Not good; do it again. Still not good; again. Still not good; go home. Many did. This kind of ferocious performance-disciplining, far from intimidating me, sends adrenaline pouring into my bloodstream. Split hairs, will you? Split this!

Becker and Fagen made neurosis and obsession rewarding and uplifting. Endless hours were spent analyzing and refining the smallest performance details without noticeably improving the music. But I must say that the two tracks I did for Steely Dan's *Gaucho*—"Glamour Profession" and "My Rival"—and the two on *The Nightfly* [Donald Fagen's first solo album]—"I.G.Y." and "Ruby Baby"—did improve my ability to constructively analyze a performance. Becker and Fagen's constant prodding, combined with their willingness to let me prod myself—even allowing me to destroy a performance they loved because I insisted on redoing the entire part—helped put titanium in my spine.

By comparison, Chaka and Arif were more like political anarchists. Unsupervised creative license was the order of the day—well, almost—but somehow discipline always seemed to settle on top of the proceedings, and a need for order, or perhaps *consistency* is a better word, wound up governing the proceedings. If there is a lesson in this, perhaps it is that the final creative product is achieved by processes unique to the performer, and that external forces, whether highly regimented or equally intense but unstructured, are no more than catalysts in the hands of a player determined to make a statement.

In March 2002 Anthony discussed pianist/composer Michel Camilo's CD Triangulo *and their 20-year continuous partnership—the longest of Jackson's career. The two met in 1979 as members of the session-musician-loaded New York octet French Toast. In 1984 pianist Tania Maria asked Camilo to open for her at Carnegie Hall with a small band, and thus the Michel Camilo Trio—with Toast-mates Jackson and drummer Dave Weckl—was born. "Anthony is a genius, a total master," Camilo says. "His playing is always special and fresh. He's also my musical alter ego; we're both perfectionists, and he instinctively knows exactly what I'm going for. I hear him when I write, and I constantly look to challenge him. That's why I think he has stayed with me: He loves to be challenged, and I get a kick out of making him work hard."*

How extensive is your knowledge of traditional Latin music?
I've developed a good, intuitive feel for the music from playing and listening to it, and loving it. I know

the various grooves when I hear them—what goes where, whether it's a 2:3 or 3:2 clave. Of course, I'm continually learning. Sometimes I alter my part and Michel and El Negro [drummer Horacio "El Negro" Hernández] tell me it's not traditionally correct—that I've got the leading tone laying here and it works better if it lands over here. Or I may play a polyrhythm that correctly subdivides the time but doesn't work with the way they're comping. When it comes to Latin pedagogy, they speak and I shut up and listen. It doesn't get any deeper than El Negro, and that has been a wonderful education for me. This is the first time I've played intensively with a virtuoso Latin drummer, and it's interesting to hear his feel and approach on both Latin and non-Latin pieces. Much of what he does is unique and involves subtleties that would not appear in anyone else's drumming. He has clearly made me a better player.

What was Michel's concept for Triangulo?

Michel views the trio as a triangle, which is how we set up onstage—thus the title. He wanted to capture the dialogue that goes on among the three of us as the music moves from intimate and introspective to heated and explosive, and as the shape and focus shifts to various corners of the triangle.

The ballad "Afterthought" is a study of the trio's introspective side.

I'm proud of that track. My part includes a descending line that starts in the upper register and doubles Michel's left hand. I use my volume pedal to swell the notes, and I play each note a little louder as I move downward. Overall, the part is so soft it's almost subliminal. The idea is to broaden and warm the piano part without overtly calling attention to the bass, and I used everything I know about touch and dynamics with both hands to bring that out. It confirms for me what I've tried to learn about the figurative side of the sine wave underneath the zero line. Everybody thinks about what's above the line: "Does the audience hear me?" But you can't ignore what's down there; you can't ignore the near silences, the introspection. These add tremendous meaning and richness to a performance, if you're willing to mine the lower floors.

Some assume you use a volume pedal to approximate a bowed upright or a fretless.

That's totally inaccurate. I use it more as an expression pedal, which is what it's called on a pipe organ. I confess to imitating one instrument: the Ondes Martenot [an early electronic instrument] and its main player, Olivier Messiaen's sister-in-law Jeanne Loriod, who passed away last August [2001]. She was my main inspiration for using the volume pedal.

Do you find you use the thumb-and-palm-mute technique more with Michel because of much of the music's Latin nature?

Actually, with Michel I've been moving back to a more open pizzicato, and I've also been using the thumb and two fingers classical-guitar-style, both muted and open—like I do in the film *Calle 54*. Certainly, though, in a Latin setting the palm mute works well in the Baby Bass tradition. One hitch is it sounds good live but often doesn't record as well. It tends to sound more muted than it actually is, and that's one reason I'm experimenting with miking my system in the studio—to get an earthier, boomier sound.

Is "Anthony's Blues" named for you?

Yes, that's a tribute from Michel to my constant use of tritones. The extremely angular melody line is a nod as well. I hear the tritone as the central interval on which to build harmonies and melodies, as opposed to the major or minor 3rd. Instead of root, 3rd, and 5th, I think root, minor or major 3rd, and augmented 4th. The tritone interval has been extremely important to me from the first day I heard a recording of Messiaen playing his own music on organ. Essentially, Michel wrote a piece that is played—and can be improvised—in two keys a tritone apart. To some ears it will sound like a standard 12-bar blues with extensions on the chords, but if you listen you can hear us moving back and forth between the two keys.

What are your thoughts on Calle 54?

See it! If it's not playing in theaters, buy it on DVD; it speaks for itself. When the film opened, most critics agreed it was the greatest music documentary ever made; audiences were applauding the onscreen performances. For me, it was a tremendous honor to appear with so many brilliant Latin musicians.

How did Michel come to pick "From Within," from his Rendezvous *album, for his segment of the film?*

Originally he was going to write a piece for the occasion—but [filmmaker] Fernando Trueba, who had been to many of our shows, requested "From Within," which is our set closer. It was just as well, because we wouldn't have had time for a new piece to really gel. We filmed two takes, the final version being an assemblage of the two. The film and audio were cut together; we recorded my Fodera Contrabass using a mic in front of my system, which included an FM Acoustics preamp, a Krell power amp, and two custom Epifani 1x12 cabinets. In retrospect I wish I had gone direct out of the preamp, although the crew did a good job with my sound.

How did you approach your solo?

I was told it was going to be short, much like the written solo Michel had me play on the *Rendezvous* version—so rather than an improvisation, I decided to try a recomposition. Fortunately I came up with something I felt was effective, and I was able to get it into the film in almost complete form. The original written solo was a two-bar phrase played four times; my recomposition is in multiple sections and is more polyphonic, with more of an emphasis on a separate bass line underpinning the counterpoint riding on top—almost piano-like in nature. The best way to understand how it was developed is to listen to the original track and compare it to the *Calle 54* version.

What has kept you and Michel together?

There are a number of factors, including musical like-mindedness and his loyalty despite political pressure at times to have an upright bassist. At the core of it all, though, we are temperamentally similar in an artistic sense: fiery, aggressive, fearless, demanding. As was the case with Al Di Meola, every album we've done has made me a better player, because each prompted a great deal of exploration through having the gauntlet thrown down at me. You're a bass guitarist? Okay, I have something for you. I always feel like he's trying to break down walls, as opposed to staying in one niche or stagnating. If you have that burning need and willingness to spill your blood on the floor whenever you play, it will be satisfied with Michel.

The late French pianist Michel Petrucciani had a steady trio with you and Steve Gadd.

That was special. I don't think I'll ever be in that kind of situation again—playing with a dyed-in-the-wool, orthodox jazz musician who had the political nerve to hire a pair of "studio" players. It was similar to the situation Michel Camilo is in, but to an even greater extreme. One French jazz critic wrote, "The only problem I have is that Petrucciani uses Steve Gadd and Anthony Jackson, and all I can say is, why?" But Michel was like Miles: He called the people *he* liked. He told us, "You're the ones I want in this band, because no one else in the world can do what you can do." That was vindication for being a fierce bass guitar partisan my whole life.

Camilo Contrabassics

Although Michel Camilo composes bass lines with Anthony Jackson in mind—and often relies on him to flesh out parts during rehearsals or even while recording—there's still a hefty amount of written notation to be interpreted. Jackson relishes the challenge. "It's all about what lies behind the notes," says Anthony. "If you listen to five pianists' recordings of a Chopin étude, they are all playing the same notes, yet each sounds different. The performer's personality has an acute effect on how the music comes across."

Example 1 tracks the main two-bar bass figure from "La Comparsa," from *Triangulo*. "The phrase markings are critical—especially the emphasis on the Bb's, which must stand out. Also, while I palm-mute the low G's at first, as the track goes on and develops, I gradually take off the mute." **Example 2** recalls the main two-bar bass line of "Las Dos Lorettas," from *Triangulo*. "The challenge here was to make this fairly busy line work with El Negro, who is also playing busily, though quietly, underneath. At times, in the phrase's second bar I lay back and give the 16th-note figure on beat *three* more of a triplet feel."

Example 3 shows the main four-bar groove of "dotcom-bustion," from *Triangulo*. "The classical term for this kind of line is *moto perpetuo*—perpetual motion," says Jackson, who keeps the notes short via light palm muting. "It works because it absolutely doesn't move while providing a foundation for the piano and drums, which play loosely. El Negro came up with the alternating bar-of-four/bar-of-three groove on a little sequencer he travels with, and then he and Michel wrote the tune with an Afro-Cuban flavor." **Example 4** illustrates the piano-and-bass break in *Triangulo*'s "Mr. CI." "It was written as a four-bar ascending and descending line, which Michel played in unison with his hands, but I decided to jump in and double the last two bars for contrast."

Ex. 1

Ex. 2

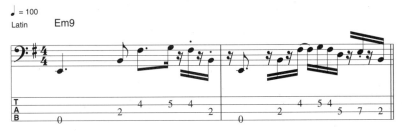

Ex. 3

Ex. 4

Ex. 5

Example 5 shows Michel Camilo's actual chart for the tutti (band unison) section of "From Within," from the *Calle 54* soundtrack. It occurs at 4:37 on the CD soundtrack, right before Jackson's solo. "The phrase markings and dynamics are key. Michel drops down an octave at bar 10, so it's important to play stronger there, and in bar 12, as noted, we all lay back on the phrase. Also, I played the last *D* in bar 17 down an octave."

A.J. Talks Shop
Setup Master Class

TRAFFIC COULD BE SEEN crawling up 6th Avenue outside New York's Bass Collective, as the merciless midday August sun seemed to drain the energy from cars and pedestrians alike. Inside, however, was a flurry of activity as the 16-member graduating class prepared for a special event: a rare master class on setup with session legend Anthony Jackson. Over the course of the informal 80-minute discussion/demonstration, Jackson—who was joined by Fodera Basses' Joe Lauricella—covered a wide range of thought-provoking issues on bass guitar setup, maintenance, and design. Some highlights, in Anthony's words:

The Nature of Wood

Little attention gets paid to setup. Setup is traditionally done as quickly and cheaply as possible to make an instrument *just* playable—but I want to address proper instrument setup and raise consciousness about the importance of getting an ideal setup. All bass guitars can benefit from this.

To begin with, remember that we play wooden instruments. As we all know, wood behaves like a living material even after it's dead; it never stops moving, never stops changing. This means over the life of your instrument you will never have an absolutely stable setup. You will continually have to tweak it yourself—or, in more serious cases, take it to a professional. Before you can do that, however, you have to develop the ability to recognize when factors like climate change have affected your instrument. Because if you're on an important session or live performance and your instrument has shifted and it throws you off, no one will listen to excuses about how your neck moved.

The Virtues of a Zero-Relief Fingerboard

Your fingerboard is laid out with calculations to the thousandth of an inch showing exactly where each fret should go. But these calculations assume the frets are lying on a *flat* surface. Whenever you hear someone say the fingerboard should have a slight [lengthwise] curvature—the reason usually being to prevent buzzing—think about it. A curved surface changes the relationship of fret spacing, which can affect tuning—although compared to a flat fingerboard the difference is admittedly quite small. More important, I believe a flat board simply feels better. So your neck should be as straight as you can get it. Yes, it's going to buzz, and you're going to have to stop the buzz. How? Proper setup.

To make a flat board usable, you must have level frets. Frets fresh from the manufacturer are seldom as level as they can be. If they were, you'd have to tack on hundreds of dollars to the cost of each instrument because it means a lot more time spent. If you suspect something is wrong with your frets, or you've been unable to straighten your fingerboard, a meticulous setup is the only cure—and a fret-by-fret inspection is one way to start. Even if you don't think anything is wrong, it's always advisable to get an immediate after-sale inspection of your new instrument by a professional luthier.

Behold the Nut

Aside from a flat [zero-relief] fingerboard contributing to an even and responsive feel, improvement occurs by balancing nut height against bridge height. With a flat fingerboard it's possible to raise the nut slightly while lowering the action at the bridge. This produces a surprisingly even response from the very lowest notes to the highest without a big increase or decrease in the strings' height across the fingerboard. Regarding the higher nut: Guard against excess here, because as one presses down on the string it always goes slightly sharp. A nut placed too high will cause your 1st-fret notes, particularly on the heavier strings, to be even more sharp. The difference must be found by trial and error. But the principle of straight neck, flat fingerboard, higher nut, and lower bridge is something you all should investigate. These adjustments absolutely must be made under the close supervision of an experienced setup person, and it may take several repeat visits to get right. It's worth it.

String Tension & Scale Length

Over the years I've learned that the quality of your instrument's sound depends partly on how tight you can make the strings. We all know pianos come in different sizes; all are tuned the same, and yet the larger pianos are louder and sound better. An important reason is the length, and therefore the tension, of the strings. When you have a given thickness of string tuned to a given pitch, and you lengthen it without changing pitch, you need more tension. A longer string, all else being equal, has a stronger, more accurate overtone series and better sustain. You may know I play an extra-long-scale instrument—36"—solely because with the same gauge of string, a longer scale simply sounds better than a shorter scale. The price I pay is more difficulty fingering.

String Break Angle

Besides scale length there's another factor that determines string tension. On some bass guitars the strings run virtually straight across the nut with almost no break [angle]. You should have some means of bringing the strings down behind the nut, even slightly. You can wind them low around the string post, but you don't want to depend on that. You want an absolutely firm system of keeping the strings bent over the nut, whether it's through the use of string trees, a C-clamp, or an angled headstock. My instrument's headstock has an extreme angle; this ensures isolation between the winding length of the string and the speaking length of the string, and it increases the tension.

More Nut & Angle Observations

Earlier I said the 1st-fret notes are always slightly sharp. Here's a good way to minimize this: When you first string up your instrument, you'll notice that the heavier strings in particular curve smoothly over the nut and therefore sit higher over the 1st fret. As the string settles in, this curve breaks a bit, creating more of an angle. The result is less distance to the 1st fret and a note that plays more in tune.

The lesson: When you string up, force the string down over the nut. You can use your thumb, but this may be uncomfortable. A better idea is to use the shank of a screwdriver; supporting the neck with your hand, lightly press down each string right in front of the nut, just until the string is about to touch the board. It's also a good idea to take a piece of paper from your string packaging and run it up under the strings to prevent them from grinding into the fingerboard when you press down.

String Spacing

You've heard of the concept of adjusting your strings for equal center-to-center distance. But think about it. Take a given center-to-center measurement from strings 1 and 2. That same measurement for strings 5 and 6 will result in those strings being closer together; because they are fatter, their edges will be closer to each other. In other words, if you maintained the center-to-center measurement and kept adding progressively heavier strings, eventually the strings would touch.

The correct spacing to maintain is inner edge to inner edge. If you space your strings equally from edge to edge they will all be the same distance apart, even though the centers are further apart. The centers are not important, because you don't feel the centers when you play; you feel the edges of the outer wrap. They're what you want to have at an equal distance.

String Spacing & Neck Width

Within the width of my fingerboard, the strings are as widely spaced as possible. Unless you have tiny hands, I think you can all appreciate a roomy feel at both ends of the instrument. Some believe that on 5- and 6-string basses tight spacing is easier to play. In the long run it really isn't. If you consider proper technique—which means keeping the thumb behind the fingerboard, instead of over the neck edge—you'll see that my instrument's neck could be even wider, yet I could still reach the strings. That said, however wide your fingerboard is, spread your strings out as much as you can if your bridge allows it. Not being cramped reduces fatigue. Your bottom string can be quite close to the edge without danger of push-off if you finger properly. Use care with the top string, however; a bit more distance is required to prevent pull-off, which is always more of a danger.

Final Thoughts

My main point is that the same setup principles apply to all fretted wood instruments. Whether or not you choose to follow my advice on what constitutes a proper setup, you must make the effort to maintain the quality of whatever setup you choose. Attention to maintenance and setup is ongoing and must be rigorous. Know your instrument and be responsible for evaluating its condition at all times. Remember, your relationship with wood is ever-changing—but I promise you, when you have a proper setup things just don't get any better.

JOHN PATITUCCI
Inner Depth, Outer Reach

Interviewed by Jim Roberts, May/June 1992; Richard Johnston, December 1998; and Chris Jisi, December 1994, July 1997, April 2000, and May 2003.

"IT'S A LONG WAY FROM SLAPPING TO THE BOW," says John Patitucci—and since his emergence in the late '80s no one has spanned the gap between traditional upright and modern electric with more facility and renown than this Brooklyn native. Expanding the territory Stanley Clarke pioneered, Patitucci mastered the groove/solo and electric/upright dichotomies with Chick Corea's Elektric and Acoustik bands and through countless record, jingle, and film dates on the Los Angeles session scene. When he left the Elektric Band in 1992 to lead his own projects, John had already recorded three well-received solo albums, including the challenging jazz/classical hybrid *Heart of the Bass*.

While refusing to be bound by stylistic preconceptions, Patitucci concedes it's not always easy bridging the metronomic demands of pop-influenced styles and the freer rhythmic concepts of small-group jazz: "If I've been playing a lot of groove music but then have to play jazz, I have to woodshed to get ready for it. When I have to go the other way I make sure I put in enough work on the electric to feel connected to it and make my time feeling natural and clear." Likewise, it takes effort maintaining his crystalline tone and nuanced phrasing on electric while keeping up his formidable acoustic chops. "There are certain things I *have* to have in my playing. Raw strength is always there from the upright, but I have to work on the electric's subtleties because the touch is so different."

In the late '90s Patitucci changed gears and returned to New York City to make a deeper commitment to his acoustic jazz side, culminating in his key role in Wayne Shorter's revered quartet (the sax titan's first acoustic group since the '60s). John's corresponding move to the Concord Jazz label and his five subsequent albums (including his 2003 release *Songs, Stories & Spirituals*), showcase not only his facility and musicality on both instruments, but his considerable growth into one of the finest bass-playing composers of the new millennium. And while his technical prowess continues to inspire many an aspiring doubler, he cautions against making too much of that aspect of his playing: "It never turns me on to hear someone just play fast when there's nothing in it, just notes swirling around. For me, it's way beyond chops and trying to impress people. It's about trying to reach into somebody's soul and move them."

John Patitucci was born on December 22, 1959, and raised in the Flatbush section of Brooklyn, New York. He was first exposed to music by his older brother, Tom, a guitarist. "When I was nine or ten, I played guitar—for about two minutes," he recalls. "It just didn't feel good, and Tom suggested I try bass so we could play together. Somebody in the neighborhood had a Telstar bass we bought for $10, and I was off and running."

Blessed with a quick ear, John mastered the fundamentals and began to play in neighborhood bands. In 1972, when his family moved to the San Francisco Bay Area town of San Ramon, he hooked up with a teacher, Chris Poehler, who proved to be a key influence. "Chris was a professional bass player, and he played both electric and acoustic. He encouraged me to learn how to read, and he hipped me to a lot of great music, like the '60s Miles Davis records with Ron Carter and Chick Corea's records with Stanley

John Patitucci

Clarke. I had been listening to James Jamerson since I started, but Chris introduced me to other great R&B players, like Chuck Rainey and Willie Weeks. I learned Willie's famous solo on Donny Hathaway's 'Everything Is Everything' when I was 12 or 13, and that was a huge influence on me."

When he was 15 Patitucci picked up the acoustic, studying with Charles Siani of San Francisco State College and plunging into classical music. After high school he studied at S.F. State for a year before moving to Southern California; he continued his studies at Long Beach State for another two years, eventually dropping out when he began to get so much work that he couldn't attend classes.

John's first big-time job was with pianist Gap Mangione (brother of flügelhornist Chuck), and he went on to work with many Los Angeles jazz notables, including vibraphonist Victor Feldman, guitarist Larry Carlton, and percussionist Airto Moreira. Then in 1985 he hooked up with Corea. "They used to have this Valentine's Day party at Chick's house every year, and a lot of musicians would hang out," John recalls. "I played there with Victor Feldman's trio, and Chick heard me. Afterward he asked if I would help out with some rehearsals he was putting together—he had to learn several Mozart pieces to play with Keith Jarrett in Japan. So I did that, and then he asked me, 'Do you play electric bass?' I said, 'Sure, that's what I started on.' He asked me to give him some tapes of my electric playing, which I did, and it turned out that he wanted to start a new electric group."

That "new electric group" became the popular and critically-acclaimed Elektric Band, which helped John launch his solo career with his 1987 debut, *John Patitucci*.

What are the advantages and disadvantages of doubling on electric and acoustic bass?

Speaking purely from a playing point of view, the main disadvantage is that you're talking about two separate instruments. The technique and touch are completely different. Upright players who double on electric usually have to work on lightening their touch because the upright is physically more demanding to play. Left-hand technique involves using the 3rd and 4th fingers together in the low positions to give you the power to play in tune, especially on stretches. This is the opposite of the electric, where you want independence of all four fingers. The right hand, meanwhile, is held differently on the two instruments. Then there are issues ranging from thumb position and playing with a bow on the upright to using your thumb and playing chordally on the electric. I have a saying. It's a long way from arco to slap.

The advantages, conversely, are conceptual to me. If you can walk on the upright, then you can adapt the proper feel to the electric. I was able to apply the hammer-ons and pull-offs I learned on the electric bass when I began playing upright. Most important, playing an acoustic instrument teaches you about tone production—drawing a pleasing sound out of the string. That's a great influence on the electric. When I first started doubling, other bassists told me they couldn't conceive of doing it for fear they'd wind up being mediocre on both. But with people like Stanley Clarke and Ron Carter as role models, I knew it could be done well. Now, each instrument is an essential part of my musical voice.

Not many people would even attempt to play both electric and acoustic as much as you do.

I always say it's just stupidity on my part! I've always felt, "Well, I'd *like* to do this," and I've been fortunate to have the kind of people around who have encouraged me. No one ever told me it was impossible. Sometimes, in the thick of it, I think, "Wow, what am I doing? I'm nuts." Playing both instruments has caused me some physical problems. It can be tough, but I see musical reasons for playing both instruments. For one thing, I get to play with a more diverse cross-section of people. Some people call me for electric and others call me for acoustic, and I wouldn't want to cut out either one.

One thing I've always been concerned about is playing both instruments with enough conviction so I don't sound watered down. That's the risk you take when you play both: being mediocre on two instruments rather than strong on one. My goal has always been to be strong on both.

James Jamerson also played both acoustic and electric—although he's certainly better known for his electric playing.

It's come full circle, in a way. Jamerson got me into playing; he was really inspiring—his feeling and groove, obviously, but also the way he constructed his bass lines. It was very compositional. And he was originally an upright bass player—a good one and a real jazzer. I went the other way, starting on electric and then adding the upright.

Anthony Jackson will tell you that James Jamerson had a huge impact on him, and that's a pretty heavy statement when you consider what a genius Anthony is. He's a unique individual on the instrument and a consummate artist—a true virtuoso.

You were one of the first players to follow Anthony's example with the 6-string. You plunged right into it, at a time when others were very skeptical about the instrument.

A lot of people were saying crazy things like, "Oh, you're going to get tendinitis. Maybe it's fine for Anthony, but that's just not going to work for you." But Anthony was dead on the money. I knew that if somebody I respected that much felt strongly enough to go out of his way to have people build this thing, then there was *something* going on. And I had to investigate it.

Did you feel comfortable with the 6-string right away?

It was really weird at first. I enjoyed it, and I had an idea of what I wanted to do with it, but I was tripping around. I got my first 6-string right before I went on my first tour with Chick in 1985. It was shock treatment—I just started doing it. Maybe that was good, because it forced me to just jump in there and play. I'm still learning how to play the 6-string—it's a constant refining process.

It must have been especially strange doing it as a left-hander who plays right-handed.

Well, I've always played bass right-handed. When I started, there were no left-handed instruments around, so I just picked up a [right-handed] bass and started playing. Later on, I noticed that the thumb stuff was hard for me to do, and I really had to work to get my right hand loose. Being left-handed has been an advantage in some ways. Other bass players have commented that I use my left hand a lot in terms of articulation—slurring and hammers and things like that. Some guys sound *really* right-handed, and they pick every note they play; I tend to do a lot more with my left hand.

How would you describe yourself as a composer?

I like to write lyrically and melodically. I've been influenced by people like Chick Corea, Wayne Shorter, and Herbie Hancock, and I've also been influenced by a lot of pop music—the R&B I grew up with—Motown, Stevie Wonder, Donny Hathaway—is very melodic. I love Latin, Brazilian, and African music—they're all melodic as well as rhythmically powerful.

Although I'm a bass player, my music isn't all written around the bass. I don't think every song has to have a bass melody and lots of overtracked basses; I like to write for *all* the instruments.

Are you encouraged when you hear young players using 5- and 6-string basses?

It seems that players are starting younger on these

 Heart of His Basses

Foremost among John Patitucci's signature Yamaha 6-strings is a butterscotch 35"-scale model with a sweepable midrange. His main backup is a cherrywood 6. Other electrics in his collection include Yamaha fretted and fretless TRB-5s, Sadowsky 4- and 5-strings, an old Fender Jazz, a Yamaha custom acoustic/electric 5, and a Fender Mustang that was the second bass he owned. He strings them with D'Addario Prisms stainless-steel roundwounds, gauged .030, .045, .065, .080, .105, .130. John's main acoustic bass is a circa-1960 Pöllmann. He also owns a 125-year-old 7/8-size Viennese acoustic and a 80-year-old Juzek. His upright strings are D'Addario Helicore Hybrid or Orchestral, and his trimmings include a Morizot French bow, a Gage Realist under-bridge pickup, an AMT clip-on mic, a Crown GLM100 interior mic controlled by a Fishman Pocket Blender, and Audix mikes.

Live over the years, Patitucci has plugged into Walter Woods heads with assorted Bag End cabinets. He then went to Aguilar gear, including a DB750 head and one or two GS410 cabinets. His cables are Planet Waves. For recording his electric, he sends his bass into an Aguilar DB680 and then direct to the board; for his upright he favors a Neumann U47 studio mike.

instruments, and some of them are pretty flexible already. The one thing I would caution them about—and I mention this when I do clinics—is to be sure they're doing their functional roles as bass players. You can get all hung up in the solo attributes of the 6-string, but your first job is to be the foundation of the rhythm section. That's really an important job; it's the reason why we took up the instrument in the first place.

What else do you cover in your clinics?

I try to show players how to come up with interesting lines. I'll take a specific groove and show them different ways to approach it. Great players like Jamerson and Chuck Rainey created lines that made every part of the song sound good. Coming up with a line like that is like threading a needle—it's difficult to teach that.

What I talk about, mostly, is listening. I tell them to really listen to players they enjoy and analyze what they do—write the music down, so they can see what goes into a good bass line. You learn a lot by transcribing great players—you see patterns and compositional thinking.

Young musicians should take advantage of the time they have and practice a lot. It's super-important to get out and play with other people, too; you have to *listen* and figure out what works in different musical situations. Different styles demand different priorities.

What about soloing technique?

That comes down to musicianship skills, really: training your ear, learning harmony, having a good grasp of the scales and arpeggios on your instrument. I went over most of these things in my second video [*John Patitucci: Electric Bass 2*, DCI]. Getting into the piano helps—if you learn some chord voicings on the piano, you can analyze the different kinds of chords and learn how to hear them. That way, when somebody strikes a chord, you'll either know, "Well, that's a 13th chord with a ♯11," or at least you'll recognize the sound and know how to play through it by ear. It will click.

Looking back, what would you say were the most important events in launching your professional career?

That's hard to say. I feel very fortunate—I think God was really good to me, because a lot of things seemed to happen at the right time. When my family moved to the West Coast, that turned out to be a good thing. You might think it was bad to leave New York, because it's such an important music town, but in the long run it turned out great for me. Living near L.A., I've been able to take advantage of a lot of different work opportunities and play with a lot of great musicians.

Have your spiritual beliefs affected your career?

What you believe has to influence the way you play and *why* you play. I didn't get serious about Christianity until I was 17. By then I had been playing for a while, and it changed my focus. I became more in touch with the gift that God had given me and wanted to use it for the right reasons, rather than getting caught up in self-aggrandizement. It's easy for a musician to get wrapped up in the "me" thing, because there are a lot of insecurities that drive us to express ourselves with an instrument. We want people to like us.

I'm very influenced by Bach's credo, "Every note for the glory of God." Bach was in touch with where his gift came from, and every note he wrote and played was in celebration of this gift. If you're doing that, chances are that the people listening to your music will enjoy it, too. It's a higher purpose than, "Oh yeah, I'm doing this so chicks will dig me." Whether you believe what I do or not, I think it's better to have that kind of focus—to try to touch people with your music and give them something of value.

When I interviewed John in April 2000 much had changed. He had left Los Angeles and his fusion-and-session-dominated workload, and returned to his native New York to refocus on his acoustic jazz side. This included the Afro-Cuban jazz journey he took for his ninth solo album, Imprint.

A large part of your career was spent in Los Angeles. How would you sum up your L.A. days?

L.A. was school for me. When I wasn't on the road with Chick Corea gaining all that knowledge, I did sessions, which is where I learned about being disciplined enough to work with other people in a lot of different styles and about contributing to their music without overplaying or forcing myself on it. A big part of the challenge was discovering the different ways to approach playing time. I can remember early Christian music and gospel dates with drummers from Oklahoma who laid *way* back, and there I was, from Brooklyn, playing on top and wanting to burn!

Basically, what I did in L.A. was come up with parts. If you want to be successful bassist in any style, you've got to learn how to create parts—how to compose on the instrument and make up a part that's the groove, that people can hang the music on. And if the part is written, you have to give it the strength and conviction to make it sound like *you* wrote it.

Where did the Imprint *concept come from?*

John Patitucci Selected Discography

Solo albums: *Songs, Stories & Spirituals*, Concord Jazz; *Communion*, Concord Jazz; *Imprint*, Concord Jazz; *Now*, Concord Jazz; *One More Angel*, Concord Jazz; *Mistura Fina*, Stretch; *Another World*, Stretch; *Heart of the Bass*, Stretch; *Sketchbook*, GRP; *On the Corner*, GRP; *John Patitucci*, GRP. **With Chick Corea:** (all on GRP) *Time Warp*; *Beneath the Mask*; *Alive*; *Inside Out*; *The Chick Corea Akoustic Band*; *Eye of the Beholder*; *Light Years*; *The Chick Corea Elektric Band*. **With Wayne Shorter:** *Alegria*, Verve; *Footprints Live*, Verve; *Phantom Navigator*, Columbia. **With Roy Haynes:** *The Roy Haynes Trio*, Verve. **With Herbie Hancock:** *Directions in Music: Live at Massey Hall*, Verve. **With Danilo Perez:** *Motherland*, Polygram; *Central Avenue*, GRP. **With Natalie Cole:** *Unforgettable*, Elektra. **With Mike Stern:** *Give and Take*, Atlantic. **With Jim Beard:** *Truly*, Escapade. **With Michel Camilo:** *Thru My Eyes*, RMM. **With Mariah Carey:** *Charmbracelet*, Def Jam. **With Victor Feldman:** *To Chopin with Love*, Palo Alto. **With Was (Not Was):** *What Up, Dog?*, Alliance. **With Peter Erskine and John Abercrombie:** *The Hudson Project*, Stretch. **With John Beasley:** *Change of Heart*, Windham Hill. **With Jay Azzolina:** *Past Tense*, Double-Time. **With Bass Extremes:** *Just Add Water*, Tone Center. **With George Benson:** *Love Remembers*, Warner Bros. **With Joanne Brackeen:** *Pink Elephant Magic*, Arkadia Jazz. **With Gary Burton:** *Departure*, Concord Jazz. **With Joey Calderazzo:** *Joey Calderazzo*, Sony. **With Edward Simon:** *The Process*, Criss Cross. **With Al Di Meola:** *Grande Passion: World Sinfonia*, Telarc. **With Dave Grusin:** *West Side Story*, N2K; *Homage to Duke*, GRP; *Gershwin Connection*, GRP. **With Lee Ritenour:** *Stolen Moments*, GRP. **With Steve Khan:** *Got My Mental*, Evidence. **With B.B. King:** *Here and There*, Hip-O. **With Renee Rosnes:** *Life on Earth*, Blue Note. **With Manhattan Transfer:** *Vocalese*, Atlantic. **With Barry Manilow:** *Because It's Christmas*, Arista. **With Roger Waters:** *Amused to Death*, Sony. **With Gonzalo Rubalcaba:** *Images*, Blue Note. **With Vinnie Colaiuta:** *Vinnie Colaiuta*, GRP. **With Jeff Beal:** *Three Graces*, Triloka. **With Jason Miles:** *Celebrating the Music of Weather Report*, Telarc. **With Everything But the Girl:** *The Language of Life*, Atlantic. **With Kenny Rogers:** *Timepiece*, Atlantic. **With Ali Farka Toure** (with Ry Cooder): *Talking Timbuktu*, Hannibal. **With Stay Awake** (with Hal Wilner and Bonnie Raitt): *Stay Awake: Interpretations of Vintage Disney Films*, A&M. **With the GRP All-Star Big Band:** (both on GRP) *All Blues*; *The GRP All-Star Big Band*.

It was inspired by the passing of my mom, to whom the record is dedicated. The process led me to ponder all the input and experiences I've had, both inside and outside of music—the traditional Italian culture I was raised in, the people I've met, the places I've been, my faith. We all have this in our lives; everything that affects us and leaves a little imprint we carry with us. The album is a collection of my imprints.

Much of the album shows an Afro-Cuban influence.

I've been around that music and studied it for some time, and I have a deep respect for bassists like Cachao, Bobby Rodriguez, Sal Cuevas, and Andy Gonzalez. But I haven't had a chance to do much of that on my records, so I wanted to experiment with it. The key was to find Latin masters with a jazz sensibility. I know [pianist] Danilo Perez from playing with him in Roy Haynes's trio, I did a tour with El Negro [drummer Horacio "El Negro" Hernández], and they turned me on to [percussionist Giovanni] Hidalgo. Rather than adhere to a strict folk tradition, my goal was to mix Afro-Cuban elements with jazz in a modern, open way, so the players could stretch and comment on the music.

That comes across clearly in the opener, "King Kong."

I thought of that as "Ornette Coleman goes to Cuba," because of its linear shape—with lines that dissolve in the middle, and the way the harmony is deliberately disguised. I brought in compositions that were thoroughly notated, and I talked about the types of feels I wanted, but what these guys came up with was beyond my imagination.

How did the additional percussion and traditional rhythms affect your bass lines?

It was tremendously inspiring. Even though he plays the kit, El Negro has a very open feel that doesn't tie you to a drum beat, and Hidalgo is a whole other education. They, along with Danilo, showed me different ways to tap cross-rhythms, like four against three, to develop my independence. Basically, I just tried to put a big anchor on everything. I was conscious of the clave and the tumbao, but I was playing a fair share of downbeats because it worked with what they were doing. Afro-Cuban music is fascinating because there's a lot of layering of rhythms and feels, with a consistent referencing to all of them. During the course of a piece, the musicians will comment on one and then stray toward another. That happened quite a bit on "Imprint": The song is in 3/4, but when we recorded it someone would lead us into 6/8, and then we'd all sense when to go back to 3/4.

It sounds as though you carry those ideas to your bass work on the straightahead jazz tunes, such as "Little Steps."

When you're playing with a drummer like Jack DeJohnette, who is continually flowing and creating, it doesn't work to stay in one groove or to walk all the way through. You have to keep changing it up, while also listening to him and to the soloist. That concept evolved largely from the great Miles Davis bands with Herbie Hancock, Tony Williams, and Ron Carter. You have a pulse and a tonal center as a reference, and around that there's room to listen and converse. As the bassist, your job is to keep that pulse and tonality in people's ears by hinting at it, while also contributing melodic and rhythmic ideas and support. A key to doing this well, which I work on with students, is to be familiar with any particular sound on the whole instrument. When you have a sound—say it's A minor—you've got to know it over the entire fingerboard, so you have the flexibility to jump around and freely choose notes while still remaining in that sound. You can't afford to be stuck in one part of the bass.

On "Postcards" you use upright for the groove and 6-string for your melody and solo.

I picked up the 6 because the melody reminded me of John Scofield. I also overdubbed the 6 at the end of "Imprint." Going in, I wanted to use the 6 in an acoustic jazz context for its different sound and color, and it was great having the upright's thick foundation to blow over. However, I also wanted to shake the notion of, Oh, he's strapping on the 6—they're going to play a funk or fusion tune. Naturally, one bass can be preferable to the other in certain situations, but I try to not have such a regimented view of what goes where. Live, I've been playing both of these tunes on the 6, which has been fine.

Your bowing on the "Japanese Folk Song" melody is very cello-like in tone and range.

I've been working on my bowing with John Schaeffer, who was the New York Philharmonic's principal bassist, and Tom Martin, the former London Philharmonic principal, and they've opened up my sound. I play French-style, and John switched my grip to put my thumb on the frog [the bow-hair support on the bow's grip end], like the old Neapolitan style, which is really cool. I prefer to use the bow more in a lyrical, cello-like setting, but I'll blow with it here and there. It's difficult to make the notes swing like you can with your fingers, but I plan to get into it more. First, I just want to build up my ability to play in tune with a big, beautiful sound.

The album closes with Mongo Santamaria's "Afro Blue," keeping your Coltrane cover link intact.

Obviously, Trane is a huge hero of mine. I've always fooled around with "Afro Blue," and I had never heard it done as a solo bass piece. So I thought it would be interesting as a duet with percussion. I brought the original key down a half-step to E minor, and when Hidalgo and I got into rehearsal I came up with a 3/4 groove based on something he played. Later, El Negro said he was hearing us in 6/8, so I guess we were in and out of both feels. I originally played through Hidalgo's amazing solo, but I took myself out in the mix because he was getting pitches on his congas and I didn't want to distract from that.

What's your vision for your bass playing?

I want to get to the point where I can play a melody without people tripping on the fact that it's a bass. To not notice the technique or the register or the intonation—just react to the melody emotionally and listen to the line's development rather than the instrument it's played on—like we do with a piano or horn or guitar. Beyond that, it's about honing my voice. [Drummer] Billy Hart once said Trane sounds like he's playing a ballad whether he's screaming a hundred notes or playing one note real soft. That's what I'm trying to do on the bass.

Web site

www.johnpatitucci.com

John's Steps

LIKE ALL GREAT DOUBLERS, John Patitucci may evoke bebop on his 6-string electric or Latin funk on his upright without batting an eye. Here are examples from a few of his 11 solo albums.

From *Now*: In a four-and-a-half-minute duet romp over the changes to "Giant Steps," John Patitucci (on his Yamaha 6), along with drummer Bill Stewart, travels both inside and outside John Coltrane's historic harmonic sequence while maintaining a lyrical approach reminiscent of Trane himself. In the second chorus (**Ex. 1a**), John begins with

Ex. 1a

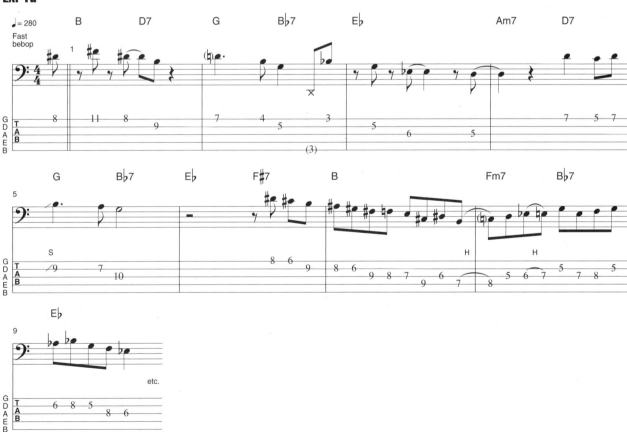

descending melodic phrases in bars 1–5 and then in bars 6–9 moves into descending and ascending bebop lines. "I use a lot of left-hand articulation when I solo," John notes. "I slur notes using hammer-ons and pull-offs to approximate the way the great horn soloists tongue some notes and 'swallow' others. That's what makes a line swing."

Example 1b lays out John's fifth chorus, starting with two ear-catching sequences in bars 1–7. "The first sequence is a series of descending triads moving down in whole-steps, which gets displaced by two beats. I got the idea from the way bassists typically walk through 'Giant Steps.' Instead of playing the roots—B, D, G, B♭, E♭—they'll play B, A, G, F, E♭ for a smoother line. I took that motion, added the triads, and then displaced them to create interesting alter-

Ex. 1b

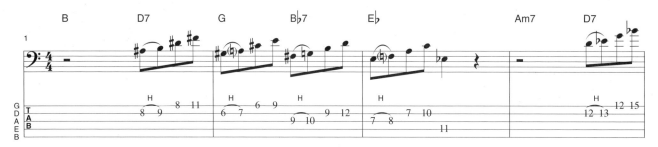

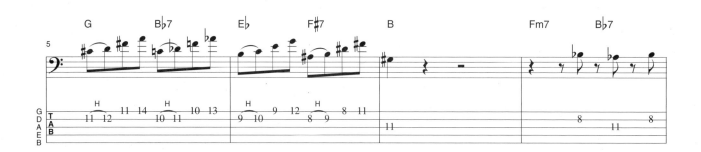

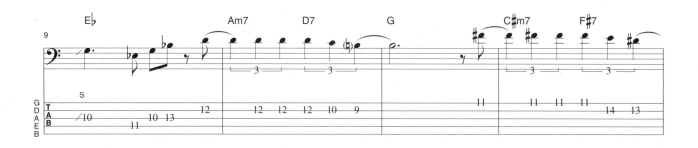

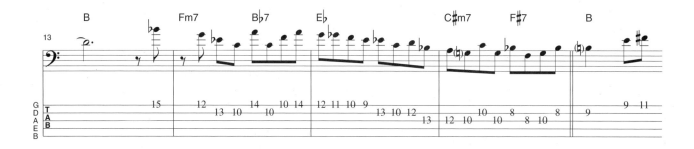

ations against the changes. For instance, the *B* triad motif against the *D7* chord in bar 1 gives you the ♯5, 13, ♭9, and 3. In bars 4–7 I moved the sequence up a major 3rd." In bars 8–13 John returns to pure lyricism with the track's most melodic phrases, and bars 14–16 explode with angular pentatonics. "I used shapes and chromaticism to free myself and go in a new direction for the next chorus, which contains a lot of open intervals and more outside material."

From *Fingerprints*: **Example 2** is inspired by Patitucci's upright solo in "King Kong." Having introduced a two-bar motif that emphasizes *Cm/maj7*, he begins to develop it over the next few bars. The motif spans more than two octaves, illustrating John's point about knowing a sound on the entire fingerboard. "I tend to break down the board

Ex. 2

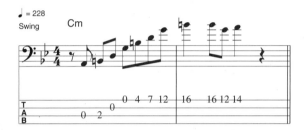

Ex. 3a

Ex. 3b

Ex. 4

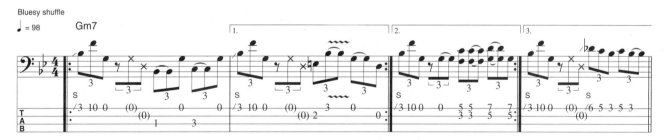

Ex. 5

into smaller sections, like arpeggios, and then link them together." **Examples 3a and 3b** come from Patitucci's version of John Coltrane's "Afro Blue." Example 3a is his opening two-bar upright groove, which he plays in a half-time three feel. Example 3b contains his upright reading of the melody's first four bars, for which he doubles the tempo. "On top of that, Giovanni Hidalgo implied some 6/8, so we had a two-against-three feel going."

From *Songs, Stories & Spirituals*: **Example 4** contains John's opening upright line from "I Will Arise," an old Baptist spiritual. "I wanted to take an African roots approach to the tune. The first part of my pattern is inspired by the way Pygmies sing—with high "whoops"—and then I embellish the second half of each bar. **Example 5** shows John's 6-string bass line from "Lei"—"That's a Brazilian *partido alto* groove."

VICTOR WOOTEN
All in the Family

Interviewed by Chris Jisi, March 1997; Bill Leigh, January 1998; Bill Leigh and Chris Jisi, February 1998; Bill Leigh, February 1999; and E.E. Bradman, February 2002.

HAS THERE BEEN A MORE INFLUENTIAL and inspiring bassist in the last 15 years than Victor Lemonte Wooten? Back when he was first featured in *Bass Player* in 1991, Wooten was a 26-year-old musical veteran just beginning to turn heads by expanding funk-bass techniques with the genre-leaping jazz/bluegrass instrumental ensemble Béla Fleck & the Flecktones. The unit featured banjo ace Fleck, keyboardist/harmonica player Howard Levy, Victor, and his brother Roy "Futureman" Wooten on percussion. With Levy's departure in 1992, Vic Wooten stepped forward in the trio format to display a staggering array of skills that quickly turned him into a bass hero of Pastorian proportions. He became known for using his impressive technical ability to play melody, rhythm, and bass parts simultaneously on his Fodera 4-string.

Wooten presented his first fully formed exposition of this concept on his 1996 solo debut, *A Show of Hands*. Filled with complex jazz, funk, and classical-style pieces all played with no overdubs, the disc was a bass-record milestone. Victor's solo vision only expanded from there, with the subsequent releases of *What Did He Say?*, *Yin Yang*, and the double CD *Live in America*. He began solo tours with drummer JD Blair and various guests, and grew in demand as a sideman. This led to three Bass Extremes discs (and countless gigs and clinics) with partner Steve Bailey [see page **52**], two albums with Scott Henderson and Steve Smith as the trio Vital Tech Tones, and tours with the Mike Stern Quartet. In 2000 Victor also launched his annual Bass/Nature Camps in Tennessee, providing perspective for young musicians.

Victor hastily points to his own roots as the key to his career success: "My brothers and parents were the foundation. They prepared me for just about anything by teaching me to keep my mind open and to learn to adapt. Musically, that means not being rigid and not having to play in a certain way." The youngest of five musical brothers, Victor began his bass career as a three-year-old when his oldest brother, Regi, began teaching him to play. By age five Victor was joining his brothers on the nightclub circuit. By the time he was in middle school, a few years after the family settled in Newport News, Virginia, he was a veteran musician. His best schooling in the art of freestyling? The daily summertime jams at the Wooten home.

Wooten is keenly conscious of his visibility in the bass world, yet he retains down-home humility, a strong sense of gratitude, and an eagerness to share the spotlight. (He regularly pulls bassists out of the audience to participate in his shows.) "My goal is to show that the bass is a complete instrument, like the guitar or piano, but to do it in a way that says, 'This is what you can do,' not just 'Look at what I can do.'" During the same week he became a first-time father, he took time to talk about his career, analyze *What Did He Say?*, and explain why he does solo work. "In the Flecktones I get to express myself in a huge way; I think I have more freedom than any bass player in any band. Still, when you're

Victor Wooten

in a band, you're sharing your ideas and compromising a lot. That's not a bad thing—when you put great minds together you come up with greater things. But as in any relationship you need some time to yourself. That's my choice in doing solo work."

What bass players had the biggest impact on you?

I would say Stanley Clarke, Jaco Pastorius, Larry Graham, and Bootsy Collins. Of those players, Stanley was the most important to me. I patterned myself after him for a long time, and you can hear it in my playing. When I was eight years old, I went to see Return to Forever—after the show I got to talk to Stanley. I didn't know what to say, so I asked him if I could have a broken string or something. He said he didn't have anything, but he gave me an address to write to. I went home and wrote a letter, and he sent me an autographed picture, a tour schedule, a Return to Forever book, and it just made my whole life. I think if Stanley had been mean to me, it would have changed things. A lot. As a result, now every time I play I make myself available to people right after the show. For at least an hour, I sit down, talk and sign autographs. Many times I'll get out my bass and show people things or answer questions.

What advice do you give to the young bassists you meet who admire your playing?

I remind them it's about music first and technique last. A lot of the players I meet nowadays I can tell I've influenced. I really like that, but I'm seeing a lot of flashy thumb licks that don't really *feel* that good—they're not *groovin'*. I tell them to focus on groove and feel first and then put technique on top of that. If all people see from me is the technique stuff, I'd much rather they spend more time listening to someone else who's concentrating more on groove.

What Did He Say? *has a very different feel than the strictly solo-bass* A Show of Hands. *Why did you choose to do this album now and that album then?*

I could have done either album first, but I had wanted to do a solo bass record for maybe ten years, so that's what I did first. I wanted to make a statement—more to myself than to the public—not to prove what I could do, but to show it could be done. I just didn't quite know how to make the record listenable for the duration. It was kind of a challenge to myself, and I was very happy with the outcome.

Even though the new album is different from most bass records out there, it's more along the lines of what other bass players are doing. Most of the time a bass record is centered around jazz and fusion, with the bass playing the melody over a band. That's great, but it's kind of standard. I want to express myself in a different way, not just to be different—it's just that I am different. Of course, I'm no more different than anyone else, but I think when a lot of people make records they try to figure out what everyone else is doing and see how they can fit in. I do what I do whether it fits in or not. With *What Did He Say?* I'm trying to express myself in a band context.

Why did you leave Virginia for Nashville?

Kurt Storey, who helped to produce both records, is a great friend; he's my longest Nashville connection. I met him at Busch Gardens, an amusement park in Virginia, where we both worked as musicians in the early '80s. Over and over he would tell my brothers and me that we "gotta move to Nashville," and he was telling people in Nashville about the five of us. Over the years we kept in touch, and in 1987 I visited him in Nashville. He introduced me to Béla, Edgar Meyer, [violinist] Mark O'Connor—the whole crew. That was when I first played for Béla over the telephone, which led to us getting together and having a jam session. Kurt also introduced me to Jonell Mosser, an amazing vocalist, who asked me to sub for her regular bass player for a month.

When I came to Nashville, I was playing quite differently than most people. Nashville musicians play incredibly well—and I hope this doesn't come off as criticism—but I was hearing people being conservative. At gigs they'd play perfectly but not stretch at all. It makes for a great show—but man, I love it when people are stretchin'! It's like if an audience is watching a juggler: If the juggling is perfect, great. But the way to really get the audience is if he almost drops one pin, struggles and struggles, and then suddenly grabs it and gets it back under control. The audience goes crazy!

So when I was first playing with Jonell, I was totally in left field, doing kind of what I'm doing now, only now people are more used to it. The first night we played out, there was one song where everybody got to take a long solo. Mine was like a solo I would take during the Flecktones' "Sinister Minister" [*Béla Fleck & the Flecktones* and *Live Art*]—you know, I really let go. Nobody was expecting that. I played a lot of the drum lines and fills, tapping and slapping and everything. The audience loved it—people freaked out. So much so that the drummer, who was supposed to take a solo after that, hyperventilated and had to be taken to the hospital. We had to get a guy out of the audience to finish the set. I don't tell that story often because it sounds like I'm boasting, but that's just what happened. It was a great night, and that led to me keeping the gig for a couple of years.

Since you're the first of the brothers to leave home, and the first to do a solo album, in a sense you're the adventurer.

I guess you could say that. Right now, I'm the one people know about. But "the brothers" is where I came from. When I do clinics with Steve Bailey, people ask me where I got this or that technique, and I often say my brother Regi taught me. One day Steve got to see Regi play, and all he kept saying was, "Now I get it! Now I get it!" Everything I do on the bass Regi does on the guitar—tapping, thumb stuff, everything. Some things we developed together, and some things I've shown him, but he's really the basis of everything I do.

In the three years between the time that you worked on A Show of Hands *and* What Did He Say?, *did any other musicians have a big impact on you?*

Yeah—Mongolian and Tuvan throat singers. The Flecktones took a trip to Asia and spent about a week in Mongolia; that's where we got turned on to these guys who sing two or three notes at a time. That totally knocked me out, so I started learning how to do it. I did a little bit on "The Loneliest Monk": once after the first bridge, and again getting some vocal overtones toward the end. I'm not great at it, but it's an amazing technique and I'm still working on it. Also, I've been getting into a Spanish bassist named Carles Benavent, who plays a lot with guitarist Paco de Lucía. I was able to find a couple of his solo records when I was in Spain.

And I'm always amazed by Oteil Burbridge. I just love everything he does.

Is there a story behind the title track, "What Did He Say?"

I have a friend from Virginia, Matt Smith, who has this amazing ability to talk in total gibberish but make people think he's actually saying something. You can hear some of it on the album ["radio W-OO-10"], but it's even funnier in person, because people try to be polite and act like they know what he's talking about. One time JD and I were laughing about it before a gig, and we started going, "What did he say? What did he say?" during soundcheck. That night during the set it came up again, and we developed this great groove around it. After we came off the road, we got the live tape to hear what we'd been doing, got together with Kurt Storey, and recorded it at my house. We did the chorus vocals using a loop. I put down a scratch vocal for the verse, but Kurt and JD liked it and wouldn't let me change it. While we were playing, our cockatiel, Cherokee, was squawking in the background. He was getting into it, so we looped him in there, too.

In the liner notes you mention there are six bass tracks on the song. Are the harmony parts separate tracks?

Yeah. For this record, wherever I thought it would sound better to play parts separately, I did. But on the first CD I made a point of playing everything at once.

There are parts of this song and others where you sound a lot like Marcus Miller. I don't remember hearing that in your work before.

It's totally new. Most of the time that's the NYC Empire bass. It's like a Fender, and since I've never owned a Fender I've never had that sound. The bass really reminded me of Marcus when I got it because it has a fatter tone. A lot of my playing was patterned after Stanley Clarke, who has a thinner tone.

The second part of the bridge sounds like it has two bass lines.

One is going down and there's another in the background, just adding fills. The melody on top is two or even three parts. For the liner notes I counted every track of bass, even if it was just an extra little part.

That's a pretty mean shuffle groove on your cover of Bobby Caldwell's "What You Won't Do for Love."

A Show of Basses

Victor Wooten's main bass—fast taking its place among the most famous 4-strings—is his 1983 Fodera Monarch Deluxe. Made of curly and rock maple, Honduran mahogany, and East Indian rosewood, it sports EMG PJ pickups and a Kahler tremolo. Other key basses include his Yin Yang Foderas in 4-string fretted and fretless and 5-string fretted varieties; a Fodera tenor bass (tuned *ADGC*); a Fodera NYC 4-string; a fretless 5-string and a fretted 6-string built by Joe Compito; a Conklin 8-string; a Nechville "Banjo Bass"; a Goldtone bass banjo; a Conklin M.E.U. electric upright; a Taylor fretless acoustic bass guitar; a 1781 Italian acoustic bass; a Juzek acoustic bass; a Kubicki Factor 4-string; a custom Keith Roscoe 5-string; a Ken Lawrence nylon-string hollowbody piccolo bass; his late-'70s Alembic Series 1, which he describes as his "first good bass"; and his actual first bass, a Univox Beatle Bass copy. His strings are Fodera Victor Wooten signature nickel roundwounds (gauged .040, .055, .075, .095). Victor also places drugstore-bought elastic ponytail holders around the necks of his basses to "clean up the ringing."

Live, Wooten plugs into an Ampeg SVT 4PRO with Ampeg BXT-410HL4 and BXT-115HL4 cabinets (which he designed with Steve Bailey), and he uses Shure in-ear monitors. He also takes a Walter Woods 1,200-watt head on some tours. Victor steps on DigiTech Whammy and GNX2 multi-effects pedals, a Morley volume pedal, and an EBS BassIQ envelope filter. His rack gear includes an Eventide Ultra-Harmonizer, a Furman power conditioner, a Roland Sound Canvas, a Yamaha 01B mixer, and a Korg DTR1 Digital Tuner. For sound sculpting, he has a custom MIDImix controller and a Yamaha MIDI controller for the Yamaha MIDI pickup on his Yin Yang 5-string. He also has the Roland V-Bass modeling system.

[*Laughs.*] A lot of that must be credited to JD. I end up playing around him a lot. When *A Show of Hands* came out and JD and I started touring, that was one of the tunes we'd play. With the Lexicon JamMan, I can loop chords and the bass line—really create the whole band all on the fly—and just play the melody on top.

This song consists of mainly three tracks: bass line, chord line, and melody. I list more tracks because there are parts where I play some harmonics, even though they're not there through the whole tune. And sometimes there are two or even three tracks on the melody. I use the tenor bass, tuned *ADGC*, for the melody, chords, and solos. Some of my solos on this tune might be more melodic than people are used to hearing me play. That's mostly Oteil's influence.

You say the song "Cherokee" is a good example of a new playing style you're trying to develop.

My goal is to use my up-and-down-thumbstroke technique to play these fast, ripping notes and make 'em pop the way trumpet players tongue fast bebop lines. You can hear me trying this on the "Cherokee" solo. I actually did quite a bit of punching-in on that bass part. I'm just not at the point where I can play like that and keep it going.

Arrangement-wise, I had come up with the idea of having everybody in at the beginning, dropping out for the bass solo and then gradually coming back, beginning with James Genus on acoustic bass and ending with the drums—kind of backwards.

What makes your thumb style unique?

I think it's mostly the way I *think* about certain things. My thumb technique is not that different from what other people are doing; I just think of it in a way most players don't. When most of us use our thumbs, we get brain-locked into playing octaves and pentatonic scales, or muted notes in neat, complex rhythms. But when we use our fingers, all of a sudden we're more creative—we play all kinds of scales and stuff. I try to think of my thumb as being no different from my fingers; it's just another way of hitting the note. I'll take the type of solo most people would play with their fingers and play it with my thumb, to get a different attack. When I started thinking like that, all of a sudden my thumb playing sounded different, just because of my note choices.

How did you develop the musical idea for "Don't Wanna Cry"?

When I'm on the road I always bring my Boss DR-5 with me. It's a 4-track sequencer in a little box, with drums and sounds so you can program the whole rhythm section. I can plug in my bass and play along— that's the way I practice on the road. When I was in Japan doing a clinic tour with James Genus, I used it to come up with the main groove of "Don't Wanna Cry." The groove sat in the DR-5 for about a year, and then at a Flecktones soundcheck the vocal idea hit me in a flash. I got a microphone, went into a dressing room, and recorded almost all of the vocals. Everything you're hearing except for the vocals and bass melody is that DR-5 program. This is the same box I used for the "piano" solo on "The Loneliest Monk."

The cool thing about the DR-5 is the buttons are positioned to simulate a guitar fretboard—six lines of six keys. It's easy for me to play because it's just like tapping. That's how I played the piano part. I had to punch in and fix some mistakes, but it wasn't sequenced. We gave it an "old" sound by playing an old record in the background.

Is that song a tribute to Thelonious Monk?

Yes and no. It's about how Monk was strange, so much so many people called him crazy. But that's what we call anybody who's out of the ordinary. The musicians we love the most are the people who are out of the ordinary, because you have to be out of the ordinary to be an original. Anybody who's an innovator or inventor has to step outside of normal thinking to get there. To me that's where we should all be.

"A Chance" is a bit of a departure from "Monk."

JD wrote that song; he had recorded it at home on his 4-track. When he played it for me, I thought,

Man—this is so cool and so funky, and it's the type of tune I wouldn't write, so I asked him if we could do it for the record. I played my Compito 6-string using the same effects he used on the demo: a DOD FX25 Envelope Filter and an Ibanez Soundtank FL5 flanger.

"Norwegian Wood" is the only solo bass arrangement on the album, and it's pretty ambitious. How did you come up with it?

A friend of mine, who works for a radio station, asked me to be part of a John Lennon tribute. I said okay, but I didn't really know any John Lennon tunes. He started naming off some things, and I remembered "Norwegian Wood."

When I'm arranging, it's best for me to try not to think about it too hard. I just hear it in my head. I found out quickly I could play the main melody in harmonics in the key of *G*—actually the key of *C* on the tenor bass. The intro chords are another Oteil influence, and then I add a flamenco type of technique. From there I had to figure out a way to get to *C* so I could use the harmonics the way I wanted. I kept experimenting, and when I got something I liked I'd record it. I kept adding to it until the end of the tune.

When I do these kinds of pieces I do fix things, but I probably end up leaving more mistakes than I fix. There's one place in the middle of the tune where I kind of lose it, and you hear me go [*sighs*]. But I came back in time in the next part, so I thought, Okay, let's just leave it. It's that idea of the juggler who almost drops one pin but gets it going again. I like that—instead of being a seamless performance, there's some life in it.

Your father sings lead on the tall tale "Bro. John." Is it based on a story he always told?

Yeah. He would tell us stories about John who could eat and eat. There's another tune Dad sings in that same bouncy, old gospel style. My dad calls this style of singing "snatchin'." "Let's *snatch* this one," he'll say. The actual groove was something I'd come up with on my Fodera yin-yang fretless while playing around with the JamMan. I thought it was cool, but since it's in an odd time I opened it up in 4/4 in the middle so my dad could sing over it. I sent him a copy of it with me singing and asked him if he would be able to do it. He got excited and started working on it right away.

You came up with a very interesting version of John Coltrane's "Naima."

I was sitting around jamming with my friend Tye North, who plays bass for Leftover Salmon. He started

Victor Wooten Selected Discography

Solo albums: (all on Compass) *Live in America*; *Yin Yang*; *What Did He Say?*; *A Show of Hands*. **With Béla Fleck & the Flecktones:** (all on Warner Bros. except where noted) *Little Worlds*, Columbia; *Live at the Quick*, Columbia; *Outbound*, Columbia; *Left of Cool*; *Tales from the Acoustic Planet*; *Three Flew Over the Cuckoo's Nest*; *UFO Tofu*; *Live Art*; *Flight of the Cosmic Hippo*; *Béla Fleck & the Flecktones*. **With Bass Extremes:** *Just Add Water*, Tone Center; *Bass Extremes, Vol. 2*, Tone Center, *Bass Extremes* (CD/transcription package), CPP Media. **With the Jaco Pastorius Big Band:** *Word of Mouth Revisited*, Heads Up. **With Dave Matthews:** *Live in Chicago*, RCA. **With Paul Brady:** *Spirits Colliding*, Mercury. **With Mark O'Connor:** *The New Nashville Cats*, Warner Bros. **With Buckshot LeFonque:** *Buckshot LeFonque*, Sony. **With Alex Bugnon:** *107 in the Shade*, Sony. **With Vital Tech Tones:** *Vital Tech Tones*; *Vital Tech Tones Vol. 2*, Tone Center. **With the Wootens:** *The Wootens*, Arista. **With Larry Coryell/Tom Coster/Steve Smith:** *Cause and Effect*, Tone Center. **With Shane Theriot:** *Highway 90*, Orchard. **With Adam Nitti:** *Balance*, Renaissance. **With Louie Shelton:** *Urban Culture*, Lightyear. **With David Wilcox:** *Underneath*, Vanguard. **With Vince Ebo:** *Love Is the Better Way*, Warner Alliance. **With Shanda Brash:** *Good to Go*, Rio Star. **With Stuart Duncan:** *Stuart Duncan*, Rounder. **With David Grier:** *Lone Soldier*, Rounder. **With Heritage:** *Heritage*, Koch International. **With various artists:** *The Country Bears: Original Soundtrack*, Disney.

playing these chords from a chord shape we both got from Oteil. I started grooving underneath it, and together we noticed "Naima" worked with it if the melody is played in half-time. I've always loved that tune; it was one of the songs Regi taught me on guitar when I was a kid. A while later, Oteil was visiting Nashville, so I called JD, my brother Regi, and Kurt. Kurt set us up, and we threw it down in two takes. I didn't really have an arrangement; I just kind of created it on the spot.

I had intended to play the melody with this Yamaha B1D MIDI-converter pickup I have on one of my basses. You can hook up a breath controller, call up a flute or sax patch, and when you fret a note, it doesn't play until you blow into a tube. It's so expressive. But when we were recording, the way Oteil played the melody sounded better than anything.

Oteil's being there gave me a chance to play a little electric upright, too—the Conklin M.E.U. Whenever my brothers and I listen back to my upright playing, we start laughing because my sound is so much out of the Stanley Clarke school—especially when I start to solo. He influenced my electric playing, too, but I've been playing electric long enough to put myself back into it. But my upright solo at the end of "Naima" reminds me of Stanley, which makes me happy because I love him so much.

I like working with other bass players even on my records, because I don't really look at them as bass records. They're just *my* records, and I want them to be the best possible. That might mean getting another bass player to play the part. I'm glad I got a chance to get Oteil on the record, and I'll probably be using more bass players in future projects, too.

Was "Sometimes I Laugh" originally a solo piece?

I've played it as a solo piece for a long time, but I thought I could enhance it by adding the other parts. I used the tenor bass on this one also. It's kind of a sad-sounding song, but there's one section in the middle where I would hear children laughing every time I'd play it. So I got a bunch of friends of mine, my two nephews, and some other children to laugh for me.

What tracks are you playing on "The Sojourn of Arjuna"?

One part that's a bass line, chords, and harmonics, another that's just a simple bass line, and I'm also doubling Paul McCandless's sax melody on fretless and fretted basses. I got that idea from Jaco, who once recorded a part twice to get a natural flanging sound.

This song started off as a solo bass groove. Later I came up with the melody, and we started playing it live with the Flecktones. My brother Joseph, who played keyboards on the tune, said it reminded him of a soldier who's going to war and hating what he has to go do. There's a similar story in the *Baghavad Gita*, where Arjuna discusses with God why he has to go to battle. When the people from Compass Records heard the tune, they suggested I get Davy Spillane to play bagpipes on it. So it's a nice, slow funk groove with an Irish melody on top.

How did you get the idea for "A Little Buzz"?

You're always trying to get rid of buzzes when recording, so I came up with the idea of trying to make them groove instead. I wrote the tune the day we recorded it, throwing out silly ideas at JD. I'd say, "I need a stupid drum beat, something that starts and stops with lots of angles—not fluid at all." And it came together. I "played" the buzz part using the exposed ends of two guitar cables.

Tell me about "Heaven Is Where the Heart Is."

That started out as a solo bass tune, too. There's just one track of bass. I had a title and I started coming up with the song when I got the idea to try to get Take 6 to sing on it. Later an even better idea hit me—to get my brothers to sing it. Together we came up with the vocal arrangements. My brother Rudy still lives in Virginia, so I added him on the bridge later.

As for the lyrics, we're always looking outside of ourselves, and most people who are looking for God do it that way. To me, the answer is *inside*. If we just go within ourselves, we'll find the answer to everything.

Web site

www.victorwooten.com

What Did He Play?

IT'S THE ULTIMATE MEETING OF TECHNICIAN AND MUSICIAN when Victor Wooten applies his revolutionary techniques to his soulful compositions and covers. **Examples 1–5** come from Wooten's "Freshness Guaranteed" column in the June and August 1997 issues of *Bass Player*, in which he discusses his "open hammer plucking" technique. Victor describes open-hammer plucking as hitting an open string with your right thumb, hammering a note with your left hand, and then plucking (popping) a note with your right index finger, typically creating a triplet. Example 1 contains the basic pattern. Example 2 shows that the hammered note can be changed to play any note, scale, or lick—here it's an *A* major scale. In Ex. 3 the rhythm changes and Victor outlines a *B* minor tonality; Ex. 4 is back to triplets outlining a *C* diminished chord. Example 5 shows that the "open" string thumb slap doesn't necessarily have to be on an open string.

Examples **6–12** are taken from Victor's "Wootcamp" lesson in the February 2002 issue of *Bass Player*. A master of breaking down his ideas into plain language, he offers his "above and below" concept as a fresh way to look at soloing when your theory knowledge just isn't enough. Explains Victor, "Let's say we are in the key of *C* major. Even if

Ex. 1

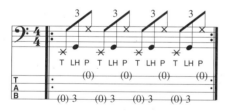

Ex. 2

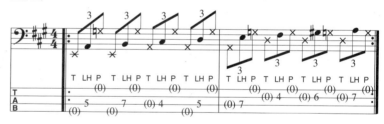

Ex. 3

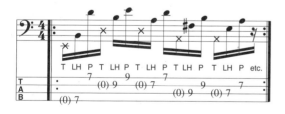

Ex. 4

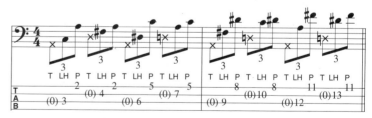

Ex. 5

Ex. 6

the chords are moving by quickly, we can usually find the 1, the 3, and the 5—*C, E,* and *G.* These are our target notes [Ex. 6]. Even if this is all we know, we can still play an interesting solo by applying this concept. Here's how it works: Instead of just playing the root note, I first play the *C#* above, the *B* below, and then the root note, *C* [first two beats of Ex. 7]. You can also do just the opposite: play the note below, then above, and then the root [last two beats of Ex. 7]. If we apply this concept to all of our target notes in the key of *C* major, it will sound like this [Examples 8 and 9].

"The way to keep the mind at ease while using this concept is to think only about the target notes. Don't ask yourself what the 'above' and 'below' notes actually are; just dance around the target notes as you please. In this exercise I chose to dance a half-step above and a half-step below, but you can use whole-steps or a combination of whole-steps and half-steps. Be creative. It's up to you.

"Let's say I have a favorite lick [Ex. 10]. Applying this concept to the first four notes, I play a half-step above them, then a half-step below before playing them in my target position and finishing the lick. This will make my old lick sound new [Ex. 11]. I can also apply the same concept by rearranging the order of the second group of four notes, thus giving the lick a different sound [Ex. 12]. You can apply this to many aspects of your playing, as well as to tempo and dynamics. If you are comfortable playing in a certain position, try playing above and below that position. Have fun!"

Example 13 is inspired by Wooten's blistering solo on "Cherokee" from *What Did He Say?* He employs his "staccato thumb/pluck" technique, in which he plays up and down thumbstrokes (see the arrows under the staff) along with index-finger plucks for fluid, horn-like phrasing. "I wanted to emulate the great bebop trumpeters, but I can't play that fast and clean with my fingers. By using this technique, I can play fast enough *and* give each note its own attack, like

Ex. 7

Ex. 8

Ex. 9

Ex. 10

Ex. 11

Ex. 12

a horn—and I can add horn-like slurs, too." As the first 16-bar "A" section of Victor's solo proceeds (following his two-bar pickup), he spins out bebop-style single-note lines, especially in bars 6–9 and bars 12–13. He used his fretted Yin Yang Fodera.

Moving over to *A Show of Hands*, **Ex. 14** contains the verse section of "Justice," his thought-provoking hip-hop homage to life on the streets (played on his Fodera 4-string). In keeping with the album's solo bass concept, he performed all of his bass parts live, without overdubs. "Whenever I play—whether I'm by myself or not—I always hear the rest of the band in my head. So I try to emulate the sound of a band, with all the rhythmic motion that occurs between the melody notes." The notes with the stems up are Victor's three-note chords, which he taps with his right-hand thumb, index finger, and middle finger, low-to-high (on the *A*, *D*, and *G* strings). Of their harmonic function he

Ex. 13

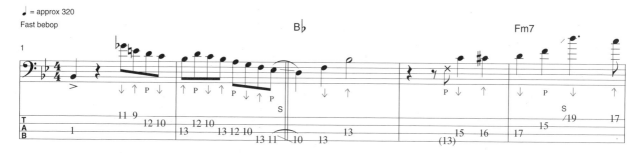

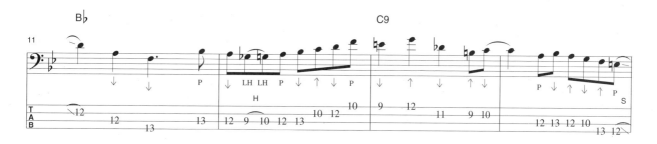

notes, "I didn't analyze the specific chord qualities—I just thought of them as moving chord sounds I liked against the song's *D* minor key. I probably got that chord shape from Oteil Burbridge or my brother Regi; a lot of times when I'm going to play 4ths I throw in the low note to get that slightly altered sound."

The notes with the stems down constitute the bass line. "I have a tendency to play phrases across the bar line, which gives this line an almost odd-time feel. With my left hand, I tapped the *D* and *C* on the *A* string and I tapped the *A*, *F*, and *G* on the *E* string. I could have played the first three notes by pulling them off on the *A* string—but I find pull-offs give a more round attack, and I wanted to attack each note here the same way, so I tapped them."

For performing the section, Victor advises, "You can either learn one part at a time or both parts one measure at a time. I'd probably learn the bass line of the first measure; then I'd learn the chords of the first measure; then I'd put those together and move on to the next measure. That's how I usually do it—I work on both hands at the same time. The hard part here is putting the two together and keeping the groove, which is tough because of the way the bottom part plays across the bar line. Style-wise, try to play with a cool, laid-back, understated attitude, and you'll be on your way."

Ex. 14

STEVE BAILEY
Fretless Extremist

HE HAS BECOME THE "YIN" TO VICTOR WOOTEN'S "YANG," but Steve Bailey, Vic's Bass Extremes partner since 1993, is a visionary of his own, having taken the fretless 6-string bass to unparalleled heights (and depths) as a solo artist, sideman, teacher, and author. From his Florida and New York training ground to his 15 years in Los Angeles to his current digs in his native South Carolina, Bailey has worked as a session and touring bassist with a broad range of artists, including the Rippingtons, David Benoit, Larry Carlton, Jethro Tull, Jon Anderson of Yes, Lynyrd Skynyrd, Willie Nelson, Paquito D'Rivera, Ray Price, and Kitaro. I got the lowdown on Steve in January 1996.

What inspired you to become a bass player?

Growing up in Myrtle Beach, South Carolina, I played

piano and then trombone in my junior high school band. One day when I was 12, some kid came up to me in school and said, "You know how to play trombone—how about playing bass in our rock band?" I went to his house that day and played "All Along the Watchtower" with one finger of my right hand and one finger of my left. I came home with two blisters—and a blistering desire to play rock 'n' roll. My early influences were Jack Bruce and Noel Redding and the bands Jethro Tull, Lynyrd Skynyrd, Black Sabbath, Led Zeppelin, and Yes. Later on, someone gave me a copy of Chick Corea's *Light as a Feather*, with Stanley Clarke on bass, and I plunged headlong into jazz.

What was the most important break you got early in your career?

After studying acoustic bass at North Texas State, I attended the University of Miami. While there, I was working five nights a week playing my upright and Spector fretless with a jazz-oriented group called the Billy Marcus Quartet. Twice a month, for a week at a time, we would back up a big-name artist, like Dave Leibman or Ernestine Anderson. One of our regular guests was Paquito D'Rivera, who really enjoyed playing with us. At the end of one semester, Paquito called and invited me to come to New York to join his band. We went on a European tour and then recorded a live album. That got me established in the music community and led to my next gig, with Dizzy Gillespie.

Steve Bailey

Steve Bailey's Gear

Basses: Aria AVB-SB-6 fretless 6-string, Moon fretted 5-string, '65 Jazz Bass, '57 Precision, Juzek 3/4-size acoustic bass, Larrivee fretless 6-string acoustic bass guitar, Warwick fretted 6-string. D'Addario EXP strings.
Amps & effects: Ampeg SVT-4PRO head with Ampeg BXT-410HL and BXT-115HL cabinets. Walter Woods 250-watt head. D-Tar Solstice two-channel preamp/mixer (for upright bass and acoustic bass guitar). EBS Octabass, Boss ODB-3 Bass Overdrive and DD-3 Digital Delay.

What do you do when you're not playing music?

I like anything athletic: surfing, snow and water skiing, mountain biking, hiking—something to get me completely away from music so that I can come back to it with a fresh point of view. However, I learned a great lesson late one night while I was at the University of Miami. I was in a car with Jaco and [steel-pans player] Othello Molineaux, and we drove up to Othello's house around 2 AM. As we were getting out of the car, Jaco said, "Listen to that! That's music!" But the car radio wasn't on and it was quiet outside. Then I listened closely, and off in the distance I could hear a train whistle blowing.

What advice do you give to aspiring bassists?

Be open to a lot of different styles and musicians. Listen to everybody's criticism, but make up your own mind. Have a life; music is a facet of life and it can be your main focus, but it shouldn't be your whole existence. If you don't go out and gather other experiences, you'll have nothing to bring back to your music. As for moving to a big city, it depends on your goals and whether you're satisfied with your present situation. The big cities offer better musicians to play with and, often, a chance to rub elbows with your heroes. But the main goal is to be happy. I know a lot of happy people playing in Ramada Inns, and I know a lot of miserable people playing in Los Angeles studios.

Web site

www.stevebaileybass.com

Steve Bailey Selected Discography

Solo albums: (both on JVC/Japan) *Evolution*; *Dichotomy*. **With Victor Wooten:** *Yin-Yang*, Compass. **With Bass Extremes:** *Just Add Water*, Tone Center; *Bass Extremes, Vol. 2*, Tone Center; *Bass Extremes* (CD/transcription package), CPP Media. **With Jethro Tull:** *Roots to Branches*, Chrysalis/EMI. **With David Benoit:** (both on GRP) *Letter to Evan*; *Inner Motion*. **With the Rippingtons:** (both on GRP) *Tourist in Paradise*; *Curves Ahead*. **With Paquito D'Rivera:** *Live at the Keystone Corner*, Columbia. **With Tab Benoit:** *What I Live For*, Justice. **With Kitaro:** *Dream*, Geffen.

Smooth Position Shifts

Steve discussed this important topic in his May/June 1995 "Fretless" column in Bass Player:

GENERALLY, YOUR INTONATION is most likely to go south during position shifts. The following exercise (**Ex. 1**) will help you improve the accuracy of your position shifts and finger spacing, and give you stronger, more independent fingers. The hard part is what to do with your fingers after they're "finished." An asterisk over a note indicates that you should leave that finger where it is until you shift. Your index finger stays down (on the *B*) while your middle and ring fingers work their way back down; then your middle finger stays on the *A* while your ring finger and pinky work their way back up. (Note that your index finger should still be holding down that *B*.) It gets worse before it gets better! As your pinky plays the *D*, begin your *smooth* shift to the next position with your middle finger on the *E♭*, and work your way down. This time your index finger rests on *B*, your middle finger rests on *D♯*, and your ring finger and pinky struggle back down. Once your left hand gets used to this, move down to the 1st position and work your way up the fingerboard. Be sure to check your pitch with open strings at the appropriate places.

Ex. 1

CHAPTER 2

Studio Savants

WILL LEE • TONY LEVIN • NATHAN EAST
ABRAHAM LABORIEL • NEIL STUBENHAUS

Before digital technology changed the recording industry, a select group of studio bassists steeped in the tradition of James Jamerson, Joe Osborn, and Chuck Rainey took the art of grooveful tracks to its musical peak. Five phenoms in particular have handled everything from singer-songwriter sides and jingles to full-tilt fusion and orchestral film dates—all with superior creativity, musicianship, and feel. Fortunately, top artists and producers continue to tap this talent pool.

WILL LEE
Sittin' in Pocket Central

Interviewed by Chris Jisi, Fall 1990 and March 2002.

STREET NOISE FILTERS IN THROUGH THE WINDOW. It's a mild summer night in New York City, and a river breeze is cooling Will Lee's SoHo loft. Reflected light glints off the gold records on the walls as Will emerges from his home studio. He prowls the room, deep in thought, then plunks down on the leather couch. "Turn on that tape recorder," he barks. "I've got something I want to say."

Hunching forward so my mini-recorder will catch every word, he begins: "Last night I was playing at the Blue Note with my good friend [guitarist] Chuck Loeb. I've been in this situation thousands of times before—standing onstage in front of a bunch of people, playing this gorgeous music, and I suddenly realized that making all the money you can doesn't give you nearly the happiness or satisfaction of making good music."

At first, these words might seem to be just another wishful proclamation from a studio veteran desperately seeking quality over quantity. But they also offer an insight into why, since the early '70s, Will Lee has been one of the most versatile and sought-after sidemen in popular music history, with hundreds of jingles and more than 750 albums to his credit.

At every session—artistically challenging or not—Lee has left his musical ego and stylistic preconceptions at the door. He has an uncanny ability to blend in seamlessly, quickly locking into a giant groove, while pumping energy and ideas into even the most routine charts. The years have added precision to his time and touch to his chops, but his trademark freshness and enthusiasm remain.

Born in 1952 in San Antonio, Texas, Will spent his boyhood in the Houston-area town of Huntsville. His family moved to Miami when he was 12, and shortly afterward he took a giant step toward his future career when he switched from drums to electric bass. Six years later, in 1971, he arrived in New York to take his place as a member of the early jazz/rock band Dreams. Since then he has successfully endured the personal and professional ups and downs of life in the high-pressure studio world, and he is now in his fifth decade as New York City's first-call groovemaster. Also a gifted vocalist and producer, Lee's voice can be heard on numerous jingles and recordings, and his production credits range from Gary Burton to Carmen Cuesta, as well as his 1993 solo effort, *Oh!*. In addition, New York club prowlers have long been able to catch Will in a variety of hip ensembles, including '70s cult faves the 24th Street Band (with Hiram Bullock and Steve Jordan), Bullock's long-running group, Wayne Krantz's experimental fuze trio, and Will's beloved Beatle cover band, the Fab Faux.

Nowhere are Will's talents more readily evident, though, than on nightly TV, originally with NBC's World's Most Dangerous Band on *Late Night with David Letterman*, and then with the CBS Orchestra on *The Late Show with David Letterman*. Whether he's thumping and jumping through the show's theme, rocking out on a '60s classic or an alternative rock chart-topper during a commercial break, or smoothly backing a musical guest, Lee generates low-end excitement. His bandmates love it. "Will gives you a feeling you just don't get with anybody else," says keyboardist and musical director Paul Shaffer, who always introduces Lee with the phrase "On the bottom, we got 'im." "His time is solid, but it's more than just solid—there's something indescribable about his playing that drives you. He can make any drummer sound good. I've played with him in a lot of situations, and it's really amazing what he can do for a band." Adds drummer Anton Fig: "Not only does Will make cool choices about when and what notes to play, but he always comes up with surprises. I never get tired of playing with him." Guitarist Sid McGinnis sums up Lee's unique abilities best: "He'll be sitting right in the pocket, and then he'll scare you by throwing in some crazy idea that sets you off in a totally new direction. With him, you always get the nasty groove, but you never know when that spark is going to hit—and it's great knowing that it can happen at any point."

What are your earliest musical recollections?

My folks were both musicians. My dad played string bass in the Houston Symphony and jazz piano with bandleaders like Gene Krupa and the Dorsey brothers. He's also a well-known music educator and author. [*Dr. William F. Lee III, a Pulitzer Prize–nominated author and former dean of the University of Miami music department, was dean of the College of Fine Arts and Humanities at the University of Texas at San Antonio. His books include* The Belwin New Dictionary of Music (*CPP/Belwin*) *and* Artistry in Rhythm (*Creative Press of Los Angeles*), *a biography of bandleader Stan Kenton.*] My mom was a big-band singer. They used to give a lot of parties that were attended by musicians, and I met people like Stan Kenton and Charlie Parker when I was two. One of the first things I can remember was the sound of Miles Davis's muted trumpet coming from the turntable in our smoke-filled living room as I wandered in from my bedroom to complain about not being able to sleep.

At four or five I was given piano lessons, but—due to the teacher—I hated it. When I was six my dad got me started on trumpet, which I ended up playing through my junior year in high school. He also bought me a set of drums, but I didn't really play them until the Beatles came out. You could say that the Beatles were my musical wakeup call. As I watched them on the Ed Sullivan Show, I did some math in my head: Drums plus Girls Screaming equal Practice. As soon as the show was over, I headed up to my room and began playing them seriously, knowing that music was what I wanted to do with my life.

When did you begin playing bass?

Sometime in the mid-'60s. The Beatles were on in February 1964, and that August my dad became the Dean of the University of Miami music school, so we moved from Texas to Florida. I recall the year because

John F. Kennedy was assassinated in November 1963, and I remember being sad that he wouldn't get a chance to dig the Beatles.

In Florida, I met some guys who were into music, and we put a surf band together. I played drums and sang lead, and we'd play at dances for $6 or something. After a while, I noticed that kids were buying guitars and drums, but nobody was picking up on bass. Our band wanted a bass player, too, so I thought: If I switch to bass, I may be working for the rest of my life. It was a pretty smart move.

I started out on a cheap Japanese bass my folks bought me. I took the money I earned with that bass and bought a brand-new white Fender Precision that I'd fallen in love with because of its beautiful shape and great feel. I used to open and close the case just to smell it.

Who were your early influences on bass?

Paul McCartney, who was the only bassist I knew about. By that point I was so obsessed with the Beatles' music I didn't feel like a fan—I felt like I was in the Beatles! Paul had so many different flavors he

Will Lee

could add to a song; to me he taught the bass how to sing. Then there was James Jamerson. I heard the bass part on Gladys Knight's version of "Heard It Through the Grapevine" jumping out of the radio speakers in my folks' pink Buick LeSabre wagon, and it blew me away. At the time, I didn't know it was Jamerson, because Motown didn't list the personnel. Later I heard Chuck Rainey, and that was it for me: his touch, his sound, the whole package.

In college you majored in electric bass, which was extremely rare at the time. How did you manage that?

When my father was hired at Miami, the deal included free tuition for his kids. I knew it was a great school, and it was only two blocks from my house, so I went in as a French horn major. In my last year of high school, I'd switched from trumpet because the band had plenty of trumpets but needed to fill out the French horn section. Unfortunately, I had a teacher who tried to change my embouchure, and it screwed me up. I was already discouraged with school because of all the non-music requirements, and then I started getting fed up with the French horn. Even music was bringing me down.

What did I have left? Drugs. I was playing bass six nights a week, six sets a night, until 4 AM, and then getting up for my 8 AM theory class. The only way to stay awake on the drive home was to get high. Pretty soon I was skipping classes and on my way to flunking out. Luckily for me, my dad had an assistant dean named Ted Crager who turned out to be a great friend. He sat me down in his office and told me that, father or not, I wasn't making it. He said he could see my self-esteem was low, but he'd heard my band and was aware that I was excelling as an electric bassist. He suggested that I make it my major. I told him I didn't read bass clef. He said he would show me some tricks and proceeded to get out some staff paper and work with me.

How did you get from Miami to New York?

Eventually I got good enough on bass to play in the University's "A" big band. It was led by Jerry Coker, a saxophone player who is also known for his jazz method books. One night Jerry and I jammed at an outdoor art festival, and a tenor player named Gary Campbell sat in with us. Gary had attended the University of Miami before moving to New York. He happened to be a friend of Michael and Randy Brecker, and when he got back up there, he told them to check me out. They were looking for a bassist to replace Chuck Rainey in Dreams. Coincidentally, among my peers, Dreams was considered *the* hip band. They weren't that well known, but at school we listened to their record daily. Anyway, Gary spread the word in New York, and I got a call from Randy to come up and audition.

What do you recall about that first day in New York?

Everything! It was in April 1971 and I was 18. The first guy I met was [Dreams' keyboardist] Don Grolnick, and I'd never encountered a character like him. He was this scary New York type who didn't say a word. It was the middle of the day, and the audition wasn't until that night, so the first thing I did was get stoned on pot. I was thinking, "Okay, now I'm cool." Then we decided to have a jam session, which—due to the drugs and all—was not happening. After that, Grolnick had to pick up a pair of glasses, so I decided to tag along. Here I am, with this guy who's like Mr. Natural in Zap Comics, and I'm a Sewer Snoid, saying things like: "Gee, what does it all mean, Mr. Natural?" And he's coming back with: "It don't mean shit!"

Finally, it was time for the audition. I was still wasted. We went to this funky place on Crosby Street, the Megaphone Company, and took an elevator down to the basement. It was one thing to know the Dreams record backward and forward, but another to walk in and see the songs written out. I was sweating, but then Billy Cobham counted off and we started playing. It was like floating through space—playing with him was the easiest thing I'd ever done. For the first time in my life, I didn't have to worry about the time or the groove; I could just play. And when those horns kicked in, with the Breckers and [trombonist] Barry Rogers, I was gone. I couldn't believe I was playing with those guys. After we finished, they asked if I could move to New York. Without hesitation I said, "I'm here."

In retrospect, I think I had two things going for me. One was that I was very much in the Chuck Rainey mold, even though I didn't know his name at the time. If I had known he was the bassist I was replacing, I wouldn't have bothered to show up. The other thing was that I sang, and Clive Davis at Columbia Records wanted the band to move in a more commercial direction.

How did you get started doing sessions?

After Dreams broke up I was ready to do an about-face and head back to Miami. The session scene appeared to be locked up by a certain clique, with no way to get in. People like Chuck Rainey and Tony Levin had all the gigs, and I figured I would just admire them from afar. At the time, [guitarist] Bob Mann and [drummer] Alan Schwartzberg were letting me stay at their house, and I was making such a nuisance of myself—emptying their refrigerator and scratching up their record collections—that they decided it was time to get me the hell out of there! So they began finding opportunities to use me. Alan got me a live gig with B.J. Thomas, and Bob got me started in the studio. He was doing arrangements of jingles, and I ended up singing and playing on one for Kentucky Fried Chicken.

My first record date was for Bob's father, Saul Mann. It was a rip-off of the soundtrack from the movie *Shaft*. The cover was designed to make you think you were buying the original *Shaft* album, but in small print it said something like: "Excerpts from the movie *Shaft*—performed by Soul Mann & the Brothers." [*Laughs.*] That session really helped me tune into what a record date in New York was like.

Eventually all the guys in Dreams started hooking me up. Steve Gadd, who was Dreams' last drummer, got me on some jingles that Tony Levin couldn't make. Mike and Randy landed me an audition with Horace Silver, and I went on the road with him. Following that, Don Grolnick got me on a Bette Midler tour. I also had some humbling experiences that taught me valuable lessons. For instance, Billy Cobham asked me to play on the demo that got him a record deal with Atlantic. I thought that meant I was going to be on the record [Cobham's 1973 solo debut, *Spectrum*]. But one day I was walking my dog by Electric Lady Studio, and I heard this familiar sound. I went inside and there was Billy, recording with Lee Sklar. The reason, Billy later told me, was that my sound wasn't happening. I was still using my white Precision, and I'd done some crazy things to it, like adding a bunch of useless pickups. From that point on, I knew the importance of having good-sounding equipment.

Before long you were a session superstar, charging double scale.

At some point in the '70s, several of us—Alan Schwartzberg, [guitarist] Elliot Randall, me, and a few others—were feeling pretty courageous, so we banded together and decided to charge double scale for albums. [*At the time, standard scale was about $130 for a three-hour session.*] We were working a lot, and we thought that by charging double we could weed out some of the sessions that were a drag. As it turned out—and this is just one of the quirky things about the music business—people started calling even more. Work came flooding in, even after we went to triple scale.

What specialized skills do session players need?

You must be able to emulate all the current styles and trends. You need the basics, too: being on time, having a good attitude, being able to read well, and, of course, being "Pocket Central," ready to lock instantly with various human *and* non-human rhythm-section

Pocket Pool

Will Lee arrived in New York City with his white Fender Precision and had moved on to a sunburst Precision as his session career was taking off. These days his main bass is a sunburst custom Sadowsky Jazz Bass—seen nightly on the *Late Show*—with a maple neck and a Hipshot XTender (which Will sets up to drop his *E* string to *C*). Other key basses include his several Sadowsky 4- and 5-strings, a Yamaha BB5000A 5-string, his Hofner Beatle Bass (used with the Fab Faux), a fretless '60's P-Bass with EMG JJ pickups, '60s P- and J-Basses, a Pedulla 8-string, an Epiphone Allen Woody short scale semi-hollow bass, a Hofner President bass, and a '79 fretless Music Man StingRay. His strings with Dean Markley Will Lee Signature SR2000s, gauged .047, .067, .087, .107, .127. He uses standard-sized heavy Pick Boy picks.

Will's amp rig is a Hartke 3500 head with one or two Hartke 4.5 (4x10) cabinets. He breaks out a "faux" Vox AC100 customized with a Hartke 4000 head for Fab Faux shows, and he roams free in all live settings via a Samson wireless unit. His ever-changing effects pedalboard includes a DigiTech Whammy pedal, a T.C. Electronic Stereo Chorus/Flanger, an EBS Octabass and UniChorus, a DOD FX-25B Envelope Filter, a Danelectro Talkback, and Boss ODB-3 Bass Overdrive, HR-2 Harmonist, and DD-5 Digital Delay pedals, plus a Boss TU-12 Tuner. In the studio he prefers his Tube Tech MP1A mic pre or Cabletek/Radial JDV Direct Box.

partners. You should also be able to offer choices to a producer, including arrangement ideas.

Session players talk about having the ability to play "on tape." What does that mean?

Realistically, it means knowing that what you're about to play is going on a permanent record. If you want to take that as pressure you can, and it used to drive me nuts. For a long time my motto was: "If I'm not worried, I'm not awake." Now, I'd rather be known as a guy who enjoys playing. My new attitude on sessions is to have a good time, and that translates musically. If I feel good, then people will feel good when they hear me play.

Why was drug use so prevalent during the peak session years? Did the competition lead musicians to do cocaine so they could work around the clock?

Nobody *has* to take every gig. You've got a choice, and if you're going to be greedy, you'll pay the price. Some guys stayed up around the clock because they were so jacked up after a session that they couldn't go to sleep. I'm talking about myself. I remember staying up for a week on blow and alcohol doing sessions with a good friend of mine. We were hyped up about ourselves and the whole scene. We knew we were at the top of the game, and we were really digging it. After a while, though, the drugs became overwhelming, and it stopped being fun. It became a chore just to go to a date. It was like my college pattern repeating itself all over again: I'd come in hours late with a terrible attitude or not even show up at all.

From 1975 to 1985, I wasn't contributing *anything* to the music. I knew it, but I didn't give a shit. I knew I had the gig and I was cocky, so I was just working within the necessary parameters. I haven't been late for a session in years, but some people still think of me as "the late Will Lee." Fortunately, there were people who kept giving me second chances, like Barry Manilow and [producer] Arif Mardin.

Why did you use drugs?

Insecurity. If I didn't have a vial in my pocket, I felt like a nobody. Instead of growing up, I got into drugs. I didn't suffer through all the pains of growing up until I decided to get sober, five years ago. After I got sober, the first thing I noticed about playing was how colorful it was. It had been black-and-white numerical patterns for a long time, but all of a sudden I saw the beauty of expression again.

What's your philosophy of bass playing?

My basic approach can be summed up in two words: The Pocket. The most important function of the instrument is creating and holding down the groove.

How do you work with the drums?

There are several ways to approach it. One is playing exactly what the bass drum is playing, plus a few other notes. I love to do that. That keeps it simple, and keeping it simple is what it's all about in most cases. Another way is to totally ignore the kick drum, at least some of the time. If the drummer is playing a strong, simple groove, you can depart from it and play some new things, and it's not going to stop grooving. Even if what you play is off the wall, if it's in time and played with feeling and sincerity, it's probably going to be a good part. That was the key to the Motown sound created by [drummer] Benny Benjamin and James Jamerson. A third type of possibility exists when the song has nothing else going for it in support. That's a golden opportunity for the bass part to shine.

What about playing with drum machines and sequencers?

I find it easy to do. You can trust where the groove is going to be, and it stays there. That allows me to move around in the pocket and make the groove breathe. The best experience is working with drummers who program; they make the machines sound and feel as good as their own playing—or even *better*. They can even fool me, and I like being fooled.

What effect have synth bass and sequenced bass parts had on the way you play?

They've changed my playing, ever since the first Scritti Politti album in 1985 [*Cupid & Psyche '85*], where I got a chance to play in unison with synth bass lines. I'd done that before, but these were real cool bass parts written by David Gamson. They rarely started on the downbeat or the tonic. That record caused me to investigate new ways to play bass, because non-bassists' hands fall in places that aren't natural to bass players.

Are there any drawbacks to keyboard bass?

Sometimes they sound stiff, because too many keyboard bassists don't know how to think like a bass player. I hear synth bass parts in my head, and if I were a good keyboard player I'd play them that way. But for 25 years my chops have been on bass, so it's easier for me to use pedals or my MIDI-bass system.

You leave the chrome neck-pickup cover on all of your basses. Why?

There are a couple of reasons. Sometimes I tap on it for a percussive, cowbell-like effect, but mostly I use it as an anchor and a guide. Being a studio player, I need to be able to switch over quickly from pick to fingers

Will Lee Selected Discography

Solo album: *Oh!*, Go Jazz. **With Bill Lee:** *Birdhouse*, CD Baby. **With Dreams:** *Imagine My Surprise*, Columbia. **With the Brecker Brothers:** (all on Arista) *Don't Stop the Music*; *Back to Back*; *Brecker Bros.* **With Hiram Bullock:** *Manny's Car Wash*, Big World; *World of Collision*, Big World; *Way Cool*, Atlantic; *Give it What You Got*, Atlantic; *From All Sides*, Atlantic. **With Paul Shaffer:** *The World's Most Dangerous Party*, SBK; *Coast to Coast*, Capitol. **With Anton Fig:** *Figments*, Planula. **With James Brown:** *Dead on the Heavy Funk: 1973–1985*, Polydor. **With Donald Fagen:** *The Nightfly*, Warner Bros. **With Steely Dan:** *Gold*, MCA. **With D'Angelo:** *Brown Sugar*, Capitol. **With Barry Manilow:** *The Complete Collection and Then Some*, Arista. **With Bette Midler:** *Bette Midler*, Arista. **With Mariah Carey:** *Emotions*, Columbia. **With Al Green:** *Your Heart's in Good Hands*, MCA. **With Roberta Flack:** (both on Atlantic) *Blue Lights in the Basement*; *Roberta Flack & Donny Hathaway*. **With Chaka Khan:** *Chaka*, Warner Bros. **With Steve Khan:** (all on Columbia) *Arrows*; *Blue Man*; *Tightrope*. **With Randy Brecker:** *Hanging in the City*, ESC. **With Gary Burton & Pat Metheny:** *Reunion*, GRP. **With Bass Extremes:** *Bass Extremes, Vol. 2*, Tone Center. **With Billy Joel:** *Greatest Hits, Vol. 3*, Columbia. **With Michael Bolton:** *The Hunger*, Columbia. **With Jason Miles:** *Love Affair: The Music of Ivan Lins*, Telarc. **With Don Grolnick:** *Hearts and Numbers*, HipPocket. **With Los Lobotomys:** *Los Lobotomys*, MIDI. **With Chuck Loeb:** *Simple Things*, DMP. **With Brian McKnight:** *Greatest Hits*, Motown. **With Pat Metheny:** *Secret Story*, Geffen. **With Gary Moore:** *After Hours*, Charisma. **With Laura Nyro:** *Angel in the Dark*, Rounder; *Nested*, Columbia. **With Elliott Randall:** *Randall's New York*, Kirschner. **With Carly Simon:** *Coming Around Again*, Arista; *Boys in the Trees*, Elektra. **With Phoebe Snow:** *Second Childhood*, Columbia. **With Spyro Gyra:** (all on MCA) *Carnaval*; *Catching the Sun*; *Morning Dance*. **With Ringo Starr:** *Ringo's Rotogravure*, Atlantic. **With Mike Stern:** *Is What It Is*, Atlantic. **With BFD:** *BFD*, Iguana. **With Richard Tee:** *Real Time*, One Voice. **With John Tropea:** *Short Trip to Space*, Marlin. **With George Benson:** *Living Inside Your Love*, Warner Bros. **With Kool & The Gang:** *In the Heart*, Delite. **With Miami Sound Machine:** *Let It Loose*, Epic. **With Diana Ross:** *Swept Away*, RCA. **With Frank Sinatra:** *Night and Day*, Warner/Reprise. **With Barbra Streisand:** *Songbird*, Columbia. **With Anton Fig:** *Figments*, Planula. **With Dennis Chambers:** *Outbreak*, ESC/EFA. **With Weather Report:** *I Sing the Body Electric*, Columbia. **With Paul McCartney and various artists:** *Concert for New York City*, Columbia.

to thumb. When I play up near the neck with a pick and rest my hand on the cover, I get a nice round sound. [*Session great Joe Osborn uses a similar pick approach.*] My basic picking technique is mainly upstrokes, by the way, because I get more power pulling upwards with the pick. When I play with my fingers, alternating my index and middle, I anchor my thumb on the cover and play just behind it. For thumb slapping, I lay my wrist on the cover, which leaves my hand in a good position near the neck. I'll move my right hand around at times, depending on the sound I'm going for, and I've found I need the cover there if I want to float around between the neck and the neck pickup.

How do you mute strings?

Always with my left hand. I play a note with the first finger and mute with the fingers behind it [middle, ring, and little]. I'm not one of those bassists who plays with a beautifully curved, wide finger spread that moves daintily up and down the fingerboard. Most of what I do comes from the right hand, because my left hand stays bunched up, unless I have to play something intricate. When I play a walking bass line and want to get muted notes, like on Donald Fagen's "Walk Between the Raindrops" [*The Nightfly*], I move my hand up and down the neck and play in positions. I've noticed that Rocco Prestia and I have this in

With a Little Help from Will Lee

Will with Beatle Bass.

IN OCTOBER 2002 MILLIONS OF AMERICANS had their post-9/11 spirits lifted by VH1's live broadcast of the Concert for New York City at Madison Square Garden. For one participant there was an extra perk: Will Lee was able to fulfill a lifelong dream by playing bass with one of his idols, concert organizer Paul McCartney. Recounts Lee, "Paul Shaffer got the call to be the musical director, with the *Late Show with David Letterman* band as the house band. When we found out Paul's group consisted of Paul on bass, Gabe Dixon on keyboards, Rusty Anderson on guitar, and Abe Laboriel Jr. on drums, a light went off in my head: What if Paul did a song like 'Let It Be,' where he plays piano? I immediately started telling people that I wanted to be involved. I told everyone—strangers on the street, my dog's vet—'I really hope I can play bass with Paul!'"

Fast forward to Manhattan's SIR rehearsal studio the Monday morning before the show. Armed with a tape of several new McCartney songs slated to be performed, Will entered the room, introduced himself to Paul (the two had met before), and offered his help. Paul said, "Sure, absolutely," and Will returned soon after to rehearse "From a Lover to a Friend" and "Your Loving Flame" from McCartney's new CD, as well as "Let it Be." Says Will, "I was screaming inside but trying to stay cool. The songs went smoothly, without any comments from Paul on what I was playing—though I could see him watching and listening to all of us."

Did Lee dare bring up the Fab Faux, his Beatles cover band that's been all the rage in New York? "I did. Just as when I told him a few years back, he gave me that rolling-eyes, oh-brother look. But I explained it's not a wig quartet—it's five guys who enjoy challenging themselves by performing the later, studio-heavy stuff that's difficult to pull off live. So he said, 'Like what? Do you do "Tomorrow Never Knows"?' And I said of course, and I told him about our upcoming shows where we'll be performing the entire White Album. He hinted that if he's in town, he'll come check it out."

During a final rehearsal at the Garden on the after-noon of the show, McCartney showed the band "Freedom," a song he'd written after witnessing the World Trade Center attacks from the window of a soon-to-be-grounded England-bound jet on the Newark airport runway. Will recalls, "Paul played acoustic guitar, and he told me to keep the bass line kind of dumb, so I kept it ultra-simple in the run-through. After we were finished, I ran into him backstage and he said, 'On second thought, add some more to the part.'" With Will's bass line in mind, McCartney later went into the studio to cut the version of "Freedom" that ended up on his Capitol CD *Driving Rain*.

By the start of the almost six-hour-long concert, Lee had other duties to attend to. Equipped with three Sadowskys (two 4-strings and his new 5), a Yamaha 5, his Hofner Beatle Bass, and his Hartke rig (a 4.5 cabinet and 3500 head), Will also played and/or sang with David Bowie, the Backstreet Boys, Destiny's Child, Macy Gray, Mick Jagger and Keith Richards, and James Taylor. After Taylor's set, he headed for McCartney's dressing room. "Right before we went on, Paul cleared out everyone except the band and led us in a little prayer. It was pretty amazing; we all held hands, and I saw a spiritual side of him I wasn't aware of."

McCartney began his set on his famous lefty Hofner bass, playing the Beatles rocker "I'm Down" and "Lonely Road," a shuffle from *Driving Rain*. He then went to the piano, and Lee came on with his righty Hofner and plugged into McCartney's Mesa/Boogie rig for the ballad "From a Lover to a Friend," also from the new CD. Following Paul's vocal-and-string-quartet version of "Yesterday," Will moved to his Sadowsky 5 for the "Freedom" debut, switching back to his Hofner for "Let it Be." "During 'Let It Be' a cavalcade of stars came onstage, and Paul had Eric Clapton take a few solos, so we just kept looping the chorus and sort of made up an ending." Also unexpected—though with enough time for Will to strap on his 5-string—was a reprise of "Freedom," which ended the concert.

The event raised over $30 million for the Robin Hood Foundation, and Columbia released *Concert for New York City*, a double CD of show highlights. Lee's thoughts on the heels of his hard day's night? "I'm still digesting it all. It was rewarding to help so many people, and to see the families of fallen heroes in attendance enjoying themselves. On a personal note, like so many others, I got my big wake-up call from the Beatles. Having been able to play with Paul, I feel like I'm at a new plateau with my career—yet it's like a big circle has been completed."

common. One advantage is that you're getting the whole arm unit behind each note, which gives you a great sound.

How did the World's Most Dangerous Band come together?

In the mid '70s I was in a group called the 24th Street Band, with [guitarist] Hiram Bullock, [drummer] Steve Jordan, and [keyboardist] Cliff Carter. Paul Shaffer produced our second album, and we had a great rapport with him. Around the time the band broke up, Paul got a call to put together some music for a comedy pilot called *Late Night with David Letterman*. He asked me if I would be interested and explained his concept of playing things like James Brown, Motown, and Beatles tunes instrumentally. He told me he was asking Steve and Hiram, too; he saw us as a self-contained unit.

Because we're a four-piece instrumental band, we have to cover vocals and other parts on our instruments. On "Duke of Earl," for example, I do the bass vocal part with my fingers while playing the original bass part with my thumb. And on "Walk on the Wild Side," which has two bass parts in contrary motion, I play both at once: I pluck the *D* at the 10th fret of the *E* string with my thumb while tapping the *F♯* on the 11th fret of the *G* string with my right-hand middle finger, and then I slide down to the low *G* on the *E* string with my left hand while sliding up to the high *B* on the *G* string with my right.

Paul Shaffer and you are the only remaining members of the original band. How did the personnel changes affect you?

After Hiram left we went through several guitarists before I had a brainstorm to try Sid McGinnis. Sid's got a different sound—more rock 'n' roll and country than Hiram, who's from the jazz and R&B side—and he also has amazing energy. He fit right in. Then Anton replaced Steve and that took a minute to get used to because they represent two separate schools of drumming. Steve is real bouncy and springy, crisp and crunchy and on top of the beat. Anton's forte is pounding the shit out of the drums. He's a very simple, supportive player with a big sound, and we've created our own pocket.

If you had to name one thing as the key to your success, what would it be?

Over the years many people have asked me questions about what I do and how I do it. But to break it down to the most basic and simple truth, the way I've been able to pull it all off is because of my ears. My whole singing and bass playing career has been about pleasing my ears—trying to do what sounds right. That's the method I'm going to stick by.

Web sites

www.willlee.com
www.thefabfaux.com

Late Night Licks

Accompanying my 1990 interview, Will Lee collected the Top Ten fills he would play during the NBC edition of the Late Night With David Letterman *theme (which was a shuffle with a different arrangement than the later CBS version). Here is Will's explanation:*

THESE ARE TEN OF THE FILLS I play during the four bars of *A7* preceding the closing riff of the *Late Night* theme. Except where indicated, all eighth-notes are played with a shuffle feel. In all versions except 8, 7, and 1, the line is based on *A* and *G*, which I finger on the 5th and 3rd frets of the *E* string. In 8, 7, and 1, I alternate *A* and *E* on the open strings, freeing my left hand to play the chordal passages.

10. Basic Line: This is the basic line played with the fingers, up to and including the closing riff. I also added a little lick I borrowed from Jaco; it's on the last two beats of the second bar.

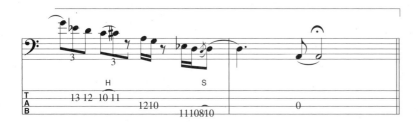

9. Basic Line with Thumb Climb: This is the basic line played with the thumb, including a climb beginning at the end of the first bar and continuing through the second bar.

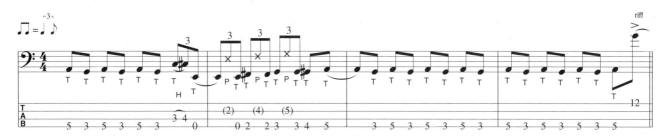

Late Night by Paul Shaffer. © 1996 Postvalda Music (SESAC). All rights administered by W.B.M. Music Corp. (SESAC). ll rights reserved. Used by permission. Warner Bros. Publications U.S. Inc., Miami, FL 33014.

8. Outlining the Changes with Hits: The double-stops in bars 1 and 2 are like horn-section hits. They outline the section's basic harmony: a bar of *A7* followed by a bar of *A7sus.* In bars 3 and 4, I use similar double-stops to quote from the chorus section of the Free song "All Right Now." I play the double-stops and the low open *A*'s together by raking a finger across the strings, starting on top with the *G* string.

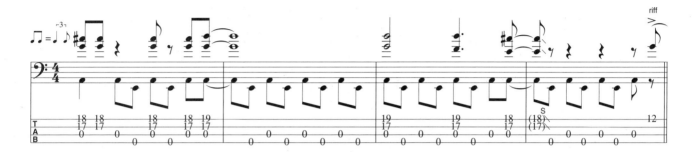

7. Crazy Chord Climb: More double-stops over an *A* pedal, implying both the basic chords and a substitute chord: bar 1, *A7*; bar 2, *A7sus* or *G/A*; bar 3, *A7#11* or *B/A*; bar 4, *A7* with the 5th on top. The double-stops over the low open *A*'s are attacked the same way as in 8, and the high *E* on the anticipation of bar 4 is played by bending up the *E♭* at the top (20th) fret.

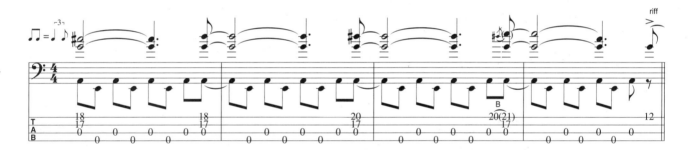

6. Shuffle with Straight-Eighth Fill: One thing we all like to do is superimpose a straight-eighth-note feel over a shuffle, as I do with this Curtis Mayfield–ish lick beginning on the last two beats of bar 2 and ending on the first two beats of bar 3.

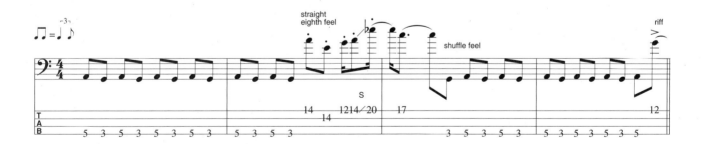

5. Shuffle with 16th-Note Fill: This is based on the same principle as 6, but with 16th-notes. I call this my "David Spinozza Lick." [*Spinozza is a New York session guitarist.*]

4. The "Soul Makossa" Lick: We've been quoting from this Manu Dibango tune since Hiram Bullock and Steve Jordan were in the band.

3. Basic Thumb Line with Fill: Here's another version played with the thumb. I create the ghost-notes in bar 2 by slapping the palm of my hand across all of the strings.

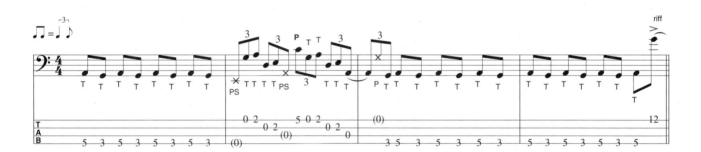

2. Tasteless Tapping Thing: This is my "Steve Stevens tapping line," which consists of alternating *D* and *A* triads in a 5–1–3 sequence. [*Stevens is best known for his lead guitar work with Billy Idol.*] The sextuplets are played this way: I put my left-hand index finger on the *D* at the 7th fret of the *G* string and tap the high *A* with my right-hand middle finger at the 14th fret. The *D* sounds when I pull off the tap. I then hammer on the *F♯* with my pinky—a four-fret stretch. The *E*, *A*, and *C♯* are played by repeating the process on the *D* string. Try this with minor, augmented, and diminished triads to inspire new ideas.

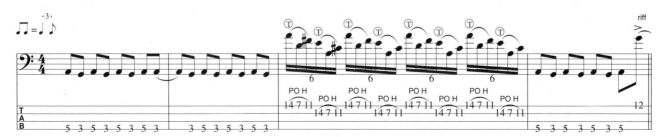

1. Fingering Fun: I came up with this arpeggiated chordal piece while fooling around with double-stops on top of an *A* pedal. The triplet chords are raked as in No. 8 and always follow in sequence on the *G*, *D*, and *A* strings. Be sure to let each note ring.

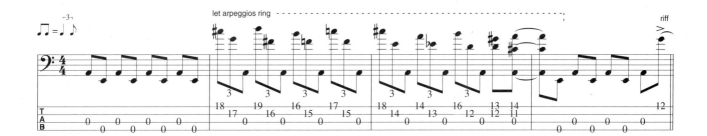

TONY LEVIN
Come Talk to Me

Interviewed by Karl Coryat, May/June 1995, and Bill Leigh and Chris Jisi, September 1998.

TONY LEVIN IS, WITHOUT A DOUBT, one of the most innovative and admired bassists in contemporary music. In addition to playing standard 4- and 5-string bass guitars and electric upright, Tony has recorded many a memorable bass line on Chapman Stick, a unique and versatile 10-string instrument played entirely by fingertapping. He's also invented a system of striking the strings with two small drumsticks attached to his fingers, which he often uses on his custom-made *3-string* bass. The veteran groovemaster has played on countless records since the 1960s and worked closely with Peter Gabriel since 1978, and he's a core member of the envelope-pushing King Crimson, whose incredibly intricate rhythms and harmonic textures have made the band a favorite of many musicians. So why didn't *Bass Player* have a Tony Levin story before 1995? He's also shy about doing interviews.

"I get embarrassed talking about myself for more than five minutes," confesses the mild-mannered Upstate New Yorker. "Also, the fact that your words are printed makes it seem as though you know what you're talking about. But lately I've been trying to grow beyond those feelings, and I feel as if I have some interesting things to talk about." Despite his initial shyness, Tony was enthusiastic about talking to *Bass Player*. We met one evening during the winter NAMM music-instrument trade show in Anaheim, California, where Tony had been fielding many of the same questions *Bass Player* readers have been asking for years: What's that board-shaped instrument with all the extra strings, what's King Crimson been up to lately, and—of course—what in the world *are* those things on his fingers?

Do you have any idea how many records you've played on over the years?
No. I'm glad I've never counted them, because that would be a silly thing to do. I have a tendency to forget things, but the figure is certainly in the hundreds and probably below 1,000.

What was the first record you played on?

I guess you could say it was a record. My dad was a radio engineer, and when I was five he took me to the studio and I recorded a little piano-recital piece for my mother's birthday. Not only was that on vinyl, it was a 78! I think my first professional session was for [keyboardist] Gap Mangione; that was sometime during the '60s.

How did you get hooked on bass?

I played piano as a little kid, and when I was ten my parents suggested I choose another instrument. I chose the upright bass, although I don't know why. I studied classical from then on; I also played some folk music, which was popular back then, and some R&B as well, but no rock 'n' roll. When the Beatles came around, I didn't say, "Oh, I must go out and get a Hofner"—I was quite happy doing what I did.

I went to the Eastman School of Music in Rochester, New York, and I played in the Rochester Philharmonic. I'm glad I did that; classical music is something I still love a lot. In fact, these days I listen mostly to classical and opera. I'm lucky that I played so much of it at an early age, because by the time I was 19 or 20, I was sick of it—even though I hadn't gone through a whole classical career, I knew I couldn't spend my life playing in an orchestra.

When I was in school, I was very lucky to meet Steve Gadd, who didn't have a bassist to play gigs with him. He got some interesting club dates, and he proceeded to show me a few things. Poor Steve was very patient—at the time I had plenty of technique, but I knew nothing about feel; I was a very straight classical musician who played inexorably on the beat. With his help I learned how to play jazz, and that's what I did for a few years. Then I made a decision to move on to rock; I grew more attracted to it, partly because I was attracted to the electric bass. I had to stop playing on top of the beat and learn to lay back a little, or at least be flexible about where to put the beat.

The location of the beat is a fascinating thing, and many drummers and bass players are experts at it. But I never learned anything specific about playing rhythm from a teacher or from reading, and I always feel funny when someone asks me about it. My experience in that realm doesn't lie in the part of my brain that expresses itself in words; it's something I learned from listening, and sometimes from the dirty looks I got from players who were better than me.

Is it something you don't like to think about?

There are many areas of music I don't want to think about—and when I joined King Crimson, I learned how much I didn't want to talk. Robert and Bill are experts at talking and thinking; when I read their interviews or hear them discussing the principles of playing music, sometimes I find I can't listen for very long. It's as if I were dyslexic—I just can't stay with it. At the same time, I know a great deal about music, and I can analyze certain things to death. Over time, I realized there are some things I just don't feel like breaking down and analyzing, although I haven't thought about why. It's not that I'm afraid I'll lose the ability to play; I just think it's the location of those concepts in my brain. They're where they belong, and I want to leave them there untouched, so they'll stay the way they are.

How did you meet Peter Gabriel?

I had worked with producer Bob Ezrin on Lou Reed's *Berlin*, as well as quite a few Alice Cooper records, so Bob called me when he was planning Peter's first solo album [*Peter Gabriel*]. When I got to the studio, I unpacked the Stick, which was kind of new for me at that time; Bob took one look at it and said, "Put that thing away!" Fast forward about ten years to the sessions for Pink Floyd's *A Momentary Lapse of Reason*, which Bob also produced; I started to unpack my bass, and Bob said, "No—I want you to play Stick on this!"

How were you first exposed to the Stick?

The instrument started to become popular in the mid '70s, and people began to tell me about it after seeing me play the bass. In those days I liked to fool around with tapping on the bass, and I'd often tap incessantly on the fingerboard between studio takes. Here was an instrument that was made to be finger-tapped, and people said, "Tony, you should get a Chapman Stick." So I did, and indeed, I had quite an easy time learning to play it. It's a great instrument for playing both bass lines and melodies or chords, but I usually just use both hands to play bass lines. Technically, that's a little like using two fingers, one on each hand, to play a bass line on the piano. But I was attracted to the Stick's unique sound, and its unusual tuning helped me to come up with unusual lines. That's something I'm always trying to do, and I'll take whatever help I can get.

How do you tune the Stick?

You can tune it however you want; normally, the bass strings are tuned in 5ths, backward. The lowest string runs down the middle of the neck, with the thinner bass strings on the uppermost edge of the fingerboard. There are different versions of the instrument—the original version has ten strings, but there's also the 12-string Grand Stick, which you can divide into six strings on each side, or five bass strings and

Tony Levin

seven guitar strings. I have one regular Stick and one Grand Stick, plus a custom Stick with one fretted bass side and one fretless bass side.

When you're recording a song, what factors make you choose Stick over a regular bass?

That's one of those things I don't quite understand—although I've had to analyze it, because often I have to defend my opinion against that of the producer. The Stick is very good at certain things; it has a terrific attack down low, it has an unusual sound, and there's a way in which I can fade it in with a volume pedal to make it sound like a bowed instrument. However, there's only one method of attack—at least only one that I can do—and that's to hammer every note with a finger. On the bass, on the other hand, there are 20 different ways to pluck a string, including where you pluck it and what you use to pluck or strike it. I like to have a lot of options, so I just listen to the song and start getting an idea for the bass part.

Let's talk about your technique of striking the strings with sticks.

I call that "funk fingers." When I was working on Peter Gabriel's song "Big Time" [*So*], I got the idea of asking Jerry Marotta to drum on the bass strings while I fingered the notes with my left hand. It took hours and hours for us to do, although in the end it came out very nicely; unfortunately, the track wasn't used in the final mix, except in one place. [*It's heard in the interlude after the first chorus.*] I had grown very attached to that part, so imagine my surprise when I first heard the final mix. This is the experience of being a bass player—you think you played on a whole song, but then you get the record and find out you played on only eight bars!

I tried to reproduce the performance live, with a drumstick in one hand, but I was struggling. One day at soundcheck, Peter said, "Why don't you attach two sticks to your fingers?" I turned around to my tech, Andy

Tony's Tony Tones

Tony Levin uses Ernie Ball Music Man basses pretty much exclusively. His main axe is a StingRay 5-string. He also plucks additional fretted and fretless fives, and his Music Man 3-string—"It's the only bass I've ever had custom made; Ernie Ball was very kind to indulge me. It has only the *E*, *A*, and *D* strings, and there are no volume or tone controls. I can't say it's the most versatile instrument in the world, but I enjoy playing it, and since the strings are further apart, I have an easier time with the funk fingers." Other bass instruments in his rotation include his NS Electric Upright, a Guild Asbory fretless, and, of course, his Chapman Sticks. He uses Ernie Ball strings; lighter gauges in the studio, heavier on the road. With Peter Gabriel he'll also play with a keyboard attached to his bass, which triggers backstage synths via MIDI. "It's a nice way to feel as though I'm playing a bass while getting synth sounds. Even though there are MIDI-equipped basses these days, I find it just as easy to play the part on a keyboard and hammer with my left hand on the bass at the same time."

Live, Levin plugs into a Trace Elliot AH600SMX head and two 1048H [4x10] cabinets. He also runs the top end of the Stick through a Trace Elliot Bonneville guitar amp.

Moore, and asked him, "Can we do that?"—meaning, of course, "Can *you* do that?" He pared down two drumsticks and found a piece of surgical tubing to attach them to my fingers. We gradually refined the system; now I use two percussion sticks, which are thinner than drumsticks, and they have scoops cut out of them to fit my fingers.

I used the funk fingers the most on the 1990–91 tour with Anderson, Bruford, Wakeman, and Howe, where I was trying to find a way to imitate Chris Squire's sound with Yes. I was also trying to approximate his phenomenal technique, which I just don't have—especially with a pick. Since then, I've wrapped the ends of the sticks in various materials to soften their attack; the bright sound was appropriate for the old Yes material, but it's too much for most record producers. I try it a lot on records, and often I'm told to "put those things away."

Another memorable bass line on So *is "Don't Give Up"—especially that deep, throbbing reggae tone at the end.*

When I went over to England to record that album I took my two-month-old daughter along. For some reason, I thought I wouldn't be able to buy disposable diapers there, so I packed as many Pampers as I could fit into my bass case. When I was looking for dampening material for the second part of that song, I opened my case and found the Pampers—so I put one under the strings, between the pickup and the bridge. Indeed, it was the deepest bottom I've ever been able to get out of a Music Man. In England they call diapers "nappies," so Peter, [producer] Dan Lanois, and I called that the "super wonder nappy bass."

You played electric upright on King Crimson's Thrak. *What was it like returning to the upright after so many years?*

It takes a terrific amount of strength compared to the electric, especially in your thumb; I didn't get that back, and I probably never will. In addition, my intonation—never the best to begin with—hasn't been helped by 20 years away from the instrument. But I did practice a great deal, and I wordlessly asked the other guys to indulge me about my pitch not being as good as it usually is. I used Ned Steinberger's NS Electric Upright, which worked really well for me, especially with the bow.

Considering how successful you've been with Crimson and Gabriel, what made you want to record a solo album?

My good friend Robbie Dupree came over to my house one day and said, "Tony, I know a kind of solo album you could do that wouldn't cut into your time at home." He knows that my home time is small and very precious to me. He said, "Why don't you get an ADAT and record with some of the players you meet around the world?" He didn't need to finish before I stopped him and said, "Consider it done."

Tony Levin Selected Discography

Solo albums: *Double Espresso*, Narada; *Pieces of the Sun*, Narada; *Waters of Eden*, Narada; *World Diary*, Alex. **With Peter Gabriel:** (on Geffen) *Up*; *Secret World Live*; *Us*; *So*; *Plays Live*; (on Universal) *Security*; *Peter Gabriel* (3); *Peter Gabriel* (2); *Peter Gabriel* (1). **With King Crimson:** *Vroom, Vroom*, DGM; *Nashville Rehearsals, 1997*, DGM; *Cirkus*, Caroline; *Thrak*, Virgin; (on Warner Bros.) *Three of a Perfect Pair*; *Beat*; *Discipline*. **With John Lennon:** (both on Capitol) *Milk and Honey*; *Double Fantasy*. **With Paul Simon:** (both on Warner Bros.) *One Trick Pony*; *Still Crazy After All These Years*. **With Gorn Levin Marotta:** *From the Caves of the Iron Mountain*, Papa Bear. **With Bozzio Levin Stevens:** (both on Magna Carta) *Situation Dangerous*; *Black Light Syndrome*. **With Yes:** *Union*, Arista. **With Anderson Bruford Wakeman Howe:** *Anderson Bruford Wakeman Howe*, Arista. **With Robert Fripp:** *Exposure*, EG. **With California Guitar Trio:** *CG3+2*, Inside Out Music; *Rocks the West*, Discipline. **With Carly Simon:** *Coming Around Again*, Arista; *Spoiled Girl*, Epic; (on Warner Bros.) *Hello Big Man*; *Come Upstairs*; (on Elektra) *Spy*; *Boys in the Trees*; *Carly Simon*. **With James Taylor:** (both on Columbia) *New Moon Shine*; *That's Why I'm Here*.

With Buddy Rich: *The Roar of '74*, Simitar. **With Paula Cole:** *This Fire*, Warner Bros. **With Chuck Mangione:** *Main Squeeze*, A&M. **With Herbie Mann:** *Discotheque*, Atlantic. **With Pink Floyd:** *A Momentary Lapse of Reason*, Columbia. **With Lou Reed:** *Berlin*, RCA. **With Warren Zevon:** *My Ride's Here*, Artemis; *Sentimental Hygiene*, Virgin. **With David Bowie:** *Heathen*, Sony. **With Ringo Starr:** *Ringo the 4th*, Atlantic. **With Robbie Robertson:** *Robbie Robertson*, Geffen. **With Richie Sambora:** *Stranger in This Town*, Polygram. **With Dire Straits:** *Brothers in Arms*, Warner Bros. **With Gov't Mule:** *The Deep End, Vol. 2*, ATO. **With T-Bone Burnett:** *The Talking Animals*, Columbia. **With Mike Mainieri:** (both on NYC) *Wanderlust*; *White Elephant*. **With Warren Bernhardt:** *Manhattan Update*, BMG Victor. **With Blue Montreaux:** *Blue Montreaux*, Arista. **With Steps Ahead:** *NYC*, Intuition. **With David Torn:** *Cloud About Mercury*, ECM. **With Tom Waits:** *Rain Dogs*, Island. **With Ivan Lins:** *Awa Yio*, Warner Bros. **With Yoko Ono:** *Season of Glass*, Geffen. **With Kate & Anna McGarrigle:** *Kate & Anna McGarrigle [Carthage]*, Warner Bros. **With Jules Shear:** *Watch Dog*, EMI. **With Peter, Paul & Mary:** *Reunion*, Warner Bros.

How would you characterize the music on World Diary?

I'm at a slight loss to describe it—it's kind of a "small" instrumental record. There are two tracks with Brian Yamakoshi, a koto player; koto and Stick is a very interesting combination. There are two tracks with a doudouk player named Levon Minassian. I did two tunes with Bill Bruford; I asked him to play the melody on electric percussion while I backed him up on Stick. There's a piece with Shankar, the violinist/vocalist who was on Peter Gabriel's tour, and another piece features a wonderful percussion ensemble called Nexus. I also did a tune with a Norwegian tenor-sax player named Bendik. After recording all the pieces, I compiled the material in the studio, and in a few cases I added another instrument—Manu Katché and Jerry Marotta played drums on a couple of pieces. I think there's something interesting about recording in a hotel; each track, in a way, reflects where it's recorded. There's nothing slick about the music, and I like that.

Did you play only Stick on the record?

I played a little bass guitar and also a little electric upright. On the tune with Levon Minassian I bowed the NS bass; it's "totally exposed" bowing, the first I've done since my last recital in music school many years ago.

How many sessions do you do nowadays?

I'm uncomfortable with the term "sessions." That's what they are, and I probably shouldn't feel the way I do about the word. But there was a time when I really was a "session musician"—and I felt okay about it. In those days there was a ton of work in New York, and if you left for a while, your work would be taken up by other musicians. It didn't involve playing with your own sound, technique, or style; any competent player could be used for any session. But at a certain point I made a decision not to be a "session musician" anymore; I decided I wanted to be a rock musician and go out on the road. I subsequently got to play on albums by people who liked the way I play the bass, and ever since then I've developed an aversion to being called a studio or session musician. My playing, too, has changed. I'm not the craftsman I was in the '70s; nowadays I try to come up with parts that express what I want to do with the music.

Does that mean you work less?

I do fewer and fewer albums as the years go by. When you do a Peter Gabriel tour that lasts a year and a half, that seriously cuts into the number of albums you can do; I would say that in the last year I must have done only three or four. I get fewer and fewer calls, too.

How can bass players increase their expressiveness?

I've been influenced by the melodies of Tchaikovsky, the orchestrations of Ravel and Stravinsky, Chuck Mangione's trumpet playing, Steve Gadd's time sense, and Paul Simon's sense of how to write a melody and how to introduce a new lyrical idea. These are things that have nothing to do with a bass line, but their value to a bass player is huge because they have everything to do with music. Like other musicians, bass players are trying to make the best music they can with whatever function they take on a particular piece. The more musicality you have, the quicker you're able to hone in on a musical part. That not only makes you happy with your own part, it makes the people you work with happy.

Peter Gabriel has called you "one of the world's best bass players, if not the best."

I find that whole subject embarrassing. I feel as though I'm a very lucky guy, because for my whole life I've been doing something I love to do: playing low notes. I feel as though I'm a good bassist, but I'm skittish about being compared to other players. In no way am I the "best" bass player; there is no such thing. Real success comes with feeling good about yourself and what you're trying to do—and if you make music, that means feeling good about the music you're able to make. We bass players are often forced to play parts that aren't the ones we'd like to play, but it's worth a bit of fighting. It's tremendously satisfying to get the *right* part onto a record—or even better, to get it out into the air in a live show, where people hear it and it's gone.

You've become something of a hero to a lot of players over the years. What wisdom would you like to share with your admirers?

Some of the beginners I've talked to in my travels think of me as someone who's very successful, and they have an idea about what it must be like to be in my position. They imagine that because of who I am, people hire me to play exactly the way I would like to play—but the reality is quite different.

I'd like to tell less-experienced bassists that sooner or later you'll have to face discouragement. It could come in the form of being kicked out of a band, being told to play a part that isn't you, or being replaced in the middle of a project. It's important to understand that this happens to all of us—not just bassists, but all musicians. All the successful players I know have had to face a lot of adversity, and they've had to learn how not to take it personally. My advice, if I'm going to be caught giving advice, is to keep in mind that these things happen to Tony Levin, they happen to Steve Gadd, they happen to Manu Katché—and not just at the beginning of our careers, but pretty continually. Playing music is full of setbacks, but you just have to keep playing—to have success, you must learn to cope with the setbacks.

Web sites

www.tonylevin.com
www.tonylevinband.com

Tony Gives It Up

ONE OF TONY LEVIN'S MOST MEMORABLE BASS CREATIONS is the mellifluous, multi-part line on Peter Gabriel's "Don't Give Up," a haunting duet with singer Kate Bush from Gabriel's 1986 *So*. Levin played the song fingerstyle on a Music Man StingRay 4-string, with his *E* string tuned down to *E♭* to accommodate the final section's low *E♭*'s. Tony, who sometimes looks to other instruments and players for bass inspiration, says the main bass figure was developed from a drum loop. "All Peter had for an idea was a drum machine part that played through the whole piece. The drums' rhythm pattern and pitches gave me the idea for the notes I played. I also made the phrase twice as long and did some other things to it." The result was the hypnotic four-bar chordal phrase that drives the song's mournful verses (**Ex. 1**).

Ex. 1

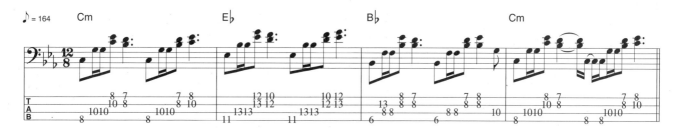

Example 2 recalls the four-bar chorus section phrase, where Levin steps back with simple, low, dotted half-notes, leaving plenty of room for Bush's sensitive vocal but keeping things interesting with upper-register slides and the arpeggio at the end of bar 4 (between vocal phrases). Says Tony, "I played the high fills live—they weren't over-dubbed—and I used a volume pedal to create the swells."

Ex. 2

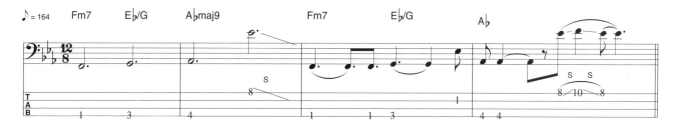

In the song's outro, the time signature changes but the quarter-note value remains constant—that is, twice the eighth-note value of the 12/8 section. **Example 3** illustrates the section's deep, skanking two-bar phrase for which Tony shoved one of his daughter Maggie's diapers under the strings near the bridge. "I heard the other parts, and I just had a sense of what I wanted to do: a dubby sound, as bottomy as possible, with short, dampened notes. I didn't know what notes I'd play until I got the dampening in there."

Ex. 3

"Don't Give Up" by Peter Gabriel. Published by Real World Music, Ltd. (PRS) for the World. Administered in N. America by Pentagon Lipservices Real World (BMI).

NATHAN EAST
A View from the Best Seat in the House

Interviewed by Chris Jisi, June 1997.

"BASS PLAYERS HAVE THE BEST SEAT IN THE HOUSE," contends Nathan East. When you consider the up-close-and-personal views he's had of such artists as Eric Clapton, Phil Collins, Whitney Houston, Michael Jackson, Madonna, Elton John, and Babyface, it's easy to understand what he means. Of course, Nathan—an easygoing sort famous for his big smile and even bigger bass pocket—is really talking about the role of the instrument. "We bassists are equally involved in the rhythm and the harmony, and we have the ability to support as well as to step out front. From a creative standpoint we can color the music in so many ways."

East's understanding of those aspects and the responsibilities that go with them are the keys to his amazing 25-year career. On his Los Angeles home turf, he's a first-call session bassist with over 1,000 albums and numerous jingles and soundtracks to his credit. On the road, he's held it down for rock royalty, pop divas, and jazz geniuses. In addition, he writes, sings, produces, and has a solo career in waiting—all of which can be heard in his work with the jazz supergroup Fourplay.

East is one of many great bassists who hail from Philadelphia. Three years after his birth there on December 8, 1955, his family moved to San Diego to accommodate his father's job as an engineer designing aircraft for General Dynamics. The East children—five boys and two girls—grew up surrounded by aviation and the sciences, but music was always in the house. Says Nathan, "We had a piano my dad would fool around with. He could play 'Stella by Starlight,' and my mom could read music and play. The first music I can recall hearing was Vince Guaraldi's 'Linus and Lucy.' I remember going to the piano to try to pick it out."

Nathan played cello in junior high school, but while viewing a rehearsal by his brother David's high school jazz ensemble, he was captivated by the sound and function of the bassist's Fender Jazz. "It sounded incredible," Nathan recalls. "I remember thinking, Wow, this guy gets to push all these other musicians along." Brothers David and Ray also sang in folk masses Nathan attended. "One day there was a Gibson EB-3 bass sitting on a stand at the altar. I picked it up and started playing with some of the band members, and I said to

myself, This is absolutely it. I knew then and there that was what I wanted to do with my life."

Equipped with a $49 short-scale Japanese bass his mom bought for him at a pawnshop, the 14-year-old set out to learn his craft and join every band he could. "I quickly realized if I stayed on the same note when the chord changed, it made a difference—and that if the chord stayed the same but I changed my note, that made a difference as well. That's how I discovered the common tone and the substitution, and learned how I could control the complexion of the music." Reaffirming his bass bloodlines, Nathan brought his axe with him on family trips

Nathan East

back to Philadelphia to visit relatives. Seeking local musicians there, he learned important lessons about groove-keeping and jazz harmony. A car ride up to Manhattan's famed 48th Street netted him his first J-Bass.

Back home, Nathan's main training tools were the record player and the radio. "I was playing along with James Brown, Motown, the Beatles, Sly Stone, Cream, Hendrix, and horn bands like Chicago, Blood, Sweat & Tears, and Tower of Power. I focused on prominent bass parts, which meant I was being driven crazy by James Jamerson, Chuck Rainey, Verdine White, and especially Rocco Prestia, whose lines I couldn't even play! On top of that, I was checking out the fusion and jazz side—Stanley Clarke, Ray Brown, Ron Carter, and Scott LaFaro."

In the midst of all of these low-end stimuli, East got his first big break. "I was in a local band called Power, and we did a Stax revue with their roster of artists. One of the artists was Barry White, and he hired our whole band for a national tour." Only 16 years old (he graduated from high school early), Nathan hit the road as a member of the Love Unlimited Orchestra. Clad in tuxedos, the group played such venues as Madison Square Garden and the Apollo Theater. East's most valuable lesson, however, was learning about the less glamorous side of life on the road. "Barry told us he could pay each of us $250 a week, although we'd be paying for our own rooms and food! We didn't know any better; we were jumping and high-fiving each other right in front of him. We criss-crossed the country in a bus while Barry flew and took limos. Most times we all slept in one or two rooms to save money. We had fun, but it was often brutal."

Upon returning home, East enrolled in the University of California at San Diego, heeding his father's advice to have something to fall back on and fulfilling a promise he'd made to his grandmother to get a college degree. During his third year he declared music as his major and began studying classical upright bass with noted pedagogue Bertram Turetzky. Three weeks before graduation and a final recital for which he would perform Jaco's "Portrait of Tracy," East received a call from guitarist John McLaughlin asking him to be in New York by the weekend to begin a tour. "Turning him down was one of the most agonizing decisions I've ever had to make, but the only thing that kept me from pulling out of school was the promise I'd made to my grandmother. Plus, deep down I felt that if someone of John's stature was interested in me, I was moving in the right direction. I even went ahead and started on my master's degree when Bertram pulled me aside and told me I'd had enough schooling—that it was time for me to go to Los Angeles and make some money playing."

While waiting for an opportunity in L.A., East got involved in the San Diego club and studio scene. "As luck would have it, Barry White resurfaced with some recording projects. I began driving up to L.A. to record with him during the day, and then I'd come back to play clubs at night." Finally, Nathan decided to move to Los Angeles and end the commuting. In the fall of 1979 he rented a tiny guest house behind an apartment building in Burbank. "I remember frequently calling the telephone company for the first few months to make sure the phone worked, because it wasn't ringing!"

On the second day of 1980, fortune smiled when Nathan got a call from renowned writer/arranger Gene Page for the bassist's first big date: a jingle for Hertz. "I walked in and there was Lee Ritenour, Ray Parker Jr., and Wah Wah Watson on guitars, James Gadson on drums, and pianist Sonny Burke. I was a nervous wreck—I told myself, It's now or never, so play your ass off. I had worked with Gene Page for Barry White, and I remembered someone telling me, 'If he likes you and starts to use you, it's worth a quarter-million a year.' Thankfully, Gene liked the fact that I could read music as well as interpret and play a lot of styles, so he started calling me for everything. On top of that, all of the musicians on the date told me I did a good job, and each one of them went out and tooted my horn. So I always say my career started on January 2, 1980, because from that day on I've worked non-stop."

You became established in the L.A. studios at a time when the bass scene was in flux.

That's right. There was a bit of a void around 1980; Chuck Rainey, Joe Osborn, Carol Kaye, and Anthony Jackson had left town, and players like Max Bennett, Wilton Felder, and Eddie Watkins had pretty much stopped taking dates. Lee Sklar and Louis Johnson were busy. My peers—Abe Laboriel, Jimmy Johnson, Neil Stubenhaus, and Freddie Washington—were all in L.A. a little before me, and they were on their way to becoming established. It was the perfect time for bassists who could read and play. I was fortunate to get a lot of recommendations from people like Abe, Patrice Rushen, and especially Jeff Porcaro. I got tight with all the drummers [*laughs*], and they've remained good friends of mine.

What were your key early projects in L.A.?

The nice thing about being in the Gene Page camp was there was always a big project going on—Dionne Warwick or Johnny Mathis sessions with 60-piece orchestras. I played on Whitney Houston's and Madonna's first records, and they were complete unknowns then. I met Quincy Jones while playing at his 50th birthday party, and he started using me. Lionel Richie was the first major artist to make a big commitment to me and use me on everything he did. "Endless Love" was my first gold record; he also wrote "Lady" for Kenny Rogers, and I played on that. The other important artists for me early on were Kenny Loggins and Al Jarreau. With Kenny I did the *Vox Humana* album and the track "Footloose." I made two records with Al, which is where I met producer Jay Graydon and got to play with Steve Gadd. Another key with Kenny and Al was the tours I did with them; that was where I really got my stage chops together, in terms of being up front singing and dancing, and learning about performing live in front of huge audiences.

Wasn't going on the road for extended periods a questionable move for an upcoming session player?

In many studio circles, yes—but I've never been afraid to leave town. I've seen too many people who were chained to L.A., and they were generally the ones who suffered burnout. I was fortunate to get away from the scene periodically—and every time I went on the road I'd find my playing would be fresher and more inspired when I got back. Overall, I've been quite blessed. When I first got to L.A., I was given a lot of good advice by older musicians on what pitfalls to avoid. My first accountant told me, "All right, I'm giving you four years in this town." That made me even more determined to achieve longevity! My credo was: show up on time with quality equipment, kick some ass, and leave. I tried to bring the best performance and the best attitude to everything I touched—and I'm thankful the phone kept ringing. I never felt the effects of mechanized music or keyboard bass, or being out of town.

Over the years, some top bass players have been critical of studio bassists for "sacrificing their artistry."

I think there's plenty to be said for someone who can create with a lot of heart for a wide spectrum of recording artists under the circumstances and pressures of the studio. The bassists who say those things are invariably bandleaders who seem to have forgotten that the nature of the instrument is supportive. I have a solo side, but I pride myself on being an excellent support system—being The Man next to The Man. A studio bassist is simply an artist of a different kind—just listen to James Jamerson.

You replaced Jamerson's part on "Lady" near the end of his career. Do you think part of his downfall resulted from his reluctance to alter his approach and sound, based on his earlier success in Detroit?

That may have been one aspect of it—but I think it had more to do with his performances not being up to his usual high standards, because of the personal problems he was experiencing. I remember being called to replace one of his parts and refusing, only to find out later that I had replaced him on "Lady."

You must have recognized that having an identifiable sound and style can be a disadvantage for a studio player.

Absolutely, because the nature of the job requires you to keep up with the shifting tides of music. Also, I figured out early on that if you become the hot guy with the hot sound everybody wants, demand is going to cool off rather quickly. I saw it was far more valuable to have a chameleon-like approach; that's why my concept has always been to do what's right for the song, and no more. I think that has become my trademark, rather than people knowing it's me based on one note

East Meets West

Nathan East has been playing Yamaha basses since 1980. "I saw Abe Laboriel playing one at a concert, and he sounded great. A short time later, on a trip to Japan, I was able to hook up with the Yamaha people." Inspired by Anthony Jackson and Jimmy Johnson, he quickly moved to a 5-string, adding yet another string soon after. By 1994, Yamaha had developed a signature bass for East; his main axe is a 36"-scale BB-series Nathan East Signature 5-string. "The extra scale length really upgrades the sound and feel of the *B* string," he says. Nathan's first-call 6 is a Yamaha TRB6. Other basses in his regular rotation include Yamaha BB East fretted and fretless 5-strings; a Yamaha 5-string acoustic bass guitar; fretted and fretless Fodera 5's; a '72 Precision with a J-Bass neck; an early '70s Jazz Bass; and a Clevinger 5-string electric upright. His strings are Nathan East Signature Elites (stainless steel roundwounds, gauged 0.47, .067, .085, .105, .130); for his Clevinger, he uses Thomastik Spirocore chrome steel flatwounds.

East chooses Aguilar for amplification; his basic setup includes a DB750 head and two stacked GS410 4x10 cabinets. Nathan occasionally steps on a Boss CE-2 Octave, a Boss CE-2 Chorus, and Moog Taurus bass pedals. An A/B box with a volume attenuator allows him to dial in separate levels for his Yamaha and Clevinger basses. East also uses an Aguilar DB900 direct box, an Aphex Bass Xciter, an Avalon U5 direct box, Korg DTR1 Digital Rackmount Tuner, TARA Labs cables, a Yamaha wireless system, and—when he needs a pick sound—his fingernails.

or a certain lick, or the tone of a certain bass. Herb Alpert once told me, "Your bass fits so smoothly and easily into the track," and I've always thought that was a great compliment.

Your first big departure from the studio scene was the Philip Bailey/Phil Collins project for which the three of you collaborated on the No. 1 hit "Easy Lover."

I had worked with Philip on his first solo album, and he recommended me to Phil. We went to Europe in 1984 to do Philip's *Chinese Wall* record, which was followed by my first European tour. After a few weeks in the studio, we had good songs and a good mix of Philip and Phil's talents—but Philip said to me at the end of the last day of recording, "We still need an undeniable hit." So, we sat down and wrote "Easy Lover" in about 20 minutes. It was amazing the way it came together; I wrote most of the music, Phil wrote the lyrics, and Philip wrote his parts. We put down a rough version with the intent of re-recording it the next day, but after hearing it the following morning, we realized that was the take.

Meeting Phil really took my career to another level and changed my perspective forever. Suddenly, I didn't care if I ever got back to L.A.! Through him I met all the English rock legends: the Stones, the Who, Paul McCartney, Sting, Mark Knopfler, Elton John, and—of course—Eric Clapton. Phil produced Eric's *Behind the Sun* album, which [keyboardist] Greg Phillinganes and I played on. At Live Aid the next year, Eric and I hung out, and he later brought me, Greg, and Phil in for *August*, which Phil produced. That led to the four of us doing a brief European tour in 1986. Steve Ferrone played drums when Phil was unavailable, and soon after, he joined me and Greg and we became Eric's band.

One of the most enjoyable things about that group was the freedom Eric gave to the three of you, resulting in funkified grooves and jazzy reharmonizations.

Because we were playing the same songs in every show, we constantly tried to tastefully push the music in new directions and make it a little deeper and better each night. The credit, though, goes to Eric; most artists want their music to be played by the book, but he's always looking for a fresh approach. He's like Miles in that he goes in the opposite direction of the flow, he never looks back, and he continually reinvents himself—as he did with the *Unplugged* album, and later when he put together his blues band. He was also generous enough to give me complete bass and vocal features.

The introduction to "Layla" became one of your playing features, during which you quoted Jaco's melody from Weather Report's "A Remark You Made."

The impact of Jaco's playing reached far beyond bass players. During one of the tours, Eric had a copy of Weather Report's *Heavy Weather*, and that's all he would to listen to. When Jaco died, we decided to do a tribute. The song "A Remark You Made" touched everybody, so we began fooling around with it during soundchecks, and it ultimately became the introduction to "Layla." Over the years it evolved and even became a major orchestral piece arranged by Michael Kamen, with two or three sections. Each time I performed it I thought of Jaco and other greats who had passed—Wes Montgomery, Jimi Hendrix, and later, Stevie Ray Vaughan.

You were almost involved in the tragic helicopter crash in Wisconsin that took Stevie Ray's life.

Eric was sharing the bill with Stevie Ray, Robert Cray, and Jeff Healey for a series of concerts at a venue called Alpine Valley. We chartered four helicopters for our band, which we had used the night before. On that night I met a young lady whose father was a pilot, and they offered to fly me to the concert site the next day. I ended up taking the ill-fated helicopter to the show, but I accepted their invitation to fly me back to the hotel in Chicago, and I invited Greg Phillinganes to come with us. Once our two seats in the helicopter became available, Stevie Ray took one and Eric's road manager, Colin Smyth, took the other. We heard about the crash the next morning, and it was probably the darkest day of my life.

You have a jazz itch that's scratched by Fourplay. How did that band form?

It was a result of myself, Lee Ritenour, and [drummer] Harvey Mason being in the studio with Bob James to record his *Grand Piano Canyon* album in 1990. After we finished, Bob asked if we would be interested in a group concept with the four of us being equal partners and everybody contributing material. He had a band name, and since he's an A&R man with Warners Bros.' jazz department, he felt he could secure a deal. A couple of months later we got together to rehearse, and then we hit the studio. Our original intent was to do it for the fun of it—but our first record sold half a million copies, and it remained at No. 1 on the Contemporary Jazz charts for six months.

Nathan East Selected Discography

With Fourplay: (all on Warner Bros. except where noted) *Yes Please*, Bluebird; *Heartfelt*; *Snowbound*; *Fourplay 4*; *Elixir*; *Between the Sheets*; *Fourplay*. **With Eric Clapton:** (all on Warner/Reprise) *One More Car: One More Rider*; *Reptile*; *Pilgrim*; *Unplugged*; *24 Nights*; *Journeyman*; *August*; *Behind the Sun*. **With Phil Collins:** (both on Atlantic) *Dance Into the Light*; *But Seriously*. **With Babyface:** (both on Sony) *Love Songs*; *Day*. **With Al Jarreau:** (both on Warner Bros.) *Live in London*; *High Crime*. **With Whitney Houston:** (all on Arista) *Just Whitney*; *Whitney*; *Whitney Houston*. **With Anita Baker:** (all on Elektra) *Rhythm of Love*; *Compositions*; *Giving You the Best That I Got*; *The Songstress*. **With Lionel Richie:** *Louder than Words*, Mercury; *Dancing on the Ceiling*, Motown; *Can't Slow Down*, Motown; *Lionel Richie*, Motown. **With Kenny Loggins:** (all on Sony) *Unimaginable Life*; *Return to Pooh Corner*; *Leap of Faith*; *Back to Avalon*; *Vox Humana*; *High Adventure*. **With Philip Bailey:** (all on CBS/Sony) *Inside Out*; *Chinese Wall*; *Continuation*. **With Michael Jackson:** (all on Epic) *Invincible*; *HIStory*; *Bad*. **With the Jacksons:** *Victory*, Epic. **With Quincy Jones:** *Back on the Block*, Qwest. **With Earth, Wind & Fire:** *Touch the World*, CBS/Sony. **With Elton John:** *Duets*, MCA. **With Peter Gabriel:** *Passion: Music from The Last Temptation of Christ*, Geffen. **With Madonna:** *Madonna*, Sire. **With Natalie Cole:** *Stardust*, Elektra; *Dangerous*, Modern. **With Chaka Khan:** *I Feel for You*, Warner Bros. **With Barbra Streisand:** (both on CBS/Sony) *Back to Broadway*; *Emotion*. **With Aretha Franklin:** *Who's Zoomin' Who?*, Arista. **With Randy Newman:** *Trouble in Paradise*, Warner Bros. **With Joe Satriani:** *Joe Satriani*, Relativity. **With Michael Bolton:** *Timeless: The Classics*, Columbia. **With Michael McDonald:** (both on Warner Bros.) *Blink of an Eye*; *No Lookin' Back*. **With Donna Summer:** *She Works Hard for the Money*, Mercury. **With David Foster:** *River of Love*, Atlantic. **With Rickie Lee Jones:** *The Magazine*, Warner Bros. **With Richard Marx:** (both on Capitol) *Rush Street*; *Richard Marx*. **With Amy Grant:** *The Collection*, RCA/Victor. **With James Ingram:** *It's Your Night*, Warner Bros. **With George Benson:** (both on Warner Bros.) *20/20*; *In Your Eyes*. **With Bob James:** *Grand Piano Canyon*, Warner Bros. **With Lee Ritenour:** (both on Elektra) *Portrait*; *Rit 2*. **With David Benoit & Russ Freeman:** *The Benoit Freeman Project*, GRP. **With Herbie Hancock:** *Sound System*, Columbia. **With Hubert Laws:** *Family*, CBS. **With Wayne Shorter:** *Joy Rider*, CBS. **With Michael Henderson:** *Slingshot*, Kama Sutra. **With the Pointer Sisters:** *So Excited*, Planet. **With the Backstreet Boys:** *Black & Blue*, Jive. **With Enrique Iglesias:** *Enrique*, Interscope. **With TLC:** *FanMail*, La Face. **With Justin Timberlake:** *Justified*, Jive. **Soundtracks:** *Bamboozled*; *The Preacher's Wife*; *Phenomenon*; *Waiting to Exhale*; *One Fine Day*; *Lethal Weapon 2*; *Rush*; *Escape from L.A.*; *Something to Talk About*; *Crossroads*; *Footloose*.

With all of our busy schedules, we have to find a window for recording and a window for touring each year. From a personal standpoint, though, Fourplay affords me the chance to be the "artist," and to stretch out in a progressive setting as a writer, vocalist, and bassist.

On the critical side, the terms "happy jazz," "safe jazz," and "fuzak" have been tossed about.

I don't know how to describe our music, since it wasn't written to fit any format—but if you're having dinner or anything else [*winks*], it works. Seriously, though, we didn't try to put any limitations on the writing or the soloing, and we didn't pay attention to any "safe" labels. On the other hand, we didn't approach it like a straightahead jazz group, and we didn't say, "Let's see how fast we can play." It's more of an ensemble sound and effort with the goal of creating good songs through both individual and ensemble writing and arranging. Live, we've been known to pull out "Seven Steps to Heaven" for the skeptics who think we can't play.

Your other steady commitment is to Babyface. When did you begin working together?

I met Babyface on a project he did for Aretha Franklin several years ago, and basically he's been calling me ever since. He is, without a doubt, the most prolific musician/songwriter I've ever been associated with, and his work is always of the highest quality. I believe he now has over 100 Top Five hits. Plus, he's a ridiculous guitarist who plays upside-down and lefty. In the '80s his music was more sequencer- and keyboard-bass-oriented, but his formula for the '90s includes the use of a live rhythm section—usually with myself, Greg Phillinganes, John Robinson, and [percussionist] Sheila E., among others. We've done everything from "Change the World" [*from the film* Phenomenon] and other soundtrack songs to Lionel Richie to Face's own roster of artists.

You mentioned a close kinship with drummers.

Absolutely. Bass and drums are the core of everything in music. Playing relationships with drummers are like little marriages, in that you begin to know instinctively what the other person is going to do, on *and* off the stage [*laughs*]. I would have to say the late Jeff Porcaro was my favorite to play with; there's such a chunk out of my heart and a void in the industry because he's gone. Still, I'm very fortunate to maintain "marriages" with people like Phil Collins, Harvey Mason, Steve Ferrone, Steve Gadd, Ricky Lawson, Vinnie Colaiuta, John Robinson, Jim Keltner, the late Carlos Vega, and other top drummers.

How do you approach playing with a drummer?

I listen to his whole kit and then zero in on his kick and snare. Bass players are the main beneficiaries of drummers' efforts; they support us and give us so much to play off, which is another big part of why I say we have the best seat in the house.

What do you think of the current state of the bass?

It's very healthy—although we're moving at a slower pace now because there's less to discover, thanks to the contributions of Jamerson, Larry Graham, Jaco, Anthony Jackson, and others. There's a lot of quality, but nobody has redefined the bass in a while. More than likely, that person will come along; on the other hand, it may never happen again to the same magnitude—just like there will never be another Beatles.

What perspective have you gained from "the best seat in the house."

That bass is a universal instrument; I know, because I've been to the four corners of the globe to help prove it! I have no complaints, though. They say if you love what you do, you'll never work another day in your life. And I love my life.

Web site

www.nathaneast.com

The Two Faces of East

NATHAN EAST HAS DONE HIS PART to uphold and advance the strong groove tradition established by studio bassists—but another area where he has helped raise the bar is as a soloist. His undeniable flair for blues and bebop improvisation has led to his being given solos in unlikely places in various pop, rock, and R&B settings. A pair of prime examples of these "two faces of East" are his groove part on "Change the World," the Babyface-produced Eric Clapton Grammy song of the year in 1997, and his classic solo on "Our Love," from Al Jarreau's 1985 concert video *Al Jarreau Live in London* [Warner Bros.].

Example 1a shows the style of Nathan's verse groove of "Change the World." Says East, who played his signature Yamaha 5, "I wanted to set up a counter-pattern to John Robinson's kick drum as opposed to matching it. We had tried quarter-notes and eighth-notes, but neither felt right. The counter-line kept the forward motion going in a fresh way." Note the fills at the end of bars 2, 4, and 6. "Having played with Eric for so long, I tried to envision the interplay that would happen between us if we were onstage, and then I tried to capture some of it on tape. I knew he was going to put his guitar parts on later, so the fills are like little telegraphed messages saying 'hello.'" Example 1b was inspired by the chorus bass line. Here Nathan steps forward with chromatic passing tones in bars 3 and 6 and tasty fills in bars 2 and 4. "Those are Jamerson/Chuck Rainey–inspired."

Ex. 1a

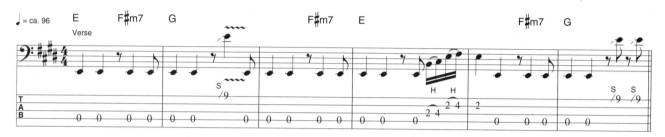

Ex. 1b

Example 2 contains the first 13 bars of East's exquisitely melodic solo on "Our Love," played on his Yamaha BB3000 5-string. "Al Jarreau loved the offbeat nature of having the bass play a solo in the middle of his ballad, so it became an established part of the show. I look at a solo as a mini-song you write on the spot—one that tells a story." Indeed, his improvisation is a collection of themes, variations, and resolutions. In bars 1 and 2, he uses ascending and descending arpeggios to state his theme around the A major tonal center. In bars 3 and 4, he retains that concept as the tonal center shifts to G♭ major. In the pickup to bar 5, a new theme starts, as the tonal center shifts to F♯ minor, the relative minor of A major. This is resolved as the chords begin to cycle back to the A major tonality in bar 7. At the end of bar 7 into bar 8, Nathan brings the resolution to a little peak; this is a nod to the unrelated substitute chords in

Ex. 2

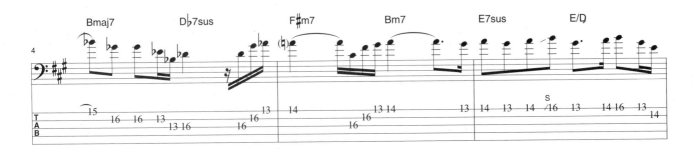

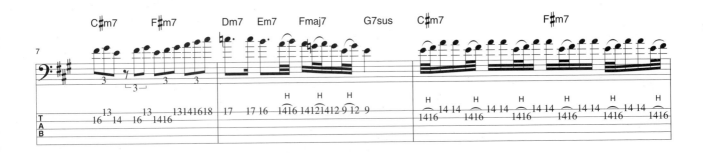

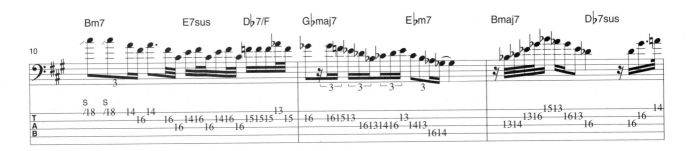

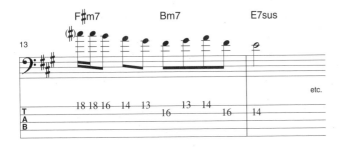

bar 8 that make up the turnaround, which leads to the second half of the solo. Nathan's ability to smoothly connect the key centers with common tones (as on the last beats of bars 2 and 9 to the first beats of bars 3 and 10) gives the solo its flow.

At bar 9 the chords from the first eight bars repeat. This time, East begins with a repetitive three-note figure with shifting rhythmic emphasis. Though not part of the *C#m7* chord, the presence of the *A* in the figure confirms the *A* major tonality. Nathan resolves the phrase in bar 10 before using similar rhythmic motion to segue to the next tonal center at bar 11. Here, his descending triplets feel almost like an exhaled breath before the rapid ascending *Bmaj7* arpeggio in bar 12. On the pickup to bar 13, Nathan restates the bold *F#m7* theme he originally stated in the pickup to bar 5; he uses slightly different notes here, but the effect is the same. The slowed-down tempo and upper-register notes serve to make bar 13 the solo's climax.

A key to East's overall melodicism is his preference for singing what he plays, either to himself or in a soft voice—a common device used by jazz soloists. "I always try to play from the heart, and singing is a natural connection. Your phrasing and melodies roll off the tip of your tongue when you sing. I would advise other bassists to do some practicing away from the bass; just sing and let it come from within. If you play only patterns on the neck, you're never going to move the listener. To really move someone, you have to be moved yourself—and that has to come from the inside. Sincerity is everything. If you mean it, it works."

ABRAHAM LABORIEL
Master of Balance

Interviewed by Richard Johnston, September/October 1995.

ON A WARM SPRING NIGHT in Orange County, Abraham Laboriel's presence fills the storefront church where he's playing a benefit for the Hispanic Association of Christians for the Arts. While he evangelizes and leads the congregation in hymning and hand-clapping, Abe also leads his band in hugely grooving tunes that often end with his trademark choreography. A final chorus is likely to find the ebullient bassist bouncing across the stage, smacking his strings with abandon while his elbows and legs fly in all directions—a marionette jerked by a mad puppeteer.

One of bassdom's most creative soloists is also a veteran of more than 3,000 sessions in myriad styles. He says simplest is best, yet he commands a mind-boggling array of mutant techniques—and he can create mighty grooves whether palm-slamming his strings in thrash fashion or plucking them classical guitar–style. These extremes come together in an amiable teddy bear of a man with a dusting of gray hair and, it seems, a hug for the whole world. For Abraham Laboriel, it's all a matter of balance. "If I become a great soloist at the expense of not having a good sense of time and rhythm, I feel that something very crucial would be lost."

That statement is a little behind the times. Laboriel is already a great soloist, judging from his solo album *Guidum*. His improvisations range from the soulful phrasing of "Exchange" and the intricate ornamentation of "Let My People …" to the explosive hammer-slap-strumming on "Bebop Drive." But the recording also bears witness to Abe's righteous groove-ability—if "Slippin' and Slidin'" doesn't quicken your pulse, you may not have one. In addition, *Guidum* (ghee-DOOM) reveals Abe's empathy with longtime collaborators Justo Almario (reeds) and Greg Mathieson (keyboards). The 70-minute album—which also features the drumming of future Paul McCartney sideman Abe Laboriel Jr.—was recorded live in the studio with only a thimbleful of overdubs. Says Abe, "When we did *Guidum*, because of all those years of making records, Greg and I felt that we wanted to capture that excitement we all feel when we're just trying to learn a song."

The strategy seems to have worked. In groove and intensity, *Guidum* is a several notches above Laboriel's first solo album, *Dear Friends*, which nonetheless cooks in its own good-natured way. Another showcase for Abe's virtuosity, *Justo Almario • Abraham Laboriel*, features the two friends playing jazz-inspired arrangements of traditional and contemporary songs of praise.

Laboriel was born in Mexico City in 1947, the child of a musician/composer/actor who started teaching his son classical guitar at age six. Abe had lost the tip of his left-hand index finger two years earlier in an encounter with a washing-machine belt. "My father taught me to play guitar with the other three fingers, and that got to be very, very difficult. By the time I was eight I quit."

At age ten Abe was inspired to take up guitar again when his brother Johnny joined a band called Los Rebeldes Del Rock. "The American publishing companies would send him records to consider recording in Spanish, because he and his band were the most important rock entertainers in Mexico in those days. I started to learn by ear by playing along with all these records, mostly just rhythm." By the time he was 17, Abe was working as a studio guitarist in Mexico City. After studying aeronautical engineering for a time, he convinced his parents music was his calling, and he soon landed a guitar scholarship to Boston Conservatory. Sensing Abe wasn't cut out to be a classical musician, a faculty member recommended him to nearby Berklee College of Music.

At Berklee Laboriel began playing electric bass—at first for a church choir, and then in a quartet led by Al Silvestri, who would later write the *CHiPs* TV soundtracks Abe recorded. Laboriel took a liking to his rented Fender Precision—though not to its wide neck—and would have switched majors if Berklee had offered an electric bass degree at the time. Nonetheless, he stuck with bass. After some studio work in Boston, he played on vibist Gary Burton's *The New Quartet* and then went on the road backing Johnny Mathis with the Count Basie Orchestra. Through that gig, the young bassist met Henry Mancini, who encouraged him to come to Los Angeles. Abe's arm-long list of session credits now covers everyone from Herb Alpert to Joe Zawinul. He's worked extensively on TV and movie soundtracks, logged road miles with guitarist Lee Ritenour and vocalist Al Jarreau, and also made four albums with Mathieson and Almario in the Christian fusion group Koinonia.

You're like three musicians—a bass player, drummer, and guitarist—all in one.
[*Laughs.*] I love music with all my heart, and those instruments are my first points of reference.
When did you learn to play drums?
Between the ages of 12 and 15 I did a few jobs on drums with rock bands in Mexico. On one occasion the electricity went out when we were playing for a dance. I was in one of those weird moods, and I decided just to keep playing until the electricity came back—and the audience kept dancing for an hour. I felt really rewarded that the dance didn't stop—that we were all able to go home at the right time. So I've always loved the drums.
How do you maintain both virtuosic solo technique and the ability to fit into any musical situation?
It has to do with being open-minded. Someone once told me, "Listening is the greatest form of loving someone." When a person feels he's being listened to, he feels loved and respected. Through the years, many people have told me things that I keep very close to my heart, and those conversations have shaped everything I do. Major Holley, one of my teachers at Berklee, said, "The bass player is the house into which all the other players come to find shelter and have a good time. If you forget that responsibility, you're leaving everybody

without shelter." That has stayed with me—that sense of responsibility. When I'm playing behind someone, I try to think, How can I play so that you're comfortable? What can I do to make your song feel the way you want it to?

When I first started to make records, I heard that most players who spend a lot of time in the studio quickly learn to become very economical—to get rid of the fat and play only the simple things that are essential to communicate the crucial feeling of that moment. If I overplay, it doesn't translate well onto tape, and some things that I feel are boring or uninspired really sound great on tape. So by trial and error, as well as by the observation and feedback of other people, I have learned what it takes to make a situation work. During really busy times I feel cheated, because I don't have time to reflect. It's a tremendous learning tool to think back on what happened and to remember how people changed their parts to make the music work.

Bass players should pay attention to instructions given to any of the other musicians at a session or rehearsal. If you're aware of what the other musicians have to do, your playing can help them to remember those things, and it can support those instructions. Steve Gadd helped me tremendously on that. He says

Abraham Laboriel

that when he plays, he doesn't know whether he's playing the hi-hat, the cymbal, the snare, or the bass drum. He listens to how his playing is affecting the overall feel of the song; he doesn't think, Should I be on the hi-hat? The cymbal? What kind of a feel should I be playing? That inspired me, so when I make records I first and foremost try to play as simply as possible. As people start making comments—"I wish somebody would do something here, this is lacking, I like this a lot"—then those passages start shifting, based on all the information I'm given.

Among all your sessions, do you recall any favorites?

There's an Al Jarreau song called "Mornin'" [*Jarreau*] that was one of the really high points, because we recorded that live. Al was singing with such *power*; the feeling was so strong and the song was so lovely, we literally could have played it all night. It was one of the rare things we got on an early take. When Ella Fitzgerald did her tribute to Antonio Carlos Jobim [*Ella Abraça Jobim*], sometimes I couldn't breathe, just from the thrill of being with her. She had all these guests, including Toots Thielemans and Joe Pass, who was incredible. And recently I had a chance to record with Joe Williams for the first time, which was also a dream come true.

Guidum *was recorded 99 percent live in the studio. Did it require a lot of takes, or was it just a matter of rehearsing the tunes and getting them down?*

We had a two-day rehearsal, and we recorded all the songs in a day and a half. Most were first or second takes; some of the endings kept lingering, and then we'd end abruptly in order to capture the emotion we were all feeling. In most sessions, *that's* the feeling we go through when we're just getting familiar with the songs, and it gets lost as things get more and more refined—"repeat this, repeat that, don't forget this part . . . ."

Abe Jr. seemed to pick up the parts pretty well.

Yeah! There's one producer who tells me that my son put me to shame on this record—"Man, you couldn't keep up with him!" It's amazing; Abe's now 24 years old, and every time I play with him, I'm surprised he understands as much as he does. His favorite music to practice at home is rock, so I never hear him play other kinds; then when we get together to play a variety of styles, it blows me away. He plays with so much *passion*.

On "Slippin' and Slidin'," it seems like you must have been standing up at the end of the song, when the vamp gets so intense.

[*Laughs.*] I always play standing up. I sit down when we're learning the music, but whenever we record, I always stand. Carol Kaye once told me that a lot of bass players have back problems from playing sitting down, because the neck is too far away from their bodies. I discovered that by standing up, you can bring in your hand a little closer, in a more natural way.

Did you play your Valley Arts basses on Guidum?

Absolutely. I used the interchangeable-neck one, so I can play both fretted and fretless. I also used the 8-string on "Exchange."

The 8-string seems to have some grit in the sound. Is that the nature of the bass, or is it something added in the recording?

It's the attack. When I play hard, I can choose which of the two octaves I favor. If it's an upstroke, the high note is favored, and if it's a downstroke, it's the low note. That variety creates a rich sound.

On the first song, "Wassup," you play the high melody on a very sweet-sounding bass. Was that a 6-string?

Yes—a Swedish-made Ares bass. This guy named Robert Sahrling was making beautiful amps, and he decided he wanted to make guitars and basses. I've been developing carpal-tunnel syndrome, so I've been asking the manufacturers to make me narrower necks; the Ares is the first smaller-neck bass I got. When I first heard it, the sound just blew me away—I knew it was going to be crucial to express all the aspects of my playing. I also played the Ares on "Slippin' and Slidin'," and I used a Warwick 6-string Thumb Bass, which has a bubinga body, on "Out from Darkness."

You also use a French-made Leduc.

Cristophe Leduc loves wood, and his craftsmanship is just unbelievable. He invented a concept called the "floating top"—it's a semi-acoustic bass guitar, the top part being a thin piece of spruce. It's really similar to a fine guitar or violin, because of the way the different woods vibrate and talk to each other. I used the Leduc for the solo on "Another Day."

I used an electric/acoustic Yamaha APX-5 for the swing part of "Guidum," backing up Justo's solo. That bass was difficult to make, and since they couldn't find a way to make it at a competitive price, they decided to stop manufacturing it.

What about your custom Jim Tyler 5-string?

I used that for the beginning of "Guidum," when I'm just talking and singing the song by myself. That's one of the great recording basses; all the producers like it. Most of Jim's basses have "tapered" frets, where the lower strings have fewer frets, but because of my chordal approach I asked him to make it full-fretted, and it's great—in tune everywhere.

Early in your career you used just one bass, a Goya Panther II. Does that help explain how you can get so many sounds just by using different hand techniques?

I think so. But also, my attention span was really short when I was first learning bass. Pretty soon I started

Abe's Arsenal

At the time of *Guidum* Abraham Laboriel was using three main studio basses: a Yamaha BB2000, to which he'd added a low *B* string; a prototype BB2000; and a '65 Precision with Seymour Duncan pickups. "Also, the Yamaha TRB series has become crucial for me in the last couple of years," says Abe, who plays a TRB5P 5-string with a piezo bridge. "The pitch is impeccable, it has a lot of punch, and it has personality. A lot of producers and arrangers like the way it sounds." As for the Fender, "This is going to get me into trouble, but I use the Fender when producers don't really want me to have personality in my playing. If they say, 'All I want is a great-sounding bass,' that's what I use. Actually, when I put Seymour Duncan pickups in the Fender, it acquired a lot of personality—but from a psychological point of view, when people see me playing a Fender, they often say, 'Yeah, what a difference.'" Abe usually goes straight into the console through an onboard Jim Tyler pre-amp and an ADL tube direct box. He sometimes uses an Ernie Ball volume pedal to get bowed-upright effects. If a producer wants an amp sound, Laboriel usually uses an Ampeg B-15 or a Walter Woods driving a Gauss 15.

For live gigs, Abe goes through the ADL and the volume pedal—which he uses to cut his signal when changing basses—and then straight to the PA. "Most soundmen don't want the bass to bleed into the drums, so when I used an amp, they were always asking me to turn down. One time as an experiment I turned off the amp, and the engineers were delighted. That's when I discovered that relying on the monitors is better—the audience gets a clearer sound, and the people onstage can ask for whatever they want." Abe concedes, though, that "about 40 percent of the time" the monitor sound is disappointing.

Laboriel uses GHS strings on most of his basses—either Brite Flats or Super Steels—and for his low *B* he prefers taper-wound strings made by La Bella. "The thin end at the bridge improves the intonation," he notes.

Over the years Abe has accumulated some 40 basses, and he concedes it's "a little excessive" trying to maintain them all. "But different producers say, 'No, don't sell that one; if I call you, I'm going to want you to bring it.' One day I think I'm going to simplify, but if producers like certain things, I'll try to please them as much as I can."

adding rhythmic and harmonic interest, just to make it sound fuller. In my bass clinics, I tell people that all music goes *oom-pah-pah*: the bass is the *oom*, and everything else is the *pah-pah*. So when you practice bass by itself, all you practice is a series of *ooms*, and there's a lot of space between them. You could say that when I was younger, I was incorporating the *pah-pah* into my thing.

What other ingredients go into the different techniques you use?

A lot of them come from wanting to imitate drummers. My thumb acts like a bass drum, and the other fingers are the snare. The *rasgueado* [flamenco-strumming] style comes from guitar—I discovered that's similar to a filigree-type thing drummers do on the hi-hat. So you have the bass drum, the snare, and the hi-hat.

When you play a basic walking line, do you always alternate your fingers?

It varies, depending on the color of sound I want. If I use the flesh of the thumb, I get a dark, warm sound, while the calluses on my index and middle fingers create a brighter sound. When the nail actually touches the string, it's much brighter still. The other two fingers also create a warm sound, but it's softer with the pinky than with the ring finger. Sometimes, depending on the complexity of the line I'm playing, I'll bring in whichever finger happens to be available.

What would you say to a student who said, "I want to play just like you—to use all the techniques you use"?

Well, the traditional answer is that what I do comes from a different place. When I play, I have either a drum-like concept or a subjective feeling I want to bring into the song at that moment. How do I get there?

Abraham Laboriel Selected Discography

Solo albums: *Guidum*, Integrity; *Justo Almario & Abraham Laboriel*, Integrity; *Dear Friends*, Bluemoon/Wigwam. **With Koinonia:** *Koinonia*, Bluemoon; *More Than a Feelin'*, Sparrow; *Frontline*, Sparrow; *Celebration*, Sparrow. **With Friendship:** *Friendship*, Elektra. **With James Ingram:** *It's Your Night*, Qwest. **With Al Jarreau:** (all on Warner Bros.) *Jarreau*; *Breakin' Away*; *This Time*; *Look to the Rainbow*. **With Quincy Jones:** *The Dude*, A&M. **With Lee Ritenour:** *Captain Fingers*, Epic; *Feel the Night*, Elektra; *Rit*, Elektra. **With Larry Carlton:** *Larry Carlton*, Warner Bros. **With Donald Fagen:** *The Nightfly*, Warner Bros. **With Paul Simon:** *You're the One*, Warner Bros. **With Ella Fitzgerald:** *Ella Abraça Jobim*, Pablo. **With Henry Mancini:** *Symphonic Soul*, Victor. **With Manhattan Transfer:** (both on Atlantic) *Mecca for Moderns*; *Extensions*. **With Michael Jackson:** *Dangerous*, Sony. **With the Crusaders:** *Rhapsody and Blues*, Mercury. **With George Benson:** *Give Me the Night*, Warner Bros. **With Chaka Khan:** *What Cha' Gonna Do for Me?*, Warner Bros. **With Sheena Easton:** *A Private Heaven*, EMI. **With Dave Grusin:** *Collection*, GRP. **With Miles Davis & Michel LeGrand:** *Dingo*, Warner Bros. **With Joe Sample:** (both on MCA) *Voices in the Rain*; *Carmel*. **With Joe Pass:** *Whitestone*, Pablo. **With Jimmy Smith:** *Sit on It*, Mercury. **With Sadao Watanabe:** *Birds of Passage*, Elektra. **With**

Rubén Blades: *Nothing But the Truth*, Elektra. **With Me'Shell NdegéOcello:** *Bitter*, Maverick. **With Stanley Clarke:** *East River Drive*, Epic. **With Herbie Hancock:** *Lite Me Up*, Sony. **With Joe Zawinul:** *The Immigrants*, Columbia. **With Airto:** *I'm Fine, How are You?*, Warner Bros. **With Juiio Iglesias:** *1100 Bel Air Place*, Sony. **With Herb Alpert:** *Rise*, A&M. **With Gary Burton:** *The New Quartet*, ECM. **With Billy Cobham:** *Picture This*, GRP. **With Michael McDonald:** *Take It to Heart*, Reprise. **With Barbra Streisand:** *Songbird*, Columbia. **With Bette Midler:** *Bette*, Warner Bros. **With Claus Ogerman:** *Claus Ogerman Featuring Michael Brecker*, GRP. **With Jeffrey Osborne:** *Stay With Me Tonight*, A&M. **With Dolly Parton:** *9 to 5 and Odd Jobs*, RCA. **With Diane Schuur:** *Collection*, GRP. **With Lionel Richie:** *Can't Slow Down*, Motown. **With Robbie Robertson:** *Robbie Robertson*, Geffen. **With LeeAnn Rimes:** *Twisted Angel*, Curb. **With Shakira:** *Laundry Service*, Sony. **Soundtracks:** *Against All Odds*; *Beaches*; *The Champ*; *The Color Purple*; *Dick Tracy*; *Distinguished Gentleman*; *A Fine Mess*; *Fletch*; *48 Hours*; *Hero*; *Ishtar*; *Jo Jo Dancer, Your Life Is Calling*; *The Last of the Mohicans*; *My Cousin Vinny*; *9 to 5*; *Outrageous Fortune*; *Pretty in Pink*; *Saturday Night Fever*; *Splash*; *Sudden Impact*; *Terms of Endearment*; *Tootsie*; *White Nights*; *The Mexican*; *Prince of Egypt*.

It's my individual way. The exact same idea in the hands of another person would take a different form. Ideally, I'd love to be able to teach people concepts and then encourage them to discover their own way of bringing the concepts to fruition.

What's your best advice for bass players?

To be honest. When I make mistakes, I make blatant mistakes—and I say, "It was me." [*Holds up hand.*] When you keep your mouth shut, it only creates problems.

Honesty in music also has to do with recognizing that the best you have to offer has already been offered, and that if there's somebody else who can do something better than you, you shouldn't get in the way. Don't try to further your own career by hiding somebody else who can help everybody to feel good: "Wow, listen to what this guy's doing—I hope nobody hears him, because then they won't hire me." I hope to eradicate that kind of mentality.

Web site

www.angelfire.com/music/worldpop/MU110

Slaps, Snaps & Strums

SOME DESCRIBE ABRAHAM LABORIEL'S STYLE as "five-fingered," but he also uses two-, three-, and four-finger techniques, a unique thumb-snap method, percussive palm work, and various types of strumming. He often combines these with left-hand hammer-ons to produce complex rhythms, sometimes with double-stops, triple-stops, and beyond. Here are some of Abe's innovative techniques to try out; he demonstrates most in his instructional video *New Bass Concepts* [Warner Bros.]

1. **Three-finger plucking.** Thumb plus index and middle fingers, alternating T–1–2. Common in triplet passages.

2. **Four-finger plucking.** Either strict alternation, T–1–2–3, or using whatever finger is available for a given string.

3. **Five-finger plucking.** Adds the pinky. Sometimes Abe uses this method to create a rolling guitar-style tremolo.

4. **Drag-and-land.** Drags the fingernails over muted strings toward the low strings, landing on a fretted tonic.

5. **Triplet hammering.** Plucks the first note of the triplet, hammers the second, and plucks the third. Abe can do rapid rhythmic figures this way.

6. **Up-and-down triplet hammering.** The same as above, except with up-and-down fingerstrokes.

7. **Bass paradiddles.** A variation of the drum rudiment, in which the hands alternate right-left-right-right and left-right-left-left. Abe's alternations combine plucks and hammer-ons.

8. **Right-hand rocking.** A rocking "drum roll" motion with the thumb against the body and the flats of the fingers on strings. Abe uses this for percussive effects and also combines it with hammer-ons.

9. **The thumb snap.** Instead of the conventional downward-motion thumb slap, Abe uses the thumb to snap strings from beneath.

10. **Thumb triplets.** A down-up motion—a downstroke with the thumb on a fretted note, then a hammer-on, then an upstroke on a fretted note.

11. **Fingernail strum-roll.** This is the *rasgueado* guitar technique. The fingernails strike the string as the fingers are flipped one by one from the thumb, like shooting marbles. Abe does this from index finger to pinky and pinky to index finger. He likens the rapid-fire sound to a drum roll on a closed hi-hat.

12. **Right-hand percussive slapping.** Just whap 'em with the flat of the hand. Usually used in combination with left-hand muting.

13. **Two-hand percussive slapping.** Both hands get into the act. Not recommended for ballads.

14. **Whole-hand strum.** Uses the fingernails for a flamenco-guitar sound.

15. **Wes Montgomery–style octaves.** Combines left-hand muting with up-and-down thumb strums.

NEIL STUBENHAUS
The Insider

Interviewed by Chris Jisi, May 2001.

Neil Stubenhaus

I N HIS 20-PLUS YEARS AS a first-call Los Angeles studio bassist, Neil Stubenhaus has seen the music business from the inside—from sessions for Quincy Jones and Burt Bacharach and on such chart-toppers as "On My Own," "Pink Cadillac," and "The Wind Beneath My Wings" to film dates for John Williams and 13 Academy Awards shows to Barbra Streisand's historic 1994 tour. All told, his tally includes more than 500 album dates (yielding 60 gold records and 40 Grammy-winning songs), close to 400 film scores, and hundreds of television soundtracks and jingles.

Neil has also had a first-hand look at the industry's changing tides, including the wave of technology and mechanization that has eroded session players' workloads. Yet Stubenhaus has persevered, comfortable in studio anonymity while always speaking his mind and championing the cause of the instrumentalist. "A musician's lifeblood is to play," he asserts. "The need to be around people performing and creating is in our soul."

A native of Fairfield, Connecticut, Neil began playing drums at age seven. His mother, a classically trained pianist, encouraged him to study keyboard—but he instead picked up his sister's guitar at age 12, inspired by Eric Clapton and Jimi Hendrix. Blessed with a quick ear, in neighborhood bands Neil spent much of his time showing bass players their parts before switching to bass at 15. He soon purchased a P-Bass and worked his way into the area's elite bands, supplementing such initial rock influences as Tim Bogert and Jack Bruce with the sounds of Motown, Sly Stone, Quincy Jones, and Miles Davis. After high school he spent a year and a half touring with Little Anthony & the Imperials, until his passion for jazz and for playing with different musicians led him to follow local pals John Scofield and bassist Chip Jackson to Boston's Berklee in 1973.

At Berklee, Stubenhaus connected with classmates such as Jeff Berlin, Mike Stern, Steve Smith, and Vinnie Colaiuta, and he studied with Steve Swallow. When Swallow departed, he recommended Neil to teach his 50 students. "It was a hectic and exciting time," Stubenhaus recalls. "Trailblazing bassists like Stanley Clarke, Miroslav Vitous, and Paul Jackson frequently came through town, and Pat Metheny and Jaco were based there doing Pat's trio, so I got to know Jaco well." A '77 call from Stern led Neil to leave Berklee and join Blood, Sweat & Tears. When the tour ended, keyboardist Gap Mangione—who had just recorded a Larry Carlton–produced album—hired the rhythm section.

While Neil was performing with Mangione at the Roxy in Los Angeles, Carlton invited him to audition for the band he was putting together in support of his solo debut. Neil got the gig and moved to L.A. in October 1978, with the understanding the session guitar ace would help him land studio work. "Larry called jingle writer Don Piestrup and TV composer Mike Post, and that was all the spark I needed. Through a

Piestrup session I met a huge record contractor, and on a Post date I met Tom Scott. By 1980 I was working every week with major artists."

What early session experiences helped your playing the most?

Probably my greatest learning experience and the key to my studio development occurred during the making of Tom Scott's 1979 album *Street Beat*, which is when I first played with Jeff Porcaro. Until that day, whenever I heard Porcaro on a record I thought he was a solid groove drummer, but he didn't impress me like Steve Gadd. Tom counted off the first tune, and I couldn't believe what I was feeling. Jeff's instinct for instantly coming up with a happening part blew me away. His musicality was beyond anything I'd ever experienced. He understood a song section by section, be it playing something slightly different to define the bridge, taking the groove to a new level in the fade, or making the perfect pause. I realized it was not about me and my bass playing. It was about the music.

How did you become Quincy Jones's first-call bassist?

I'm not sure, but I'm honored and amazed to this day. I first met him around 1981 during a pretour rehearsal for his album *The Dude*. Louis Johnson couldn't make it, and [trumpeter/arranger] Jerry Hey recommended me to sub for the day. I was a huge fan of albums like *Walking in Space*, so when we played through that material I knew it cold. Quincy has a gift for letting the music come out of his artists and musi-

 Stubengear

Neil Stubenhaus began his session career on a mid-'70s Fender Precision with Seymour Duncan PJ pickups. He also had several early-'60s Jazz Basses; everything was strung with Rotosounds. His main instrument now is a custom James Tyler 5-string. The white-with-blackburst bass features Seymour Duncan PJ pickups and a rosewood fingerboard. His backups are identical red-and-white Tyler 5's. Also in his cartage case are a fretless Pedulla PentaBuzz 5, a semi-hollow fretless Rick Turner Renaissance 5, a Tyler PJ 4-string, a Washburn AB35 5-string acoustic bass guitar, a Sadowsky 4, and a Ken Smith 5. Neil strings most with .045–.130 Rotosound RS66 Swing Bass sets.

In the studio, Neil usually records through a custom SWR Super Redhead, which includes a talk-back mic and an active direct box with a Jensen transformer. "The transformer warms up the sound," he notes. Also at hand is an SWR Interstellar Overdrive preamp, a Yamaha SPX990 (for chorus, pitch shift, or reverb with fretless bass), and a Korg tuner. For home-studio sessions he carries a Raven Labs APD-1 direct box. Onstage Neil plugs into an SWR SM-900 head with two stacked Goliath III 4x10 cabinets, via Monster cables. On Barbra Streisand concerts he uses an SWR Workingman's Twelve combo.

cians naturally before he adds his input and pieces everything together, and the results speak for themselves.

Veteran producers and arrangers often credit the bass player with making or saving a track, yet many session greats feel they were undercredited and underpaid for their contributions to hit records.

Bass is probably the most undercredited instrument, because it has the ability to drive the music in a particular direction without the listener—and often the other musicians—knowing it. When the bass player moves in a successful new direction, everybody falls in so instantly and seamlessly it's usually not immediately apparent why. To drive a whole song on bass, or for a rhythm section to come up with a killer arrangement, and be paid a flat labor wage just doesn't seem fair. Especially when the rest of the business doesn't work that way. Songwriting and publishing all pay again on radio, TV, and film, but what the sideman contributes doesn't. It's not something I'm bitter about, but I can think of plenty of sessions like that in my career.

On a typical session do you get to interpret charts?

If I think the written or demo bass line is lacking—and it's not being doubled—the first thing I do is change it to what I think is better. Ninety percent of the time the reaction is, "That's great, Neil." If they're

Union Labeled

Through the Recording Musicians Association of the American Federation of Musicians (**www.rmaweb.org**; **www.afm.org**), Neil Stubenhaus is active in projects such as improving working conditions, developing relationships to create more work, pursuing ancillary payments, and educating musicians. Says Neil, "My objective is to increase pay and raise the level of respect. [At the time of this story the union's base side-musician scale for a three-hour "phonograph" session is $290; for a TV or film session, $260.] I'm passionate about elevating our status. If you're a stockbroker you learn early on about 401(k)s and IRAs, and your company contributes to your retirement fund. Too many musicians don't even think about such issues. And most don't know there's over a billion dollars in the union pension fund, which members can collect on from age 55 for the rest of their lives, if they're smart enough to participate."

married to the part, they'll say, "Stick to the ink there." The key is having the confidence to try your own idea in the first place.

What I've seen more in recent years is no chart at all—not even a chord chart. You just learn and memorize the tune as you go. I enjoy the challenge, especially if it's a great song.

What about the reputed hazards of a session bassist having an identifiable sound and style?

Having something in your playing that stands out is terrific for individuality, but it can limit you. In most situations producers want the bass to blend in and not draw attention to itself, especially now with everyone wanting low end more than ever because it's technologically possible. So a bassist with a distinctive sound may be passed over for a session. I may not have as distinct a sound as some of my peers, but people still know it's me by the notes I play.

There's a twist to the sound issue, however. I can't tell you how many times producers or engineers have me tweak my tone while playing alone or just with the drums, without taking into consideration how the bass is going to sound when combined with all the other instruments. That's a big fallacy in recording bass. You need to judge the sound in the context of everything else on the track.

What are your typical preamp, EQ, and pickup settings?

In the studio I very rarely use my onboard preamp. I prefer the true passive sound, and I realize the studio has far better electronics than my bass has. I keep my balance pot dead center, so both the P and the J pickups are full up. The treble and bass knobs are flat, though on live gigs I may add a touch of either one.

What do you like to hear in the headphone mix?

I like to hear as much of everything that's pertinent to the track, and then hear my bass one increment above that, above where it would normally be in the mix. Good or bad, bass players become conditioned to hearing ourselves a bit above everybody else; that comes from years of us standing in front of our amps on live gigs.

How do you work with click tracks?

I'm comfortable with the click. I embrace it and play with it as if it's a drummer playing just quarter-notes. The key is to like the click, feel it, and feel your time with it so you enjoy having it there. If it makes you nervous you'll have trouble. If you start to pull away from it or your time is floaty, the first thing to do is turn it up—to the point of pain if need be!

What are your right- and left-hand techniques?

I basically use a finger-per-fret with my left hand. In the right I alternate my index and middle fingers to pluck, occasionally adding the thumb or ring finger. When I slap, my right thumb is angled toward the headstock so it's neither perpendicular to the strings nor straight up and down. For muting, I use my right palm and pluck with the thumb or with a pick, and I also do some left-hand muting. But I believe there's no set, standard technique for playing the electric bass.

Neil Stubenhaus Selected Discography

With Quincy Jones: (all on Qwest/Warner Bros.) *Basie & Beyond*; *From Q with Love*; *Q's Jook Joint*; *Back on the Block*. **With Tom Scott:** *Target*, Elektra; *Desire*, Elektra; *Street Beat*, Columbia. **With George Benson:** *The George Benson Collection*, Warner Bros. **With Billy Joel:** *The Bridge*, Columbia. **With Elton John:** *Duets*, MCA. **With Anita Baker:** *Rapture*, Elektra. **With Patti LaBelle:** *Winner in You*, MCA. **With Was (Not Was):** *What Up, Dog?*, Alliance. **With Manhattan Transfer:** *Bodies & Souls*, Atlantic. **With Rod Stewart:** *Vagabond Heart*, Warner Bros. **With Frank Sinatra:** *L.A. Is My Lady*, Warner Bros. **With Barbra Streisand:** *Timeless*, Columbia. **With Rickie Lee Jones:** *Flying Cowboys*, Geffen. **With Milton Nascimento:** *Yauarete*, Columbia. **With Ray Charles:** *Ain't It So*, Atlantic. **With Don Henley:** *Actual Miles*, Geffen. **With Natalie Cole:** *Everlasting*, Capitol. **With John Fogerty:** *Eye of the Zombie*, Warner Bros. **With Randy Newman:** *Land of Dreams*, Reprise. **With Smokey Robinson:** *One Heartbeat*, Motown. **With Roberta Flack:** *Oasis*, Warner Bros. **With Bette Midler:** *Divine Collection*, Atlantic. **With the Corrs:** *Forgiven, Not Forgotten*, Atlantic. **With Brenda Russell:** *Paris Rain*, Hidden Beach/Epic. **With Luther Vandross:** *Luther Vandross*, J-Records. **With Neil Diamond:** *Heartlight*, Columbia. **With Glenn Frey:** *Soul Searchin'*, MCA. **With Michael McDonald:** *The Very Best Of*, Rhino. **With Al Jarreau:** *Breakin' Away*, Warner Bros. **With Regina Belle:** *Passion*, Sony. **With Willie Nelson:** *The Great Divide*, Universal. **With B.B. King:** *Anthology*, MCA. **With Gino Vannelli:** *Nightwalker*, Arista. **With Bonnie Raitt:** *Nine Lives*, Warner Bros. **With Brian McKnight:** *Brian McKnight*, Mercury. **With Lionel Richie:** *Dancing on the Ceiling*, Motown. **With Selena:** *Dreaming of You*, EMI. **With Mario:** *Mario*, J Records. **With Vinnie Colaiuta:** *Vinnie Colaiuta*, GRP. **With Pages:** *Pages*, Epic. **With the Nielson/Pearson Band:** *Neilson/Pearson*, Capitol. **With Karizma:** *Document*, Hudson Music. **Soundtracks (a few of Neil's favorites):** *Heartbreakers*; *Down to Earth*; *Isn't She Great*; *The Story of Us* (with Eric Clapton); *Bowfinger*; *Payback*; *Rosewood*; *Sleepers*; *Passenger 57*; *Hook*; *Tequila Sunrise*; *Romancing the Stone*; *Return of the Jedi*; *The Toy*; *Some Kind of Hero*.

Do you have a regimen for practice and warm-up?

Usually I just play whatever comes to mind to loosen up my fingers. I also don't pick up my bass every day if I'm not working. I believe if you get away from your instrument for a few days you come back fresh, with some new ideas. But remember, I'm not a virtuoso soloist type. I play more from my gut, and I can execute whatever I think of 99 percent of the time. But if I'm hitting the road with Karizma and have to kick into high gear, I'll warm up and shed more.

When did the session scene start to take a downturn?

Well, the day synthesizers showed up on sessions in the early '80s was the day I couldn't hear myself in the headphones anymore. I'd never asked for more bass in the Fender Rhodes days, but suddenly I couldn't hear a note I was playing, and thus began this process we called "begging for bass." The mechanization all happened at once: synths, drum machines, keyboard bass became the choice; people were understandably grooving on the new technology. The problem was those tools made it easier for musicians, including less-talented ones, to create plausible music on much smaller budgets.

The first to fall off was TV music. TV composers tried to save money by doing everything themselves, and once the studios caught on, the budgets were drastically reduced. Viewers didn't complain, and that sealed it. Jingles were next. Then the record scene followed. Between self-contained grunge bands and home studios, the pace slowed. Being called in to overdub by yourself instead of playing with a rhythm section became common. With less demand for artistry on all fronts, the quality level diminished. The least affected was motion picture work, which has largely retained its quality and remained lucrative thanks to bigger budgets. Also, it has a better residual system than record work.

Movie sessions can range from orchestral dates, where the musicians read the music and watch the conductor—who follows the film—to small-band situations where we just read the music and sometimes have the option of following the film on a monitor. I've been very fortunate to work with all of the major composers, including the great John Williams. John's score for *Sleepers* was memorable. Beforehand, he approached me and told me the main theme throughout the movie needed a sound, which I decided should be my fretless Pedulla. Right before the cue, in front of 80 musicians, he said to me, "Okay, Neil, you'll deliver the message." Now, having to watch the conductor in a variable tempo, read the notes on the page, and keep an eye on the fingerboard for intonation is a challenge in itself—but if it's John Williams, you're already as scared as hell, because after two takes he's moving on. Thankfully, it all came together.

What advice can you offer to aspiring session bassists?

There's not a lot of major session work for bassists in L.A. anymore. The players I compete with for calls have been the same for over a decade. I think the answer is to emulate the current music scene and embrace the technology. Hone your bass skills, but also develop some keyboard and songwriting skills. Then take out a loan and get a home studio together. Learn about the gear and the software and how to program, and start putting grooves and tunes together. From there you can begin collaborating with other home studio owners, including playing bass on their tracks.

In other words, create an underground session scene.

Exactly. We've reached the point where a whole generation of artists has been raised entirely on machines and synthesized sounds. If enough home-studio-savvy bass players counter this by adding real bass on the projects they're involved in, the session bassist—and the instrument—will maintain a healthy existence.

Web site

www.neilstubenhaus.com

Stubengrooves

LIKE MANY STUDIO VETS, Neil Stubenhaus can name standout sessions from among the thousands he's done. Here are a few examples, plus a sample of his groovework with Karizma, a recent project with keyboardist David Garfield, guitarist Mike Landau, and drummer Vinnie Colaiuta. **Example 1** shows his style on the chorus of Tom Scott's 1982 classic "Desire." Using his mid-'70s PJ Precision, Stubenhaus took the basic sketch and made the bass part his own with slurs and ghost-notes. **Example 2** shows Neil's prominent P-Bass part on Smokey Robinson's '87 hit "Just to See Her." In classic Jamerson/Motown style, both the intro/verse (shown) and a later verse break down to just bass, voice, and drums. "I improvised from a lead sheet, and the vibe of the song dictated what to play." **Example 3** shows Neil's killer shuffle verse on Quincy Jones's "Cool Joe, Mean Joe (Killer Joe)," from '94's *Q's Jook Joint*. "Quincy didn't have a particular groove in mind, so I started playing this line on my Tyler 5, which is sort of a nod to Ray Brown's part from Quincy's *Walkin' in Space* version of the tune." Note Neil's cool fill in the second ending, which imply new chords that the band added.

Example 4 was inspired by Stubenhaus's improvised groove behind David Garfield's piano solo in "Heavy Resin," from Karizma's live CD *Document*. Of note is the tricky odd-time meter, which Neil and Colaiuta give a smooth, half-time funk feel. Stubenhaus played his Tyler 5. "Each bar is divided into six beats and five beats, and Vinnie plays the kick-and-snare backbeats on *three* and *nine*." In support, Neil always plays on *one* (the downbeat of the first six beats) and *seven* (the downbeat of the second five beats). In between he adds cool color tones on syncopated upbeats.

Ex. 1

Ex. 2

Ex. 3

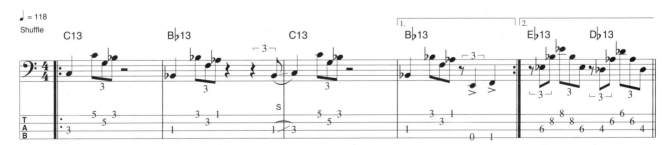

Ex. 4

"Heavy Resin" by David Garfield & Dean Cortez: © 1983 Creatchtunes Music (ASCAP) Wavytunes Music (BMI).
All rights administered by See No Evil Music and Hear No Evil Music. Used by permission.

CHAPTER 3

Fusion Flamekeepers
JEFF BERLIN • JIMMY HASLIP • VICTOR BAILEY
GARY WILLIS • MICHAEL MANRING

A phalanx of talented bassists followed in the updraft created by low-end liberators Stanley Clarke, Jaco Pastorius, Alphonso Johnson, Michael Henderson, and Percy Jones. As time wore on, the less-gifted faded, others slid into a steady sideman groove, and some settled on successful smooth jazz careers. A handful have remained steadfast, continuing to explore the outer edges while keeping the torch lit.

JEFF BERLIN
The Return of a Player

Interviewed by Chris Jisi, January 1998 and August 2001.

JEFF BERLIN'S PASSION FOR BOXING HAS ALWAYS SEEMED APPROPRIATE, given his relentless, aggressive playing style and his confrontational views on music education. Still, after more than two decades as one of the defining solo voices on the electric bass guitar, Berlin was about to throw in the towel on his recording career as he approached twelve years without a label deal. "I decided the writing was on the wall—that people apparently didn't want what I had to offer as a contemporary bassist and musician," he admits. "Artists come and go in this business every day, so I'd pretty much come to terms with it." Jeff wasn't exactly idle, though. He opened the Players School of Music in Clearwater, Florida, in 1995, and remained busy with sessions and live gigs. Deep inside, however, Berlin's prizefighter heart refused to let him quit. Lo and behold, his perseverance led to late-round knockouts with the release of *Taking Notes* in 1998 and *In Harmony's Way* in 2001.

Taking Notes packs a potent punch, with Berlin leading collaborators such as Tribal Tech keyboardist Scott Kinsey and drummer Cliff Almond on a whirlwind musical journey through sassy big-band blasts, deft solo chordal ballads, brooding Latin romps, updated Americana, and sweeping jazz-rock fusion movements. On *In Harmony's Way*, he plunges into straightahead jazz with the help of former Pat Metheny drummer Danny Gottlieb and Florida pianist Richard Drexler, plus guests Mike Stern, Dave Liebman, and Gary Burton. Amid the ride-cymbal grooves and block piano chords, Jeff's solos seem more penetrating and assured than ever, while his walking lines swing with upright-style intensity. All in all, Berlin's comeback finds him in better shape than in his late-'70s/early-'80s heyday as a prizefighter bassist in the weight class of Stanley and Jaco. Says Jeff, "The truth is I've always been a musical late-bloomer."

Jeffrey Arthur Berlin was born in Queens, New York, on January 17, 1953, and raised in Great Neck on

Long Island. Early on Jeff acquired a love of classical music from his father, an operatic baritone, and his mother, who played piano as a hobby. His father started him on violin at age five; Jeff took to the instrument immediately and prodigiously, winning awards as a soloist at recitals, competitions, and festivals with chamber groups and orchestras. Lured from the classical world by the arrival of the Beatles and other rock 'n' roll bands, he pondered a switch to drums, only to be told they were too loud to practice in the house. Instead, at age 14, he emulated a neighborhood bassist and bought a Hagstrom with his paper-route money. "I saw that it had four strings like the violin, so I figured I could play it with a modicum of ease," he recalls. Almost immediately Jeff began to explore forward-thinking melodic directions on his new instrument, thanks to his violin background as well as the atypical approach of his new hero, Cream bassist Jack Bruce.

At age 18, smitten with the jazz guitar chords he heard while working in the pit band of a touring Broadway show, Berlin headed to the Berklee College of Music in Boston. At Berklee he absorbed the influences of faculty and peers such as Pat Metheny, Gary Burton, Mick Goodrick, Steve Smith, John Scofield, and Mike Stern. Anxious to ply his trade with a long list of favorite musicians, Jeff returned to New York and hooked up with drummer Carmine Appice and guitarist Ray Gomez. He also worked briefly in a trio with guitarist Allan Holdsworth and the late drummer Tony Williams. After traveling to Europe in 1975 to record an album with Yes keyboardist Patrick Moraz, Berlin returned to New York City at the height of the fusion era. There, his experience ballooned through club gigs, loft jams, and record dates with such artists as Pat Martino, Bill Evans, Gil Evans, Toots Thielemans, Al Di Meola, Larry Coryell, George Benson, Lenny White, and Herbie Mann. (Jeff's most memorable missed gig: A call from drummer Al Foster to play with Miles Davis.)

In 1977 Berlin received an invitation from former Yes drummer Bill Bruford to play on *Feels Good to Me* and join Bruford's band, which featured Allan Holdsworth. This led to three more hugely popular discs—including the bass tour-de-force *Gradually Going Tornado*—while also giving life to such Berlin bass anthems as "Joe Frazier," "5G," and "Palewell Park." Three years later, at the request of Musicians Institute founder Pat Hicks, Jeff moved from Boston (where he had been studying with teaching guru Charlie Banacos) to Los Angeles. By day he helped launch the Bass Institute of Technology, bringing in such luminaries as Jaco Pastorius, Geddy Lee, and Billy Sheehan. By night he forged a fusion club scene with such rising stars as drummer Vinnie Colaiuta and guitarists Scott Henderson and Frank Gambale. Meanwhile, Jeff's Bruford-induced popularity among L.A.'s vast rock community led to a brief stint with Frank Zappa and jams with Rush and Eddie Van Halen. (At one point Eddie asked Jeff to join Van Halen, an offer he declined due to his jazzier musical focus.)

The mid '80s saw the release of the solo albums *Champion* and *Pump It!*, which boasted members of Rush, Journey, the Dixie Dregs, and Chick Corea's Elektric Band, as well as ex-Hendrix drummer/vocalist Buddy Miles. Bass landmarks on those records ranged from his classic solo-bass arrangement of "Dixie" [*Champion*] to the funky remake "Joe Frazier II" to Jeff's note-for-note reading of Eric Clapton's solo on a cover of the Cream version of "Crossroads" [both on *Pump It!*]. After meeting his future wife while on tour in Venezuela, Jeff left the daily grind of L.A. in 1990 and relocated to Florida to raise his family. From his Clearwater home base, he has since toured with Yes (filling in for an ailing Tony Levin), Billy Cobham, Joe Walsh, Jermaine Jackson, and Kazumi Watanabe. He has also returned to L.A. for sessions with k.d. lang, Jerry Lee Lewis, James Burton, and Jeff "Skunk" Baxter, as well as concerts with Chick Corea, Isaac Hayes, and Edgar Winter.

Berlin's frustration with the current state of music education—a frequent topic during the ten-year run of his *Bass Player* column, "Beyond Chops"—led him to open the Players School, which he describes as a rhythm-section school offering instruction in bass, guitar, keyboards, and drums. It was there that he spoke with me about his career.

What were the key ingredients to the early development of your style?

The Beatles, for one. Their tonality caught my ear and made me want to play rock 'n' roll, which led me to switch to bass and give up the violin. My ten years of classical training also had a big impact; having to prepare pieces long before I performed them gave me a sense of vision and a desire to break free of the rules. As a result, I already knew I wanted to make an original statement on the electric bass without being constrained by the instrument's function. I started out attempting classical pieces and Beatles songs, because playing melodies was what I knew. A little later, when I heard Jack Bruce playing with so much originality and freedom, it was a revelation. He opened my ears to improvisation and exploration, which changed my approach permanently. I wanted to find notes that other people didn't

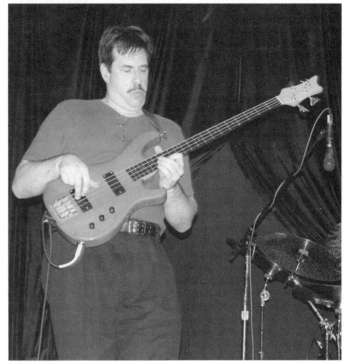
Jeff Berlin

play, like Jack did. I'd join bands and immediately start improvising in the upper register with no regard to doing my job as a bass player. A lot of people refused to play with me, and rightfully so. It's difficult to put up with any self-serving musician who's not playing for the group.

Was your attitude and determination a product of your upbringing?

Yes. Both of my parents had tough upbringings. My father is a Holocaust survivor who twice escaped death sentences, and my mother endured her share of problems. As a result, much of their pain was passed on to me and my siblings. My problem was I couldn't relate to people—they were the enemy. I was uptight, angry, and competitive, and that came through in my playing and my attitude. Throughout the '70s and '80s I paid a great price for lacking social skills. It cost me work, and it cost me friends. It wasn't until the '90s that I underwent intensive therapy to sort things out and make peace with myself and the rest of the world. I realize now that had I related better to people, my entire history might have been rewritten. But that's 20/20 hindsight.

Besides Jack Bruce, what other bassists were important influences?

Tim Bogert—he played some phenomenal bass with Vanilla Fudge and Cactus; John Entwistle, for his stylistic and sonic innovations; and Paul McCartney, although I was too into hard-playing, chops-oriented bands to appreciate his brilliant subtleties until later on. When I returned to New York from Boston, I began doing a lot of R&B gigs, and I really got into James Jamerson, Chuck Rainey, Jerry Jemmott, and James Brown's bass players. From there I moved to funk—Larry Graham, Bootsy Collins, Paul Jackson, and my all-time favorite groove player, Rocco Prestia. Of course, Stanley Clarke had a *huge* impact on me, and then Jaco hit and knocked me out again. I got caught up in his style at first and bought a fretless—but I quickly sensed that everyone was going to try to play like him, so I decided to go back to the fretted bass and find my own voice. It was at that point that I created a vacuum for myself; I stopped listening to other bass players and trusted my own musicality. I began living by a mad principle, which I've stuck to for 20 years: If a prominent player becomes known for a certain style, technique, instrument, amp, or effect, I'll purposely avoid it. I can't bring myself to copy someone else's invention as an artist, even if it prevents me from using certain universal bass devices, like slapping or harmonics.

What impact did moving to Boston have on your development?

I now know I wasn't completely formed as a musician until my 30s—but considering how green I was when I got to Berklee and how much I'd improved by the time I left three years later, I would say it was the greatest learning period for me. I was so hungry for information I would practically run over people asking them all kinds of questions. I can remember calling out to teachers from down the hall and seeing them duck the other way! At the time, Berklee had only an upright bass program, so I was told to get an acoustic bass; I played it for three months, but I realized it wasn't for me. Instead, I would go down to the basement library and get trombone music to work on. Gradually, through school ensembles and local gigs, I learned how to function as a bassist—but I still took it right up to the line in terms of how many notes I played. In fact, it was my chops that got me work in Boston and then New York, because even though I wasn't musically developed as Stanley and Jaco were, we were regarded as the only three electric bassists with considerable technique at the time.

What are your memories of the New York scene in the mid '70s?

It was a very exciting, creative time, with the heaviest collection of unbelievable players I'll ever see in my lifetime. Electric fusion pioneers were jamming with burning straightahead jazzers in clubs and lofts everywhere. I was still growing, but what a scene to grow in! I could go from playing in Al Di Meola's band with Lenny White, Brian Auger, and the Brecker Brothers one night, to sitting in with Bill Evans the next. Here's a typical example of how healthy the scene was then compared to today: I played a sold-out gig with Herbie Mann at the Bottom Line with an expanded rhythm section, which also included Will Lee and Tony Levin on bass—and Herbie picked us up in limousines!

How would you describe your time in Los Angeles?

On the surface, it was fun playing in the clubs and meeting all of the big '80s rock stars. But at the core, L.A. was the toughest scene I ever encountered. Although I played with just about every top session musician from the time I arrived in 1980 until I left for good in '94, I couldn't crack the lucrative studio scene. Obviously, I carried a lot of baggage reputation-wise at first, but it went beyond that. I remember getting called to do a piece in a movie score; the composer had written a very difficult bass line, and someone had recommended me. I came in and nailed it, and the guy went nuts: "I've never seen such a demonstration of bass virtuosity; I'm paying you double scale, and I'm calling you for *everything* from now on!" Three months later you could hear the crickets in the background while I waited by the phone. From a business standpoint, L.A. is not a friendly town.

What are your reflections of the Bruford band?

I met Bill through Patrick Moraz and Ray Gomez, and we hit it off immediately. Like Ginger Baker, he had a unique, English approach to drumming that was more angular and accent-oriented than the straight timekeepers I was used to—but for some reason, we jelled right away. At the time I was still hopping from project to project, afraid that if I committed to any one group, my progress would stop. But with Bill I finally felt ready to be in a band. His compositions were excellent, and along with Allan Holdsworth and [keyboardist] Dave Stewart, we had a real chemistry and made some great music.

What's the inspiration for your trademark chordal pieces?

That came from my desire to sound more orchestral on the 4-string bass without having to rely on harmonics. Also, I knew that guitarists and pianists have the ability to play melody, harmony, and rhythm all at once when performing solo, and I recognized this as an untapped area for bass. I started playing chords, gradually adding tonalities and tensions inspired by guitarists and pianists. From there, I got into moving chordal passages and voice leading, and I started to come up with arrangements of everything from national anthems to pop tunes.

How does your commitment to the 4-string affect your feelings about the 5 and 6?

If I were involved in full-time studio work—where you're hired to do a job—I would own a fretless and a 5, but probably not a 6. I have a problem with the thin, non-bass-like sound of the notes on the top end of a 6-string. As for my own music, the 4 is where I came from, and I'm satisfied with its three-octave range.

During my brief time with Frank Zappa, he handed me a complicated piece of music called "Pedro's Dowery," written in treble clef. I took it home and transposed it onto my bass, and when we rehearsed, Frank discovered he'd given me the guitar part by mistake. He loved the way it sounded, though, and he told me to keep playing it. So I've had both the want and the need to go lower and higher—but it's those same limitations that have often inspired me to find something new on my instrument. If the 4-string is eventually replaced by the 5 or the 6, though, that's fine; evolution and change are important in music.

What do you practice?

At this point, my fundamental playing skills are established, so I consider practice a process of improvement and exploring new areas. I transcribe and play through solos by the great jazz improvisers; I work on my lessons from Charlie Banacos; and I examine 20th-century classical piano music and

Equipment Lite

Taking a ten-year absence from his solo career may have had little effect on Jeff Berlin's playing and writing—but it has wreaked havoc on his gear roster. Gone from Berlin's one-time collection of 12 basses is his much-recorded Bruford-era Fender hybrid, as well as a handful of the signature-model Peavey Palaedium basses he helped design. In fact, all that remains is a John Buscarino 4-string, a brown Peavey Palaedium, and his main bass, a signature-model Dean 4-string with an alder body, ebony fingerboard, Bartolini JJ Humbuckers, and a Leo Quan Badass Bridge. He always backs off varying degrees on the neck pickup to get his signature growl. His strings are Carl Thompson roundwounds, gauges .040, .060, .080, .100.

A Crate and Dean endorsee, Berlin plugs into a Crate BXH220 head and various BX-series cabinets. He's also enthusiastic about his T.C. Electronic Stereo Chorus/Flanger pedal. "One thing I have discovered is how to use my equipment to serve me. I used to play very hard—but now I have no calluses, because I turn up the volume on the amp and play with a lighter touch. You need to play bass strongly, but not *physically* strongly. The strength is in the attitude you play with, which comes from knowing your instrument and knowing the music."

orchestral scores to learn some of the voicings used. Recently, I heard a Prokofiev piano-and-violin sonata in *F* minor that blew my mind, and I had to investigate it. Whenever something piques my interest, I'm there dissecting and analyzing.

You've played with many of the top drummers of the last 30 years. What do you look for in a rhythm-section relationship?

It's essential that the drummer and I hear the quarter-note in the same way. If we agree on the quarter-note, then no matter how we play off each other and subdivide the beat, it's going to be happening. Like anybody else, I prefer a drummer with a hard-kickin', swinging feel that breathes in any style of music. Of the great drummers I've been fortunate enough to play with, I can tell you the main reason their feels are legendary is they know their instrument—and the music they're playing—inside and out.

How do you feel about the bassists who are currently admired the way Stanley, Jaco, and you were in the late '70s?

To be frank, some deserve it and some don't—but that's largely a product of the '90s being a weak musical era, both in the originality and creativity of the artists and in the demands of the listener. Simply put, a lot

Jeff Berlin Selected Discography

Solo albums: *In Harmony's Way*, M.A.J.; *Taking Notes*, Denon; *Pump It!*, Passport Jazz; *Champion*, Passport Jazz. **With Bill Bruford:** (all on Polydor/Editions E.G.) *The Bruford Tapes*; *Gradually Going Tornado*; *One of a Kind*; *Feels Good to Me*. **With Allan Holdsworth:** *Road Games*, Warner Bros. **With k.d. lang:** *Even Cowgirls Get the Blues*, Sire/Warner Bros. **With Kazumi Watanabe:** (both on Gramavision) *Spice of Life Too*; *Spice of Life*. **With Patti Austin:** *End of a Rainbow*, CTI. **With the Players:** *Players*, Passport Jazz. **With Gil Goldstein:** *Pure as Rain*, Chiaroscuro. **With Dave Liebman:** *Light'n Up, Please!*, Horizon. **With Patrick Moraz:** *i*, Atco. **With the Nathan Cavaleri Band:** *Nathan*, MJJ. **With Ray Barretto:** *Eye of the Beholder*, Atlantic. **With David Sancious:** *Just as I Thought*, Arista. **With Don Pullen:** *Montreux Concert*, Atlantic. **With Gil Evans:** *Tokyo Concert*, WestWind. **With Herbie Mann:** *Mellow*, Atlantic. **With Pete Levin:** *Solitary Man*, Gramavision. **With T Lavitz:** *Gossip*, Wild Cat. **With Clare Fischer:** *Crazy Bird*, Discovery.

of heralded bassists have gained notoriety playing someone else's style. Still, there are great players and innovators in every era, and I believe there always will be. I think Victor Bailey, Marcus Miller, Victor Wooten, Gary Willis, John Patitucci, Jeff Andrews, and Oteil Burbridge are all remarkable bass players.

The opening track of Taking Notes, *"Stung, McCartney'd & Bruced," is an ear-grabbing statement in the tradition of "Joe Frazier." Tell us about the title.*

All three are musicians I very much admire, because they're honest bass players: they play *themselves*. Jack is my hero—the most original-sounding rock bassist I've ever heard—and Paul and Sting are two of the greatest pop songwriters who ever lived. I would love to be able to put down eight bars of bass solo on any one of their songs. As for the piece, I tried to use one of Paul's trademarks: He's noted for writing songs that keep developing into new sections, like "Uncle Albert" and "Live and Let Die." I start off with the bass melody, and the track goes through five or six different sections before the melody returns.

"Clinton Country" and "Tears in Heaven"—two additions to your solo chordal repertoire—feature extensive left-hand legato work, à la Allan Holdsworth. Is this a new development for you?

Yes. It evolved as a result of my wanting to match the long lines and smooth attack of all the great melodic horn improvisers who have influenced me, from Cannonball Adderly to Sonny Stitt to Michael Brecker. Playing with Allan—who pioneered and mastered that style on guitar—had an impact on me as well. Basically, the technique involves left-hand hammering with selective right-hand plucks, while being conscious of horn- and vocal-like phrasing. I've always played with very low action, so I didn't need to make any changes neck- or string-wise. Another technique that evolved out of my solo pieces is fingerpicking a chord rapidly with my thumb, index, and middle fingers for a tremolo-like effect. What's important is that the notes come first; they establish the requirement for the technique. Some people work on technique with no musical goal, which is backwards.

What was the concept behind your cover of "Imagine"?

John Lennon's melody is so eternal and pure, I knew I could reharmonize it without changing its integrity. I came up with an arrangement utilizing a combination of modulations, jazz changes, and Lennon's original triadic harmony. I realized I wouldn't be able to match the expression of a human voice with the electric bass if I played the melody as John sang it, so I decided to augment it slightly with grace notes and fills.

Your jazzier approach on In Harmony's Way *is typified on "Everybody Knows You When You're Up and In."*

That's a 16-bar tune that leaps around harmonically; it's sort of like my "Giant Steps." Actually, it was inspired by Coltrane's "One Down, One Up" [*Dear Old Stockholm*]. Dave Liebman just eats up the changes in his tenor solo. I wrote the tune because I wanted the challenge of having to reach beyond my soloing capabilities. That's one of the paramount elements of my musical life: to reach for something I don't do well. I don't think it matters if you even succeed, but you've got to reach for something in life.

What's going on in "Reggae Ricardo"?

It's essentially a horns-and-groove tune to feature Mike Stern and my rhythm-section bass work. I added an interlude that goes *G7 | B♭7 | A7 | C7 | B♭7 | D♭7 | C7 | A7 | D7* before returning to a *Gm7 | C7* vamp for Mike's solo. Toward the end, at 6:45, I take two little one-bar breakdown solos, in which I mirror Danny Gottlieb's 16th-note hi-hat pattern using right-hand, two-finger alternating plucks.

If your two CDs constitute a "return," where does your career go from here?

I plan on continuing to make albums and perform them live. What I could really use is a Marcus Miller or a Don Was as a producer; somebody like that would really help both from a sonic and a musical perspective. I'm also committed to the Players School and the ethic we've established. I'd like to do more mainstream sessions, because in recent years I've come to thoroughly enjoy the sideman role: being able to contribute a good, solid part to various artists' songs. I'd love to work with a gifted composer like Wayne Shorter, and I've long wanted to tour in a major rock band to satisfy that side of my style. In short, my career as an artist and an educator is very rewarding—but first and foremost, I'm a *player*; I always have been, and I always will be.

Web site

www.jeffberlinmusic.com

Talking Notes

CHIEF AMONG JEFF BERLIN'S MANY SKILLS on the electric bass guitar is his unparalleled mastery of melody. You can find six excellent contrasting examples of Berlin's melodic bent in groove and solo mode in *Taking Notes* and *In Harmony's Way*.

From *Taking Notes*: **Example 1** occurs at the 4:01 mark of "Stung, McCartney'd & Bruced," halfway through Rob Lockhart's alto sax solo. Up to this point, Berlin has been improvising a 16th-note funk line over *E13* and *G13* chords. As bar 1 of Ex. 1 begins, he locks into a stricter, repetitive line, adding ear-grabbing melodic tones through chromatic movement between the *G#* and the *E* on beat *two* of bars 1–4. Explains Jeff, "My two goals were to be melodic and rhythmic at the same time, and to be true to the style. It's essentially my take on James Jamerson, Chuck Rainey, and Jerry Jemmott."

Example 2 is from "Clinton Country," a chordal solo-bass arrangement that incorporates "The Star Spangled Banner" and "America." The example begins at the 2:28 mark, after Jeff has already performed "America" once. As he plays the melody a second time, beginning in bar 1 (note stems up), he adds a counterpoint line underneath (note stems down), recalling his classic arrangement of "Dixie" [*Champion*]. "Counterpoint involves a melodic line unto itself that also suggests a harmony under the original melody line. Classical composers are master contrapuntalists, and counterpoint was a big part of my training growing up." Although two-handed tapping would appear to be an option for playing the two lines together, Jeff uses his right-hand thumb, index, and middle fingers to pluck both lines at once, with a few added hammer-ons. In bars 5, 6, and 7, he plays the last four melody notes rubato (indicated with fermatas), adding left-hand legato, arpeggiated ornamentations in between.

From *In Harmony's Way*: Example 3 shows the percussive yet melodic samba-like ostinato Berlin plays on "Runaway Train." "I didn't want to follow the crowd and slap, but I wanted to achieve a similar effect, so I used left-hand muting and right-hand plucking and patting." **Example 4** contains two bars of Berlin's bebop-heavy solo at the 2:41 mark of "Emeril Kicks It Up." Back in melodic groove mode, **Ex. 5** features the opening bass line of "Reggae Ricardo." Dig Jeff's cool altered-chord treatment and wide intervallic leaps. "To get a thunky, muted sound, I stuck a rag under the strings back by the bridge—a first for me." Finally, **Ex. 6** shows Jeff's trademark close voicings on the first four chords of the ECM-ish "A Place of Know."

Ex. 1

Ex. 2

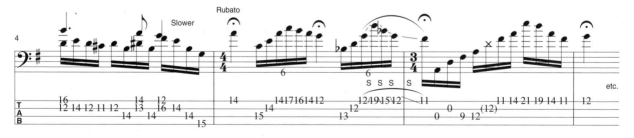

Ex. 3

♩ = 158   Dm

Jazz samba

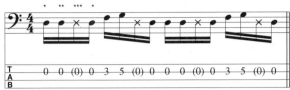

* = index finger pluck
** = index downstroke w/ back of nail
*** = right-hand pat

Ex. 4

♩ = 136

Jazz shuffle

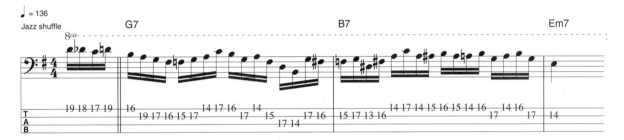

Ex. 5

♩ = 86

Reggae funk

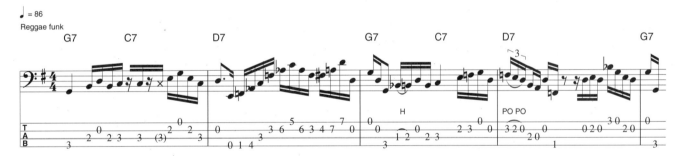

Ex. 6

♩ = 138

Half-time ballad

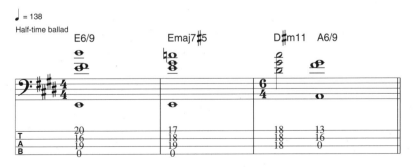

JIMMY HASLIP
Lyrical Lefty

Interviewed by Alexis Sklarevski, July/August 1992; Ed Friedland, December 2000; and Karl Coryat, June 2002.

ONE OF THE RAREST GIFTS among the session bass elite is the ability to switch from being a faceless sideman who fits seamlessly into any track to being an instantly recognizable stylist with a trademark tone and approach. Few, if any, fit that description better than Jimmy Haslip. As a top bassist on the Los Angeles scene, Haslip has worked with a huge list of artists in every style from rock, pop, and R&B to funk, fusion, and jazz. At the same time, he's renowned for having one of the most unique voices in all of bassdom as a member of the jazz supergroup the Yellowjackets (for whom he also composes, arranges, and produces).

Born in 1951 in the Bronx, New York, Haslip started on drums at the age of seven and went through a host of other instruments, including the trumpet and tuba, before settling down with the electric bass. Left-handed and self-taught, Jimmy turned over a right-handed axe and proceeded to forge his unique "upside down" technique. (If you go to a Yellowjackets concert expecting to learn how to play a line by watching him—forget it!) After traveling extensively and living in several different cities throughout the late '60s and early '70s, he settled in Los Angeles in 1975.

Soon after his arrival, Haslip became a founding member of the Yellowjackets along with pianist Russell Ferrante. (The group debuted in 1978 at the Roxy Theater in L.A., as the backup band for guitarist Robben Ford.) Over the years, the 'jackets have been nominated for numerous Grammys and have won two—thanks, in large part, to Jimmy's fluid, lyrical lines and impeccable grooves.

Why did you decide to become a bass player?

I grew up in a household where I heard a lot of music, and when I was a little kid the one style that really grabbed me was salsa. It had an infectious groove. I grew up listening to Machito, Tito Puente, Mongo Santamaria—all of the Latin artists. My older brother Gabriel turned me on to a lot of music; he was deeply into jazz and classical music. From my peers, I heard all the Motown and R&B stuff, and I was completely consumed with music. I started on drums when I was very small and played trumpet in elementary school. Then one night I was at a junior high dance, and there was this band with an electric bass. That did it! It grabbed me and shook me, and I thought, "Wow, I like that!"

What was your first band?

It was called the Soul Mine, and it was made up of a bunch of my athlete buddies from high school. We played Doors, Beatles, Hendrix, Cream, and a lot of soul tunes. I was about 16 or 17, and we worked at parties and school dances.

What were you playing in those days?

I started out on a Japanese bass called a Zimgar; it cost 50 bucks. I had that for about a year, and I learned quite a few tunes on it. That really got me into the idea of playing bass.

What bass players were you listening to?

James Jamerson was *the* influence at the time, although I didn't find out who he was until 15 years later. And Paul McCartney, for two reasons: I loved the Beatles, and he played left-handed! Also Chris Squire from Yes, Peter Cetera from Chicago, Jack Bruce, Noel Redding [with Jimi Hendrix], Jack Casady [with the Jefferson Airplane],

Phil Lesh [with the Grateful Dead], and Berry Oakley [with the original Allman Brothers Band]. Oakley was really an inspiration, because he used a lot of modal ideas. I also listened to Ron Carter, Scott LaFaro, Jimmy Garrison, Reggie Workman, and other acoustic jazz players.

Did you take lessons?

I got together with a guy named Ron Smith, who played tuba with Elvin Jones, and later I went to a small private music school for a bit. That didn't work out at all—the teacher didn't understand what I was doing. I'm naturally left-handed, so when I got a bass I just flipped it over

Jimmy Haslip with drummer Marcus Baylor.

and started figuring it out that way. The teacher kept telling me to play right-handed, but I didn't want to do that.

I made up my own rules as I went along. I've always played upside down, with my *E* string [at the bottom of the fingerboard] where the *G* string would be normally. At first I just used my thumb—not slapping with it, just plucking. Then I started to pick with two fingers, which is the technique I still use most of the time.

Is it difficult to slap with the strings upside down?

Yes, but I've developed two techniques. One is to slap everything with just the thumb and not use any pops; one place you can hear that is on the tune "Sylvania" [Yellowjackets, *Samurai Samba*]. The other method is to use my index and middle fingers to pick and the thumb to get a popping sound; I did that on "Monmouth College Fight Song" [Yellowjackets, *Casino Lights*]. I've also started to use down- and upstrokes on the same string with just the thumb.

How much do you practice now?

I'll practice five hours a day when I'm on the road, usually at night after I get back from the gig and I'm all warmed up. I spend most of my time improvising over chord progressions. I'll take a form like a 12-bar blues or Rhythm changes [the chord progression of "I Got Rhythm"] and solo for hours. I'll also take Yellowjackets tunes and do the same thing, especially if it's something in our set that I solo over.

Over the years I've spent quite a bit of time practicing with a metronome and playing all my scales and arpeggios slowly through two or three octaves. I always try to incorporate what I've been practicing into what I do with the band, whether it's an idea for a sound or a lick I've discovered. One cool thing about being in the band is that I have a place to experiment with all these ideas. With the Yellowjackets, there are no borders—we'll try anything and everything. That's a great situation to be in.

When and why did you start playing 5- and 6-string basses?

I started playing 5-string in 1985, but I didn't move on to the 6-string until March '91. Around 1983 I heard Jimmy Johnson at a club in L.A. Jimmy had been using a 5-string for a long time, and I just loved the sound. There were all these great low notes coming out, and at first I thought he had some sort of pedal. Then I realized it was the bass itself.

Going from a 4-string to a 5-string was a bit of a chore, although I think a lot of it was psychological. Within a couple of months I felt pretty comfortable playing it. Going from a 5 to a 6 was not nearly as hard.

When did you begin playing fretless?

I got my Tobias 5-string fretless in 1987, and at first I used it very little due to the intonation problems. I practiced hard that whole year, and by 1988, when the Yellowjackets went in to do the *Politics* album, I used it on that. I also played it on a Gino Vannelli tune called "Wild Horses" [*Big Dreamers Never Sleep*].

The more I worked with it, the more I decided to dedicate myself to the fretless bass. After *Politics* came out we went on tour, and I brought only the fretless—it was a sink-or-swim situation! I spent five months on the road playing fretless, and by the end of that year I felt I had a handle on it.

How did you develop your fretless sound?

At first I had to concentrate on intonation. I met Jaco in the '70s, when he had just joined Weather Report, and I took a few lessons from him. One of the things he taught me was to put the fingertip of your fretting hand right on the fret marker to get the true note. The center of your finger has to be right on the line. Once I got a feel for the intonation, I started working on my vibrato. Mstislav Rostropovich, the master cellist, was a big inspiration for that technique—he's truly incredible.

How big an influence was Jaco?

I was certainly inspired by him. I listened to him quite a bit, not to copy his playing, but just to learn more about playing fretless. As time went by, I realized how expressive the instrument could be.

Jaco was a master. I really liked him, not only as a musician and a composer, but also as a person. We ran into one another many times on the road, and I always felt he was my friend. He did so much for *all* musicians, not just bass players. He had a special place in my heart, and when he passed away I was very disturbed.

My book, *The Melodic Bass Library*, is dedicated to Jaco and James Jamerson. Those two guys, along with Anthony Jackson, were huge influences on my playing. I don't think I sound like any of them, though; we all have our own personalities.

You were credited with playing fretless on Gino Vannelli's Brother to Brother, *but you didn't start playing fretless until nine years after the record came out. How did you get that sound on a fretted bass?*

I used a very quick hammer-on technique leading to the note I wanted to ring—it's like a fast series of grace notes preceding a specific pitch. With a little chorus, it becomes even smoother. By the time I did that record I'd already hung out with Jaco, and I wanted to emulate the sound of a fretless.

How did you develop your phrasing?

I listened to horn players and guitarists. A lot of it has to do with the way I hear music and how I incorporate that into the way I play. Going back to Jaco again, one thing he told me was that he studied players like Charlie Parker, Miles Davis, and John Coltrane because they had the best phrasing.

Did you transcribe solos?

A little—I would figure out portions of solos. I collected any kind of information that would help me to develop a library of phrases. As time went on, I realized that a lot of these things came from scales and arpeggios, so I started studying scales and melodic patterns very thoroughly. Through that process I started to find my own ideas, and I became much more comfortable with the idea of soloing.

How much do the Yellowjackets rehearse?

Not a lot. If we're going on tour we'll get together for two or three days, and that's it. If we're preparing to record we'll rehearse for two weeks or more, because we're learning new songs and trying to give them some personality, to make them feel comfortable, and to play from the heart.

How many takes of a tune will the band record?

At the most we'll do three takes. We do enough preproduction before an album so we're comfortable with the music. We strive for spontaneity.

How often do you record live with a full band?

The 'jackets record live and a few other projects have been done live, but that's about it. As a session player, I usually get called to overdub on finished tracks, which can be a pretty lonely task.

When you play a session as a sideman, what's the most important factor in coming up with a solid, unobtrusive accompanying line?

Sometimes I'll walk in and my part is on paper, so I just have to decide which bass I'm going to use. Most of the time the people I'm working for have something specific in mind, and they'll articulate that to me. I'm heavily influenced by the phrasing of the melody, particularly on vocal tunes. I like to hear the tune a couple of times, just so I can get a feel for it. No matter what, though, I always want to be locked in with the drums.

How good a reader are you?

My reading is fair, and I'm completely self-taught. If I know upfront that I'm going to be doing a reading project, I'll practice and get my chops up for it. I don't get called very often *just* to read, though—usually, I'm asked to conceptualize a part for a tune. With the

Haslip's Haul

Jimmy Haslip favors Mike Tobias basses in both the Tobias and MTD varieties. These include fretted and fretless Tobias 5- and 6-strings, his MTD 635 6, fretted and fretless Tobias "Killer B" bolt-on 5- and 6-strings (which he helped design), an MTD fretless 7-string, a fretted Keith Roscoe LG3006 6-string, a Yamaha TRB fretted 5-string, a Yamaha BB1200 fretted 8-string, a Yamaha fretless 5-string acoustic bass guitar, a Jim Tyler fretted 5-string, and a Moon fretted 4-string. His strings are D'Addario Special Medium Light Prisms, gauged .027, .047, .067, .087, .107, .127, with a .020 *F* on his 7-string.

His stereo SWR 'jackets rig consists of SM-400 and SM-500 heads with two Goliath Junior 2x10 cabinets or 6x10 Goliath Sr. and 4x10 Goliath cabinets. He splits his signal with a T.C. Electronic SCF chorus. He'll also use a Super Redhead combo, a Baby Blue combo, and an SWR Mr. Tone Controls parametric EQ. In the studio he prefers a Cabletech or Westlink direct box, sometimes splitting his signal into both. If needed he'll mic an SWR Redhead.

Yellowjackets, we write out most of our music. That's good, because I get to practice on my own. By the time the band finishes doing a record, my reading has gone up three or four notches.

How would you evaluate your playing at this point in your career?

I think I get a little better every year. As long as that keeps happening, I feel good about what I'm doing. The bottom line, though, is that when I finish a record project it's hard for me to listen to it right away. Especially with the Yellowjackets! I usually can't listen to a 'jackets record for months—maybe even a year after it's finished. I'm probably much more critical than I need to be. I hear things I'm sure no one else does, but they bother me every time they go by. I care about the music and try to be very conscientious. That keeps me humble—and it also enables me to continue to grow.

In 2000 Ed Friedland talked with Haslip about his second solo disc, Red Heat, *a simmering Latin-jazz project inspired by the traditional Latin music he heard while growing up. Jimmy also addressed soloing and recording techniques, and tackling the 7-string:*

Is this your first excursion into true Latin music?

It's the closest I've come with the tradition in mind, although it's still my own interpretation. Even though it's inspired by the traditional Latin music I grew up with, Joe Vannelli and I were open to creating more unusual rhythmic and harmonic treatments. Joe has a beautiful harmonic understanding—together we spent a lot of time experimenting with combinations of loops and samples. We wanted to dig deep and find something unusual yet appealing.

At the same time, I listened to a lot of old recordings by artists my father turned me on to when I was young: Tito Puente, Eddie Colon, Celia Cruz, Tito Rodriguez, Mongo Santa Maria, Eddie Palmieri, Ray Barretto, and Machito.

What influenced your tumbaos, and where did you draw your inspiration from?

One inspiration was a couple of DAT tapes Steve Khan made for me filled with tunes performed by contemporary Latin artists—music that combined modern sound, harmony, and compositions with the Latin tradition. I listened to Issac Delgado, Gilberto Santa Rosa, Groupo Galé, Candido Fabré, Jovenes del Barrio, Africando, and Tito Nieves, to name a few. My wife and I also went dancing to live Charanga bands at a Latin club here in L.A.—that was incredibly inspiring, and it definitely filled my head with ideas for timba and montuño grooves. Joe Vannelli also has a great sensibility for using technology in a natural and organic-sounding way. But the most inspiring thought was putting this music together in memory of my father—he ultimately inspired the entire work.

What goes on in your head when you're soloing?

I don't want to think of anything in the moment. I'd say it's a true connection between my heart and my soul. I have some ideas about how I'd like to approach the solo, but truthfully I have no preconception of what will actually happen in the improvisation state. I practice at least four hours a day; that's a good time to analyze and concentrate on phrasing, melody, patterns, and tonality. I believe practicing will prepare you for open improvisation. Consciously, I'm listening to the accompaniment, the form of the solo section, the rhythms, and things that might inspire me to instantly interact with what's happening. But the bottom line is the solo has to be expressive; I want to express my emotions, whether it's sadness, joy, anger, fear, or love. That doesn't mean it has to be technically perfect.

How do you solo in the studio?

On this project I mostly overdubbed on separate tracks and made composites to create a cohesive statement—something I felt worked for the composition. However, I did the solos on "Los Feliz," "Vaya," and "She Never Has a Window" in one take. I like being in the studio on a creative level, but you have to be careful not to get too critical and suck the life out of the music.

How do you make your recorded solos feel alive?

I've done lots of overdubbing sessions since the late '80s, so I've figured out how to absorb the music and lock into whatever is already there. You just have to focus entirely on the existing tracks and react as if you were there to begin with. I'd rather be in a conversation with live musicians—but when that's not possible, I just make believe they're there.

Do you think the 7-string bass is here to stay?

Yes—the 7 has enormous potential, especially live. With an extended-range instrument I can hold down the bottom *and* play melody or solo in the guitar range. I've also worked hard on emulating acoustic bass on the electric, and that gives me three distinct hats I can wear during a performance. With effects and MIDI you can extend the instrument infinitely and contribute in an extremely diverse way. I like having that kind of freedom and creative options with one bass guitar; it makes me think beyond the instrument's traditional realm, and that's exciting.

How practical is it for you to play the 7 live?

Very practical! Michael Tobias built me my first 7-string bass just in time to feature it on the new release.

I plan to tour with it and promote *Red Heat* at some point soon. I used the MTD 7 tuned *BEADGCF* and a Keith Roscoe 7 tuned *F♯BEADGC* on an L.A. gig with a wonderful Brazilian guitarist named Sandro Albert. I like to challenge myself on all levels, and this is a good way to continue to grow as a musician. I never let things get too comfortable—I want to keep myself on my toes.

How to you get a fat sound from the high strings?

I use medium-light D'Addario Prism strings, and we also recorded the melodies and solos in stereo using a chorus pedal as a splitter box, adding a bit of delay or reverb or both to one side. We sometimes used the chorusing, and we used an envelope filter on a couple of tracks. Using stereo really gave the instruments a lot of clarity and presence in the mix.

How do you record your acoustic bass guitar?

I've recorded my fretless Yamaha 5-string a few different ways, but this time we just went direct into the board. We wanted a big, solid sound, and that's what we got. I was trying to get an Ampeg Baby Bass sound, but I don't feel I accomplished that completely. There's another challenge for my next attempt at recording Latin music.

Do you use any amplification when recording your electric basses?

I used either an SWR Super Redhead or an SWR Workingman's Combo amp for a little extra room sound and overall girth.

How has playing left-handed with the bass strung upside-down affected your style?

In some way it's given me a different perspective looking at musical patterns, and in some ways perhaps a small technical advantage. I've never felt normal playing this way, that's for sure! But then again, I don't spend a lot of time thinking about how I play. I like to submerge myself in the music and set myself free to express the music the way I hear it.

Does the stringing make it harder to play "normal" material?

Not at all. At one time I thought it would hinder my playing, but eventually I saw anything is possible—even upside down. It boils down to your confidence and how

Jimmy Haslip Selected Discography

Solo albums: *Red Heat*, Unitone; *Arc*, GRP. **With the Yellowjackets:** *Time Squared*, Heads Up. *Mint Jam*, Yellowjackets; *Club Nocturne*, Warner Bros; *Blue Hats*, Warner Bros.; *Dreamland*, Warner Bros.; *Run for Your Life*, GRP; *Like a River*, GRP; *Live Wires*, GRP; *Green House*, GRP; *The Spin*, MCA; *Politics*, MCA; *Four Corners*, MCA; *Shades*, MCA; *Mirage a Trois*, Warner Bros.; *Samurai Samba*, Warner Bros.; *Yellowjackets*, Warner Bros. **With the Jaco Pastorius Big Band:** *Word of Mouth Revisited*, Heads Up. **With Jing Chi:** *Jing Chi*, Tone Center. **With Bruce Hornsby:** (both on RCA) *Hot House*; *Harbor Lights*. **With Steely Dan:** *Gold*, MCA. **With Gino Vannelli:** *Slow Love*, Verve Forecast; *Big Dreamers Never Sleep*, Epic; *Black Cars*, Mercury; *Brother to Brother*, A&M. **With Marilyn Scott:** *Walking With Strangers*, Prana Entertainment; *Avenues of Love*, Warner Bros.; *Take Me with You*, Warner Bros; *Smile*, Sindrome. **With Crosby Stills & Nash:** *CSN*, Atlantic. **With Bob Mintzer:** *Quality Time*, TVT; *One Music*, DMP. **With Pages:** *Pages*, Epic. **With Anita Baker:** *Rapture*, Elektra. **With Ron Wood:** *1234*, Columbia. **With Cher:** *Cher*, Geffen. **With Rod Stewart:** *Foolish Behaviour*, Warner Bros. **With Diana Ross:** *Ross*, Motown. **With Neil Larsen & Buzzy Feiten:** *Full Moon*, Warner Bros. **With Chris Botti:** *December*, Sony. **With Robben Ford:** *Inside Story*, Elektra. **With Kevyn Lettau:** *Police*, Universal. **With Lee Ritenour:** *Portrait*, GRP. **With Brenda Russell:** *Get Here*, A&M. **With Tom Scott:** *Street Beat*, Columbia. **With Bobby Caldwell:** *August Moon*, Sindrome; *Carry On*, Sindrome. **With Jeff Richman:** *Live at the Baked Potato, Volumes 1 & 2*, Tone Center. **With Dave Samuels:** *Natural Selection*, GRP. **With Jimmy Barnes:** *Soul Deep*, Mushroom/Atlantic; *Two Fires*, Atlantic. **With Michael Penn:** *March*, RCA. **With various artists:** *Wouldn't It Be Nice: A Jazz Portrait of Brian Wilson*, Capitol/Blue Note; *Wired: Original Soundtrack*, Varese. *Casino Lights*, Warner Bros.

much you really want to play the music. I do have to practice a lot to learn some of the music I'm playing, just because it's hard no matter how you play the instrument. If you want to play challenging material, you have to spend time learning and assimilating it. If you're having difficulty with something, play it slowly and build yourself up to speed—it's the best way to learn difficult music.

Web sites:

www.jimmyhaslip.com
www.yellowjackets.com

Heated Grooves

JIMMY HASLIP'S *RED HEAT* contains some hot grooves, as does *Jing Chi*, a 2002 CD by an improvisational trio of the same name, featuring Haslip, Robben Ford, and Vinnie Colaiuta. Beginning with *Red Heat*, **Example 1** is a fast-moving tumbao from "Los Feliz." Be sure to honor the eighth-note length on beat *four*, and palm-mute to approximate an authentic Baby Bass sound. **Example 2** shows the tumbao from "Dalle del Sol." The bass pattern underscores the tune's unique chordal harmonies and its otherworldly melody to create an ethereal Latin sound. (Palm-mute on this one, too.) **Example 3** contains the "Vaya" tumbao section. At 3:21 Jimmy gets more aggressive with the line and throws in some great variations—listen to the bass "bark" as he digs in.

From *Jing Chi*, **Example 4** shows Jimmy's Larry Graham–esque octave ostinato during the solo section of "The Hong Kong Incident." **Example 5** recalls the bass line of "Tengoku," which Haslip built from an Oriental-sounding scale the trio came up with. **Example 6** has the ZZ Top–inspired jammed bass line from "Man in the Ring," while **Example 7** shows the Led Zeppelin–meets–Frank Zappa unison riff from "Aurora."

Ex. 1

Ex. 2

Ex. 3

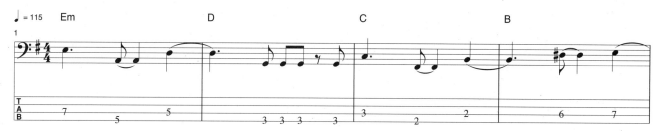

Ex. 4

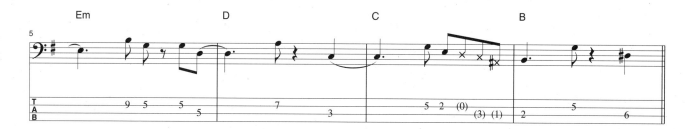

Ex. 5

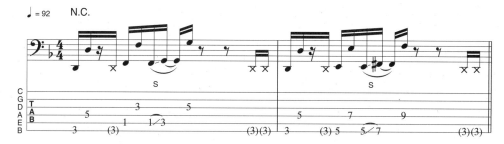

Ex. 6

Ex. 7

"The Hong Kong Incident" (R. Ford, J. Haslip): © Tamale Music, LaViera Music/BMI. "Tengoku" (R. Ford, J. Haslip, V. Colaiuta):
© Tamale Music, LaViera Music, Spherical Music/BMI. "Man in the Ring" (R. Ford, J. Haslip, V. Colaiuta): © Tamale Music,
LaViera Music, Spherical Music/BMI. "Aurora" (V. Colaiuta): © Spherical Music/BMI.

VICTOR BAILEY
Bass Happens

Interviewed by Chris Jisi, September 1999 and November 2001.

ALTHOUGH VICTOR BAILEY BREATHES THE RAREFIED AIR of the bass elite, there's an element of unfairness to his career. After meeting the monumental challenge of replacing Jaco Pastorius in Weather Report in 1981, Victor was poised to lead the second generation of talented fusion bassists through the doors blown open by Jaco, Stanley Clarke, Alphonso Johnson, and other low-end revolutionaries. Victor in particular had worshipped at the altar of Bird and Trane in order to take electric bass soloing to new levels. Alas, fusion turned to fuzak, often reducing Bailey and his ilk to overqualified ostinato operators. Even sadder, Victor became mired in major-label mediocrity as a sideman and managed just one solo album, 1989's dazzling *Bottom's Up*.

Having weathered the smooth jazz storm in the ten years since his debut, Bailey returned in 1999 with *Low Blow*. Featuring hornmen Bill Evans and Kenny Garrett, keyboardist Jim Beard, guitarist Wayne Krantz, and the over-the-top drumming of Dennis Chambers and Omar Hakim, the ten-track disc is a major bass offering. Victor takes a broader view: "I'm a musician trying to use all of my skills and talents to create an album of my music. One of those skills happens to be playing the bass." Indeed, Bailey's decade of growth is most evident in the disc's overall musical cohesiveness.

Still, for all of *Low Blow's* forward-thinking fusion and funk, its centerpiece and subsequent crowd favorite is Bailey's stirring vocal/bass cover of the Jaco classic "Continuum" [*Jaco Pastorius*]. Victor asks, "Do you know who Jaco was?" and tells the tale of the fallen bass genius through poignant lyrics that uncannily match Jaco's melody and solo. Like the rest of *Low Blow*, the track will ensure that you know who Victor Bailey is.

Born in 1960 in the bass-hot city of Philadelphia, Bailey took up drums at age ten. Five years later, during a basement rehearsal with his brother's band, the bass player quit and Victor volunteered to step in. He strapped on the instrument and discovered an immediate affinity for it. In 1980, following two years at Berklee College of Music, he moved to New York City and began playing with South African trumpeter Hugh Masekela and vocalist Miriam Makeba, in whose band he met drummer Omar Hakim. When Hakim got the gig with Weather Report soon after, he recommended Bailey, and the tandem recorded four albums with maestros Zawinul and Shorter before the group broke up in 1987. Victor joined Omar to backup Madonna on her 1993 world tour. He then moved to Los Angeles in 1997 and joined the Zawinul Syndicate, where he began planting the seeds for a solo return.

Victor Bailey

Why ten years between albums?

Mainly because at the time I made *Bottom's Up* the contemporary jazz scene was starting to make the transition into smooth jazz—and that's not what I wanted to do. Looking back now and seeing what many other solo bass artists did, I probably could have made records for small labels or put them out on my own. But because of my sideman work the people I knew in the business were all at major labels. So I would meet with them every few years, but all they wanted was safe airplay material.

What finally ended the dry spell?

I'd known Joachim Becker of ESC Records for years through working with Bill Evans and other artists. We had discussed my doing an album for a few years, but I think once I got back with Zawinul— where I'm fortunate to be up front and featured—it gave him a sense of what I could do as a solo artist. I played him a demo of the *Low Blow* songs, and it was a done deal. I brought the musicians I wanted into the studio, and we cut the album in a week, mostly live.

The title track is reminiscent of Jaco's "Teen Town," with its scurrying bass melody.

I actually wrote that on keyboard and my Yamaha QY70 sequencer while touring with Zawinul. I didn't necessarily intend for it to be a bass melody, but whenever I compose I also jot down the music in bass clef. When I went to record the demo I picked up my bass to read the melody. It sounded pretty good, so I stayed with it.

How did you get the slide effect in your solo?

I'm playing a series of ascending four-note arpeggios on the *G* string by plucking and then sliding to each note. For example, the first arpeggio is a *C♯m7*, so I slide up and pluck the *E* at the 9th fret, and then I re-attack the *E* and slide down to the 4th-fret *B*. I re-attack the *B* and slide up to the 6th-fret *C♯*, and finally I re-attack the *C♯* and slide down to the 1st-fret *G♯*. The concept came out of all the John Coltrane solos I transcribed when I was at Berklee. He used a lot of slurs so his lines sounded like one continuous thought instead of a bunch of notes strung together.

What inspired the 3/4 funk of "Sweet Tooth"?

Some years back I went to see saxophonist Steve Coleman in Europe. He writes some strange, interesting music. Somehow after hearing him I came up with the angular bass line that opens the track. I didn't even have a time signature, but as I added parts at the keyboard it ended up as a funk-in-three groove.

Bailey Audible

Dubbing himself a purist, Victor Bailey has remained faithful to the 4-string. For years his main bass was his 1988 Pensa-Suhr, which featured a koa body, maple neck, rosewood fingerboard, EMG JJ pickups, onboard Pensa-Suhr preamp, and Badass bridge. The instrument influenced his current line of Fender Signature Jazz Basses. Following the 2002 theft of his prototype Fender, his prime bass has been his second signature Jazz Bass. He strings it with DR Hi-Beam roundwounds gauged .040, .060, .080, .100.

Victor's live rig is a 620-watt EBS Fafner head with two EBS-410 cabinets. He also has EBS-210 and EBS-115 cabs. His effects include a Line 6 Bass POD and an EBS Octaver.

What technique are you using in the first part of your "Feels Like a Hug" solo?

I'm tapping the notes on the fingerboard with my right index finger in conjunction with hammer-ons and pull-offs. Like a lot of bassists, I started tapping in the late '70s, probably inspired by rock guitarists like Eddie Van Halen. In this case it seemed to fit the music, even though conceptually I'm coming out of a horn bag. It's similar to the legato technique Jeff Berlin used on *Taking Notes*.

That tune, "City Living," and "She Left Me" all have strong radio potential. Was that a consideration?

No. I never target tracks for radio. I just write, and different sides of me come out. I don't worry about whether my music is radio-friendly. The problem is that radio is not music-friendly.

In contrast, you penned a pair of full-blown fusion tracks in "Knee Jerk Reaction" and "Brain Teaser." To what do you attribute your writing's range?

A lot of it comes from my dad, Morris Bailey Jr. He's a great writer known for his R&B work with Philly Sound artists like Patti LaBelle, the Spinners, and Harold Melvin & the Bluenotes—but he's also a heavy jazz composer and arranger. Inspired by watching him, I started writing R&B and jazz at age 12, and he offered tips and suggestions. I always say my roots are bebop and funk—I have a jazz mind and a funky heart.

You alter your sound and approach considerably on the straightahead trio track "Baby Talk."

When I play swing or walking lines I don't want to cut through the band as much as wrap *around* it. So instead of my usual punchy, back-by-the-bridge tone, I turn my treble knob all the way down and move my plucking hand up over the neck to about the 15th fret. I'm not trying to sound like an upright bass, but I am trying to emulate the atmosphere of it. On this track I stayed with that technique for my solo as well, because I wanted to stay inside the changes and make a warm melodic statement.

What's the story behind "Do You Know Who/Continuum"?

Shortly after Jaco died in 1987 I was on a plane to L.A. when the inspiration hit me to write lyrics to "Continuum." I had transcribed it when I was 16 and practiced it daily, so I was able to put words to every note Jaco plays. I grabbed a pen and wrote the whole thing in ten minutes! I would sing the lyrics any time I heard the record, and I actually performed it twice in New York in 1997. When I finally got my deal, I made an arrangement with a few reharmonizations and a military snare groove, which Omar made his own. I recorded the bass first and then took a few passes at the vocal. It didn't have to be perfect because I was telling a story from my heart. In fact, if you play my version and Jaco's version and listen closely, the lyrics are all there in his bass part. It's like I didn't really write them. They came through me.

"Graham Cracker" recalls another of your bass influences. Do you change your pickup settings when you slap?

I always have the back pickup wide open with a bit of the front pickup to add some body. For slapping I turn the front pickup almost all the way on, and I strike the strings just below the neck. For me "Graham Cracker" is like if Larry Graham went to Berklee and then wrote another "Hair."

What's your take on the late-'90s bass scene?

There's a whole lot of phenomenal bass playing on albums—from slapping and tapping to solo pieces—but there's not a lot of great music. You can talk about the artistry of Stanley or Jaco without even mentioning their bass playing, because they created and were involved in such incredible music. That's what's missing for me. Hopefully it will change.

Will you wait another ten years to record?

Don't even joke! I plan on continuing to make records and touring with the goal of having the freedom to grow like jazz musicians did from the '20s to the '70s. It seemed to come to a halt in the '80s, but all we need is one artist to break through and open things up again. I would love to be that person.

True to his word, Victor quickly followed up Low Blow *with* That's Right!, *which featured Omar Hakim, Bill Evans, Jim Beard, Dean Brown, Lenny White, and Bennie Maupin. He also ended his sideman run with Joe Zawinul's blessing and became a full-time solo artist equipped with a new Fender Signature Jazz Bass:*

What was your concept for That's Right!?

I was planning to make a more bass-oriented record, but the bass-heavy songs didn't stand up to the other material I had, and I'd rather create an album of good music than just a bunch of bass melodies and solos. I did, however, concentrate more on the sound of the bass—looking to find different colors for the tunes. I was never big into effects as a sideman, but as a leader I've been trying out various things. Also, my new signature Jazz Bass played a key role.

How did that come together?

Mike Lewis of Fender approached me at Bass Day '99 and said, "I notice you're always playing Jazz-style basses, but not Fenders. Why is that?" So we got together and spent two years designing an instrument. We started with a koa body because I like the tone—but it's not a real bottomy-sounding wood, so we put a maple back on it, which adds tight bottom. On the other end, koa isn't bright enough for slapping, so we put a tiny slice of rosewood in the middle to help there. I also wanted some of the sustain of a neck-through while retaining the punch and funk of a bolt-on Jazz Bass, so we designed pickups with a ceramic magnet under the polepieces. That eliminates the magnetic field at the top of the pickups, which pulls at the vibrating strings and reduces sustain. Then we fine-tuned a 3-band preamp.

What gear did you use on the CD?

I played a prototype of the signature Jazz—which is similar to the finished version I have now—strung with Dean Markley NickelSteel Bass roundwounds, .040–.100. I went direct through a Countryman DI, and I also miked my live EBS rig. The direct signal gave me the tone, and the miked rig gave me the body I wanted. My outboard effect was a Line 6 Bass POD.

The opener, "Goose Bumps," as well as "Nothing but Net" and "The Rope-a-Dope," feature some of your trademarks: groove-oriented "A" sections that lead to more complex bridges.

Yep, that's me all right! "Nothing but Net" is a tune I played with my first band in 1989. I always go through all of my tapes for album material; I wrote a new A-section melody, but the rest is the same. On "The Rope-a-Dope" I wanted to solo during the bridge so I could blow over some interesting changes, and I wanted to use another sound to go along with the bass. I accidentally dialed up a weird harmonizer patch on Pro Tools and ended up keeping it.

There's already a buzz about your Funkadelic cover, "Knee Deep/One Nation Medley."

It's kind of my response to the latest smooth-jazz trend where everyone is covering old songs, except they

Victor Bailey Selected Discography

Solo albums: *That's Right!*, ESC; *Low Blow*, ESC; *Bottoms Up*, Atlantic. **With Joe Zawinul:** *Faces & Places*, ESC; *World Tour*, ESC. **With Weather Report:** (all on Columbia) *This Is This!*; *Sportin' Life*; *Domino Theory*; *Procession*. **With the Jaco Pastorius Big Band:** *Word of Mouth Revisited*, Heads Up. **With Steps Ahead:** *Vibe*, NYC; *Yin Yang*, NYC; *Magnetic*, Elektra. **With Michael Brecker:** *Now You See It, Now You Don't*, GRP. **With Lenny White:** (both on HipBop) *Renderers of the Spirit*; *Present Tense*. **With Bill Evans:** *Touch*, Zebra; *Escape*, Escapade; *Petite Blond*, Lipstick. **With Jim Beard:** *Song of the Sun*, CTI. **With Billy Cobham:** *Picture This*, GRP. **With Omar Hakim:** *Groovesmith*, Oh Zone. **With Urban Knights:** *Urban Knights*, GRP. **With Mary J. Blige:** *My Life*, MCA. **With Faith Evans:** *Faith*, Bad Boy. **With the O'Jays:** *Emotionally Yours*, RCA. **With Regina Carter:** *Regina Carter*, Atlantic Jazz. **With Force MDs:** *Touch & Go*, Tommy Boy. **With Kevin Eubanks:** *Shadow Prophets*, GRP. **With Will Downing:** *Dream Fulfilled*, Island. **With Special EFX:** *Just Like Magic*, GRP. **With Najee:** *Tokyo Blue*, EMI. **With George Howard:** *Love and Understanding*, GRP. **With Alex Bugnon:** *Love Season*, RCA. **With Carlos Santana:** *Dance of the Rainbow Serpent*, Columbia/Legacy. **With Bob Berg:** *Riddles*, GRP. **With various artists:** *Who Loves You? Tribute to Jaco Pastorius*, Concord.

do them exactly like the original or even water them down. I wanted to take "(Not Just) Knee Deep," which I've been playing since I was a kid, and turn it inside out and do a real arrangement of it. I sequenced the groove on my little Yamaha QY70 [hardware sequencer] while on the road with Zawinul; then I sat at the keyboard and tried to find new harmonies that felt natural without sounding too "out." Interestingly, I wasn't aware I went into the melody of "One Nation Under a Groove." It just happened—I realized, wait a minute, that's a different song!

The slap solo is interesting.

That was a struggle. I wanted to solo, but I couldn't figure out the vibe; my usual fingerstyle bebop-flavored stuff wasn't working. Finally, I backed off the bridge pickup slightly to favor the neck pickup, and I started slapping and popping. It's a different sonic and conceptual approach for me, and it really fit the track. We also pulled out an old Pultec EQ, which gave the bass a fat analog sound without clouding the tone. It didn't change the sound of the bass—it changed its shape.

"Where's Paco?" has a unique bass tone as well.

I was going for a bluesy, B.B. King–like sound to double my vocals. I ended up using the "pig foot" setting on my Bass POD for a smooth, sustained overdrive.

What was the inspiration for the poignant ballad "Joey"?

That's a sad tale. My cousin, Joe Bailey, was robbed and killed in Philadelphia last January. I went to Philly for the funeral, and when I came back I sat at the piano and wrote the whole song in five minutes. On the track I played the melody using a smooth distortion from the Bass POD's "rodent" setting.

"Steamy" is a departure for you.

That's an old Bennie Maupin tune the Headhunters played but never recorded. Bennie was coming to my house in L.A. to look at some of the music before we headed east to record, and I told him if he had a tune to bring it with him. As soon as I heard the doubled bass clarinet and bass line, I loved it. On my records I've never had just a long, open groove with no changes. I thought of taking a bluesy solo, but there was such a cool vibe rolling along I didn't want to interfere with it. I just played the ostinato with my right hand positioned over the bottom of the fingerboard for a warm, deep, upright-like sound.

What's the origin of "Black on the Bach"?

I got the idea to do a solo bass piece incorporating classical and blues—as if Bach and B.B. King wrote a tune together. There's an accompaniment track and a melody/solo track, which has a touch of reverb and is panned around. I recorded and mixed the piece to an Alesis ADAT at my house, burned it to CD, and then we dumped it into Pro Tools and mastered it.

On the fusion-burner title tune you play a blistering, string-crossing bass line.

I tapped it on the fingerboard, alternating between my left-hand 2nd finger and right-hand index finger. I reached over the top of the neck with my left arm, because it's hard to tap lower-string notes when reaching around from under the neck. I wrote "That's Right!" on the bus while touring with Zawinul. Believe it or not, the initial inspiration was the groove of Sly & the Family Stone's "Dance to the Music."

What led you to halt your sideman career and focus on being a full-time leader?

The first step was leaving Zawinul's band at his encouragement. He told me I had records out and that it was time for me to be an artist. On sideman gigs I use only a portion of my capabilities, because no matter how much freedom I have, my job is still to play the bottom. While I love doing that, there's much more I can do on the instrument—and if I'm going to develop it, I've got to go out and play my music every night. I'm on a mission.

Web site

www.victorbailey.com

Low Blowing

IN ADDITION TO HIS WORLD-CLASS SOLOING SKILLS Victor Bailey can swing a funk groove like no one else. "Bill Withers once told me, 'Man, you have a jazz mind and a funky heart,'" says Bailey. *Low Blow* and *That's Right!* are rife with solos and bass lines that illustrate his gift for putting notes in his own special place in the pocket.

From *Low Blow*: **Example 1** shows the first half of the main bass melody of "City Living," which was originally inspired by the Mu-Tron III+ pedal Victor uses on the track. "The effect's sound changes depending on how hard you attack the notes, which along with the slides and hammers adds to the overall expression." **Example 2** contains the blistering four-bar main groove from "Knee Jerk Reaction." Victor is a master at making busy fusion lines groove. "I just try to lock into the overall feel, listen, and stay out of the soloist's way."

Example 3 illustrates the first 18 bars of Victor's sizzling "Brain Teaser" solo, a live take he later scatted along with. The first phrase trills around a descending *F* triad before reinforcing the *A* minor tonality with the *E7* altered-chord tones in bar 2. After working his way down the neck in bar 3, Victor climbs back up through the *Dm* chord using chromatic movement to nail to the chord tones. "That's some bebop trumpet stuff people like Miles and Wallace Roney are known for." Having nicely negotiated the *B♭7sus* tonality in bars 6 and 7, he eases into the solo's main theme in bar 8, developing it tastefully by changing one note each in bars 9 and 10. Although the harmony takes an unrelated turn in bars 11–14, Victor keeps developing the four-note motif to fit the changes' whole-tone sound. "That's some-

Ex. 1

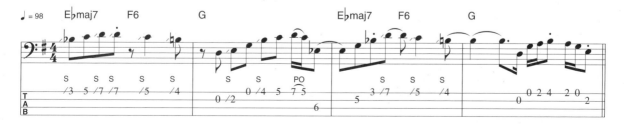

Ex. 2

Ex. 3

Ex. 3 (continued)

Ex. 4a

Ex. 4b

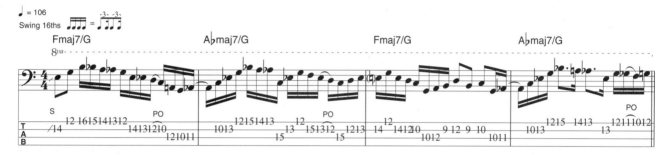

Ex. 5

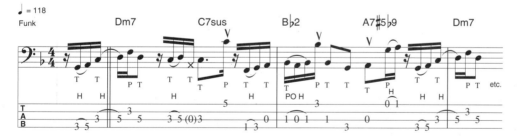

Ex. 6

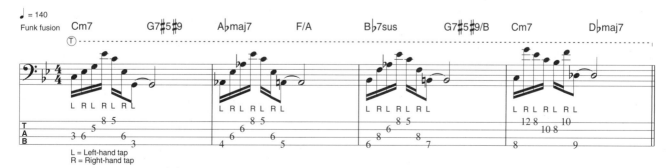

thing I learned from Wayne Shorter. He'll continually develop an idea by adding or changing one little thing in each bar." The theme resolves triumphantly in bars 15–17 before the killer lick in bar 18 leads back to the original *A* minor tonality. "The first half of that lick is right out of the *Slonimsky Thesaurus of Scales*, which Trane made famous."

From *That's Right!*: Example 4a shows the opening groove of "Goose Bumps." Victor varies the note durations, which helps the funky line swing. **Example 4b** contains Victor's second solo interlude (at 2:21), to which he added a bit of Pro Tools chorus. "I could almost hear a rich, big band orchestration in that section, so I blew some bebop-flavored lines over it." **Example 5** shows the slapped groove during the second *B* section of "Knee Deep/One Nation Medley," at 1:59. Even though the tune has a straight-16th feel, Victor implies a subtle swing presence with popped accents on the last 16th of bar 1's beat *three* and bar 2's beat *one*. **Example 6** shows the title track's terrifying, tapped main bass line, first heard at 0:13 (see the interview to learn how he did it).

GARY WILLIS
Tribal Technician

Interviewed by Chris Jisi, April 1993, February 1999, and January 2001.

AN UNDERGROUND INSTITUTION, Tribal Tech savors its role as a survivor in the post-fusion wasteland of soulless fuzak. Supplying the subterranean spark for the band is Gary Willis, who, along with co-leader Scott Henderson, has sought to revolutionize rather than merely revive vintage fusion. Renowned for his solo flights on a fretless Ibanez 5-string, Willis has also unleashed some of the baddest groove innovations since Jaco redefined the 16th-note. Add to that his forward-searching compositions and his well-organized approach to technique and touch, and Willis easily qualifies as one of the most important bass voices of the '90s and beyond.

Born on March 28, 1957, in Longview, Texas (some two hours east of Dallas), Willis early on gravitated toward instrumentals by the likes of the Crusaders, Tower of Power, War, Sly Stone, and the Allman Brothers. "They appealed to me because without words, the interpretation wasn't as defined—you could use your imagination," Willis explains. Gary took a few lessons on the family piano and tinkered with an old guitar, but his future course was set after his parents presented him with an electric bass for his 13th birthday. On weekends his father played gospel-style piano in church, and soon Gary was joining in on bass.

Willis's love of harmony led him back to guitar and toward jazz, thus beginning an eight-year conflict between guitar and bass that was finally resolved when he enrolled at North Texas State University in 1978. "I realized that everything I played on guitar, no matter how important, was on the top, so I had little control over how the band sounded as a whole. On bass I was able to have a bigger influence on the music by directing the rhythm and feel of the band." At North Texas Willis was required to study classical string bass while absorbing such influences as Miles Davis, pianist Bill Evans, and bassists Jaco Pastorius, Paul Jackson, and Rocco Prestia.

Though he was gigging regularly in Dallas and had recorded with several fusion bands, Willis gladly moved to L.A. when his wife was offered a job there in 1982. Before long, a combination of jam sessions and word-of-mouth referrals led him to a successful audition with guitarist Phil Upchurch. "That was pivotal because it was my first real groove gig; I had to settle down and refine my playing fast." While working with Upchurch, Willis met guitarist Henderson, who, after discussing music with Willis, informed the bassist that he wanted to start a band. Starting as a sextet, the unit played local clubs for years before finally heading to the studio in 1985 in search of a deal. Following the release of their fourth disc, 1991's *Tribal Tech*, the band—by then a quartet co-led by Willis and Henderson—took to the road, where they continue to ply their tribal trade.

Gary Willis

How do you approach a solo?

The best analogy I can make is that soloing is like speaking a language. In conversation you may express the same ideas and use the same words, but each time there are different inflections and variations. The first step, however, is to develop a vocabulary. What I did was listen to and transcribe soloists on other instruments, people like Bill Evans, Clifford Brown, Michael Brecker, George Benson, and John Scofield. Although it was never in my nature to just take a lick and repeat it, playing other people's ideas expands your ears and lets you view the neck in new ways. The goal is to get to the point where neither your ears nor your technique holds you back—to become fluent enough so the search for, and connecting of, ideas comes from your subconscious and relates to the overall picture, rather than consciously applying notes or scales to certain sections of a song.

The most exciting aspect of your playing is your ability to blur the line between soloing and groove playing.

That's due to the influence of jazz, where the rhythm section has a responsibility to listen and respond—to go places with the soloist. It makes the music more interesting to listen to, so we try to include that in all of our tunes. There are certain set sections and parts, but a lot of the solo sections are not as specified, so we can develop the groove as the soloist develops his solo. Consequently, the music takes on different forms from night to night.

How does that affect the bass/drums relationship?

It opens things up. You're still responsible for timekeeping and for creating a "locked" feel with the drummer, but if you latch onto certain figures, especially with the kick drum, it can be a problem if one of you changes. So you have to focus on the whole kit and develop your instincts to get an intuitive sense of where you should play together and where you're free to try ideas.

The foundation for a lot of your improvisational grooves is the 16th-note pulse made popular by two of your influences: Jaco Pastorius and Rocco Prestia.

They're the inspiration, sure. But it's something I worked on after hearing bassists who were technically limited to playing eighth-notes get left behind when the soloist and drummer kicked the energy up a notch by playing 16ths. I wanted to be in control enough to hear and execute ideas in that pulse, so I could participate and make things happen. The most important element is the use of ghost notes; they provide the illusion of space and the accents that really propel the groove. If I played a pitch on every note, the bass lines would be far too busy.

For right-hand technique you emphasize using three fingers and playing with a light touch.

Most bassists learn music through their left hands, with their right hands sort of tagging along. By

Willis Ware

After years of building custom basses for Gary Willis, Ibanez introduced the Gary Willis Signature Bass in 1998. Based on the SR885 body shape, the fretless 5 (and a twin fretted model) feature numerous Willis refinements: A light-ash body; an ebony fingerboard and maple fret lines on the fretless and a rosewood board on the fretted; a deeper cutaway; a height-adjustable "Willis Ramp" running from the pickup to the neck; a single Willis-designed passive/active Bartolini pickup curved to match the ramp and board; a 2 + 3 headstock configuration; and Willis-designed round tuners for reduced weight, better balance, and easier string changes. In addition to his main natural-finish fretless signature model Gary's collection includes his "Bass Lite"—a custom fretted Ibanez ATK305 5-string—and a modified fretted Ibanez SR506 6, which he uses for teaching. His strings are GHS Progressives, gauged .045, .065, .085, .105, .135.

Onstage Gary plugs into an Aguilar DB750 head and one or two Aguilar GS410 cabinets. Other sonic ingredients include his Lexicon MPX1 multi-effects, a Visual Volume Pedal, and Monster Cables. When recording *Bent* and *Thick* Gary went direct into his Retrospec Juice Box all-tube DI and occasionally his Eden Navigator preamp. He kept his Eden D210XLT close by so he could feel the lows while tracking.

addressing the right hand independently, you can gain the kind of control that will eventually help you to develop a style. Using a three-finger technique allows me to play things that wouldn't normally occur with just two fingers.

As far as using a light touch goes, once I got good equipment I started playing softer and got a better sound. Playing a note softly will result in the same attack as playing a note hard, but the tone will be fatter. Plus, you have more range and control of dynamics when you play with a light touch. For me, that's most effective when I'm grooving because I have to move a lot of air on the dead notes to feel the accents.

Basically, my right-hand technique can be broken down into two systems: *closed position*, where the first and second finger play on one string, with the third finger ready to play the next higher string or dampen the original string if I move to the next lower string; and *open position*, for playing ideas that spread across three strings, where the first and second fingers play the low notes and the second and third fingers play the high notes. In both cases my fingers remain on the strings at all times for the purpose of muting. At times I use my right-hand palm to mute the strings while playing with my thumb and fingers.

For the left hand you've broken down the neck into three positions.

I've since revised that with a system that breaks down the neck into just two positions. It involves looking at a key center starting from either your 2nd or 4th finger and allows you to go anywhere on the neck using a combination of the two positions. By reducing everything that happens under your fingers to one key, to get to any other key you never have to shift more than one fret away. I've found that too many bassists follow harmony in several places around the neck—when the chord changes, their hand jumps to another area.

Even though you play fretless, you tend to stay away from slides and heavy vibrato.

Sliding is easy and available on the fretless, but I don't hear it, personally, because it's not something you do naturally with your voice. The same is true of exaggerated, nervous-sounding vibrato. Coming from playing barre chords as a guitarist, I worked on getting my first finger where I wanted it and where it was in tune. That meant spending two years with my head bent forward, eyeing the fingerboard. But eventually you learn the neck of your bass and develop muscle memory.

A good way to work on intonation is to record a drone note and play against it, making it any part of the harmony—the root, the 3rd, the 9th. Then play different scales around it. That helps you to get into the habit of relating everything you play to something else.

How would you define Tribal Tech's musical concept?

The focus is as much on the writing as it is the playing. Too often you hear great musicians rip through boring or poorly written material, in a hurry to get to the solo sections. On the rare occasions when you hear great compositions, even if they're played by average musicians, you come away with a much more rewarding musical experience. So what we try to do is maintain a high level of both composition and improvisation. Stylistically, I would describe our music as a combination of jazz and rock with a lot of funk thrown in.

How do you and Scott develop the material?

Actually, we don't co-write—we're pretty independent. The main thing we do is check with each other to be sure we're not writing the same grooves. Then we'll play ideas over the phone and make comments and suggestions. When we get to rehearsal, the whole band participates in a sort of co-arrangement

through suggestions and experimentation. Our common goal is to create interesting music featuring strong melodies, without being repetitive or derivative. That's the challenge of writing: to test your imagination and get it to go somewhere new and different.

I understand you write on keyboard, with the help of a Macintosh computer.

That's right. I didn't write with any regularity until around 1986, when this band gave me the opportunity. But I've always written on keyboards. It's good to compose on a different instrument, because it prevents you from falling into familiar patterns on your main instrument. Since I'm not a good keyboard player, the Mac lets me find my ideas and then plays them back for me. Probably the only tune I've written mostly on bass is "Renegade" [*Nomad*], which was written around an improvised bass line.

Your tune "The Big Wave," which opens Illicit, *pretty much trashes contemporary fusion. Why?*

Much of it lacks depth. A lot of so-called fusion out there, especially in the "Wave" format, projects a one-dimensional, feel-good, safe, happy mentality. Not only is there little challenge in creating that music, it doesn't reflect reality—it doesn't relate to what's happening in people's lives day to day. It's a corporate-established format having nothing to do with art.

Where is Tribal Tech headed?

We're optimistic about the future even though we have two cultural strikes against us. The way the music industry is structured in this country, radio play is critical to a band's success and so is having a video. There's a whole generation that can experience music only by watching videos. We refuse to limit our music to fit into those formats; instead, we're just going to continue to bring it to live audiences. As listeners we want to be inspired by music, so it validates what we're doing when people come up to us at shows and tell us our music inspires them. It's especially rewarding when that sort of feedback comes from non-musicians. To know that our music affects people in everyday walks of life—that's what keeps us going.

Gary's words proved prophetic. When he spoke to Bass Player *six years later, Tribal Tech had been shunned by radio, dropped by labels, and logistically locked out of the domestic touring circuit. Undaunted, he marched on, quietly becoming one of the most influential voices on his instrument. In 1999 Tribal Tech released the jam-written* Thick, *and Willis unveiled his second solo effort,* Bent—*featuring Tribal-mate Scott Kinsey, saxophonists Bob Berg and Steve Tavaglione, and drummer Dennis Chambers. We discussed both albums and his Ibanez signature bass.*

How did Bent *come about?*

Alchemy Records gave the green light to begin my second album, so I went back to the Musicians Institute, where I had recorded *No Sweat*. We tracked *Thick* with Tribal Tech at the same time. I approached *Bent* much like my first record: a mix of written material, a few heads, and a lot of jamming.

The opening track, "Hipmotize," features your "Bass Lite," an instrument you used on No Sweat *but didn't identify.*

People kept asking if I played guitar on *No Sweat*, so I figured I'd come clean. The Bass Lite is a fretted ATK 5-string Ibanez made for me. I tuned it like the top five strings of a 6 with light gauges—.025, .030, .035, .045, .065. On certain tunes I needed a different voice besides my fretless, and the Bass Lite turned out to be valuable. I've used it since in a lot of settings.

You slap the Bass Lite on the Bent *title track. Is slapping a recent development for you?*

Not at all. In the '80s I was slapping as a sideman with everyone from Phil Upchurch to Wayne Shorter. For the live studio tracks I tuned my fretless's *B* string down to where it was almost lying on the fingerboard—and then we just jammed, with no melody or key.

How did you get the fat, multi-layered sound on "Cadillac"?

That's the Yamaha G50 Guitar MIDI Converter and the Bass MIDI pickup, which I mounted on my fretless. I usually use the G50 for writing. I've always said you should try not to write on the instrument you play, to avoid falling into patterns—but I came up with some melodies by improvising and experimenting with the G50. As a result this record is a little more linear than *No Sweat*.

You use an interesting technique during your "Emancipation" solo.

I wanted a non-traditional, more Eastern fretless approach. I played a lot of hammer-ons and pull-offs, using my 1st and 4th fingers five frets apart, so I was hitting mostly unisons and 4ths over basic *E* minor and then *G* major tonalities.

What's the story behind Thick?

After seven "composition" records we all felt it was time for a change. We'd been jamming in concert for a while, and the successful nights led us to want to try it on record, so we just went into the studio and started jamming. Playing-wise this puts more responsibility on you because you have to figure out your role: Are you playing a bass part, a melody, noise, or what? From there we took the tracks home, added our individual input, and then compared notes. We wanted to keep the original vibe, but for balance it became necessary to contrast, say, a one-chord groove by adding a solo over changes. There were times when I'd tell one of the guys I wanted to change a bass part, and he'd say, "You can't—I wrote something around that!"

What led you to use "prepared" basses?

My college roommate and I made a cassette recording using rubber bands and other items on our guitars. The way I view it, a synth player has access to hundreds of sounds; on bass I can get a variety of tones with my hands, but it's limited by comparison. Screwing with the bass gives me more sounds and roles I can assume.

"Clinic Troll" takes manipulated instruments to the extreme.

While Henderson wasn't looking I wove a piece of discarded bass string into his guitar strings. I also played a more percussive part with random hammer-ons on my fretless and ran it through the Lexicon MPX1's touch-sensitive pitch transposer. When I tapped hard the pitch would take a dive, and if I let it sustain it would climb back up. I actually prepared my bass on "Somewhat Later" and "Party at Kinsey's" by weaving a bunch of Popsicle sticks into the strings. You sort of have to tune the sticks by putting them at angles, and often you have to loosen the strings to get all the notes to sound, so any reference to standard bass is out the window.

There's a Cream/Hendrix flavor on "What Has He Had," which sounds like you're using a slide.

I'm bending the thinner-gauge Bass Lite strings all to hell, along with distortion and octaver. I also scrape the strings with my thumbnail to get those overtones. I didn't contribute much to the original jam, but at home I took out the keyboard tracks, picked up the Bass Lite, and got into the psychedelic, power-trio vibe.

You've inspired a lot of players to use palm muting. How did you develop that?

I stumbled on it in the '80s while trying to play reggae grooves in various bands. At first I put my palm on the strings and used a pick, but I quickly abandoned that and used my fingers instead. I've incorporated it more and more over time for a number of reasons: It sounds bigger and moves more air, and it fits better underneath guitar and keyboards. I can also maintain high levels of energy and note activity without getting in the way. Musically I like the control it gives; as the intensity picks up I can gradually back off into regular tones or sometimes start individual notes muted and remove the palm pressure, letting them swell into full-blown notes.

How did your light right-hand touch come about?

From not ever having a bass teacher and having to discover techniques myself, as well as from my early frustration playing too hard due to crappy amps and loud drummers. I took a "physics for musicians" class in college and learned that if you pluck a string softly and crank the amp, it produces the same attack as a string plucked hard—but the tone is fatter for the duration of the note.

When you play a groove or a solo, even at high volumes, a lot of the feel is determined by your dynamics. By training yourself to use a lighter touch at all intensity levels you're still able to vary your dynamics when everything is cranking. Another factor is that on fretless there's a fine point to attacking the string so it will sing, which is why I need a volume pedal to back off some notes at very low stage volumes.

You appear to be having more fun on Bent *and* Thick, *as opposed to the serious attitude that prevailed in earlier years.*

It's probably because I've learned to accept my status in the industry—or lack of it—so I'm not as concerned with how much demand there is for what I do. I just do it. In my band and in Tribal Tech, most of the time we're just trying to have fun, and I think that's finally starting to translate.

Web Sites

www.garywillis.com
www.scottkinsey.com/TribalTech.html

Bent to the Task

"LITE," PREPARED, AND MIDI'D BASSES may give Gary Willis more colors on *Bent*—but there's no mistaking his combustible 16th-note grooves and soaring, singing solos. **Example 1** follows Gary's muted bass line and Bass Lite line at the 3:40 mark of the Headhunters-reminiscent "Hipmotize." The bass part comes from the original jammed track, while the Bass Lite part was overdubbed. Says Gary, "When I'm grooving I like to use a bigger phrase early in a section and reduce it later on, which really increases the momentum."

Example 2 features the first 20 bars of Gary's gorgeous solo on the jazz-waltz "It's Only Music" on *Bent*, starting at 2:59. The section shown is a virtual study in jazz improvisation. Gary begins with a melodic shape centered around *B♭* and *C* in bars 1–7. Bar 4 marks a temporary resolution; then the motif sets up a call-and-response figure on the last beat of bar 5 and beat *two* of bar 6 before finally pausing for a breath in bar 7. Heading into the next section, in bar 9 Willis sets up the *A♭* tonality with a tasty bar-8 bebop run that outlines the II–V (*B♭m7/E♭7*) with a tritone substitution (*A7*). Working through the *A♭maj7* in bar 9 with chord tones, he anticipates the upcoming *Am7♭5* chord on the last half of bar 9's beat *three*; he then moves up the neck to match the intensity of the dramatic harmonic shift, initiating a cycle back to *E♭*. Gary begins the final chorus idea on bar 12's last beat, and in the next two bars he displaces it by a half-beat while altering it slightly to fit the harmony. Anticipating the end of the chorus, in bar 15 he descends in 4ths and ascends favoring the V chord's 13 and ♭9 to build to a sweeping climax at the end of bar 16. Using the *D* at the very end of bar 16 as a starting point, he introduces a new four-note motif to start the second chorus. In bars 17 through 20 he cleverly alters the figure while dropping the fourth note (*G*, *G♭*, *F*, and *E*) by a half-step each time.

Moving over to Tribal Tech's 2000 release, *Rocket Science*, Willis provides the groove thrust on the band's jam-constructed ninth CD. **Example 3** contains his blazing muted four-bar ostinato at the 1:59 mark of "Saturn 5." **Example 4** shows his greasy one-bar groove from the title track, at the 1:14 mark. Finally, **Ex. 5** rocks out with Gary's two-bar ostinato during Scott Henderson's guitar solo on "Space Camel" (at 3:56). Notes Willis of the jam-writing process, "We've discovered the hardest part is getting that first idea. We're all good enough musicians to react, so coming up with complimentary parts is easy—but finding that first spark is difficult."

Ex. 1

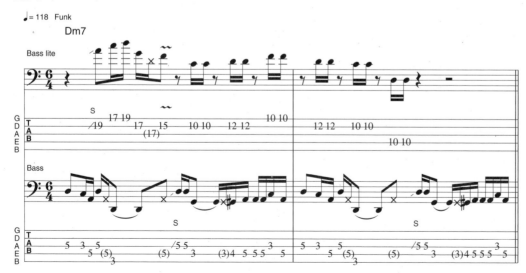

Ex. 2

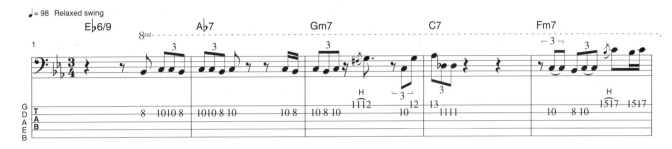

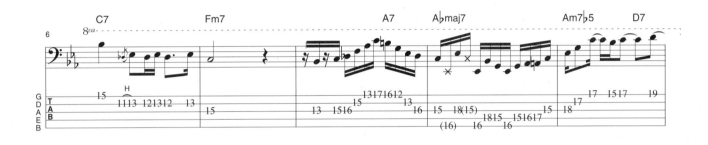

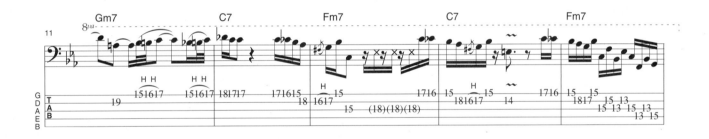

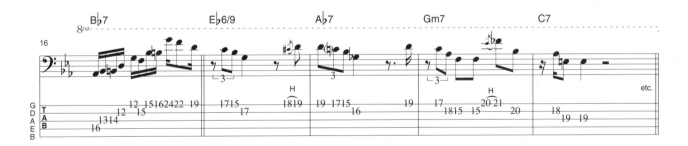

Ex. 3

Ex. 4

Ex. 5

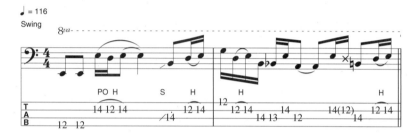

MICHAEL MANRING
Eclectic Electric Explorer

Interviewed by Jim Roberts, May/June 1991 and January/February 1994; and Richard Johnston, December 1998.

HAVING EMERGED IN THE 1950s, the electric bass guitar is still a young instrument. During its brief history, there have been a few players who showed the way—visionaries whose artistry and technical innovations expanded the possibilities for the rest of us. Add the name Michael Manring to that list.

Manring has mastered the entire encyclopedia of modern bass technique, from plucking and picking to slapping, tapping, and a variety of chordal strums—sometimes on two or three basses at once. In his search for new sonorities, he has experimented with dozens of altered tunings. Although Michael's playing is often astounding, he has consciously downplayed what he refers to as the "circus" aspect. "One of my goals," he explains, "is to integrate the different techniques into a whole. With some people, it's 'Here's my tapping section, and now I will slap.' It's more interesting to get them all to work together."

The son of a Navy pilot, Michael Manring was born in 1959 and raised in the Virginia suburbs of Washington, D.C. His interest in bass guitar was initially piqued by something he heard on television. "I had a passion for the sound of it right away. My mother thought it was an organ, so she signed me up for piano lessons—I was eight or nine at the time. Eventually I figured out what I had heard was a bass guitar, and my parents let me buy one for my tenth birthday. I got this used violin-body bass for 50 bucks. Boy, was it a dog! Later on I got a Gibson EB-3, which was a big improvement. I remember being in junior high school and actually running home to play that bass, because it was such a gas."

After playing both electric and acoustic bass during high school, Manring attended the Berklee College of

Music for a year. When the spring semester ended, he hit the road with a band of fellow students. "We were all Berklee-ites, and we started out wanting to be a fusion band. But reality caught up to us, so we switched over to Top 40. And it was the height of the disco era. Being on the road was exciting for about a month or two, but it was hard playing stupid music every night. I quit after about six months."

Manring returned home and joined Natural Bridge, a fusion ensemble that was signed to make an album for Tappan Zee, a CBS affiliate. The record was never

Michael Manring

released, but Michael stayed with the group for two-and-a-half years. During this period, he began to play with guitarist Michael Hedges, a kindred spirit who was also interested in exploring the outer limits of his instrument via altered tunings and unusual playing techniques.

In 1983 Manring moved to New York City, where he put his expanding chops to work in a series of jazz gigs and studied with Jaco Pastorius. "Jaco had just been in Bellevue, and he was pretty well cleaned up at the time," recalls Michael. "I took only a couple of lessons, but he was very helpful and supportive. I would play a piece of his and ask him about it—how he fingered it and how he phrased it, things like that. He could be very sweet, one to one, but as soon as he had an audience it was different. It was a sobering experience. Jaco was such a hero, and he had what all of us wanted—but it was sad to meet him and find out what a mess he really was. It made me think, and rethink, about what I wanted from music."

Manring didn't find New York to be an hospitable musical environment. "I wasn't doing anything that felt like something I really wanted to do. And there were a lot of drugs in the jazz scene at the time, which I wasn't comfortable with. At the same time, I was getting more and more excited about what was happening with my friends in California." Before his move to New York, Manring had played on a record Hedges had made for a fledgling label called Windham Hill. Manring soon found himself commuting regularly to the West Coast to play on other projects for the company, and in 1984 he moved back to Virginia to begin work on the material that was eventually released as *Unusual Weather* two years later. Once the record was finished, Michael resettled in the San Francisco Bay Area.

From his first record Manring's interest in bass as a solo instrument has distinguished his work. "I've always been in love with the sound of the bass. It has so many other sounds *within* it, and solo playing seemed like a natural way to take advantage of that. I was doing it almost from the time I started playing, although people tried to discourage me. 'Nobody is going to want to hear solo bass. Don't bother.' I kept writing solo pieces anyway."

During the 1994 interview Jim Roberts and Manring talked extensively about Thonk, *which was a radical departure from Michael's previous work.*

THONK FEATURES THE LOUDEST AND MOST AGGRESSIVE MUSIC Michael Manring has ever done. Produced by John Cuniberti—perhaps best known for his work with guitarist Joe Satriani—*Thonk* has a powerful, pounding, in-your-face sound that's sure to amaze those who had dismissed Manring as a granola-munching new-age nerd.

Although bassists have always found much to marvel at in Manring's work, *Thonk* adds more dimensions. In addition to once again showcasing Michael's remarkable command of just about every technique imaginable, from straightahead single-note grooves to multi-instrument two-handed solo pieces, there are such revelations as the hair-raising sound of fretless played with an EBow through a wide-open Marshall, a piece played with *two* EBows held in his right hand, and another piece played on *three* basses simultaneously. As usual, though, the technical innovations are there to serve the music, and Manring emphasizes that he considers himself "a composer whose medium is bass."

"Big Fungus" kicks off the disc with a wail of feedback and a thunderous drum roll. The screaming "guitar" lead is actually Manring cranking his Zon Hyperbass through a Marshall, and his only accompanist is Primus drummer Tim "Herb" Alexander. Michael's hookup with Herb is a clue to the origins of *Thonk*. "Herb actually lives nearby," explains Manring. "Somebody had told me I should check out Primus, and I loved the band right away. Les Claypool is great, and I was blown away by Herb's playing. I got in touch with him through some mutual friends, and we got together to play. It was really fun.

"I guess I had gotten kind of tired of doing new-age music. It felt a bit limiting to do everything with taste and restraint. If you take taste too far, it's not tasteful anymore. I had wanted to do an all-solo record next, but Windham Hill didn't like that idea, so I wasn't sure what I was going to do. I had been going out to hear some of the bands that live around here [in the Bay Area], like Primus and Faith No More. And I had worked with [guitarist] Buckethead on Will Ackerman's recent record [*The Opening of Doors*]. So I ended up making demos of music like that—some pretty ugly stuff! I didn't think Windham Hill would be interested in it, but they were."

Michael is quick to point out that his interest in rock is not a new development. "When I was growing up, I played the requisite number of Led Zeppelin tunes. That's *always* been a part of where my music was coming from. Most of my friends grew up the same way, playing in garage bands and studying bebop at the same time. I've always liked all kinds of music, and I like to bring all of my influences together. That's what I've done with this record, and I hope people will pick up on that."

Like Manring's previous discs, *Thonk* features his solo work. There are four solo pieces: "Monkey Businessman," "My Three Moons," "Adhan," and "The Enormous Room." The most unusual—at least in terms of performance—is "My Three Moons," which is played on three instruments simultaneously. "I travel with three basses, and since people have seen me play 'Watson & Crick' [on two basses] and noticed the third one there, I started getting asked, 'Why don't you play all three of 'em at the same time?' I realized eventually I was going to have to live up to that challenge! But I have to say I wouldn't ever have performed or recorded the piece if I hadn't felt good about it from a *musical* standpoint. There are a lot of fun things in there. For instance, I'll play a pattern with one hand and then switch it to another bass; since it's in a different tuning it'll be a different sound. Of course, to realize that you'd have to try to play it—and I don't suppose many people will do that!"

Michael played the other solo pieces on the Hyperbass alone, although each has a twist. "Adhan," which has an eerie, atmospheric sound, was played with two EBows held in Michael's right hand. "They're kind of big, so I can activate only the two outer strings [tuned *B♭* and *F*] with them. It makes for some curious left-hand fingerings!" The funky "Monkey Businessman," played in a *CFB♭E♭* tuning, uses mostly slapping and strumming techniques. It was recorded with a combination of direct and room sounds: "We recorded it to an Alesis ADAT with a separate [magnetic-pickup] signal from each string on its own channel and the transducers on another channel. We put those five channels into the board, and then we sent the sound from the magnetic pickups to an amp in the room and the sound from the transducers to the studio monitors. Then we miked the room and recorded that." The result is a gigantic sound that makes the Hyperbass sound as if it's a hundred feet tall. The disc closes with "The Enormous Room," which takes full advantage of the retuning capabilities of the instrument. "That one has the most tuning moves of any piece I've ever done. I haven't counted, but there are somewhere between 12 to 16 basic tunings and maybe a hundred tuning switches. But this piece is more about composition than it is about any of the techniques themselves. This piece was a chance to explore thematic playing. It doesn't have a typical AABA structure; it has themes that are presented in different ways. I'm really proud of it as a composition."

The rockers have a slightly different focus. "I wanted those tunes to be simpler than ones I've done in the past. I thought it was important to write some stuff that could be jammed on." The jammers included guitarists Steve Morse, who played on "Snakes Got Legs" and "You Offered Only Parabolas," and Alex Skolnick, who is on "Disturbed" and "Cruel and Unusual." "It's interesting, because both of them feel they've been pigeonholed unfairly. This record gave them a chance to break out of that." Manring says former Journey drummer Steve Smith, who played on four tunes, also found the *Thonk* sessions liberating. "People thought of him for a long time as just an arena-rock drummer, but he's got a lot more music in him than that. I think he's managed to get rid of that perception recently and be taken seriously as a jazz drummer."

"On a Day of Many Angels" features Smith and pianist Phillip Aaberg. "That's one of the pieces I composed to bridge the large stylistic gap between tunes like 'Bad Hair Day' and 'The Enormous Room.' It was

Michael Manring Selected Discography

On Windham Hill unless otherwise noted.

Solo albums: *The Book of Flame*, Alchemy; *Thonk*, High Street; *Drastic Measures*; *Toward the Center of the Night*; *Unusual Weather*. **With Michael Hedges:** *Torched*; *Taproot*; *Live from the Double Planet*; *Watching My Life Go By*, Open Air; *Aerial Boundaries*; *Breakfast in the Field*. **With Attention Deficit:** *The Idiot King*, Magna Carta; *Attention Deficit*, Magna Carta. **With Sadhappy:** *Good Day Bad Dream*, Periscope. **With the Skol-Patrol:** *The Skol-Patrol*, Grey Streak. **With William Ackerman:** *The Opening of Doors*; *Imaginary Roads*; *Conferring with the Moon*; *Past Light*; *A Windham Hill Retrospective*. **With Montreux:** *Let Them Say*; *Sign Language*; *A Windham Hill Retrospective*. **With John Gorka:** *Company You Keep*, Red House; *Temporary Road*, High Street; *Jack's Crows*, High Street. **With Patty Larkin:** *Perishable Fruit*; (both on High Street) *Angels Running*; *Tango*. **With Peppino D'Agostino:** *Acoustic Spirit*, Shanachie. **With Darol Anger:** *Heritage*, Six Degrees. **With Mike Marshall:** *Brasil: Duets*, EarthBeat. **With Darol Anger & Mike Marshall:** *Chiaroscuro*. **With Heritage:** *Heritage*, Koch International. **With Holly Near:** *Early Warnings*, Appleseed; *Sky Dances*, Redwood. **With Opafire:** *Opafire*, RCA/Novus. **With Barbara Higbie:** *Signs of Life*. **With John Durant:** *Anatomy of a Wish*, Alchemy. **With Carl Weingarten:** *Escape Silence*, Multiphase. **With Henry Kaiser & Wadada Leo Smith:** *Yo, Miles!*, Shanachie. **With Suzanne Ciani:** *Meditations*, Seventh Wave. **With Danny Heines:** *One Heart Wild*, Silver Wave. **With Scott McGill & Vic Stevens:** (both on Free Electric Sound) *Controlled by Radar*; *Addition by Subtraction*. **With David Cullen:** *Equilibré*, Acoustic Music. **With Monks of Doom:** *Forgery*, IRS. **With Altazor:** *Concurrencia*, Redwood. **With Mike Mainieri:** *Come Together, Vol. 2*, NYC. **With various artists:** *Windham Hill Guitar Sampler II*; *A Winter's Solstice I–VI*; *Summer Solstice, An Evening with Windham Hill Live*.

Manring's Menagerie

Michael Manring's relentless search for new horizons has led him to experiment endlessly with both musical form and musical instruments. During his career he's been through a whole roomful of basses, including axes by Music Man, Steinberger, Paul Reed Smith, Riverhead (fretted and fretless Unicorns), a Larrivée 5-string acoustic bass guitar, and a Fretless Paroutaud Music Laboratories Infinite Sustain 5-string prototype.

Michael's main basses are graphite-neck Zons, and he is actively involved in their design. He has three prime basses, all of them 4-strings: The first is the Zon Michael Manring Hyperbass, a unique fretless that took more than a year to develop. It has a three-octave fingerboard and can be retuned to dozens of different combinations, thanks to four Hipshot Xtender Keys on the headstock and a special bridge with two levers for raising and lowering the saddles. The electronics feature both a quadrophonic Bartolini pickup and four Fishman transducers, three mounted in the body and one in the neck between the nut and the first fret. The Hyperbass can be operated in either mono or quad mode. Manring's second Zon bass is a stock Legacy Elite II Special fretless—well, *almost* stock; it does have two Hipshots. His third axe is a one-of-a-kind Zon headless with a small poplar body and a fretted graphite neck. Its twin pickups are Bartolini multi-coils, and the tuning bridge was made by ABM. In addition to being small enough to stow in an airplane's overhead compartment, it can be strapped on low and played simultaneously with the Hyperbass for performances of "Watson & Crick," from *Drastic Measures*. (For the three-bass performance of "My Three Moons," Manring needs an assistant to hold the Elite II.) Michael's strings, which come in *lots* of different gauges, are D'Addario XL220 nickel roundwounds. He likes to change them before each performance or recording session.

Manring also has a Zon fretted headless prototype, a fretless Zon Legacy Elite 6-string, and a Zon Legacy Elite 10-string. For a normal person, that would mean it's a 5-string bass tuned *BEADG* with a lighter-gauge string doubling each bass string one octave up. For Michael, though, it means he's got ten strings he can (and does) tune to ten different notes.

In addition to his mastery of plucking, slapping, and tapping, Manring has also pioneered the use of the EBow with the bass guitar. A small electronic device held in the picking hand, the EBow was designed to give guitarists the kind of endless sustain violinists take for granted. The device contains an electromagnetic oscillator that sets a string in motion and keeps it going; manipulating its position over the string offers different timbral possibilities, and placing it over a magnetic pickup produces "interference effects" that can sound quite startling. Although it's difficult to get a big bass string going with an EBow, Manring has found that the combination of ultralight strings (the Hyperbass set is .020, .032, .042, .052) plus various "string-starting" techniques allows him to take full advantage of the EBow. He has five: Two are what he calls "old EBows," which have a slightly different oscillation pattern—and thus produce a slightly different sound—than his two newer models. The fifth EBow is a special model that works only on harmonics.

Although Manring's instruments are complicated, his stage rig is fairly simple. For clinics and small venues, he uses an SWR Baby Blue combo. His rack has three Rane equalizers (one for each bass) and a Lexicon LXP-5 multi-effects. To route the signals into the LXP-5, he uses a MIDI-Man Mini-Mixer. On the floor he's got a Boss tuner and a Digital Music Ground Control pedal for switching effects settings. To generate MIDI continuous-controller information, he uses a Boss volume pedal. Other effects include an ADA MP-2 preamp, a Lexicon Vortex and JamMan, an Alesis Quadraverb, a Yamaha SPX-90, a DigiTech RP10, a Deltalab Effectron II, an MXR 01 reverb, a Zoom 9002, and "a bunch of stompboxes." To record he usually takes the signal out of an SWR Baby Blue directly to the tape deck. When he's working in large hall, Michael either rents a high-power rig or plugs into the house system.

an attempt to do a power ballad that wasn't corny. The harmony is pretty jazzy, but I wanted to play it using some of the rock techniques I used on the other songs. There's a *lot* of EBow on that one."

Although Manring notes *Thonk* takes him in a bold new direction from his first three solo albums, it has one defining thread: "I feel it's true to myself."

Web site

www.manthing.com

Manring for the Rest of Us

For the December '98 Bass Player, *Richard Johnston got Michael Manring and John Patitucci together to discuss their current albums. Manring's was* The Book of Flame, *whose grooves inspired this lesson.*

So maybe you're not into playing a 10-string, tuning to minor 2nds, or performing on three basses at once. There's still lots of stuff you can learn from Michael Manring. Beyond oddities of instrumentation and execution, many of Michael's tunes are based on solid grooves he twists in unique ways.

Example 1a shows the foundation of "Adult Content/Brief Nudity": a syncopated one-note line that draws much of its motion from Michael's surgically precise articulation. Over that Manring lays a squirty-toned counterpoint (**Ex. 1b**). You can combine the two parts, however, and add Michael's 16th-note synth squiggle for a Bootsy-meets-Webern

Ex. 1a

Ex. 1b

Ex. 1c

line that's sure to worsen your drummer's nervous tics (**Ex. 1c**). In the brief contrasting section that starts at 0:40 (**Ex. 2a**), Michael makes those 16th-notes pinprick-sharp, including the Jaco-ish fill that ends with a skittering triplet. **Example 2b** shows his melodic variation of that fill. (We've avoided putting key signatures on these modal lines; the chord symbols reflect the overall modal colors.)

Though **Ex. 3a** looks daunting, it's actually fairly easy to play the harmonic-accented whole-tone line from "The Book of Lies"—if you tune minor-7th/whole-step/whole-step. (It takes agile left-hand work, though, to cop the correct note lengths.) We liked the idea of using harmonics to outline a whole-tone sound, however; **Ex. 3b** shows a standard-tuning version centered on *C*. Your own explorations will yield other interesting possibilities.

Ex. 2a

Ex. 2b

Ex. 3a

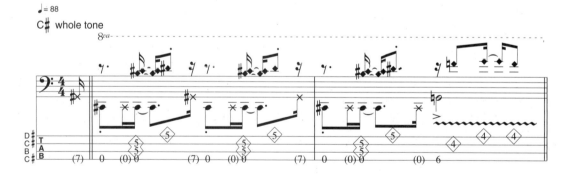

Ex. 3b

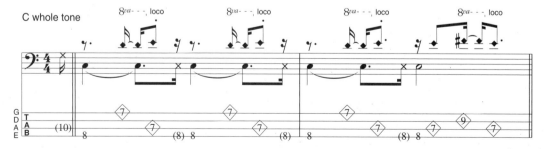

Careful articulation is again crucial in the sputtering line from "Theseus in the Rain" (**Ex. 4a**). The tonality combines whole-tone and diminished scales. To bring the lick back to the real world, turn the *F#*'s into *G*'s. Voilà!—a funk line in *C*, complete with bluesy 3rds in bars 2 and 8. Michael tosses in a little lunar night music with the slower contrasting section that starts at 2:39; **Ex. 4b** shows the 5-string-friendly part that starts with an unctuous *F*-to-*D* slide.

Ready for re-entry? The **Ex. 5** line from "Your Ad" is simple, fun, and funky. Run it through the cycle of 5ths and try it with octaves instead of ♭7's. Then take a well-deserved break.

Ex. 4a

Ex. 4b

Ex. 5

CHAPTER 4

Dazzling Doublers
CHRISTIAN McBRIDE • CHRIS WOOD • BRIAN BROMBERG

Often elusive to even the most exclusive acoustic and electric bassists, the art of doubling has come a long way from Jamerson to Clarke to Patitucci. Today's loftiest doublers display equal parts wisdom, craft, and vision—in the process, frequently developing two distinct musical voices.

CHRISTIAN McBRIDE
Vertical Climb

Interviewed by Chris Jisi, October 1998 and May 2003.

CHRISTIAN McBRIDE'S HORIZONS CONTINUE TO EXPAND. While he maintains a hectic pace as a jazz sideman—working with everyone from Diana Krall and John Scofield to Wayne Shorter and McCoy Tyner—he has also joined former young lions such as drummer Brian Blade and trumpeter Roy Hargrove in shedding the musical confines of the jazz purist's three-piece suit. McBride's recent output extends to jazz-related artists such as George Duke, Natalie Cole, David Sanborn, and Kenny Rankin. It also has reached beyond to mega pop stars Sting, Paul Simon, and Carly Simon, and hip-hoppers D'Angelo and D'Angelo/Roots drummer Ahmir "?uestlove" Thompson, with whom McBride formed the phat-grooving Philadelphia Experiment.

The quality of Christian's solo work has been responsible for much of this growth. Since the 1998 release of his third album, *A Family Affair*—in which he first exposed his Philly-fueled groove and solo chops on fretted and fretless electric bass—the industry has taken notice. Says McBride, "I can't tell you how many times someone from the R&B or rock or smooth jazz world has said to me, 'With your sense of rhythm I would've called you in a heartbeat had I known you play electric.'" More important, McBride's merging of acoustic and electric jazz, which he explored further on 2000's *Sci-Fi*, is helping him shape his own musical voice. McBride's most definitive statement can be heard on *Vertical Vision*. Having explored the possibilities of blending electric current and acoustic attitude, he at last sounds at home manning his upright on a funk tune or bestowing bebop with his fretless—thanks largely to the finest edition of the Christian McBride Band to date.

Born in the bass-rich city of Philadelphia on May 31, 1972, McBride first leaned toward the low end via his dad, Lee Smith, who played electric bass with various Philly soul stars and Cuban percussionist Mongo Santamaria. When Christian was nine his mother bought him a Kingston electric, and he began playing along with R&B records and radio. Two years later—inspired by his uncle, jazz upright bassist Howard Cooper—Christian took up the acoustic bass at home and in the school orchestra, and dove headlong into jazz. In 1986

Wynton Marsalis heard Christian play at Philly's fertile High School for the Creative and Performing Arts and encouraged him to set his sights on New York City. McBride arrived there three years later, at age 17, carrying a partial scholarship to Juilliard. But his studies were eventually derailed by gigs with jazz notables such as Bobby Watson, Freddie Hubbard, Benny Green, Joe Henderson, and Ray Brown and his SuperBass band, with John Clayton.

Christian McBride

Early in '03 I met the congenial Christian at his Upper East Side Manhattan apartment to take a look at *Vertical Vision* as well as his career.

What's your main issue when going between acoustic and electric bass?

The fact that they're two different instruments with two different touches. The upright requires more sheer muscle and stamina to play and to get a tone out of—especially with regard to left-hand articulation, which is the key to projecting a big sound. That's different from the electric bass, where much of the sound comes from the pickups and amp. As a result you almost need less muscle and more relaxation. I learned that lesson when I first came back to playing a lot of electric with Joshua Redman and my own band after a seven-year layoff. At first I found my chops were getting tired much quicker than they did on the acoustic. Then I realized I was thinking about how the electric enabled me to play more fast, technical material—but I was using an upright touch to do it. It was like a boxer going into the ring and throwing everything he's got in the first round. Another problem was the callus on my right-hand middle finger had gotten so big and hard from the acoustic that I couldn't feel anything. So I had to learn how to play Gary Willis style: lighten up and play with less force, and let the amp do some of the work. By the way, the same thing happened to me on upright during my "purist" period, when I was encouraged to play without an amp. I figured I would have to really dig in to be heard and I ended up developing tendinitis in both arms, and I had to lay off for two months.

How did you correct that situation?

The first thing that opened my eyes was seeing Paul Chambers on the famous 1960 Miles Davis film with the Gil Evans big band. He was playing so cool and so light, and he was still getting a huge sound. Then watching Ray Brown and Ron Carter live confirmed that approach. Another major influence was [former *Tonight Show* bassist] Robert Hurst. He maintains a comfortable, medium action on his acoustic, and he plays with his right-hand fingers perpendicular to the strings whether he's walking or burning through a solo. So he always gets a big, meaty, consistent sound. Most acoustic bassists move their fingers perpendicular to the strings—electric-style—only when they have to play fast or take a solo, and they lose a lot of tone.

Do you have a preference between the two basses?

Right now I'd say I need both instruments to express whatever voice I've developed to this point. I love the challenge of playing the fretless, yet I still have to practice more on acoustic to keep my chops up. I started on electric, so that music is my roots, but the acoustic is Mother Earth for me, and you always have to go home to Mom!

Most acoustic bassists who play fretless go for unfinished fingerboards and a dark, woody, upright sound; you have a more singing, modern tone.

Jaco gave the instrument such an identity, and I wanted to come out of that tradition—the same way the upright has a traditional sound I try to achieve. Beyond that, hopefully something original and musical comes out when I pick up the fretless. Actually, when I covered "Havona" [a Jaco tune on Weather Report's *Heavy Weather*] on *Sci-Fi*, I felt uncomfortable tampering with the original, so I figured the best thing to do was cover it as is. But then I thought if I play electric on it that might border on blasphemy! So I decided it might add a twist if I played it on upright.

Many say the fretless is harder to play in tune than the upright.

It certainly is; for one thing, there are no landmarks with regard to the shape of the neck or the body as there are on the upright. I purposely didn't get fret lines on my bass, so I could really focus on getting my intonation together. I remember for the first couple of months I was ready to take it back; I just couldn't seem to get it together. I was cool in the lower positions—but once I got further up the neck, look out!

What's your groove philosophy?

I like what guitarist Freddie Green said when asked how he was able to swing so hard with Count Basie's band: "Man, I just stay out of the way." In any style of music, the keys to finding a groove and locking into that zone are listening and not playing too much.

Who are some of your early groove heroes?

My father, Lee Smith, with Mongo Santamaria and on Philly International sessions; Ray Brown, of course, who was like my other musical dad; Paul Chambers; Ron Carter; Jimmy Blanton; and Sam Jones—I think he's unsung. On electric: James Jamerson, Larry Graham, as well as Bootsy Collins, Bernard Odum, and the rest of the James Brown bassists. For funk, the James Brown/Bootsy period is my favorite—yet my most frustrating. I've mentioned the importance of simplicity, but Bootsy's lines on "Sex Machine" and "Soul Power" are far from simple. There's a James Brown/Bobby Byrd duet called "Since You've Been Gone" with Bootsy and [drummer] Clyde Stubblefield. Now, you can talk about lopsided funk with rhythm sections like Paul Jackson and Mike Clarke with the Headhunters or Rocco Prestia and Dave Garibaldi with Tower of Power—but man, if you're not paying attention on this track, you will *not* find the *one*, because no one hits it!

What was your concept for Vertical Vision?

It's a continuation of the *Sci-Fi* direction, which is my attempt to combine the acoustic and electric sound—not just on bass, but with keyboards, and this time adding flute with tenor and soprano sax. The main difference is this CD is much more band-oriented. This is the first group I've had where everyone is on the same page; we've been together since September of 2000 and we know and trust each other's musical instincts. Geoff Keezer is my X-factor, he's known as a straightahead pianist, but he's way into funk and classical and he even dabbles in heavy metal guitar. [Saxophonist] Ron Blake is my rock, he's hung in with me through several editions of my band. And [drummer] Terreon Gully brings the whole sound together and into focus. All three are fearless and I need that from my band, considering how we cross styles. These guys don't back down from anything.

To me, Terreon is the key because he keeps everything firmly seated in jazz.

Exactly! I know a lot of drummers who can play both sides—jazz and groove—but they do it almost *too* authentically; they sit all the way in each bag, which is good in a general sense. But in my band I'm looking for the diversity to visit certain idioms without setting up camp there. Terreon provides that while retaining a jazz sensibility. He reminds me of Jack DeJohnette: When he plays groove-oriented music it's still very loose and has that link to the early R&B feels that so many cherish and strive for now.

So you would describe yourself as a jazz musician.

Absolutely—everything I do is rooted in a jazz. That's what the music has always been about to me: someone taking a standard, show tune, or Latin piece and making it a jazz vehicle. I want to keep that concept and add some electricity, like Weather Report or Herbie Hancock's Mwandishi band did. I'm not doing anything special or new, but maybe I'm one of the few guys who's not scared to shake up his reputation. Like many of my peers, I'm searching and trying to find my own voice, and the only way to do that is to take chances. At this point I couldn't care less if I get bad reviews; I think when an artist takes risks it will ultimately lead to good musical results.

What's the story behind the "false" opener, "Circa 1990"?

Bridal Gear

Vertically, Christian McBride favors a 3/4-sized German upright of unknown origin. It sports a David Gage Realist pickup system, D'Addario Helicore light-gauge strings, and a John Norwood Lee French-style bow. His backup is a 3/4-sized Juzek. Horizontally, Christian plucks a maple-fingerboard Pensa J-Bass–style fretless, a '75 Fender Jazz, and a Ruyou Motoyama fretted 5-string. All are strung with D'Addario Prism stainless-steel roundwounds.

Live he plugs into a Glockenklang Soul Bass head with Epifani 4x10 and 1x15 cabinets. For smaller jazz gigs he takes his Acoustic Image Clarus head, a popular choice among New York upright players. His pedalboard includes a Morley A/B switch, Boss PS-5 Super Shifter, Electro-Harmonix Big Muff, Dunlop Cry Baby wah, Ernie Ball Volume Pedal, Boss SYB-3 Bass Synth Pedal, Boss RV-3 Digital Reverb/Delay, Voodoo Lab Pedal Power 2, and Line 6 MM4 Modulation Modeler. On *Vertical Vision* he recorded his upright through a combination of Neumann U47 and U87 mics and direct signal from the Realist pickup to an Avalon U5 DI/preamp. His electrics went to the board through the Avalon.

It's a little joking stab at the way the so-called young lions were perceived during that period—in our suits and ties playing traditional jazz. Then we abruptly rip into "Technicolor Dreams." When we mastered "Circa" we took out all the highs and lows and added some sampled vinyl record static to get that thin 1930s sound. On the flip side, I've done three electric discs now, but I'm definitely going to make another straightahead album at some point. I love swinging and playing that style of music, and as Ray Brown taught us, the bass player's job first and foremost is to play some time—if you want to keep some money in the bank and food in the fridge, you'll walk!

Did your desire to play electric music genuinely wane circa 1990?

To a large degree, yes. I was young and I got with a certain crew of straightahead musicians who brainwashed me against electric music—even though as a kid I was into playing all styles on both basses. Around 1995 I started to come around. I did David Sanborn's CD *Pearls*, and someone said, "That's very unlike you." It suddenly hit me that people actually think I don't like other kinds of music—that I'm a real jazz Republican. I put my first band together around that time, and I knew I would eventually incorporate electric bass. When I told people—even the musicians in the band—I'd get strange looks!

What was the inspiration for "Technicolor Nightmare"?

People think it's funk or fusion, but it's mostly rock 'n' roll: Led Zeppelin with John Paul Jones and Jon Bonham, early Yes, John Entwistle. I was trying to blend all of that with a jazz concept. I realized I could have itched too badly to play electric and really rock out, so I decided to stay on acoustic and drive it from there, and it worked well. In addition to miking my upright, we went direct from the Realist pickup to an Avalon U5 [DI/preamp], which is a first for me on my albums. On a hard-driving song like this I knew the mic would be too broad, so we used a bit of DI to get some punch in there. I also overdubbed the head bass line on my '75 Jazz Bass to tighten it up—plus Geoff plays it on organ.

The straightahead "The Wizard of Montara" is a good example of your pushing the stylistic envelope.

I didn't want it to be just a traditional jazz tune, in keeping with the album's concept, so I pondered what I could do. I played the walking groove on upright, but I told Geoff not to play any acoustic piano—and of course he took it a step further and played a detuned Moog synth! Then I decided to take my solo on my '75 Jazz Bass and overdub a track on which I double the solo on bowed acoustic bass; I needed a couple of days to learn my own solo and practice it with a bow. There were a couple of notes I couldn't quite figure out, so I said let me pretend I'm playing electric—what do I *think* I would have done here?—and then I got it. The two-bass tandem can also be heard on the little solo breaks between sections.

How do you incorporate bowing into "Lejos De Usted"?

For the intro I overdubbed three bowed notes behind Ron's flute. Later the melody was laying so nice that I didn't want a typical solo over changes, so I told the guys to loop the melody and I sort of answered it in the holes. I wanted to do something like Miles Davis's *Nefertiti*, where instead of soloing, Miles, Wayne Shorter, and Herbie Hancock play off of each other through the melody. Then I asked the engineer, Joe Ferla, to give the notes a washy sound, so he used his rack gear to add some stereo flanging.

Who are your bow influences?

Mainly Paul Chambers and some Slam Stewart, but for the kind of lyrical playing here I was coming more from an Edgar Meyer and David Murray approach.

Live you use effects on both electric and upright. Why and how do you use them with your upright?

I can't recall too many other players using them—aside from Melvin Jackson with AACM [the Association for the Advancement of Creative Musicians]—but since my musical M.O. with my band has always been about growth and non-conventionalism, I figured, why not? My pedalboard has a Morley A/B switch, so both my electric and acoustic are looped in. From there I just let the musical moment dictate what pedal to try— sometimes I'll use them with the acoustic like I would on electric—for funk ostinatos or soloing, and other times I'll try something more radical, maybe using the bow or on a straightahead tune. The only problem I run into is feedback, particularly with the Big Muff and the Boss Digital Reverb/Delay, so I have to experiment more to see if I can control it with touch or gear settings.

"The Ballad of Little Girl Dancer" is another track with an interesting solo-section approach.

The head at the beginning and end of that song is heavily inspired by a track on Wayne Shorter's *High Life* album called "Midnight in Carlotta's Hair"—Wayne is my main influence as a composer. However, the middle goes to an open one-chord vamp. I told both Geoff and Ron to solo in whatever style they felt, and they played off of each other. It's another thing we're getting into that we borrow from the Weather Report canon—where nobody is soloing, yet everybody is soloing. I like the sketchiness of—is somebody blowing, or what exactly *is* going on?

You hold up your end with a prominent improvised fretless groove. How did you develop that ability?

Since the open section was a gray area, I sensed Geoff and Ron were moving cautiously, so I figured I could help boost them along a bit while still trying to stay out of their way. Overall, the key to playing that style is having your improvisational skills together. Jazz teaches you to think every bar, to constantly search for something new and find different ways to make the music happen. Whereas in rock or R&B you're usually taught to be disciplined—to find a groove that makes the entire song work and not stray from it too often. So the benefit of being able to do both is you can lay down a groove yet keep it loose and find fresh ideas on top.

"Song for Maya" has an Afro-Cuban edge.

That's Ron's tune; he lives up in Washington Heights [upper Manhattan], where that music is playing constantly. We tried to give it some Eddie Palmieri attitude. Actually, I feel a little uncomfortable with that track because I played a sort of floating, pseudo–Afro Cuban part, and then Danny Sadownick overdubbed some really authentic percussion, but I didn't have time to change my part to better fit what he played. It takes me back to a mid-'90s session I did for Jeanie Bryson [*Tonight I Need You So*] with folks like Danilo Perez, Ignacio Berroa, and Paquito D'Rivera. I was the only non-Latino, so I knew right away I was in trouble. They counted off the first song, a fast samba, and we didn't get past the *second* bar before I heard, "Wait! Hold It! Hey, McBride . . ." They all came over and gave me the crash course in what to play, but I loved gettin' schooled. Now I can feel the clave and I know whether it's 2/3 or 3/2, but I'm still far from being an expert.

Is your cover of "Boogie Woogie Waltz" inspired by the original Weather Report version on the 1973 album Sweetnighter?

Not really. But let me say that Miroslav Vitous—who played upright on that track along with saxophonist Andrew White on electric bass—is one of the baddest cats ever. His *Infinite Search* is a desert island disc for me. Our inspiration comes more from bootlegs with Jaco or Alphonso Johnson, especially an intense 1974 version at Northwestern University with Alphonso. I decided to start with just the wah bass, which is my fretless through a Big Muff. Then the held notes are full throttle: plucked and bowed upright, fretless, Jazz Bass, keyboard bass, and organ bass—our intention was to blow your speakers out! The main groove is all fretless with a drop of upright about one minute into the tune. Toward the end I reharmonize the melody with different pedal tones, and then the wall of overdubbed basses comes back. The design of the track is that each section gets bigger than the one before.

Christian McBride Selected Discography

Solo albums: *Vertical Vision*, Warner Bros.; (all on Verve) *Sci-Fi*; *A Family Affair*; *Number Two Express*; *Gettin' to It.* **With the Jaco Pastorius Big Band:** *Word of Mouth Revisited*, Heads Up. **With Sting:** *All This Time*, A&M. **With Joe Henderson:** (both on Verve) *Lush Life*; *Double Rainbow.* **With Chick Corea:** *Remembering Bud Powell*, Stretch. **With Geoff Keezer:** *Turn Up the Quiet*, Sony. **With Benny Green:** *Naturally*, Telarc; *Greens*, Blue Note. **With Joshua Redman:** *Mood Swing*, Warner Bros. **With Ray Brown and John Clayton:** *SuperBass, Vol. 2*, Telarc; *SuperBass*, Telarc. **With the Philadelphia Experiment:** *The Philadelphia Experiment*, Ropeadope/Atlantic. **With David Sanborn:** *Pearls*, Elektra. **With Benny Carter:** *Legends*, Musicmasters. **With Roy Haynes:** *Té Voux*, Dreyfuss. **With Wallace Roney:** *Obsession*, Muse. **With Roy Hargrove/Stephen Scott Trio:** *Parker's Mood*, Verve. **With Roy Hargrove:** *Public Eye*, RCA Novus. **With Joe Lovano:** *Tenor Legacy*, Blue Note. **With Johnny Griffin:** *Chicago, New York, Paris*, Verve. **With Milt Jackson:** *Burnin' in the Woodhouse*, Qwest. **With Jim Hall:** *Jim Hall & Basses*, Telarc. **With Freddie Hubbard:** *Live at Fat Tuesday*, Music Masters. **With John Scofield:** *Works for Me*, Verve. **With Kathleen Battle:** *So Many Stars*, Sony Classics. **With Bob James:** *Straight Up*, Warner Bros. **With George Benson:** *Absolute Benson*, GRP. **With Pete Belasco:** *Get It Together*, Verve Forecast. **With Kenny Kirkland:** *Kenny Kirkland*, GRP. **With McCoy Tyner:** *What the World Needs Now*, GRP; *Prelude and Sonata*, Fantasy. **With Diana Krall:** *The Look of Love*, Verve; *Love Scenes*, Impulse. **With George Duke:** *Face the Music*, BPM; *After Hours*, Warner Bros. **With Jimmy Smith:** *Damn!*, Verve. **With Natalie Cole:** *Ask a Woman Who Knows*, Verve. **With Russell Malone:** *Heartstrings*, Verve. **With Dean Brown:** *Here*, ESC. **With various artists:** *Fingerpainting: The Music of Herbie Hancock*, Verve.

How did your work with Sting come about?

My guess is he heard me on Chris Botti's CD *Night Sessions*, because everyone on that disc—Kipper, Dominic Miller, Manu Katché, and Chris—is in Sting's band. They knew Sting wanted some acoustic bass on the record he was working on, *All This Time*, so they recommended me. I knew a few Police songs and I covered "Walking on the Moon" on *Sci-Fi*, but I wasn't totally familiar with his work. So I got a Police box set and all of his solo records, and I did a crash course for a week before flying to Tuscany for two more weeks of rehearsing. The *All This Time* DVD was my first gig, so I had all my little chord charts and cheat sheets onstage.

What sort of direction did he give you?

He stayed on me a lot at first, probably because I didn't know his music cold and he wasn't that familiar with my style—plus I was playing his instrument—bass. But it was cool, because I wanted to learn the music thoroughly. He'd coach me on a song, but not stylistically. Once I got the parts down he'd let me embellish them and make them my own. The jazz flavor of the band and the jazzy versions of some of his tunes obviously suited me, and his R&B/Motown-ish arrangements of "All This Time" and "If You Love Somebody Set Them Free" were right up my alley.

Did you play any electric?

Only on a few songs in the first rehearsals, otherwise no. He plays his old Fender on some songs, so he made a rule: "This band ain't big enough for two electric bassists." I picked his bass up once and played a fast crazy run, and he gave me this look of death [*laughs*]. But it's all in fun; there's always some ribbing going on. The rest of the band and crew say, "Sting, you've got big balls hiring a guy who's better than you!"

We do several concerts a month, and I recorded some tracks in L.A. for him. He actually did a song with us on *Vertical Vision*. I wrote a tune and some lyrics with the idea that he would come in and finish it and make it his own, which he did. But we only had a day in the studio and we couldn't get the vocals down exactly like we wanted, so we're going to save it for my next CD.

While he was there he asked to hear some of the other tracks. I'd play them and he'd ask if he could have a look at the bass part, and I could see him playing air bass along with the music. He has a real hunger for knowledge and tremendous respect for all music, which is why to me he's hands-down one of the greatest musicians of any generation.

Who's on your list of bass favorites these days?

All the usual legends: The late Ray Brown, Ron Carter, Paul Chambers, Dave Holland, James Jamerson, Larry Graham, Bootsy, Stanley, Jaco. Among upright peers I dig John Patitucci, Robert Hurst, Peter Washington, Ira Coleman, and Eric Revis, and there's a young player working with Dianne Reeves named Reuben Rogers—he's one of those rare guys who has a great feel for both acoustic and electric. On the electric side I love Matt Garrison—he's *sick*—as well as Marcus Miller, Victor Wooten and Oteil Burbridge, and Richard Bona.

What challenges do you face as a bassist/bandleader?

I've found that my biggest challenge has nothing to do with music: It's the traveling. There was a time when you'd go the airport and a ticket agent would see an upright bass and the rest of the instrument cases, realize that it was a band, and either waive the excess-weight charges or add on $50. Since 9/11 they've gone by the book, and almost every airline has raised their excess rates—especially in Europe. Our first flight on tour in summer 2001 was from Italy to Switzerland and they wanted to charge us $4,000 to put all our gear on the plane. Now I try to set up the tour route so we can take buses instead of planes all the time. Other than that, I just have to sweat bullets about whether I'm going to bring home any money! [*Laughs.*]

Web site

www.christianmcbride.com

Vertical Decisions

CHRISTIAN McBRIDE'S *VERTICAL VISION* PALETTE includes bowed, plucked, and effected upright, and fretted, fretless, and effected electric—colors he swirls by using them in nontraditional settings.

    Example 1a shows the main groove of "Technicolor Nightmare." Although Christian played it on upright, he advises us to "keep it in the rock spirit in which it was created." **Example 1b** captures the head-ending band unison riff. In bar 2 he plays the descending *B♭*, *F*, and *C* (starting on the "and" of beat *two*) with his fourth finger, making for a tricky position shift leap to play the ascending *E♭*, *A♭*, and *D♭* that follow with his index finger.

Ex. 1a

Ex. 1b

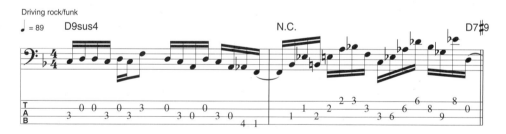

Ex. 2a

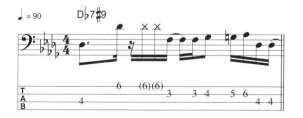

Ex. 2b

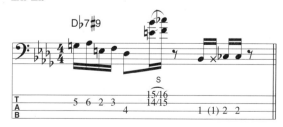

Examples 2a–2d recall four fretless Pensa groove interpretations during the open blowing section of "The Ballad of Little Girl Dancer." Example 2a sets the basic shape. Example 2b introduces cool melodic movement utilizing lower approach notes (keep the first note short), as well as an ear-catching double-stop. Example 2c adds more bluesy melodicism (anticipate the first note slightly), as beat *one* becomes the variation point in most measures. In Ex. 2d he again varies beat *one*, grabbing greasy ascending octaves starting on the dominant 7.

Example 3 contains the first seven bars of "Precious One." Christian played upright on the tune. "The line was written out by Geoff Keezer, who doubles it with his left hand, so it's obviously very pianistic. Practice it slowly at first, especially bar 6, which comes down the *G* string until the *F♯*."

Turning to Christian's first electric outing, 1998's *A Family Affair*, **Example 4** recalls a portion of his arco solo from "I'm Coming Home." "The bow allows you to play some real greasy, nasty stuff on this kind of groove because you can hold notes a long time, alter their tone, and really bend them." **Example 5a** is the main 5-string groove from "Brown Funk (For Ray)," which McBride originally wrote for the *SuperBass* album with Ray Brown and John Clayton. "Ray asked me to write something funky, so he got Ray Brown by way of James Brown. This version is a lot more over the top, with a heavy Marcus Miller influence." **Example 5b** contains part of Christian's 5-string-with-wah-pedal solo. "I hadn't planned on soloing at all in the tune, but the rest of my band insisted." **Example 5c** has a segment of McBride's 5-string fuzz bass solo (via his Boss Bass Overdrive) from "Brown Funk." "Bootsy and Larry Graham definitely influenced my fuzz approach."

Ex. 2c

Ex. 2d

Ex. 3

Ex. 4

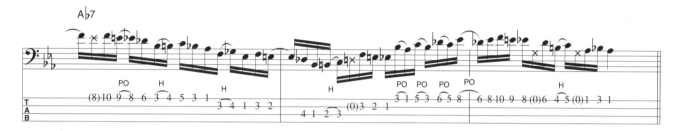

Ex. 5a

Ex. 5b

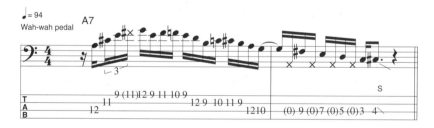

Ex. 5c

CHRIS WOOD
Jam Man

Interviewed by Chris Jisi, October 1998 and June 2002.

THE BOOMING UNDERGROUND JAM-BAND SCENE has brought format-busting sounds into all corners of contemporary music, and it's had the same effect on bass, both electric and acoustic. There's no better example than the work of Chris Wood of Medeski Martin & Wood, the veteran avant-groove New York trio that has become one of the elected leaders of the Jam Nation. Through his groove-intensive improvisations with keyboardist John Medeski and drummer Billy Martin, Wood has captured the bass world's pulse. Ponder any of the early millennium trends in bassdom—feel over flash, jams as opposed to set compositions, doubling on electric and upright, retro gear and grooves, low-end-loaded mixes over full-range bite—and Chris fits the profile. But Wood's gift goes deeper than en-vogue vamps. His extensive jazz training and "Downtown"-sharpened instincts have enabled him to distinguish subtle shadings both in the sounds of the electric and acoustic bass and the various hybrid feels he explores. His resulting visionary spin has shed new light on the concept of groove.

Born in Pasadena, California, and raised in Boulder, Colorado, Wood expressed his first musical impulse at age 12 when he took to a Gibson-copy electric bass his parents mistakenly bought for his older brother (who wanted an electric guitar). With the guidance of a local teacher and his high school band director—who encouraged him to also play upright—and with the sounds of Larry Graham, James Jamerson, Jaco, Stanley, Paul Jackson, Charles Mingus, and Cachao in his ears, Chris headed to the New England Conservatory of Music. There, he experienced lengthy, mind-expanding one-on-one sessions with Dave Holland, lessons with pianist Geri Allen, and performances with drummer Bob Moses' band of young genre-crossing musicians, including John Medeski.

Chris and John moved to Manhattan in 1991, figuring on careers as straightahead jazz sidemen and hooking up with Billy Martin on a trio gig at the Village Gate. Martin's organic style, shaped by his stints with Downtown heroes John Zorn and John Lurie, ignited a like-minded approach in Wood and Medeski, and MMW was born. Individual gigs with Downtowners ranging from Marc Ribot to the Lounge Lizards added experience and funds. Soon the trio took to the road in Martin's old Ford van, hitting coffeehouses and small rock clubs and building a young fan base along the way. More than a decade later, they've brought live jazz to a large, more mainstream audience, while Chris has inspired a legion of young jam-scene-initiated bassists to take on the challenge of the upright.

You started on electric before focusing more on the upright through college.

Playing the electric first helped me technically because I was working on a lot of four-finger left-hand exercises. Although I learned traditional acoustic bass technique when I started playing upright, the finger-independence concepts from the electric came in handy. In general, I think electric bassists are missing something if they never play acoustic bass. Sonically, there's a whole other world of sounds you can get. And physically, you've got this giant resonating chamber you can feel the vibrations coming from.

What was it like when you returned to the electric in earnest with MMW?

It was rough at first. I brought my Music Man on some of the early tours, and when I heard the board tapes it sounded horrible. I was overplaying and digging in so hard the strings were constantly clipping the pickups. No matter what instrument you're playing, it should be effortless. That doesn't mean without muscle; it just means relaxed. When you've reached that point where it's completely effortless, the sound comes out naturally. It's got to originate from a quiet place inside of you, and the only way to achieve that is through knowing your instrument cold, which takes a lot of practice. The acoustic bass in particular is like a drum: If you really crack a drum it'll be loud, but it doesn't sound good. Or you can hit it softer and get this incredible sound that's just as loud.

What's your groove approach with MMW?

Simplicity is a huge factor. When I'm trying to find a part and it doesn't feel quite right, I'll leave out one note or let it hang for a while—and usually it all falls right into place. The best grooves have conversations going on, little subtleties that kick them up to the next level and add excitement. Simplicity is what makes you tap into that, because when you leave space you listen. When you hear what everyone else is doing you can answer them.

Chris Wood

What was the concept for Uninvisible?

Coming off *The Dropper*, which was pretty experimental, we had the idea of a dub record—but really we just wanted something that had a more consistent groove throughout. As always, we jammed and came up with material and recorded the core tracks at Shacklyn, our Brooklyn studio, with Scotty Hard, our producer. From there we brought in guests who we felt would augment the music, and we did some additional recording and overdubbing at Bearsville up in Woodstock. We've found that if the music is organic enough it's amazing how you can add and combine elements. That's why we play the way we do: We try to leave open possibilities for new things to happen that we wouldn't even think of.

The opener, "Uninvisible," has a cool descending variations-on-a-theme bass line.

We're big believers in the magic that occurs the first time you play something, so we try to keep that and build on it. This tune is a good example; I'm literally developing my bass part as you hear it. I had my '65 P-Bass going through an Electro-Harmonix Micro Bass Synthesizer, and I'm just reacting to the dirty sub-octave sound. I was thinking along the lines of the Jackson 5's "I Want You Back," with Wilton Felder on bass—applying the Jamerson trademark of never playing quite the same thing twice.

Your feel is loose and almost sloppy on "First Time Long Time" and "Nocturnal Transmission."

The way we describe that concept is to play "stupid," or "stoopid." It refers to playing like someone from the street as opposed to sounding like a schooled musician. Marc Ribot had a huge influence on me in that way. He was the first artist I toured with, and at one point he had me playing guitar because he wanted someone who wouldn't fall back on all the guitar clichés. He has even studied autistic children in music programs to understand the pure, simplistic state of a child touching an instrument for the first time. When called for, I try

Wood's Shed

Chris Wood's main electric bass is a 1965 banana-yellow Fender Precision with a rosewood fingerboard. He also plucks a Hofner Beatle Bass, a sunburst '63 P-Bass, a Danelectro DC Bass (heard on "The Edge of Night"), and a '61 Ampeg Baby Bass. His strings are D'Addario XL160 nickel roundwounds (.050, .070, .085, .105); Dunlop makes his Pyrex glass slide, and he uses heavy-gauge guitar picks. Chris's 1920s Pfretzschner upright sports Gage Realist and Underwood pickups and Pirastro Olive gut-core/chrome-wrapped strings. He uses a German-style bow.

On *Uninvisible*, Wood recorded his electrics direct and via his miked Ampeg B-15. (He also has a B-18.) His effects included Electro-Harmonix Bass Micro Synthesizer and Deluxe Memory Man pedals, and a SansAmp DI for distortion. He recorded his upright direct via his Realist pickup and through his miked B-15. Live, Wood sends his electrics into an old Ampeg SVT head with an SWR Goliath 4x10 cabinet, and his upright goes through the B-15.

to get into that mindset, like not even knowing the names of the strings. Physically I'll even use a cruder, rougher approach; I may keep my left hand in one position and play mostly root-5-octave lines, and I'll use only my index finger to pluck the strings.

That's a difficult space for a schooled bassist to get into.

It's easy to get caught up in the belief that you always have to sound good or be a slick player in order to be accepted. Sometimes that eclipses the matter at hand: You have to make *music*, whatever it takes. Schooled musicians are often programmed to think that all the hours they put into their instrument means they should play it that way. There's a fear of sounding bad or taking risks or making mistakes. But that's limiting, because sometimes when you make a mistake, it's the hippest thing you play—especially when you're improvising. In MMW we find a lot of the times when something happens that we didn't expect, it's the best part. That's how we discover new sounds. It's the old "no such thing as a wrong note" adage. We've also discovered that when things get loose, that's often when your personality comes out.

What can you practice to open up that side of your playing?

It's valuable to spend some practice time playing completely freely, with no rules; just experiment with sounds and techniques that you don't normally work on. You'll discover ideas you wouldn't have otherwise, and you'll learn what it feels like to not be attached to anything you're supposed to play. That's important to get familiar with, because then you can bring it into a more structured musical format while retaining that sense of freedom and of being completely relaxed and open—almost like the instrument is playing itself.

How did "Your Name Is Snake Anthony," with Col. Bruce Hampton's spoken part, come together?

We called Bruce, who we've known forever, and asked him to contribute. He sent us a DAT with that story on it. We had an improvised piece of music that wasn't complete, so we decided to put his voice over it. It has become an MMW tradition; we did that with a Steve Cannon spoken piece on *Combustication*, and we even took a solo Sun Ra saxophonist Marshall Allen played for us on *The Dropper* and used it on a different track. Bruce's story is sort of this abstract tale about us. Snake Anthony is Bruce's name for MMW because Anthony is John's middle name. And he makes all kinds of offbeat references—such as "small Japanese woman," which refers to our love of Japanese food.

"Take Me Nowhere" and "Ten Dollar High" feature your upright work.

On both of those I actually redid the original electric bass parts at Bearsville. "Nowhere" was an improvised tune, but I didn't like the bass sound. I added the upright part, and I think it ended up improving the whole piece; the bass rides the fine line of making melodic statements while keeping the groove going. "Ten Dollar High" was a progression by John we were fooling around with, and at some point someone said, "Okay that's fine"—but I felt my part wasn't quite there, so I went back in later. The upper-register solo stuff at the beginning is just me reacting to the tune while overdubbing upright.

How do you decide when to stay back and groove and when to step forward in more of a solo vein?

To begin with, being a trio allows each of us to go beyond the traditional roles of our instruments, which for me can mean having a bass line with a little more melodic content. Our songs are based on collective improvisations, so I'm pretty much always functioning in the dual role of providing the groove and stepping forward when there's a place that calls for it. Aside from my getting an open featured solo spot live, our concept is that we aspire to improvise all the time, but in a groove context.

Do your jazz roots come out more when you pick up the upright?

Not consciously, but I'm sure my jazz hat may go on a bit because I can't help but think of Charles Mingus when I'm holding the upright. He's my biggest bass influence and a hero of mine—talk about a schooled jazz musician with amazing technical prowess who could still play "stoopid"! Generally, though, whether to pick up an electric or the acoustic is a decision I make spontaneously. I see it more in terms of sound. I get interested in an instrument

Chris Wood Selected Discography
With Medeski Martin & Wood: *Uninvisible*, Blue Note; *The Dropper*, Blue Note; *Tonic*, Blue Note; *Combustication*, Blue Note; *Farmer's Reserve*, available exclusively at www.mmw.net; *Bubble House*, Gramavision; *Shack Man*, Gramavision; *Friday Afternoon in the Universe*, Gramavision; *It's a Jungle in Here*, Gramavision; *Notes from the Underground*, Accurate. **With Stanton Moore:** *Flyin' the Koop*, Blue Thumb/Verve. **With John Scofield:** *A Go Go*, Polygram. **With Marc Ribot:** *Yo I Killed Your God*, Tzadik. **With Karl Denson:** *The Bridge*, Relaxed; *Dance Lesson #2*, Blue Note. **With Chris Whitley:** *Perfect Day*, Valley. **With Iggy Pop:** *Avenue B*, Virgin. **With DJ Logic:** *Project Logic*, Ropeadope/Atlantic. **With Gov't Mule:** *The Deep End, Vol. 1*, ATO. **With John Lurie:** *African Swim and Manny & Lo*, Strange & Beautiful. **With John Zorn:** *Film Works Volumes 3 & 4*, Tzadik. **With Bob Moses:** *Nishoma*, Grapeshot. **With Oren Bloedow:** *Luckiest Boy in the World*, Knitting Factory. **With Chocolate Genius:** *Black Music*, V2/Virgin. **With Ned Rothenburg:** *Real and Imagined Time*, Moers. **With Ken Shaphorst:** *When the Moon Jumps*, Accurate.

because it has a sound that makes me play a certain way; it's like I'm taking advantage of what that bass does best. That's why I use a number of basses—they all have totally different personalities.

Is Mingus the inspiration when you hit the bass like a drum, pull the strings off the neck, and play furious chordal strums?

Without a doubt. He did an album with Duke Ellington and Max Roach called *Money Jungle* that's total bass genius. The story goes that Mingus was pissed off at Duke because he wouldn't let him do any of his own songs. So in response Mingus started messing around and stretching all over the place with some amazing results, pulling strings off the neck and getting all these weird sounds. His attitude alone is what inspires me to try anything. I'll use a bow on my electrics and a pick on my upright. I must say the best techniques occur on the spot; the preconceived ones are never as good.

Several years back my upright was severely damaged on the road, and I had to play a show on a borrowed bass. The bridge was angled skyward to begin with, and it seemed to move even more as we went along. Sure enough, it came time for my solo and—right at the climax—the bridge just snapped. Well, that got the biggest hand of the night. After our next show a fan actually complained to me that I didn't snap my bridge!

Who else influences your experimental techniques?

A lot of it comes from the 20th-century composer Krzysztof Penderecki—such as the portamento/

Theremin effect I get with a slide on the electric or a drumstick on the upright. On the upright I can get interesting overtones and create vocal sounds such as whale calls. I also use another stick to hit the strings below the bridge to get a sound similar to gamelan music from Bali. The microtonal influence comes from one of Coltrane's favorite saxophonists, Joe Maneri, a teacher I met at the New England Conservatory. He can hear over 70 notes in an octave! Downtown-scene guitarists like Marc Ribot, Fred Frith, and Elliott Sharp have especially influenced my electric playing and use of effects. And producer/bassist Bill Laswell—there's an album he produced called *Night Spirit Masters* that features Gnawa and Moroccan trance music and a bass instrument called the zinteer.

How did you get the raw sound on "I Wanna Ride You"?

I always wanted to get a tone like that, and this was the right tune to try it out on. I used my '63 P-Bass with the tone knob all the way up. Then we put it through my old B-15 turned up real loud, so you can feel the way the tubes compress the sound. It's a strange, nasal tone that reminds me of '60s boogaloo tracks. John wrote that piece beforehand; he brought it in and showed us the changes and some key lines, but the vamp sections are more open.

You get a contrasting P-Bass sound on "Smoke," which rides your bass melody.

That's actually the same bass; we did that whole track at Bearsville. We were jamming and messing around with Jimi Hendrix's "Fire," and we ended up playing it slow, hence the name "Smoke." The opening figure develops into counterpoint with John's organ line, and the track becomes more conversational than improvisational. That's something we do a lot, inspired by folks like James Brown, Sly & the Family Stone, and Fela Kuti. In their bands there was a certain way all of the parts fit together and all of the rhythms combined to form a counterpoint that created the piece's overall rhythm.

"Retirement Song" has an interesting sonic hue.

That was a slightly different approach and a challenge. First Billy built up a drum and percussion track via overdubs. Next I had to go in and—inspired by Billy's tracks—create a bass line that established the mood, harmony, and song form. Then John built up the harmonies and added melodic context. We did this once before on "Hey-Hee-Hi-Ho," from *Combustication*. I played upright here, but I was thinking about some of the African fretless bassists, like Bakithi Kumalo and his sliding lines with Paul Simon.

You use double-stops throughout the album, from 10ths to the major 2nds on "The Edge of Night."

I just love the sound of double-stops on bass, particularly on a 4-string electric. I know it's common on 6-string, but for me the magic is in the 4-string range because the intervals create vibrations or beats that have their own rhythm—especially if you're playing, say, a major 7th or 2nd. John liked the major 2nds on "The Edge of Night" because they create a definite tonal center, but you don't know which of the two notes is the root, so it's less restrictive. My main influence double-stop-wise is Michael Henderson with Miles Davis, especially on "Sivad" from *Live Evil*.

Who are some of your lesser-known bass influences?

Pals have turned me on to early boogaloo albums and songs where I don't even know the band, much less the bassist. One is a great Junior Parker record called *Love Ain't Nothin' but a Business Goin' On*; it has amazing bass playing. [The bassist was likely Mike Leech and/or the late Tommy Cogbill, although Leech couldn't tell us for sure who played bass on the record.] Another one with a killer bass line is that old hit "Express Yourself." [The song is from the Warner Bros. album of the same name by Charles Wright & the Watts 103rd Street Rhythm Band; the credits list bassists James Jamerson and Ray Brown.] Also inspirational were early blues records by John Lee Hooker, Freddie King, and Jimmy Reed, and aside from Willie Dixon, I don't know who any of those bassists were.

Why do you use two different pickups on your upright?

They provide different sounds. The Gage Realist, which goes under the foot of the bridge, has a more natural, mic-like sound, which is good for recording. The Underwood, which goes in the hole of the bridge, has more of a "pickup" sound that can be turned up loud onstage. When I record I usually use the Realist for a direct signal in combination with a mic. Onstage I favor the Underwood for an amp sound.

How do you deal with the sonic challenges of playing upright live, especially in large venues?

Through constant adjustment and overcompensating. My main problem is being able to hear the notes clearly so I can play in tune. In most venues, especially the larger ones, I get plenty of low-end boom from the house system reflecting off the back wall. So in my monitors and my amp I end up going for a trebly, high-end tone so I can clearly hear my intonation over a loud band.

How do you feel about MMW's seminal status in the jam-band movement?

I used to feel a little weird about it because I felt it was reflecting on our music, but now I realize it's just a description of a scene—a convenient marketing label for bands on the fringe or in the cracks. There are many different-sounding groups under the jam-band umbrella, ranging from Southern rock to bluegrass to acts like Soulive, or us. The common thread is improvisation, based on a band's particular influences. That said, it has been wonderful for us. We're grateful for the wide-ranging audiences we get to play for. And the mix of styles that occurs at jam-band-oriented shows has been opening up ears all around.

Web Site

www.mmw.net

Stoopid Grooves

ON MMW'S TENTH DISC, *Uninvisible*, Wood is in peak form on electric bass and acoustic upright. His retro-rooted boogaloo P-Bass parts sparkle with 21st-century polish, while his hip-hop upright lines twist and prod with Mingus-like bravado. Overall, his ability to spontaneously deliver musically enlightened ideas with a gritty, "stoopid" edge gives his lines their state-of-the-bass distinction.

Example 1 is inspired by the constantly evolving main two-bar groove of the title track. Wood used his '65 P-Bass and an Electro-Harmonix Bass Micro Synthesizer, playing the part up at the 12th fret. "If you're not using any effects, start at the 5th fret of the *D* string," he advises. "Feel-wise, think about aiming for the downbeats, even though there are a lot of upbeats." **Example 2** contains the main two-bar P-Bass figure of "Your Name Is Snake Anthony," which Wood continually varies in MMW style. Note bar 2's *A♮*, which works as a passing tone against the *F* minor tonality. "Try to play as legato and flowing as possible," Wood cautions.

Example 3 features two bars of Wood's six-bar upright solo on "Ten Dollar High." "It's more of an interjection; I really just stepped forward in an open spot when I overdubbed the part, and I tried to keep the groove and bass-line flavor going." It's back to the '65 P-Bass for the three-bar groove during the second section of "Nocturnal Transmission," shown in **Ex. 4**. "I'm in my James Brown/Michael Henderson bag. The phrase is three bars long because that's the way Scotty Hard cut and looped it." **Example 5** recalls the main two-bar P-Bass groove of "First Time Long Time." Though the track has a slightly swingy hip-hop lilt, Chris plays the 16ths more to the straight side, enhancing the part's "stoopid" flavor.

Ex. 1

♩ = 96
Boogaloo feel

Ex. 2

♩ = 89
Film Noir funk

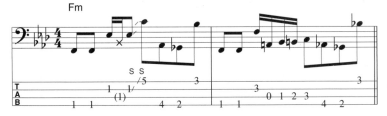

Ex. 3

♩ = 92
Upright funk

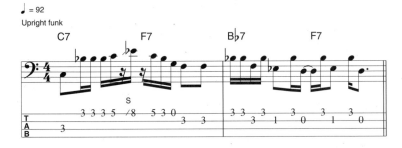

Ex. 4

♩ = 118
James Brown funk

Ex. 5

♩ = 90
Funk

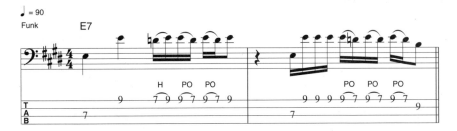

Ex. 6a

Ex. 6b

Ex. 7

Ex. 8

Ex. 9

Ex. 10

"Stoopidity" is also present on *Combustication*, MMW's seventh album. **Example 6a** describes the main bass theme of "Just Like I Pictured It," which Chris played on his Hofner Beatle Bass. "The tune started with the bass line, which I'd written previously. When I come up with bass parts on my own, they tend to be more melodic because I'm playing by myself." **Example 6b** is inspired by Wood's slide solo. "I use a standard guitar slide, which sounds especially good with the Hofner. Delta blues guitar is definitely the inspiration."

Example 7 shows the style of Wood's ever-evolving acoustic bass line on the spoken work piece "Whatever Happened to Gus?" "The whole part is inspired by Sun Ra's band in general and Sun Ra bassist Ronnie Boykins in particular." **Example 8** illustrates the main acoustic ostinato from "Latin Shuffle." While this line is played in a half-time swing feel, Billy Martin's drums buzz through double-time polyrhythmic Latin grooves. John Medeski (on acoustic piano) alludes to both feels. Reports Chris, "My part just happened as we all played together, and it became a sort of theme. The vintage sound, the feel, and the notes are all influenced by Charles Mingus and Wilbur Ware."

Example 9 shows a portion of Wood's funky Hofner groove from "Coconut Boogaloo." He executes the ghost-notes with left-hand muting. "I'm just learning about boogaloo feels from Ray Charles recordings and early-'60s soul-jazz albums on Blue Note by artists like Grant Green and Herbie Hancock. My part is a conversation with Billy's drums, within a groove context, while John adds his own colors." **Example 10** contains a portion of another Woods funk groove from "Church of Logic." Chris used his Danelectro DC Bass, played with a heavy pick. "I tried to play with a Marc Ribot–like attitude. The line is far from crisply executed, but the hammer-ons and pull-offs give it variety and character."

BRIAN BROMBERG
Bass Comes First

Interviewed by Karl Coryat, March 1993; Chris Jisi, December 1997; and Ed Friedland, March 2003.

LIKE JOHN PATITUCCI, BRIAN BROMBERG is among the few bassists who can handle the acoustic and the electric with an equally high level of virtuosity. A fiery funkster, Brian can also blow wicked 16th-note solo lines on acoustic at nearly impossible tempos. But he doesn't stop there: He does much of his soloing on piccolo bass, twisting his sound with distortion and other effects, often playing long, legato Allan Holdsworth–style leads over complex changes. He can groove hard on conventional 4-string and the "4-string contrabass" (tuned *BEAD*), and he also likes to produce rich, rubbery timbres on fretted and fretless nylon-string basses. And he can play the drums. Yikes!

As versatile as he is, Bromberg considers himself first and foremost a *bass* player. "Some people believe that just because you have a solo career, you're a star and you don't want to groove—that you just want to play fast stuff all night. For me that's just not true. I love soloing, because it's my chance to sing, but I also love to play *bass*—and the bass functions as a rhythm instrument." On acoustic Brian covers the entire fingerboard, but his lines never seem out of control because his timing is so accurate. "When I play a walking bass line, I'm soloing in quarter-notes. But I'm not just playing the bass without caring; I'm very much aware of what I'm doing. I'm singing my lines, just like when I'm soloing—I'm just singing in quarter-notes.

"A lot of people don't realize that 90 percent of my living is made as a bass player, doing sessions and touring. I've prided myself on developing good time, having a good sound, and playing in tune. Soloing is just a fringe benefit. That's one reason why the bass lines on my records are very simple; they're approachable, listenable, and readable. It's my way of saying, 'See? I can actually play *bass.*'"

Born in 1960 in Tucson, Arizona, Bromberg grew up in a jazz-filled household. His father and his older brother are jazz drummers. "I loved the feel, the spontaneous creativity, and the energy of jazz," Brian says, "and jazz was all around me. My brother had Led Zeppelin records, but he listened mostly to guys like John Coltrane and Miles Davis. For a young kid like me, that was some pretty deep stuff." It's not surprising that Bromberg soon found himself playing drums, although at 14 he began to move to bass. "I had played cello in elementary school, and when I got to junior high school there were a whole bunch of cellists but no bassists, so I was encouraged to make the switch."

As an overweight teenager, Brian was mercilessly teased by his high-school classmates. "It caused me a lot of pain, and it made me withdraw from people. I ended up transmitting the pain into my music." Through hard work and sheer discipline, Bromberg lost 70 pounds over a period of two years; he also dropped out of high school to practice his new instru-

Brian Bromberg

ment. "I don't recommend that anyone do that. But here I was playing music with 40-year-old guys who respected me as a musician and treated me as an adult, and then I'd have to go back to school and deal with these *kids.*" Brian took the GED test to earn his diploma, and he began to study music at the local university while getting jazz and symphony work.

At age 18 Bromberg received his first big break. Pianist Bill Evans came to Tucson to perform and give clinics, and Brian hung out with Evans and made friends with his bass player, Marc Johnson. Many months later Johnson recommended Bromberg when Stan Getz was looking for a bassist. "I was blown away that Marc even remembered me," Brian says. Getz called the next day, and on his 19th birthday Bromberg left Tucson to tour the world.

Getz's gig required electric bass, and Brian soon found himself sweating over a Fender fretless. "To play an electric was bad enough, but without frets? Forget it!" Brian worked with the Fender steadily, though, and the axe grew on him. Before long, Bromberg was a serious acoustic/electric doubler. He was still a straightahead jazz devotee, though. "Then something happened—I grew up. I realized that we don't have the right to judge anyone for their music—or for anything, really. When I was young, I was very closed-minded and tunnel-visioned. I condemned many styles of music: rock, country—everything but jazz and classical. As I got older, I discovered there were feelings inside me that were a lot bigger than I was. I realized we all have those feelings, and if the feelings about my music are valid for me, then they're valid for everyone, no matter what kind of music they play."

With his mind opened to disparate musical styles, Bromberg began writing tunes and performing them with his own band. In the mid '80s he hooked up with a generous investor who financed his first recording, *A New Day.* He followed that up with *Basses Loaded* (1988), *Magic Rain* (1989), and *Bassically Speaking* (1990). With 1992's *It's About Time: The Acoustic Project*—a return to Brian's straightahead roots—his solo career was well on its way.

Bromberg's Bag

Brian Bromberg rotates among over a dozen electric basses, all built from a design he came up with in 1981. Most feature graphite necks and piezo pickups. These include his new Dean B^2 signature 4- and 5-strings; Peavey-built B-Quad 4 fretted and fretless 4-strings; a B-Quad 5 fretted 5-string; B-Quad 4 piccolo basses with nylon and steel strings; fretted and fretless 4-strings built by Robert "Bob" Mick of Tucson, Arizona; Dean Performer ABG and Exotica acoustic bass guitars, both strung with steel piccolo strings; and a 4-string built by the Netherlands' Jan Knooren. All are strung with medium-light La Bella Slappers or La Bella custom piccolo strings. Bromberg plays an 18th-century Italian upright by Matteo Guersam. It's slightly smaller than 3/4-size, and he keeps the action very low. The bridge is fitted with a Rick Turner prototype piezo pickup, which Bromberg helped design; he also has Fishman Full Circle and David Gage Realist pickups. Brian feeds the signal through a Turner buffer preamp and into Fishman Bass Blender and then to the PA. His electric upright is a BSX bass. His bow is French-style and his strings are medium Thomastik Spirocore Weichs.

For live amplification, Bromberg has used Peavey, Walter Woods, Genz-Benz, and Bold Concepts gear. When he's not carrying his own equipment, Brian asks for a mixer, a power amp, and two cabinets. His stereo rack—which handles his standard electric and upright, MIDI, and piccolo bass needs—includes a line mixer, a multi-effects unit, a Yamaha G50 MIDI controller, and a Yamaha MU100R MIDI module. He also stomps on EBS Octabass, EBS DynaVerb, and DigiTech RP50 Amp Modeler pedals. Bromberg generally records direct. "All of my basses have line-level outputs, so I don't need a DI; I can go straight to the board or into Pro Tools or an ADAT. If I want a particular sound I may use a tube preamp; sometimes I process it later. I want to record the bass as organically as possible." When recording his Italian upright, he gets a warm, natural sound by using a DPA tube microphone blended with about ten percent of the direct feed from his pickup through an Avalon 737 mic pre. "In the last ten years or so a lot of bass players have gone back to trying to get that old, thumpy, indistinct sound of 50 years ago. There's no clarity or sustain, but you can really feel the air movement. With modern recording techniques and a good setup, you can get that sound but with more presence and focus." Brian points the mic straight at the *f*-hole, about a foot away. "I put it on the *G*-string side because I tend to make sounds when I play, and I want to keep the mic as far away from my mouth as possible."

By 2003 Brian Bromberg had amassed a catalog of eight solo albums featuring his skills on upright, electric, and piccolo basses. With Ed Friedland he discussed two releases: the tribute Jaco *and* Wood, *an award-winning upright tour-de-force.*

How did Jaco *come about?*

I had never thought to do a Jaco tribute record, but Susumu Morikawa of Japan's King Records had the idea to do this CD with me as the producer—ten tracks, ten different players. Naturally, I was excited and honored. But every single player we asked wound up canceling. I had already started preproduction and suddenly there was no record. I called the label to ask how I should handle it, and they said, "Make it a Brian Bromberg Jaco tribute." And so it was.

How did you feel about interpreting performances by the man who changed the way the bass is played?

Part of me was thrilled to have this chance, but another part was scared to death. I thought everyone would judge me against Jaco's achievements. Then there was the question of how to arrange all these tunes by myself when the originals are still breaking ground 25 years later. If you listened today to "Portrait of Tracy" or "Teen Town" for the first time, you would think it was the most amazing thing you'd ever heard. The music and his performances are timeless. Eventually, I decided to take the music in a different direction. One of the main ways was to use upright bass as a lead instrument.

The disc opens with "Come On, Come Over."

That's a real feel-good tune. R&B was such a big part of who Jaco was, and he grooved his ass off, so I had to do it. This track is close to the original's vibe, but I chose to play the groove on 5-string to give it foundation. I brought in the original bass line the second time through as a background line. We also included an instrumental version with [saxophonist] Eric Marienthal playing his ass off. We thought we would have two versions so the smooth jazz stations would have something to play.

"Continuum" includes a gorgeous string introduction.

On the original the tune is this wandering cycle of improvisation with a core melody and chord structure. I wanted to show people how absolutely beautiful the melody is, so I wrote the string introduction and just played the acoustic bass over it. I played fretless for the melody and doubled it on acoustic piccolo bass. It was a vehicle for me to use the different basses in a valid, musical way to convey the composition's beauty.

You slow down "Teen Town" and play upright on it.

The original is so incredible you can't mess with it—don't even try. Playing it on upright was one way to make it more my own. I could have practiced it and played it fast like the original, but what's the point? I thought it was cool to slow it down; the tune really lends itself to that, and it lets the bass speak. For the guys who want to hear it fast, I double-timed it on the second verse on fretless as an answer to the acoustic bass. It's almost like Jaco's ghost floating by. Originally I wanted to have a screaming rock guitar solo on it, but when I was tracking

Cutting *Wood*

RELEASED in April 2002, Brian Bromberg's *Wood* is a straight-ahead jazz-trio record featuring pianist Randy Waldman and brother David Bromberg on drums. The Bromberg brothers' bond is apparent in their seamless rhythmic interplay. Waldman's greatest challenge was to establish his place in a trio dominated by such a strong bass presence; he solos daringly, beautifully orchestrates under Brian's bass solos, and interacts as if he were a third family member.

Of special note are the four tracks Brian plays unaccompanied. He brings new life to the Lennon/McCartney classic "Come Together" and creates an interesting rhythmic twist on the funk-jazz favorite "Freedom Jazz Dance." He transforms Miles Davis's "All Blues" into a bass tour-de-force, playing chords, melody, and the famous bottom line. The CD's last track is Bromberg's solo take on "The Star Spangled Banner." He grooves the tune into the ground,

resulting in what must be the most in-the-pocket solo-bass arrangement of the anthem ever recorded.

Reveals Bromberg, "On my beautiful old Italian bass the *E* string is probably 30 percent softer than the other strings. It's always been a problem. But while recording *Wood*, somehow the weather and the bass gods got together, and for the first time in all the years I've owned the bass, my *E* was the same volume as the other strings."

Wood represents the first time the Bromberg brothers have recorded together since Brian's 1991 recording *It's About Time.* "I love playing with my brother—he swings his ass off. Because he lives in New York and I'm in L.A., we don't get to play together much. But soon we're going to co-lead a CD. In addition to being a great drummer, he's a talented jazz composer and arranger."

Brian Bromberg
Selected Discography

Solo albums: *Jaco*, A440; *Wood*, A440; *You Know That Feeling*, Zebra; *Brian Bromberg*, Nova; *It's About Time: The Acoustic Project*, Nova; *A New Day*, Blackhawk; *Bassically Speaking*, Nova; *Magic Rain*, Intima; *Basses Loaded*, Intermedia. **With Stan Getz:** *Live by the Sea, Cannes 1980*, Music Club; *Autumn Leaves*, Koch; *Stan Getz*, Prestige. **With Dave Grusin:** (both on GRP) *Homage to Duke*; *The Fabulous Baker Boys*. **With Arturo Sandoval:** *Dreams Come True*, GRP. **With Billy Cobham:** *By Design*, Cleopatra. **With Kenny Rankin:** (both on Private Music) *Here in My Heart*; *Professional Dreamer*. **With Toots Thielemans:** *The Brasil Project, Volumes 1 & 2*, Private Music. **With Nancy Wilson:** *With My Lover Beside Me*, Columbia. **With Shirley Horn:** *You're My Thrill*, Verve. **With Jeff Kashiwa:** *Another Door Opens*, Native Music. **With Michel Legrand:** *Michel Plays Legrand*, LaserLight. **With Lalo Shifrin:** *Return of the Marquis de Sade*, Aleph. **With Mike Garson:** *The Oxnard Sessions, Volumes 1 & 2*, Reference. **With Kevyn Lettau:** *Simple Life*, Samson Music. **With Peter White:** *Songs of the Season*, Sony. **With Gary Meek:** *Step 7*, A440. **With Mike Melvoin:** *Oh Baby*, City Light. **With Rob Mullins:** *Jazz Jazz*, Sindrome. **With Anita O'Day:** *In a Mellow Tone*, DRG. **With Phil Upchurch:** *L.A. Jazz Quintet*, Pro Arte. **With Dan Siegal:** *Clairvoyance*, ULG. **With Kim Waters:** *One Special Moment*, Shanachie. **With Turning Point:** *A Thousand Stories*, A440.

with the upright, I just started blowing and it turned out cool, so I left it that way. It's one of my favorite things on the record. The second version is what I originally heard in my head, with a screaming, guitar-type piccolo bass solo on it. The rest of the track is the same as the acoustic-bass solo version.

How did piccolo bass originally become a key part of your voice?

For me, it was the result of a creative accident early on. I had an 8-string bass—a 4 with octave strings—and I took off the low strings to see how it would sound. It freaked me out! Suddenly I could play chords that didn't sound like mud. I became more aware of melody and turned into a musician instead of just a bass player. It's such a melodic instrument, and the register allows me to "sing" more. And I've increased the range by tuning up an octave and a 4th—*ADGC*—so on my 24-fret basses I'm virtually in a guitar's high range.

The ballad "A Remark You Made" includes some former Jaco sidemen.

Right, [saxophonist] Bob Mintzer and [percussionist] Alex Acuna are on this track; Alex played on the original version of this beautiful song written by Joe Zawinul. The track evolved from the keyboards up. The melody sounds gorgeous on the upright; it sounds more jazz. I love the conversation I'm having with Mintzer. He cut his tracks in New York and sent them to me, and I assembled it, but it totally works. I did some of the keyboard programming. I'm not a keyboard player, but for certain things that I want played a particular way, I'll do it myself.

On "Portrait of Tracy" you play the opening harmonics on upright.

Yeah, and just playing them on electric is hard enough—on upright it's a bitch! This is another example of how beautiful Jaco's melodies are. His version was groundbreaking because of the harmonics—but when you get through the shock of the technical ability and come to the actual melody, it's beautiful music. I didn't want to repeat his approach on the song, so I played the melody on upright, changed the time signature, and added strings and percussion. I wanted it to feel like all the elements of the earth—really fundamental. Using a real string section made it so organic; sitting in the middle of that is breathtaking. I had heard Marcus Miller's version on the Jaco tribute album *Who Loves You*, and it was brilliant and funky. I knew I had to go in another direction.

You give an odd-time meter to "Three Views of a Secret."

That came to me fairly quickly. I thought it would be great to do it in 7/4; I know an arrangement works when the tune sounds as though it had been written that way. The chord changes were the hardest thing for me to solo over on the whole record. My favorite part is the entrance of my solo coming out of what Mintzer is playing; we're playing the same note. I love the way it came out.

"The Chicken" gets a close-to-the-original reading.

This is the only tune the label specifically requested for the CD. I had heard Jaco play it live several times, and each time it was different. I wanted to keep it pretty straight; the only difference is I play it on upright. There's a cool little turnaround in the sax-solo form.

"Tears" is an original composition.

I wrote it a while back and wanted to give it a home. The name sums it up; you have to think of tears when you think about Jaco's tragic end. The melody is emotionally powerful. In a way, this tune doesn't fit musically with the rest of the record; it's not pyrotechnic and it's not harmonically heavy, but it's something a non-musician could relate to—I feel it's an honest tribute to Jaco. I orchestrated it with the fretless as well as upright, nylon-string piccolo, and steel-string acoustic piccolo.

You get to burn on "Slang(ish)"

I originally finished the CD without this track and sent it to the label in Japan. They called me back and said, "We love the record, but how come you don't go crazy?" I explained that the CD wasn't so much about the playing as it was about the music; I just didn't feel like going there. But they asked me to please go crazy on a track. Jaco used to do a solo thing live with a loop pedal, and he called it "Slang." I tried to find a way to go crazy with it in my own way. I thought it would be cool to do the loop figure and move it up in minor 3rds. I also thought it would be cool to make it a conversation between the fretless and fretted bass. The fretless I used has a graphite neck and piezo pickups, so you can slap and do the two-handed stuff and really hear it. The fretted bass was the polar opposite: passive with single-coil J pickups. The intro part, well . . . I probably shouldn't have put that on there. I just plugged in and started improvising, and whatever happened happened. I probably played too much, but it was fun.

Web site

www.brianbromberg.net

Life of Brian

Both *Jaco* and *Wood* find Brian Bromberg in peak form, grooving, blowing, and playing melodies on both upright and electric.

Example 1 recalls the main repeated 5-string groove of "Come On, Come Over," from *Jaco*. Note the pickup on beat *four* of bar 2, which echoes Jaco's original line. **Example 2** contains a portion of the bridge bass line, with Brian again capturing the flavor of Jaco's groove while adding his own identity. **Example 3** shows a portion of the fretless melody from "Tears." Be sure to mind the pull-offs and the hammer-on. Switching to *Wood*, **Ex. 4** contains Brian's funky opening groove from his arrangement of "The Star Spangled Banner." Note the Chuck Rainey–style double-stop in bars 1 and 3. Lastly, **Ex. 5** is inspired by the melody to "Goodbye." As in Ex. 3, the inflections are a key part of the performance.

Ex. 1

Ex. 2

Ex. 3

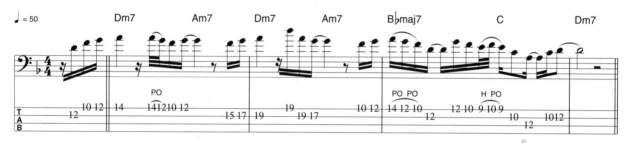

Ex. 4

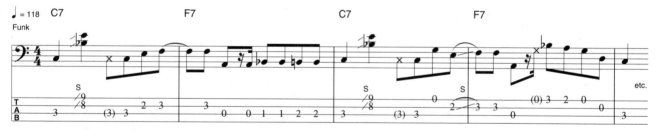

Ex. 5

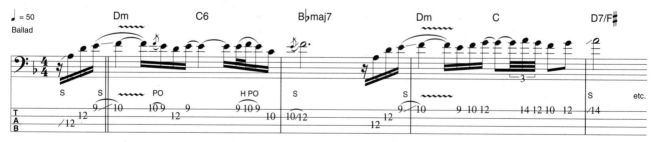

CHAPTER 5
Super Sidemen
PINO PALLADINO • DARRYL JONES
DOUG WIMBISH • BAKITHI KUMALO

Charting bass courses for artists ranging from the Rolling Stones, Eric Clapton, and the Who to Miles Davis, Paul Simon, and D'Angelo is not for the faint of heart nor the light of skills. A unique core of globetrotting groove-masters has redefined versatility, support, and studio and stage presence along the way.

PINO PALLADINO
Fretless Magician to R&B Wizard

Interviewed by Chris Jisi, March 1992, December 1996, May 2000.

WHETHER VIEWED FROM ACROSS THE ROOM or from the upper deck of a stadium, Pino Palladino's imposing physical presence—he stands 6'4"—belies his polite, soft-spoken manner. On paper, the reverse is true: The term "bass" next to his name somehow falls short of describing his enormous contributions on recordings (with such artists as Paul Young, Don Henley, D'Angelo, Eric Clapton, and Tears for Fears) and onstage (with Jeff Beck, the Who—replacing the late John Entwistle—and at the Queen's Jubilee Jam in 2002, backing up a Who's Who of musical stars).

Palladino first entered the bass world's collective consciousness with his soaring, melodic fretless lines (sometimes bolstered by a Boss octave pedal) on hits such as Young's "Everytime You Go Away," Henley's "New York Minute," and Chris DeBurgh's "Lady in Red." Before long, he became one of the most recognizable and imitated fretless players of his generation—and undoubtedly the most mimicked in his genre. As the fretless craze died down in the '90s, the "real" Pino emerged: a roots R&B–loving grooveaholic who has been in his element (at times plucking vintage flatwound-strung fretted basses) with neo-soulers like D'Angelo, Erykah Badu, Musiq, and Roy Hargrove, while maintaining his steady schedule of mainstream sessions. Notes Pino, "I've always loved rhythm, and I loved the sound of the bass and the role it takes in the music—the whole concept of not playing much but having a big impact."

Born in Cardiff, Wales, on October 17, 1957, Palladino first got into the groove via the radio-borne sounds of Motown and Stax/Volt and through hearing a jazz trio at a local restaurant. Inspired by a guitar-playing priest's folk masses in Catholic school, he started strumming on his sister's acoustic. This led to classical-guitar lessons and eventually to his first rock band. "I had a double-neck guitar and was into Led Zeppelin and Yes, but I always enjoyed playing rhythm more than lead. One day when I was about 16, I picked up our

Pino Palladino

bass player's Rickenbacker just to mess about, and I immediately felt at home. So I got my dad to buy me a Fender Precision and made the switch to bass."

Gradually Pino plucked his way to a top local gig at a Cardiff TV station. In 1980 he was recommended by a saxophonist friend to audition for ex-Squeeze keyboardist Jools Holland, who was forming a boogie-woogie band. After landing the job and moving to London, he entered the studio to record *Jools Holland & the Millionaires*; Pino is shown on the cover holding an upright bass, an instrument he doesn't play. (He used a fretted P-Bass for the sessions.)

Holland's band then took to the road, touring Europe and the United States. Sharing the bill on a number of dates in England was a soul group called the Q-Tips, featuring lead vocalist Paul Young. Pino and Paul "got on well together," laying the groundwork for their exciting collaboration on Young's 1983 debut, *No Parlez*. That album established Palladino's reputation for studio creativity, and the phone began to ring.

Many of your ideas seemed to come together on Paul Young's No Parlez. *What were the key events in that process?*

While I was on tour with Jools Holland, I happened to visit Sam Ash Music in New York City, where I purchased a fretless Music Man bass. I'd owned a fretless Precision previously, but it hadn't really grabbed me. When I got back to London, a Welsh drummer friend of mine, Chris Slade, had left a message saying that Gary Numan was looking for a fretless bass player and that I should come down and audition. So I took the Music Man and went over and played through a bunch of his songs. They all had simple changes, which gave me a lot of room to try different things. I ended up touring and doing a record with him called *I, Assassin*. That was great, because it was the first time I got to express myself in the studio with something other than typical bass parts. I remember hearing the sound of the fretless on a playback and thinking, "Hmmm—there's something here for me."

Around that time Paul Young was about to record his first album. My girlfriend—who's now my wife—was singing backup for him, and Laurie Latham, who'd worked on Gary's album, was producing. Laurie called me in to help out on a Marvin Gaye cover called "Wherever I Lay My Hat (That's My Home)." All that was down was a drum machine, keyboard pads, and a guide vocal. Laurie asked me to play something melodic on the fretless as a lead-in to the vocal. I tried to give it a sort of Jaco vibe, which seemed to work out well. We did four or five more tracks, and then I went home and forgot all about it. When I heard the mixes a while later, I was in shock. The bass was so loud; I thought, "They've got to be joking. What will people think?" But there was an affinity between the voice and bass, and that was really the start of it. When "Wherever I Lay My

Hat" became a hit in Europe, word spread, and I got calls to do sessions with people like David Gilmour, Joan Armatrading, and Go West. It was amazing.

How did you hook up with Don Henley?

That's an odd story. I had recorded an album with a singer called Nick Heyward, and his manager told me that Don had heard the album and was interested in hiring me. I took it with a pinch of salt and didn't do anything for about two months. Finally, I plucked up the courage, rang him, and explained the situation. He said he didn't recall telling anyone that—but he also said the he and his partner, [guitarist/producer] Danny Kortchmar, were familiar with my playing and would be interested in doing some recording with me.

It seems that your style reached its fruition on Paul Young's 1985 album, The Secret of Association.

The key factor was that we were given a much bigger budget. That enabled us to be a lot more indulgent with time, especially with regard to the bass parts. Most of the tracks were laid down before I played on them, and then we went through and tried different things. By "we" I mean myself; keyboardist/musical director Ian Kewley, who had a great vision; and Laurie Latham, again, applying his concept of bass featured with voice and its placement in the mix. Those two, along with Paul, helped me to create what's on the record.

You used the Boss octave pedal very effectively throughout, particularly on "I'm Gonna Tear Your Playhouse Down." Where did you get the idea for that sound?

Mostly from growing up and hearing Stevie Wonder's great bass lines—those heavy funk grooves with big, fat keyboard bass. I always wanted to capture that sound. While I was doing an earlier session for Laurie, we had laid out a bass line and I thought it would sound good if I doubled some of the riffs an octave higher. As it turned out, I doubled the entire part; that gave me the idea to get the Boss octave pedal to duplicate the effect live. It doesn't track much below *D* on the *A* string—sometimes you can get away with *C*—but the sound is awesome.

Who were your important bass influences?

Early on, James Jamerson, of course. It was gratifying to acknowledge that by recording "For Once in My Life" for the Jamerson tribute book [*Standing in the Shadows of Motown*, Hal Leonard]. Also, Danny Thompson, a great upright bass player in England. I used to sit transfixed in clubs watching him play slides, double-stops, and harmonics. Even though I was playing guitar when I first heard those two bassists, it all went into my head.

When I took up bass I started practicing with records, playing along with people like Larry Graham, Will Lee, Marcus Miller, Abraham Laboriel, and Anthony Jackson. Anthony's recordings with Chaka Khan in

 Pino Pals

Of his trademark fretless Music Man StingRay 4-string, Pino Palladino says, "I think it's about a '79; the strings go through the back of the body." The stock sunburst axe also has a rosewood board with no fret lines and one double pickup with active bass/treble boost. "With the bass and treble knobs turned midway and my plucking fingers right over the pickup, it has this one versatile, warm sound that speaks to me." Other prominent basses in his early career included a Pedulla Buzz Bass 4-string with fret lines, and a Warwick Thumb Bass 5-string. His move back to vintage-style fretted basses was led by his natural '63 Fender Precision. He also digs his black Moon Larry Graham Signature 4-string and his Lakland Joe Osborn 4-string (both with J/J-style pickups). His strings are Rotosound Swing Bass stainless-steel mediums gauged .040, .060, .075, .095, though he also praises his La Bella heavy-gauge flatwounds.

Live, Pino moved from Trace Elliot to Eden amps, and he now plugs into Ashdown gear: He has an ABM900 head and two BP150 cabinets (with a 1x15, a 2x10, and a switchable horn). His prime effect remains his Boss OC-2 Octave pedal.

particular kill me. I recently saw Francis "Rocco" Prestia with Tower of Power in London, and that was the closest I've come to being a punter [average person] again. He was absolutely marvelous; I've never heard or felt a groove stronger than his. But above all it was The Master, Jaco Pastorius. When I was a long-haired rocker, a keyboardist friend of mine turned me onto fusion: Chick Corea, Weather Report, John McLaughlin, and Stanley Clarke. Then I bought Jaco's first solo record, put on "Donna Lee," and was blown away. I didn't even understand it at first; it was a whole new dimension. He really opened it up for all bass players.

As a mostly self-trained musician who doesn't read music well, where did you learn the advanced harmonies that you play, especially when you move high on the fingerboard?

It's all by ear—I play what sounds good to me. I'm not proud of the fact that my reading skills are below average, but 98 percent of the time I'm called in to improvise. I studied for a while with a great American-born bassist here in London, Joe Hubbard, and learned about the modes and some other things, but overall I'm not very hip on theory. Like a lot of longtime players, I can pick up things very quickly by ear, so its hard for me to go back and learn the proper way.

Can you talk about your right- and left-hand techniques?

Mostly I pluck with two fingers on my right hand. I started that way on bass, probably because of the classical-guitar lessons and because the sound appealed to me. Occasionally I'll use the third finger on, say, a ballad, because I can get a warm tone with it. My thumb technique, which I don't use much anymore, is the basic slap-and-pull approach. I've also been using a muted technique where I dampen the strings with my right palm and pluck with the thumb; I used that on "Stop on By" [Paul Young, *Other Voices*]. With the left hand, I usually use finger-a-fret spacing, again from the classical guitar, although my vibrato on the fretless is anything but classical. I tend to move my whole hand back and forth as opposed to rolling the fingertip.

Can you offer any tips for achieving good intonation on fretless?

I never think about intonation, because when I do that's when I have trouble! When I first started playing the Music Man, I thought to myself, "This is amazing—I can even play chords in tune." It was like the instrument was built for my hands. It has no fret lines, but I do use the dot markers on the side of the neck. One thing I always try to do is think ahead, as far as positions and shifts, because there are so many ways to get from one note to another. It's not like playing on a fretted bass, where you can take your eye off matters more readily.

The fretless requires more concentration, yet it allows for more spontaneous expression.

Absolutely. The one thing you can't plan exactly is when to apply vibrato, or when to slide into certain notes, because that's intrinsic in the music. That's where a great vocal performance is invaluable—you react to a sung note or phrase.

When you're recording a track, how do you decide when to step forward musically?

I find there are two methods. When I listen to the demo, or when we first play the song through, I'll sense if it requires a straight-away part that can be completed within a few takes. Then I'll think about whether I'm going to play with the kick drum pattern or against it, and if there's room to add any little melodic things, chords, harmonics, whatever. The other approach involves putting down a basic track with the drummer or drum machine, and then going back to find if there's room to add something nice. Usually I deal with the latter method, but I really enjoy the former, too—especially when I'm working with a great drummer like Manu Katché or Vinnie Colaiuta, who can inspire you to do incredible things on the spot. Being able to work with different artists and top musicians in the studio is immensely challenging and rewarding. In fact, if I had to sum up my role at this point in my career, I would mostly describe myself as an enhancer of great songs—and an enjoyer of great fortune.

Pino Palladino Selected Discography

With Paul Young: (all on Columbia) *Crossing*; *Other Voices*; *Between Two Fires*; *The Secret of Association*; *No Parlez*. **With Don Henley:** (both on Geffen) *The End of the Innocence*; *Building the Perfect Beast*. **With D'Angelo:** *Voodoo*, Virgin. **With Eric Clapton:** (all on Reprise) *Reptile*, *Pilgrim*, *Journeyman*. **With Pete Townshend:** *White City*, Atlantic. **With Erykah Badu:** *Mama's Gun*, Motown. **With Musiq (Soulchild):** *Aijuswanaseing*, Def Soul. **With Tears for Fears:** *The Seeds of Love*, Polygram. **With Roy Hargrove Presents the RH Factor:** *Hard Groove*, Verve. **With Nikka Costa:** *Everybody Got Their Something*, Virgin. **With Chris Botti:** *First Wish*, Polygram. **With Melissa Etheridge:** *Breakdown*, Polygram; *Yes I Am*, Island. **With Jeff Beck:** *Who Else!*, Sony. **With B.B. King:** *Deuces Wild*, MCA. **With Michael McDonald:** *Blink of an Eye*, Warner Bros. **With John McLaughlin:** *The Promise*, Polygram. **With Phil Collins:** *But Seriously*, Virgin. **With Elton John:** *The One*, MCA; *Ice on Fire*, MCA. **With Peter Gabriel:** *Come Home to Me Snow*, Kizna. **With Oleta Adams:** *Circle of One*, Polygram. **With Seal:** (both on Sire) *Seal* (1991); *Seal* (1994). **With Chris DeBurgh:** *Into the Light*, A&M. **With Gary Numan:** *I, Assassin*, Beggars Banquet. **With Go West:** *Go West*, Chrysalis. **With Julia Fordham:** *Porcelain*, Virgin. **With David Gilmour:** *About Face*, Columbia. **With Rod Stewart:** *Human*, Atlantic. **With Nick Heyward:** *North of a Miracle*, Arista. **With Chaka Khan:** *Destiny*, Warner Bros. **With Joan Armatrading:** *The Shouting Stage*, A&M. **With the Bee Gees:** *Still Water*, Polydor. **With Paul Rodgers:** *Muddy Water Blues*, Red Ink. **With Paul Carrack:** *Blue Views*, Ark 21. **With David Crosby:** *Thousand Roads*, Atlantic. **With Youssou N'Dour:** *Joko from Village to Town*, Sony. **With Fema Kuti:** *Fight to Win*, MCA. **With Al Di Meola:** *Orange & Blue*, Bluemoon. **With David Sanborn:** *Songs from the Night Before*, Elektra. **With Dominic Miller:** *Second Nature*, Blueprint. **With Manu Katché:** *It's About Time*, BMG. **With Duncan Sheik:** *Duncan Sheik*, Atlantic. **With Ryuichi Sakamoto:** *Beauty*, Virgin. **With Celine Dion:** *Let's Talk About Love*, Sony. **With Jools Holland:** *Best Of*, Coalition. **With various artists:** *Party at the Palace: The Queen's Jubilee Concert*, Virgin. **Soundtracks:** *Standing in the Shadows of Motown*, Artisan; *Bamboozled*, Motown.

Eight years later Pino had resurfaced in R&B groove mode with D'Angelo, who was being hailed for reinventing contemporary R&B via his blend of hip-hop sounds and the untidy grooves of classic soul.

When did you hook up with D'Angelo?

We met in 1997 while doing a track for B.B. King's *Deuces Wild*, and we hit it off right away. He saw me playing my '63 P-Bass and said, "That's a Bootsy bass, right?" I said yes and mentioned that James Jamerson also played one, and he went crazy over that. It turned out the Jamerson/Bootsy/Larry Graham approach I'd been focusing on was just the concept he was looking for. He already had [Roots drummer] Ahmir Thompson in place, and after the date he asked me to do some tracks with them for what would become *Voodoo*.

How did you all come together on the D'Angelo groove?

It was a meeting of minds and influences and sounds, but the feel is 100 percent Dee; you can hear it all when he sings and plays keyboards. He hears everything in his head before he records a note, and his concept has the drums right on the beat—almost pushing—with the keyboards and bass hanging back in their own places. At points it can even sound polyrhythmic—some of it reminds me of music I've heard in Africa. When we first recorded he'd explain how far back he wanted me, and it felt pretty natural. I'd just try to lay back with the keyboards and listen to the overall feel. Still, there were times when I'd wonder if it was *too* far back—

if people would get it. But when he'd finish putting his vocals and sound collages on top, the whole track would work splendidly.

How did you record and perform the bass parts?

Dee comes up with amazing bass parts in his left hand. He would play me about 80 percent of a line, and the remaining 20 percent was open to my interpretation. My approach, which Dee encouraged, was to constantly develop the line with subtle variations, *à la* Jamerson. Another key is that Ahmir's drumming is very Motown-like; he leaves plenty of room for the bass because he just plays straight, heavy time, without a lot of fills. What's interesting is both Dee and Ahmir are pure hip-hop artists, so everything has a swung-16th-note feel. Ahmir can take that old swung soul feel and give it a contemporary sound by adding an edginess to the beat that didn't exist back then. The three of us cut all the scratch rhythm tracks as a trio, and in most cases I ended up replacing my part later, with Dee.

What equipment did you use to record, and to play live?

I played either my '63 P-Bass tuned down to D [*DGCF*] or my Moon Larry Graham signature 4-string tuned down to C♯ [*C♯F♯BE*]. Both had heavy-gauge La Bella flatwounds, which can be rough on necks; that's originally why I tuned down the Precision. I plugged into a miked Ampeg B-15, and I'm pretty sure that was the only signal we took. I've also got my Boss octave pedal, which I used on one track. Live I use the P-Bass tuned to *D*, a Lakland Joe Osborn tuned to *C♯*, and a new Moon 4. My stage rig is an Eden Navigator preamp, their WT-800 head, and two 4x10s

Considering your fretless legacy, some will view this as a new direction for you.

I'm actually showing more of my original influences now. Ultimately, it's all about keeping yourself inspired as a player. The fretless phenomenon was something that just happened, and I'm grateful for it. I got to work with a lot of amazing people on an instrument I loved playing, and I developed much of my vocabulary on it—especially in the higher register. But R&B is what's in my heart, and D'Angelo is a very special artist. He has helped to bring back some great music with real depth at a time when it's truly needed.

Web Site

www.pinopalladino.com

Full-Tilt Fretless Meets Fretted Funk

PINO PALLADINO'S EARLY RECORDINGS with Paul Young and Don Henley put his fretless style on the map. From slides, smears, detuned pedal tones, and harmonics to singing melodic phrases, doubled-octave keyboard-style lines, crisp slapped passages, and staccato 16th-note grooves, Pino's entire bass spectrum is audible in his work with those two artists.

Examples 1a and 1b are inspired by Pino's fretless work on tunes like "Everytime You Go Away." Example 1a recalls Pino's Music Man–played double-stop verse fills, beginning with tasty double-stops in 4ths and ending with a double-stop that exploits the 7 and ♭9. Example 1b illustrates a typically classic "Pino-ism"; a memorable sub-hook (bar 2) that answers the vocal.

Example 2 shows a typical chorus-fade line Pino might play on Pedulla Buzz Bass plus octave pedal on a tune such as Paul Young's "I'm Gonna Tear Your Playhouse Down." Pino completely alters his original line and pumps 16ths that outline a *Gm11* arpeggio in bar 1 and a finger-twisting variation in bar 3.

Examples 3a–3c take their inspiration from Don Henley's "New York Minute." Examples 3a and 3b recall Pino's soulful fills leading into the first and second choruses, played on his Music Man. Example 3c shows the kind of jazzy fill Pino is likely to bring to a bridge.

On D'Angelo's *Voodoo* Pino eases into a vintage-fretted vibe, evoking the spirit of James Jamerson with spontaneously improvised variations-on-a-theme parts that sit loose and way back in the pocket (a D'Angelo feel trademark).

Examples 4a and 4b recall "Playa, Playa," on which Pino plucked his *D*-tuned '63 P-Bass (the tablature is written using standard tuning). Example 4a shows his basic chorus part, to which he added his octave pedal. Note the tasty bend on the high *D♭*. Example 4b contains Palladino's basic verse part; the octave pedal is off, allowing him to grab the cool chords in bars 3 and 4: "I was thinking about Stevie Wonder in the choruses and P-Funk in the verses."

Example 5 is from "Send It On," a smooth soul ballad with a half-time 6/8 feel (though it's transcribed in 3/4). It shows Pino's melodic P-Bass line as the song ends. Bar 4's triplet-based fill is another classic Pino-ism. And it doesn't get any more raw or nasty than **Ex. 6**, Pino's main P-Bass part on "Chicken Grease." The harmony is somewhat ambiguous, a frequent D'Angelo device—but Palladino felt *B7* as the overall tonality.

Finally, Pino's basic part on the melodic hook of "One Mo' Gin" (**Ex. 7**) contrasts the Delta-dirty bass and keyboards on the tune's verse. Following a lead-in lick, he uses 10ths and other arpeggio shapes to add interest and color to the sparse track. He played his *C♯*-tuned Moon bass; again, the tab is in standard tuning.

Ex. 1a

Ex. 1b

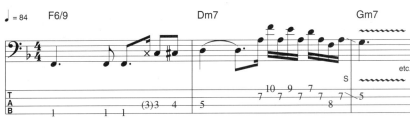

Ex. 2

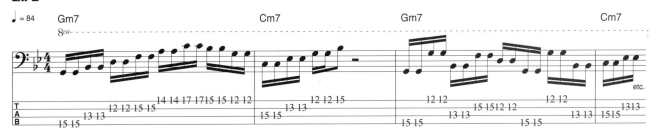

Ex. 3a

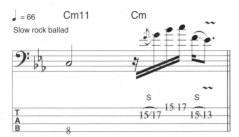

Ex. 3b

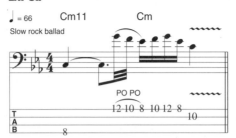

Ex. 3c

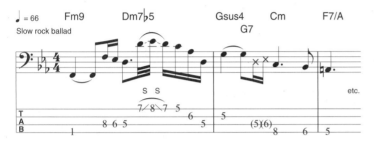

Ex. 4a

Ex. 4b

Ex. 5

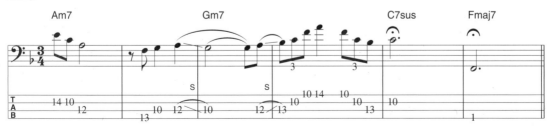

Ex. 6

Ex. 7

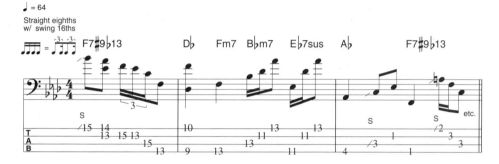

DARRYL JONES
Like a Rolling Stone

Interviewed by Chris Jisi, January/February 1995, and Karl Coryat, February 2003.

DARRYL JONES HAS HAD A CAREER THAT FORREST GUMP WOULD ENVY. Rising from relative obscurity ten years ago to join Miles Davis's band, "The Munch" has gone on to provide the punch for Sting, Peter Gabriel, Madonna, and now the Rolling Stones. In the process he has forged a résumé that reads like a Hollywood script (and, in fact, includes appearances in such films as Sting's *Bring On the Night* and Madonna's *Truth or Dare*). Most impressively, he has accomplished all of this with a musical concept so basic even the simple Southerner of big-screen fame would appreciate it. "People ask, 'How have you had to change your style to play with the Rolling Stones?'" says Darryl. "My answer is, I *haven't* had to. With the Stones, I'm doing what I've done with everyone else. My approach to all music is: break it down, cut away the excess, and get back to the fundamentals."

Jones was born on December 11, 1961, on Chicago's South Side. After eight years of exposure to jazz recordings and pop radio at home, he requested lessons from his father, a drummer. Darryl then saw his neighbor, Angus Thomas, playing bass guitar in a talent show, and he decided to make the switch not long after. With financial help from his older brother, Darryl bought a Hofner Beatle Bass copy and began studying with Thomas. Sold on a career in music, he entered Chicago Vocational High School, where he took theory courses, played electric bass in stage bands, and bowed a string bass in the orchestra. Upon graduating he began to

Darryl Jones with Ron Wood

establish himself on the local scene, eventually landing gigs with pianist Ken Chaney and guitarist Phil Upchurch.

One of Jones's regular Windy City rhythm-section mates was drummer Vince Wilburn Jr., a nephew of Miles Davis. Wilburn told Miles about Darryl during a Japanese tour in 1983; when he returned, Miles called to Chicago. "He wanted to hear me play over the phone," Jones remembers. "I ran around looking for my bass, and when I came back, he asked me if I could be in New York the next day. I said yes, and then I asked if he still wanted to hear me over the phone. He said, 'Well, you can play, can't you?' I said, 'Yes,' and he said, 'Good, because if you can't, I'm going to kill Vince.'" Darryl auditioned in person and a week later found himself onstage in St. Louis with Davis, guitarist Mike Stern, guitarist John Scofield, saxophonist Bill Evans, percussionist Mino Cinelu, and drummer Al Foster.

Concluding a two-year run that was documented on *Decoy* and *You're Under Arrest*, Jones—with Miles's blessing—moved on to join Sting at the recommendation of saxophonist Branford Marsalis. The ex-Police man and his "jazz band"—Jones, Marsalis, drummer Omar Hakim, and keyboardist Kenny Kirkland—proceeded to turn the pop world on its ear with *The Dream of the Blue Turtles* and subsequent tours. When the project ended, Jones settled in New York and spent two years at the core of the Big Apple's contemporary jazz scene, working with Stern, Scofield, guitarist Hiram Bullock, the Gil Evans Big Band, and Steps Ahead. Growing weary of his gig-to-gig cycle, Darryl returned to Chicago in 1989 determined to focus on writing and performing his own music. Demand for his rock-solid feel, however, kept him busy as a sideman on tours with Herbie Hancock & the Headhunters, Peter Gabriel, and Madonna, and on recordings with everyone from Eric Clapton to Spike Lee.

In 1994 Jones relocated to Los Angeles. He was attempting to put down roots while hanging out and playing with members of the *Tonight Show* band when the Stones came calling.

How did you land the gig with the Stones?

I got to meet Mick Jagger in 1985 while I was working on the film *Bring On the Night* with Sting, and I met Keith Richards in 1987 through Charley Drayton and Steve Jordan, who were working on his *Talk Is Cheap* record. When I found out Bill Wyman was leaving the Stones, I called Mick Jagger's management and left a message saying I was interested in auditioning. I also tried to send messages to the Stones through friends. I don't know which method worked, but I got on the list.

Why did the gig appeal to you?

When I saw Keith with the X-Pensive Winos, I began to think it might be interesting to play rock 'n' roll. My first thought was that if Keith's gig became available, I'd be into trying out. It didn't, but when Bill Wyman left, I thought, Well, why not the Rolling Stones?

What was the audition process?

I was asked to come to New York in June 1993. We played through a bunch of hits: "Brown Sugar," "Miss You," "Tumblin' Dice," "Start Me Up." Everything felt good and I thought, No matter what happens, I've had a lot of fun—and maybe I'll hear from them. They called again in October; this time they wanted to play through material they'd written for *Voodoo Lounge*. After that, they asked me to come work on the record in Dublin. When we finished, there were rumors of a tour, but nothing official was said.

In March '94 I went to hang out with Mick and Keith at a mixing session. Keith told me I had just missed Charlie, and he related a conversation they'd had that day:

Charlie: "We're going to use Darryl on the tour, right?"

Keith: "Yeah. He played on the record, and we dug it, so, yes—he's doing it."

Charlie: "Well, don't you think we should tell him?"

Keith: "I guess you're right."

Then Keith said, "So, I'm telling you." [*Laughs.*] I didn't tell anyone, though, until the band formally announced it.

Having a mutual jazz background with Charlie Watts must have been a factor in your hiring.

I'm sure it didn't hurt, but I think it was more that he felt comfortable playing with me—I know I felt comfortable with him.

How did you research for the audition?

I didn't research much. Basically, I got a few of their "best of" records and listened and played along. Instead of learning Bill Wyman's parts verbatim and then trying to sound like him, I learned the form of the songs and the general shape of the bass lines, and then I added my own interpretations. I felt it was important to play in my own style so they would be hiring me for *me*. On certain songs, however, I play the lines note-for-note because they're essential parts—like in "Start Me Up" and "Satisfaction."

There are a few Wyman-esque lines on Voodoo Lounge—*like the opening riff of "I Go Wild" and the octave climbs in the bridge and fade-out of "Suck on the Jugular."*

I can't think of any sections where I tried to cop his exact style. I actually borrowed the octaves on "Jugular" from Jaco Pastorius's line on "River People" [from Weather Report's *Mr. Gone*]. It's my little tribute to Jaco.

What's your assessment of Wyman's playing?

Even though he usually isn't in the forefront when people talk about the Stones sound, Bill Wyman is, in my estimation, a good musician and an underrated bassist. I've been listening to his lines, the different approaches he took to songs. He obviously knew a lot about this music after playing it for so long.

Did your preparation include listening to the early blues that influenced the Stones?

I've listened to some Muddy Waters records, but I didn't really go back that far until after the fact. I'd hang out in Keith's room late at night listening to old blues records, and he'd point out passages that had inspired his writing or playing. My whole approach—even from before the audition—has been to try to conceptualize what I would have sounded like and what instrument I would have used if I were playing rock 'n' roll with the Stones in the '60s and '70s.

Did you feel obligated to use a vintage bass?

That was my first inclination, and I did use a Fender for the audition to make that point. Since then I use Fenders and my Sadowsky, which functions better in this style of music than you might expect. That became especially clear when we recorded.

You apparently don't feel the need to slap, tap, or use any 5- or 6-string basses with the Stones.

No, those things don't seem appropriate. In fact, I use a pick when we play "Satisfaction" live—I think it really calls for that sound.

How did you come up with your parts for the album?

For the most part we all played live; we'd learn the tunes and then record different versions over a few days, which was similar to the way Miles recorded. In some cases I'd just pick up the bass and play whatever I felt was needed for the song, and that worked well. On other songs Mick might ask me to drive a section harder or move from straight eighth-notes to a figure—or he'd sing a line and I'd work it in. He would always say that if I wasn't comfortable with something he suggested, I didn't have to play it—so I was given a lot of freedom. Mostly, I just used my intuition.

The steady eighth-note pattern seems to be the staple of rock bass playing.

That's often the case, and I've certainly gained a better understanding of the intricacies involved. There are a thousand ways to play eighth-notes with respect to left-hand articulation, right-hand attack, note choices, note duration, use of space, phrasing, and overall feel. Then again, sometimes I'll start playing an eighth-note line with two right-hand fingers, only to find out that using anything more than one finger is overkill.

After playing with so many world-class drummers in different styles, what was your approach to working with Charlie Watts?

The only thing I did—and I do this with all drummers—is *listen*. My first order of business is to listen and lock in, to build the foundation of the house; everything else comes after that. My attitude is: Let's nail the song to the floor so it can go out as far as it needs to go.

Charlie has been great to work with. One of the fascinating characteristics of his style, which I've come to appreciate, is that he sometimes plays his fills slightly ahead of the beat. I've heard other drummers do this, and I wouldn't be surprised if they got it from Charlie. That little edge he puts on the fill creates an interesting tension in the music.

You get around quite a bit onstage. Were you given any stage direction?

Nothing was said. But I don't use just my fingers and ears to play bass—I use my whole body. I also use my eyes to connect with what everyone is doing around me. That all goes back to Miles; I used to watch him take tiny steps backward across the entire stage, and I'd see people's eyes glued on him.

It seems that playing with Miles exposed you to much of what you would later encounter with pop and rock acts.

That's true. Miles played the blues, and he played pop songs, like [Cyndi Lauper's] "Time After Time." He performed in front of huge audiences, and there was a vast amount of media attention. When I joined Sting's band, people would ask about the difference between playing behind a trumpet and playing behind a voice, and I'd say, "Man, Miles *is* a voice."

Did you and Sting ever have any bass-intensive conversations?

Not really, but he wrote some great bass lines, and my ear was open to that. What impressed me most about Sting, besides his obvious gifts as a composer and lyricist, was that he combines idioms so well—and that allows him to create his own music and his own market. He's not trying to "do" anyone else.

Your stint filling in for Tony Levin with Peter Gabriel bears similarities to your current situation with the Stones. What are your reflections on that period?

In addition to being a great artist and vocalist, Peter has the ability to sort of become the thing he's singing about onstage. When I played with Peter, I was aware of Tony's work—but as with the Stones, sometimes I'd play parts exactly like his while other times I'd play something completely different.

What was your musical approach with Madonna?

Because of the nature of the music, a lot of the bass lines were doubled on synth, so they needed to be played pretty much verbatim. But that's fun, too—for me, anyway. Herbie Hancock once said that Wah Wah Watson played the same guitar solo for a whole tour, every night—but every night it got better. That's partly the school I'm from as well: It's possible to play the same thing over and over again, but each time with a little more energy, so that by the end of the song or the end of the tour, you're going through the roof. You're changing what you *can* change about it.

Is there anyone else you'd like to play with?

I'd love to do some gigs with James Brown and maybe with a great blues player like John Lee Hooker. Those two immediately come to mind, but there are more. As I've said before, I have a fascination for musicians who have been doing what they do for a long, long time. There's so much to learn from playing with that kind of artist.

Some people still have a problem with seeing an African-American musician in a rock 'n' roll band. Have you encountered any trouble in that regard?

Not so far. There's no denying where some people are on that issue, so I won't comment. On the positive side, though, I will say I hope I'm living proof that if there's something you want to do, you should just go out and do it. It might be difficult, but nothing is impossible.

Who were the key bassists in your own development?

Angus Thomas, of course, who was my first teacher. I used to bring my bass over to his place, and we would play through a wide range of tunes—everything from the Staple Singers, Sly Stone, and Earth, Wind & Fire to Hendrix, Led Zeppelin, and the Allman Brothers. Beyond Angus, I would say Larry Graham, Stanley Clarke, and Jaco were the key players. Larry opened my ears to what the instrument could do, both sonically and technically, through slapping and popping and his use of effects like the fuzztone. Stanley broadened that concept, in terms of my thinking about soloing and developing the facility to play challenging music. Those two, in turn, allowed me to appreciate Jaco, who expanded my focus on a more musical level. Like a lot of people at the time, my reaction to Jaco was: This isn't a bass player—this is a musician who plays bass. There was so much music coming out of him, whether he was playing alone or fronting his big band. I also have to mention Paul Chambers, Ray Brown, Ron Carter, James Jamerson, Bootsy Collins, and Anthony Jackson as important influences.

 Munchables

Darryl "The Munch" Jones has played a number of basses during his tenure with the Rolling Stones, starting with his much-loved '66 Fender Jazz and including a "custom black" '65 Jazz, a sunburst '58 Precision, an Ernie Ball Music Man Sterling, an Albey Balgochian fretless, and two Sadowsky 4-strings. On the Stones' 2003 tour Darryl mainly played his white Lakland Darryl Jones Signature J-style. He also carries two other basses: his '66 Jazz, two '60s Fender Precisions, a Lakland hollowbody he'll use if the band plays Keith Richards's "You Don't Have to Mean It," and a turquoise Fender Custom Shop Jazz Bass built by J Black, who duplicated Darryl's '66. He strings all his basses with standard-gauge DR Stainless Steels, except his Lakland hollowbody and '66 Jazz, which both sport old flatwounds. His picks are standard-sized Ernie Balls, in heavy and extra-heavy gauges.

Darryl uses a two-channel Shure wireless system, one for his main Jazz and one for a Precision. Two Avalon U5 DIs send his signal to the house—one before and one after the effects and preamps, which are run through a Rocktron Patchmate switcher. The switcher sends the signal to a T.C. Electronic programmable EQ, a Triode Distortion stompbox, and sometimes a Line 6 FM4 Filter Modeler, as well as to one of two Ashly preamps, which have different EQ and gain settings for the J- and P-Basses. A Meyer Sound processor feeds the signal to two Crown Micro-Tech 1200 power amps (which each drive four Meyer UPA-1 1x12 cabinets) and two Crown Macro-Tech 2400 power amps (both of which power a pair of Meyer USW-1 2x15 cabs). Darryl also uses an Avalon U5 DI on the smaller "B" stage, where he plays the Custom Shop Jazz through an Ampeg B-15 reissue with EL34 tubes and a prototype speaker. "That's the stadium rig, but we cut it down for smaller venues," says Dave Rouze, who has been Darryl's tech since the '94 Voodoo Lounge tour.

What are your thoughts on the whole experience with the Stones to this point?

I'm thrilled to have become a part of their history. When I was a kid I didn't say, "I want to be Michael Jackson"—I'd say, "I want to *play bass* for Michael Jackson." Fortunately, my career has been the realization of many of those dreams.

In the eight years before he spoke to Karl Coryat in 2003, Darryl completed a second world tour with the Stones and had begun a third. He also expanded his cinematic side, scoring the 1997 film Love Jones *and acting in several movies, including* Village of the Damned *and* Gridlock. *Most important, he continued to refine his groove skills, and he shared the process with* Bass Player *readers.*

What's different about playing with the Stones this time?

We play better now. These guys are getting to be better musicians, even now. [Drummer] Charlie Watts is playing better than I've ever heard him play, and I think he and I are playing together better than ever. It's just one of those by-products of two people playing together over a long time.

What subtleties have you noticed about Charlie's groove?

Charlie is a rock drummer with jazz sensibilities. When he plays a fill, you start to realize his influences are more like Kenny Clarke and Max Roach than any of the early rock drummers. He doesn't really go [*mimics a straight 16th-note fill ending with a cymbal crash*], but more like [*mimics a looser, more explosive jazz-style fill*]. Also, his pocket is different. Jeff "Tain" Watts once told me that when you play drums, you want to shuffle with *everything*—hi-hat, bass drum, both hands. He said that even when you're playing a non-shuffle funk beat, there should be just a *whisper* of that shuffle in it. I think that's ever-present in Charlie's playing, because of his jazz sensibilities.

Do you think his style works better with your playing than with Bill Wyman's?

Bill Wyman is a great musician, but he isn't the same kind of player that I am. Charlie and the others seem to have gotten comfortable with someone who's more of a rock-solid player, and a little more sonically present, than Bill was. People have different opinions on whether that's good or bad for the Stones. But I'm benefiting from being more aware of what Charlie will do, and I'm better able to play with him—and I think the same is true from his side. Sometimes Charlie will play a fill and I'll play a fill, and they'll be exactly the same, or very similar—or they'll fit together like a puzzle. Playing with other musicians is like sex: Even if it's good to start out, if you stay interested it gets even better. You understand better how to do these little things that are kind of unmentionable—it's difficult to put it into words exactly what is occurring. Over time, you learn to fill up little cracks that may have existed due to a lack of familiarity.

What's the best way for a bass player to stay interested like that?

You have to keep actively listening to the drummer over the long haul. For any musicians who play together live, if they don't keep that in mind, it's a danger. It's like the difference between talking to someone who's looking past you—glancing around at everyone else in the room—as opposed to really looking in your eye and actively listening to you. When you talk to someone in that way, it creates a confidence to share certain things, and it's no different with music. When musicians know they're actively listening to each other, you open the door for a lot of magic to happen. The more you exercise this skill, the more you open that door.

How do you exercise it?

You can do it just by listening to a record. If you're listening to the Funk Brothers [Motown's '60s backing band], you'll get a great example of what it's like to be in the pocket and never leave it. And maybe then you'd listen to your own band's tape to hear what it's like not to be in the pocket. In either case, you're listening *actively*; you're still giving it your full attention. In fact, you should aim to give it so much attention that you disappear for a little while—other thoughts don't enter your mind, almost like you're meditating. You have to give so much attention to listening that it *becomes* your attention. You're no longer thinking about listening, and you're no longer even aware that you're listening—you're just listening. As long as you make yourself more sensitive to those vagaries, you'll make yourself a more sensitive listener, and therefore a more sensitive musician.

Do you ever tire of playing the same old rock 'n' roll songs night after night?

No, because with the Rolling Stones I don't have to play the same thing every night. Somebody else might disagree, but the bass lines aren't written in stone. A big reason why my style works with the Stones is that for them, rock 'n' roll meant those Motown records, in addition to a lot of other influences. And to me, rock 'n' roll is what the Stones did, so we have that merging point.

How much do they welcome your input during rehearsals?

We were recently learning a new tune Keith wrote, and I asked him, "So, how does the bass line go?" He looked at me and said, "I don't know—*you're* the bass player!" And Mick doesn't tell me to play such-and-such, because I'm the one who's been playing bass for 30 years. It's rare for someone to tell me what to play on the bass. They just don't think that way.

You've been playing with world-class musicians for a long time. But what advice do you have for a working bassist who's stuck with mediocre bandmates?

Let's say someone asks me how I get to do the gigs I do. I'll ask him what kinds of gigs he does, and he'll say, "Man, I'm in this cocktail band, and the drummer drags. It's just a drag—it isn't even a gig." And I'm like, "How do I do what I do? Not by thinking like that!" When you go on a gig, you have to remember that it's a privilege to play any kind of music—even sitting in your house by yourself. Music is this wonderful, universal language. It's meditative and spiritual. A lot of people get caught up in the frustrations, and they lose it, the way a preacher loses the calling. When you pick up an instrument, realize how blessed you are. It doesn't matter whether you're playing for 50,000 people or by yourself. I'm not saying I'm a master or guru of this stuff. It's just that when I pick up a bass, I'm conscious of how much it has given me, and I try to take that onstage with me wherever I go.

Web Site

www.therolling-stones.com/Band/darryl1.html

Darryl Jones Selected Discography

With the Rolling Stones: (all on Virgin) *Forty Licks*; *Bridges to Babylon*; *Stripped*; *Voodoo Lounge*. **With Miles Davis:** (both on Columbia) *You're Under Arrest*; *Decoy*. **With Sting:** (both on A&M) *Bring On the Night*; *The Dream of the Blue Turtles*. **With Madonna:** *Truth or Dare* soundtrack, Sire. **With Eric Clapton:** *Journeyman*, Epic. **With John Scofield:** *Still Warm*, Gramavision. **With Buckshot LeFonque:** *Buckshot LeFonque*, Columbia. **With Spike Lee & Branford Marsalis:** *Mo' Better Blues* soundtrack, Columbia. **With Philip Bailey:** *Inside Out*, Columbia. **With Joe Cocker:** *Organic*, Sony. **With B.B. King:** *Deuces Wild*, MCA. **With Randy Brecker:** *Toe to Toe*, MCA. **With Joan Armatrading:** *What's Inside*, RCA. **With Adam Holtzman:** *In a Loud Way*, Manhattan. **With Carmen Bradford:** *Finally Yours*, Amazing. **With Pee Wee Ellis:** *Blues Mission*, Gramavision. **With the Chieftains:** *Long Black Veil*, RCA. **With Chris Hunter:** *Chris Hunter*, Atlantic. **With Lenny White:** *Renderers of the Spirit*, Hip Bop. **With Mark Ledford:** *Miles 2 Go*, Polygram. **With Tania Maria:** *Outrageous*, Concord Picante. **With Nicklebag:** *Mas Feedback*, Lizard Group; *12 Hits & a Bump*, Iguana. **With David Murray:** *Tip*, DIW. **Soundtrack:** (bassist and composer) *Love Jones*, New Line Cinema.

Perfect Practice Makes Perfect

For his February 2003 interview with Karl Coryat,
Darryl wrote the following lesson on improving your groove.

YEARS AGO IN THE DAYS OF LP RECORDS, engineers would prepare a master by dropping a needle on a disc of acetate and actually cut the record—the needle would carve a groove into the disc as it went around and around. Now, if the engineer did this carefully—paying close attention that everything was going where it should be going—when you went to play that record back, it would play exactly the way it's supposed to play. But if the engineer was helter-skelter about the way that needle was cutting the groove, going crazy all over the place, when you played it back, that's how the record would play: helter-skelter and crazy.

I'm making an analogy about the way you practice. Practice doesn't make perfect; perfect practice makes perfect. Here's a great exercise: Pick a simple bass line, like the Staple Singers' "I'll Take You There" [David Hood on bass] Patrice Rushen's "Forget Me Nots" ["Ready" Freddy Washington] Elvis Presley's "In the Ghetto" [Tommy Cogbill], or James Brown's "Lickin' Stick" [Tim Drummond] and play it over and over and over again. Try to find that place where you're breathing and you're comfortable and actively listening to what you're doing. Play the bass line for at least 20 minutes. By doing that, you record this serious groove into your sense memory. And when you go back to "play that record"—to lift the needle arm—your sense memory will pick up right where you left off. So instead of sounding like you're all over the place, you'll be right there. You become a different kind of musician this way. And let me tell you something: People can feel it. The other musicians can feel it, the people sitting there listening can feel it, and that cute girl in the front row who can't stop wigglin'—she can feel it, too.

The more you familiarize yourself with the feeling of being really in the pocket, the more your body will go to that pocket—no matter what you're playing. You give yourself a kind of steadiness that not everyone else has, and you really begin to separate yourself as a groove player. A woman once came up to me after I sat in at a club, and she said, "Son, you looked like you were having a religious experience up there." It's true—when you're that far gone into the simplicity of something, you create something spiritual. And other musicians want to have that on their gig. I think that's part of the reason why I've been able to move in the circles I've moved in: because somewhere in my playing, there's always a little of that feeling.

Now, I'm not saying I sit at home and play "Satisfaction" or "Brown Sugar" for 20 minutes. But years ago, I spent 45 minutes playing the bass lines of songs like "I'll Take You There." I even played bass in the mirror, trying to get my body into it. My goal was to create this unified thing—physically, emotionally, and spiritually—so that when I'd go to play that bass line, it would sound like the world was coming to an end.

I once had a student who was working on "I'll Take You There" in the key of *F*. He was playing it like **Ex. 1a**, and he was having a real problem making it groove. I told him I knew that was the "proper" way to play it, but then I suggested that he play it like **Ex. 1b**—where you shift position to land on the *B♭*—and it made all the difference. When I'm trying to play a bass line and it isn't settling in just right, I ask myself, What note am I trying to land on and make feel a certain way? In this case, it's that *B♭*: I want to move to that note, and to me, that makes the line feel different. So sometimes just a fingering change makes a line settle into the groove more easily. When you're doing the 20-minute exercise, make sure you have the best fingering to make the line groove.

Ex. 1a

Ex. 1b

DOUG WIMBISH
Busting Out of the Loop

Interviewed by Chris Jisi, June 1997 and June 1999.

DOUG WIMBISH LEADS THE CHARGE as Jungle Funk takes the stage. Encamped stage left with his vast array of floor and rack effects, the group's unspoken leader stomps madly on pedals that color deep, loop-doubled grooves, furious pops and slaps, and soaring lead lines. His body tenses and relaxes in time with the music as his mouth silently mimics each new sound.

Any list of cutting-edge bassists from the post-Jaco era boasts an impressive crop of names. But check which of these bassists have been involved in a cross-section of cutting-edge *music*, and a single name dominates: Doug Wimbish. With his return to New York from the U.K., Doug brings along a bi-continental session ace reputation and budding bass-hero status. More important, Jungle Funk may at last bust him out on his home turf. Formed in Europe with drummer Will Calhoun and ex-Sting percussionist/vocalist Vinx, the innovative trio combines state-of-the-art technology, quality songs, and serious musicianship, all with a club-savvy dance sensibility. The resulting shows and eponymous live album are collages of high-energy drum 'n' bass and hip-hop grooves, smooth, passionate vocals, and heady sonic improvisation.

Born in Bloomfield, Connecticut, on September 22, 1956, Doug Wimbish started on guitar at age 12 but had switched to the more-in-demand bass by 14. Raised on radio R&B, he took lessons at the nearby Hartford Artist's Collective, where he met guitarist Skip McDonald. Eventually the two joined Wood Brass & Steel, a funk horn band signed by All Platinum (soon to be Sugar Hill). In 1979 Wimbish and McDonald teamed with drummer Keith LeBlanc to form the Sugar Hill house rhythm section that put rap on the map and "the bass in your face" with such pioneering hip-hop classics as Grandmaster Flash's "The Message" and Flash & Melle Mel's "White Lines."

Doug Wimbish

Seeking to continue their radical, anything-goes approach to track-making, the trio split Sugar Hill and the fickle Stateside music scene and headed to London in 1984. They soon hooked up with experimental dance producer Adrian Sherwood to create a match made in club heaven. Calling themselves Tackhead, the new foursome altered the face of British music from the dance floor up. In addition to its own Mark Stewart and Gary Clail, Tackhead provided the pulse for a wide range of seminal rap, industrial, dub, post-punk, and acid-jazz artists, ranging from Depeche Mode and Erasure to reggae balladeer Bim Sherman and mixmaster Tim Simenon. As Tackhead's underground sound began permeating the mainstream throughout Europe and back in the U.S., Wimbish found himself in heavy demand for sessions with Madonna, Annie Lennox, Seal, Squeeze, Jeff Beck, Billy Idol, and Carly Simon, and producers Arthur Baker and Peter Wolf.

Mick Jagger tapped Wimbish for two solo albums and tours, which led to an offer to audition for the Rolling Stones and Doug's later appearance on 1997's *Bridges to Babylon*. Instead, he accepted an invitation from Vernon Reid to replace Muzz Skillings in Living Colour. The union produced 1993's *Stain* and showed great promise—but Reid broke up the band soon after. Wimbish headed back to Europe with an even more global focus, working on trend-setting world-beat, trip-hop, ambient, and drum 'n' bass projects with artists such as Björk, Indian tabla savant Talvin Singh, Tehran vocalist Sussan Deyhim, and multi-instrumentalist Richard Horowitz. Returning to New York City and his Connecticut home (where he built his Nova Sound Studio) in the late '90s, Wimbish and frequent project partner Will Calhoun joined Vernon Reid and Corey Glover in the re-formed Living Colour. While the band was preparing their next release, Doug was working with rapper Mos Def and his own project, Head Fake, with Calhoun.

With all of its complex technology, how does Jungle Funk function onstage?

Despite the technology we approach Jungle Funk in a very organic way. Essentially we're a song band made up of two percussionists and a bassist. But because of our collective musical backgrounds and the equipment at hand, we can cover a lot of ground and assume various roles. What we do within each song is spontaneously explore and recreate textures and frequencies, so every night is different. The challenge is to keep a balance between the song, the performance, and the technology, while always maintaining a high level of communication and energy.

To clarify your role, can you explain what you use and play on the album's opener, "Ugly Face"?

On that tune we play to a preprogrammed loop that has a drum beat and a bit of keyboards, which I trigger from the Planet Phatt in my rack. Against the loop I play a bass line with my Spector 4-string, a DOD Envelope Filter, and a bit of chorusing from my T.C. Electronic 2290, which I always have on. For the deep, dubby groove at the end I just turn the bass EQ knob on my Trace head all the way up.

Rackhead

A look at Doug Wimbish's gear and signal chain may evoke visions of trying to land a jumbo jet while playing Twister. But Doug doesn't find his stage surroundings quite so imposing. "I rarely have more than a few effects going at any one time. If I had to, I could recreate the whole vibe from a couple of floor pedals. This is more about having a lot of sound options."

The "mothership" of Wimbish's setup is his rackmounted stereo T.C. Electronic 2290 Dynamic Digital Delay. Its floor controller and "assign" pedals enable him to sample up to 11 seconds at CD quality and access various delays. His other four rack effects include a DigiTech 2112 Studio Guitar System for "psycho effects," a DigiTech 256XL Multi Effects Processor for various effects, a DigiTech IPS33B Super Harmony Machine for harmonizing, and a Planet Phatt Swing System JV1080 for multi-timbres as well as drum and keyboard sounds and loops. These are all hooked up in parallel to the 2290, which then goes into the effects-send jack of Doug's amp. Joining his rack and amp head on top of his cabinets are a Yamaha REX50 for reverb, a Novation MIDI keyboard trigger for use with the Planet Phatt, and a Lexicon JamMan for samples and loops (activated from a footswitch pedal). "I have up to a minute of sample time on the JamMan, but it's not the same sonic quality as the 2290, so that's my main sample/loop unit."

Spread in front of him onstage are his array of effects pedals. "I don't mark the settings on them, and I unplug them after each show—so I'm tweaking knobs. I like getting a fresh start each night. I just need to know their basic frequencies, because the same pedal can sound vastly different from room to room. Also important is arranging them so you have the most flexibility sonically and musically. I put my tone shapers first (SansAmp Bass DI and GT2 Distortion, Line 6 Bass POD, Danelectro Daddy-O Distortion, and Snarling Dog Blue Doo Tube Emulator); then my 'bendy' pedals (DigiTech Whammy, DOD FX25 Envelope Filter, Dunlop Cry Baby 535Q and GCB100 bass wahs, Boss AW-2 Auto Wah, and Snarling Dog Mold Spore Wah); then my sound processors—all the 'wobbly' stuff (Boss BF-2 Flanger, Boss PN-2 Tremolo, Ibanez PH5 Phaser, and Ibanez FL99 Flanger); then my delays and reverbs—anything that messes with the time (Boss DD-2 Digital Delay, DSD-2 Digital Sampler Delay, and SYB-3 Bass Synth); and finally, my Ernie Ball volume pedal as a master on/off control. The only pedal I'll move around is my DOD envelope filter." Between rack and floor effects, Wimbish attacks his samples and loops with the 2290, the JamMan, the Planet Phatt (for drums and keyboards only), and the Boss DSD2 Digital Sampler and DD2 Digital Delay.

Wimbish's main axes are Spectors and Ibanezes. His Spectors are 1987 NS-2 4- and 5-strings (both with EMG PJ pickups), a 1988 fretless 4, a 1999 6, 2000 fretted and fretless 5's, and a fretted 6. His Ibanezes comprise his signature DWB3 4-string with EMG PJ pickups and neck-through-body design—"I mostly use neck-throughs because with the amount of effects I run I need a flat, even response throughout the full range of my bass. I even know what basses work best with what effects.")—older prototype signature 4-, 5- and 6-strings; and an upcoming Ibanez 5-string with his new design features. His remaining assortment includes his Sugar Hill '72 Jazz Bass, a '57 P-Bass, two Steve Chick/Peavey MIDI basses, Warwick Streamer 4- and 6-strings, an Ovation 5-string acoustic bass guitar, an NS Design electric upright, several Guild Ashbory basses, and a Harvey Citron acoustic/electric 5-string. His strings are Rotosound steel roundwounds in three different gauge sets: .040, .060, .075, .095; .040, .060, .080, .100; or .045, .065, .085, .105, all with a .030 C string and a .120 B string when required.

Doug plugs into SWR gear: two SM-900 heads powering two Goliath 4x10 cabinets and a Son of Bertha 1x15. A Power 750 drives his Big Ben 1x18 cabinet. He also uses his Megoliath 8x10 in some settings. His connections are made via Monster Cables. Other keys to Wimbish's setup are "a good soundman and a good monitor system. Generally it all comes down to frequencies, textures, and dynamics. Ultimately, it's all about the air and how you work it."

How do you get those dive-bombs in some of your fills?

Those are foot-triggered from my Boss Digital Sampler pedal. Sometimes I'll turn off my volume pedal between tunes and quickly sample a technique or an effect pedal on the fly to have ready for the next tune. In this case, I used the Boss to sample myself detuning the *E* string, and then I applied it in the tune. I'll also use jelly jars like a slide to play real-time dive bombs down the neck.

"Trance" seems to have a doubled bass line.

We play to a DAT that Will triggers, which contains a full track I did three years ago for a solo project. It has live drums and a lot of studio-manipulated bass. All of the sounds you hear at the top—except for the chanting and the didgeridoo—are my Warwick 6-string on the DAT. The groove starts with me playing a repetitive rhythmic figure on my low *D*, and I double that live with the Warwick, adding accents, pops, and fills with various effects. The main ones are my Boss Flanger set for quick tremolo, and a delay time of compound triplets on the 2290 that I tapped in right before the tune. The guitar-like lines are from my DigiTech Whammy Pedal pitched up two octaves and my Danelectro Daddy-O distortion pedal.

What's the distortion effect at the top of "September"?

That's my Spector 4 through my Cry Baby Wah and Daddy-O distortion with some 2290 delay added. At the end of those eight bars I have to stop the distortion, turn off the delay, start the envelope follower, and pan from back pickup to both pickups—all in a split second. You learn the value of fast footwork, good balance, and flat-soled shoes! What's also interesting on this tune is that Vinx creates a live loop. He starts by playing a drum loop from a Keith LeBlanc CD on a MiniDisc recorder, and then samples live on one of his two JamMans, and then we play to that. By the end of the song, we've dropped out and he becomes a one-man band with both JamMans linked up playing samples.

How do you get the helicopter effect at the end of some of the two-bar phrases throughout "Temporary Love"?

That's a combination of my envelope filter and what I call "flamenco slaps." I lightly fret a low *D* on my Spector 5 so there's no pitch, and I position my right-hand index finger and thumb as if I were about to pinch the *B* string down at the end of the fingerboard. Using a fast back-and-forth wrist motion, I alternately tap the fingerboard with my index finger and pull out the string with my thumb. I start soft and get louder so the envelope filter opens up in response. At certain points I also use my Boss Bass Synth pedal, which has a preset overdrive, flanger, and long delay that carries the effects colors into later beats, like waves. There are no loops or DATs on this track; it's all played live, as is "Torn" and "Still I Try."

In contrast, there's more of a mechanized, industrial, drum 'n' bass flavor to "Cycles" and "People."

Those tracks came from the drum 'n' bass project Will and I were doing, so there's more of an ambient, sampled groove happening, with less vocals. We played to DATs and pretty much stayed in that vibe. Since our JamMans are linked together, one of us can start a groove and the other two can punch in overdubs and build a whole track, which is something we've been doing more of lately. In addition to bass loops, I can do live drum and keyboard loops through my Planet Phatt and Novation keyboard.

How did you first get into effects and loops?

I've been into effects since I started playing. I always loved the imagery of the sound of effects, whether it was Hendrix, Led Zeppelin, Anthony Jackson on "For the Love of Money," or Jaco with his MXR digital delays. In the early '70s I had a Fender Mustang with an MXR Phase 90, a Mu-Tron, and an Echoplex. I first became aware of looping through using the Echoplex, but looping and sampling really came into play when I moved to London in 1984 and met Adrian Sherwood. We did a lot of experimenting with rack gear and pedal effects in the studio, and I tried to recreate that live with Tackhead. It all came full circle when I got the T.C.

Doug Wimbish Selected Discography

Solo album: *Trippy Notes for Bass*, On U Sound. **With Jungle Funk:** *Jungle Funk*, Zebra. **With Living Colour:** *Collideoscope*, Sanctuary; *Pride*, Epic; *Stain*, Epic. **With Tackhead:** *Strange Things*, SBK; *Friendly as a Hand Grenade*, TVT. **With Sugar Hill (various artists):** *Sugar Hill Records Story*, Rhino. **With Grandmaster Flash:** *The Message*, Castle. **With the Rolling Stones:** *Bridges to Babylon*, Virgin. **With Mick Jagger:** *Wandering Spirit*, Atlantic; *Primitive Cool*, Columbia. **With Seal:** *Seal*, Warner Bros. **With James Brown:** *Star Time*, Polydor. **With Annie Lennox:** (both on Arista) *Medusa*; *Diva*. **With Joe Satriani:** (both on Sony) *Time Machine*; *Extremist*. **With Jeff Beck:** *Flash*, Epic. **With Madonna:** *Erotica*, Warner Bros. **With Carly Simon:** *Letters Never Sent*, Arista; *Spoiled Girl*, Epic. **With George Clinton:** *Some of My Best Jokes Are Friends*, Capitol. **With Herb Alpert:** *Colors*, Almo Sounds. **With Al Green:** *Your Heart's in Good Hands*, MCA. **With Mos Def:** *Black on Both Sides*, Rawkus. **With Mos Def & Faith Evans:** *Brown Sugar*, soundtrack, MCA. **With the Yohimbe Brothers:** *Front End Lifter*, Ropeadope. **With Nicklebag:** *Mas Feedback*, Lizard Group; *12 Hits & a Bump*, Iguana. **With Little Axe:** *Hard Grind*, Fat Possum; *Wolf That House Built*, Wired. **With Mark Stewart & the Maffia:** (all on Mute) *Mark Stewart & the Maffia*; *Red Zone*; *Hysteria*. **With Gary Clail:** *Tackhead Tape Time*, Capitol. **With Africa Bambaataa:** (both on Tommy Boy) *Looking For the Perfect Beat*; *Planet Rock*. **With Depeche Mode:** *Ultra*, Mute. **With Bim Sherman:** *Need to Live*, EFA; *Rub-A-Dub*, EFA; *Miracle*, Mantra. **With Richard Horowitz & Sussan Deyhim:** *Majoud*, Sony. **With Peter Wolf:** *Come as You Are*, EMI. **With Freddie Jackson:** *Don't Let Love Slip Away*, Capitol. **With Billy Idol:** *Cyber Punk*, Chrysalis. **With B.B. King:** *King of the Blues*, MCA. **With Ron Wood:** *Slide on This*, Continuum. **With Michael Bolton:** *The Hunger*, Columbia. **With Rose Royce:** *The Very Best of Rose Royce*, Rhino. **With Bomb the Bass:** *Clear Cut*, Universal. **With Force M.D.'s:** *Touch and Go*, Warner Bros. **With Audio Active:** *Spaced Dolls*, Dream Machine. **With David Garza:** *Overdub*, Atlantic. **With Dhafer Youssef:** *Electric Sufi*, Enja. **With Wood Brass & Steel:** *Wood Brass & Steel*, Turbo.

Electronic 2290 in 1987. Being able to play along with myself really opened me up to a whole other head; it made me a better bassist and writer.

What was it like being involved in the roots of rap with Sugar Hill?

It was an incredible, invaluable experience. Like Motown's Funk Brothers, we were there at the dawn of a new musical form, so there were no rules or traditions to follow. As a result, we had the freedom to experiment and be completely creative using our backgrounds in R&B, jazz, and rock. I threw in anything I could think of—harmonics, double-stops, detunings, slaps and taps, dive bombs, fuzz bass. Skip's guitar style was sparse and percussive and Keith favored the lower half of his kit, so I really got to step forward musically and in the mix. The three of us worked around the clock as players, writers, arrangers, producers, and engineers for over 30 different artists from 1979 through 1985.

What advice do you give bassists who want to get into effects?

The key is to figure out your personality and the kind of sound that will reflect it. Start simple with one pedal, and try to match it with the sound you're looking for. A flanger is a good place to begin because it will give you chorus as well. Or try an envelope follower, which is something you can use on gigs. Spice things up however you want from there. What I like is that I can get other sounds out of my instrument, and that can only help bass players since we now have to compete with synths, keyboard bass, and samples.

How about bassists who want to get into looping?

There are a lot of quality multi-effects units with sample-and-hold functions, but to get the full benefit of looping—which is the ability to play along with yourself and compose—the key is to get the most time, and that involves a larger economic step.

Start by playing a basic groove, sample and loop it, and then keep playing against it, layering samples, the way I did on "Perculator." It's like having your own little studio—and it's a great disciplinary tool, because you hear what you sound like. If you have effects or interesting techniques, throw them all at the machine and see what comes out. The whole process creates a natural progression of inspiration that will broaden your vocabulary. Also, you'll find new and different uses for your most tired, clichéd licks.

What wisdom can you offer bassists who want to pursue a career as diverse as yours?

Develop your skills as much as possible, but be aware that it's equal parts skill and luck. Don't put all your tones in one basket, and listen and learn from every project you do, whether it's a good or bad experience. Also, try to team up with positive people who are on the same page conceptually; music is a reflection of your life, and how you live comes out in your playing. Most important, be someone who is easy and enjoyable to work with—because ultimately your attitude is going to determine your altitude.

Web Site

www.dougwimbish.com

Is It Live or Is It Doug-Effects?

THE MOST INTRIGUING AND MUSICALLY REWARDING ASPECT of Jungle Funk is the trio's ability to blur the line between man and machine. Case in point: Doug Wimbish's helicopter fills on "Temporary Love." "I'll use different pedals and samples quickly, before the ear catches on, and mix them in with straight bass and the techniques I've developed. So in that sense *I'm* an effect." Here are four prime examples of processed Doug, and, as a bonus, two examples of pure Doug from his Sugar Hill heyday.

Example 1 recalls the main four-bar groove from "Worship." Wimbish thumbed his Spector 5 with some envelope filter and chorus, and he stepped on his flanger (in a fast tremolo setting) for the pickup notes at the end of bars 1 and 5. Played to a DAT drum loop and live drums, the part has a subtle Afro-Cuban feel. "It wasn't intentional when I wrote it, but in drum 'n' bass music the bass ostinatos tend to have a deep tone and leave a lot of space due to the double-time/half-time feel going on. So there is a stylistic correlation to Latin bass."

Example 2 illustrates Wimbish's late-in-the-track, two-bar subharmonic groove on "Ugly Face," which he subtly alters as he goes. Note the ghost-notes and the move up a half-step at the end of the second bar. "That's sort of my 'A Love Supreme' meets 'Inner City Blues' trippy vibe. When I'm in groove mode with Jungle Funk, I apply what I call the 'peekaboo theory.' I lay it down while patiently waiting to find and place those few tasty notes that will enhance Will's drumming. To me, playing a groove is like pushing water in a tub. Eventually it comes back; there's an ebb and flow. Occasionally I'll make a splash—but then I'll let the water settle."

Example 3 recalls the four-bar theme from Wimbish's bass anthem "Torn," which he plays live on his Spector 4 with a "Vibrolux, Leslie-like" setting from his DigiTech IPS33B. Listen for the open *G* in bars 1 and 3, which rings as Doug grabs the 5ths on the *A* and *D* strings, and the melodic use of close and wide intervals in bars 2 and 4. "I originally wrote this in 1994 during a Mick Jagger session. I wanted one of those end-of-concert, huddle-together songs with the lighters held in the air. Will, Vinx, and I rewrote the lyrics for Jungle Funk."

Example 4 is inspired by the eight-bar opening and verse figure from "Still I Try," which continues in the chordal bass anthem tradition of "Torn" with the help of some pedals. "Even with all the resources at hand, we always retain a basic, minimalist approach. I love putting together songs that can work with just a singer and a bass." Operating above the 12th fret of his Spector 4, Wimbish plays the ascending arpeggios in bars 1–6 with false harmonics by lightly touching his right index finger to the string halfway between his fretted note and the bridge, and then plucking just behind with his thumb as he lifts his index. Already running delay and chorus from his 2290, he colors the held notes in bars 2, 4, 6, and 8 with additional effects. For the high *G* in bar 2 he steps on his Boss Auto Wah "to get the wobbly effect"; in bar 4 he opts for no effect; in bar 6 it's back to the Auto Wah; and for that *Ebadd9* chord in bar 8, it's the flanger.

Example 5a takes us back to the dawn of rap, with a verse groove similar to the ones Doug played on tunes like Grandmaster Flash & Melle Mel's "White Lines." "I tried to be simplistic, through the use of just two notes—but at the same time I wanted to create the illusion of two bass parts overlapping." says Doug, who typically used a '72 Fender Jazz. **Example 5b** shows the kind of riffy line Doug played to create contrast in the verse.

Ex. 1

Ex. 2

Ex. 3

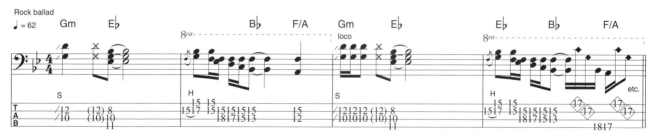

Ex. 4

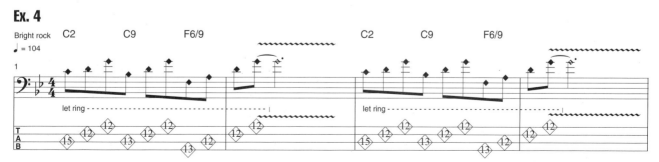

Ex. 4 (continued)

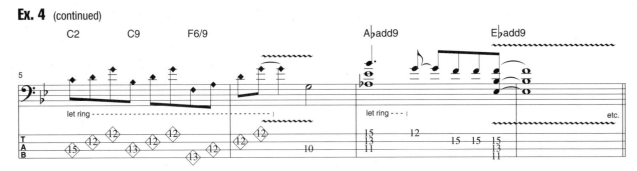

Ex. 5a

Ex. 5b

BAKITHI KUMALO
From Graceland to Gotham

Interviewed by Gregory Isola, April 1996, and Chris Jisi, May 1998.

FOR MOST OF US, Paul Simon's *Graceland* served as an introduction to Bakithi Kumalo (Bah-GEE-TEE Koo-MAH-low). The multi-platinum 1986 album wasn't Kumalo's first appearance on record—but it was his first work outside his native South Africa. Says Simon, "I still remember the first time I heard the enormous, *incredible* sound Bakithi got out of his fretless bass—almost like a horn, but so primal." Since then, the soft-spoken, affable bassist has recorded with artists ranging from Herbie Hancock and Laurie Anderson to Cyndi Lauper and Mickey Hart. In addition, he has released two solo albums, and his foray into the New York jingle scene has assured him a place in all of our homes. Whether it's propping up images of Kentucky Fried Chicken or UPS delivery trucks—or guiding the Paul Simon–penned theme from *Oprah*—Bakithi's soaring, singing bass is here to stay.

Under African Skies

Born in the South African township of Alexandra on May 10, 1956, Kumalo grew up in nearby Soweto, surrounded by music. "My mother had a band," he recalls. "She was a singer and my dad played guitar. My uncle had a band, too; he was a saxophone player, and I was always checking him out when he was practicing." Early on, Bakithi did more than just listen. "One time my uncle's bass player got drunk and couldn't make it for a wedding gig. I knew the set—it consisted of simple I–IV–V songs and traditional South African music—and my uncle asked, 'Can you handle it?' 'Oh, yes! I'm ready,' I said. I was seven years old; the bass was so heavy, and my fingers were *small*. But I had to play, and I held the groove for them."

After formally joining his uncle's band, little Bakithi hit up every local musician he could find for information and instruction. "I was a troublemaker," he laughs. "There were a lot of good musicians around home back then. At all of their rehearsals, the bass players would be saying, 'Oh, no—here he comes again!'"

Bakithi Kumalo

Despite his uncle's chiding ("He used to say, 'Music in this country doesn't pay; I don't want you to end up like me!'"), Kumalo was determined to become a professional musician. When he was ten years old the lure of a good bass and steady gigs enticed him to join an 18-month showband tour of Zululand in the remote South African province of Natal. It was a formative experience for the young bassist, in many ways. "We played schools and hospitals and prisons, and it was very rough. My strings would break and there were no music stores, so I had to patch them and keep playing. My fingers would bleed all over the neck. And since there weren't any supermarkets, either, we ended up not eating much—just living on bread and oranges and sugar cane."

It was on this bare-bones tour that Bakithi made a radical change in his playing technique. "In Zululand I got the dream. Before, I was playing everything with my thumb; my uncle's bass player used a pick, so I had never seen anybody play with his fingers. Then I dreamt of somebody playing bass with his fingers, although I couldn't see the person's head. The next morning I woke up and tried to play with *my* fingers. It was a bit difficult, but I worked on it. That dream saved me."

Kumalo's welcome home from Natal was almost as rough as the tour. "My mother could hardly look at me, because I looked so bad from being on the road so long. She said, 'You have to get a regular job. If you go back to play music one more time, you're not staying in my house!' I said, 'Mommy, no way! You mean I've wasted all my time going to Zululand and studying my playing and struggling? I can't go back.' Luckily, some of my friends called with some recording work. That's when the whole thing started."

Bakithi soon found himself in demand throughout Soweto. "I was really happening! I did a lot of local records and got involved in studio work. I was playing 12 songs a day, for about ten rand a track—which is about five dollars [*laughs*]. There were a lot of studios where they liked my playing, but the other bass players really hated me; I was so little and so young and everybody wanted to work with me. Most of the bassists I grew up with lost work. But I just wanted to play, and I was really open to learn."

Throughout the '70s and early '80s, Kumalo cemented his reputation as one of South Africa's top session bassists. Along the way, he picked up a Washburn B-40 fretless bass. "It was the cheapest bass in the store, because nobody wanted to play it. I bought it because I could afford it." He quickly found an affinity for it.

Kumalo's Cache

Bakithi Kumalo has remained a Washburn fan since his first B-40 fretless, which he played on *Graceland*. His stable has grown to include 4-, 5-, and 6-string fretted and fretless exotic wood Washburns, a Washburn 8-string, fretted and fretless Washburn 5-string acoustic bass guitars, a fretless Modulus Quantum 5, a Warwick Thumb 5, and an Alembic 5. He strings all of his basses with DR Hi-Beams (gauged .030 .045, .065, .085, .105, .130).

Onstage, Bakithi plays through a Warwick Mark Four 800 head and Warwick 4x10 and 1x15 cabinets. He generally records direct in the studio and eschews effects pedals.

"It's a beautiful instrument. Fretless is not at all easy, but you can really make it sing. Growing up in South Africa, I heard traditional singers from a lot of different tribes. Their music is so open, and that's what I try for with my bass playing; I like to hold down the groove, and then I find my space to sing." In addition to steady studio work, he often accompanied major international stars on the South African legs of their world tours. Still, he never left his homeland—and he always dreamed of America.

Here Comes Rhymin' Simon

In early 1985 Paul Simon traveled to Johannesburg in search of musicians to help him with his new project—an ambitious fusion of American pop and South African styles that would become *Graceland*. One of the first people he contacted was veteran producer Hendrick Lebone.

"I had done a lot of traditional Sotho music with Hendrick," Bakithi says, "and he knew I was a good bass player. So when Paul said he was looking for musicians, Hendrick called me up. I said, 'Paul Simon? Who's Paul Simon?' [*Laughs.*] So he started to sing 'Mother and Child Reunion' and 'Bridge Over Troubled Water.' Aahh, okay, *him*. I knew the songs—but I didn't know who Paul Simon was."

Kumalo and Simon hit it off from their first meeting. "I brought in my fretless and we started to play some grooves, and it just happened. I was tense at first—you know, 'I'm working with Paul Simon, so I'd better knock down these tracks!'—but Paul loved everything I played. Then he said to me, 'I'm going to take you to New York to finish all the tracks.' I said, 'Oh God, yes! Please, it's my dream!' I was really ready to come to the States. I started to listen to British radio for an hour a day to get my English together."

Once in New York, Bakithi gave the rest of the world a taste of Soweto with his work on *Graceland*, and the expatriate bassist found himself exposed to a world of bass playing many of us take for granted. "I heard about Stanley Clarke and Jaco Pastorius. And when I first heard Weather Report, I thought, Wow, that bass sounds like the bass I'm playing! Then my ears were really open to everybody playing bass. I listened to Marcus Miller, Victor Bailey—*everybody*."

After they finished recording *Graceland*, Simon and company embarked on an international tour that was by far the biggest gig Bakithi had ever played. Of course, Paul wasn't the least bit worried. "As a bassist in a live setting," Simon explains, "Bakithi is extraordinary. He's a very good analyst of rhythm: he lays down a really fundamental groove and he's very solid, but there's always space for the singer."

Kumalo, on the other hand, was terrified. "It was scary! The first gig we played was in Germany, and I'd never played for so many people. I couldn't face the audience; I just felt like crying. I was praying and meditating before the show: 'Please, I don't want to make mistakes.' And when we played 'You Can Call Me Al,' the people knew the bass solo was coming I could see they were saying, 'Is this the bass player on the record? We'll find out when that solo comes!' When it was close, they started to watch me. And, man—when I played that solo, I just knocked everybody down! [*Laughs.*] After that, the other shows were like a piece of cake."

You Can Call Him Al

Three minutes and 44 seconds into *Graceland*'s sixth cut is a two-bar bass break that has confounded as many bassists as it has inspired. "That was my idea," says Bakithi of the wildly descending lick in the first bar. "We were recording that song on my birthday, and there was a space to fill, so Paul said, 'Go ahead, Bakithi. Do what you like.' I just played—and they *loved* it. It was one take. Listening back, I didn't know what happened; I thought it was from God, you know? I never planned it."

Now for the tricky part: the second bar of the solo is actually the first bar played backward. Engineer Roy Halee simply flipped the tape over and spliced the two parts together. "People have tried to cop those licks," notes Simon, "but it's physically impossible." So the next time your band covers "You Can Call Me Al," forget about trying to duplicate Bakithi's mutant solo and take a tip from Paul: Just do what you like.

Biting the Big Apple

After touring the world with Simon, Kumalo's professional profile grew considerably, and he spent several years commuting between Soweto and New York City. One of his favorite collaborations during this period was with Hugh Masekela. "I met Hugh during the *Graceland* tour," Bakithi remembers, "and I really wanted to work with him. I hadn't even been born when he left South Africa because of the problems there, but he became like a father to me. Of course, his music is a good challenge—lots of cues and stuff—so I couldn't play my fretless. I always had to see his face and hands, so I just played the fretted because I don't have to look at it."

In 1983 Bakithi committed himself to living in New York year-round, and he hasn't looked back. "Friends I met through *Graceland* and the tour introduced me to a lot of people. And my manager sent out tapes to the jingle houses, just to let people know I was in town. Since then, I've been busy. Will Lee told me, 'Man, people call me and want me to play like Bakithi!' He said, 'Daddy, you'd better take care of business!'" The experience has enabled Bakithi to showcase his diversity. "Just because I'm from South Africa doesn't mean I have to play South African music." And what better place to mix it all together than New York? "Aahh, yes," Bakithi agrees. "I hear everything here. Being around so many great musicians is a challenge, but it's great. My dream has come true."

Web Site

www.boneinthenose.com

Bakithi Kumalo Selected Discography

Solo albums: (both on Siam) *In Front of My Eyes*; *San Bonan*. **With Paul Simon:** (all on Warner Bros.) *You're the One*; *Capeman* soundtrack; *Rhythm of the Saints*; *Graceland*. **With Herbie Hancock:** *Gershwin's World*, Verve. **With Mickey Hart:** *Supralingua*, Rykodisc. **With Cyndi Lauper:** (both on Epic) *Hat Full of Stars*, *A Night to Remember*. **With Anton Fig:** *Figments*, Planula Records. **With Gloria Estefan:** *Destiny*, Sony. **With Hugh Masekela:** *Hope*, Triloka; *Uptownship*, BMG. **With Harry Belafonte:** *Paradise in Gazankulu*, EMI/Manhattan. **With Chris Botti:** *Caught* soundtrack, Polygram; *Midnight Without You*, Verve/Forecast. **With Randy Brecker:** *Into the Sun*, Concord Jazz. **With Laurie Anderson:** *Strange Angels*, Warner Bros. **With Edie Brickell:** *Picture Perfect Morning*, Geffen. **With Hiram Bullock:** *Carrasco*, Fantasy. **With Eileen Ivers:** *Crossing the Bridge*, Sony. **With Miriam Makeba:** *Eyes on Tomorrow*, Verve. **With Grover Washington Jr.:** *Soulful Strut*, Columbia. **With Paul Winter:** *Celtic Solstice*, Living Music. **With Ruben Rada:** *Montevideo*, Big World Music. **With Tony Cedras:** *Vision Over People*, Gorilla.

Diamonds & Soul

TO CREATE THE SOARING FRETLESS LINES that are the lifeblood of Paul Simon's *Graceland*, Bakithi Kumalo drew from his extensive knowledge of the music of his native South Africa. **Example 1** shows the kick-drum pattern of a Zulu groove in the popular South African musical style of Mbaqanga [Mm-bah-KANG-ga]. Says Bakithi, "The kick drum plays the most important beats: the "and" of *one* and the "and" of *three*. The bass line must lock with the kick drum." **Example 2** shows the essential bass groove; note how Bakithi plays the lower note of the octaves when matching the kick-drum figure. **Example 3** is a variation in which Bakithi uses more ghost-note motion. "The 16th-note pulse comes from the hi-hat. I use the ghosted notes to help me keep the feel, which I got from listening to Jaco." **Example 4** shows a typical Bakithi fill. "Traditionally, the bass plays fills in the spaces between vocal sections, but overall its most important function is to keep the groove." Recorded examples of two of Bakithi's Zulu-style grooves and fills can be heard on "Diamonds on the Soles of Her Shoes" and "You Can Call Me Al," from *Graceland*.

Example 5 is the kick-drum pattern of a Sotho [SOO-too] groove in the Mbaqanga style. (Zulu and Sotho are two of the 11 South African tribes.) "It's basically a bouncing shuffle, but the "and" of *one* and *three* remain important beats." **Example 6** shows the essential bass groove with its shuffle-triplet feel; the last note of each triplet is usually accented. **Example 7** is a variation with sliding double-stops for color. "Traditional Sotho has no bass, so I listened to the accordion player's left hand and borrowed from that." **Example 8** doubles a vocal line; it can also be used as a fill between vocal sections. A recorded example of Bakithi's Sotho-style grooves can be heard on *Graceland*'s "The Boy in the Bubble." He also recommends checking out South African recordings in record stores' World Music sections. Overall, Kumalo advises, "Start slowly and practice with a metronome. Clap or play the kick-drum patterns first to get used to the rhythm, and then move on to the bass lines. Also, tape yourself so you can hear your progress."

Ex. 1

Bass drum pattern

Ex. 2

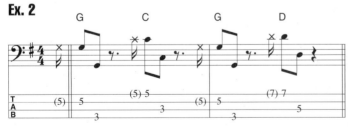

Ex. 3

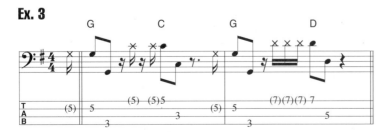

Ex. 4

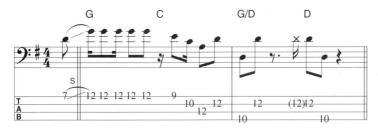

Ex. 5

Bass drum pattern

Ex. 6

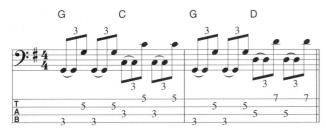

Ex. 7

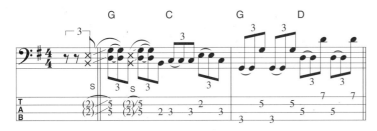

Ex. 8

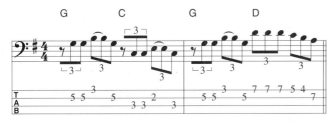

CHAPTER 6

Rock the Boat

FLEA • LES CLAYPOOL • MIKE GORDON

The '90s brought us a number of exceptional explorers who carried on in the bold tradition of Jack Bruce, John Entwistle, Paul McCartney, Geddy Lee, and Billy Sheehan. Working in three diverse but equally adventurous bands, they sailed the high seas of sound while still anchoring the groove.

FLEA

Rock Funk Bass Magik

Interviewed by Karl Coryat, January/February 1992; Scott Malandrone and Karl Coryat, February 1996; and E.E. Bradman and Chris Jisi, August 2002.

F EW HAVE INSPIRED MORE POST–P-FUNK BASS GROOVES THAN FLEA. Lickety-split slap work and nimble fingerstyle lines on an Ernie Ball Music Man StingRay first made the Red Hot Chili Peppers groovemaster super-popular with bassists in the late '80s. The Peppers themselves caught fire with millions of fans with their signature punk-funk style and over-the-top stage antics. On the band's first four albums—*Red Hot Chili Peppers* (1984), *Freaky Styley* ('85), *Uplift Mofo Party Plan* ('87), and *Mother's Milk* ('89), Flea mixed the thumping innovations of Larry Graham and Louis Johnson with his own style, built on punk-rock abandon. On *Blood Sugar Sex Magik* ('91), he had already begun to forsake slapping for a more melodic, song-serving fingerstyle, and 1995's *One Hot Minute*, 1999's *Californication*, and 2002's *By the Way* were further proof Flea and the band were growing and changing. "My biggest strength as a musician is that I sound like myself, not anybody else," Flea asserts. "I think the main point of music is expression, not trying to sound like other people."

Michael "Flea" Balzary was born on October 16, 1962, in Melbourne, Australia, and moved with his family to New York when he was four years old. His mother later divorced his father and moved to Los Angeles, where she married Walter Urban, a jazz bassist who favored serious bebop—Flea recalls happily rolling around on the floor listening to jam sessions at home. At age 11 his stepdad encouraged him to learn trumpet, which he played all through junior high school and high school in the jazz bands and orchestras. In high school he met Hillel Slovak, who asked the trumpeter if he wanted to play bass in his band. Flea bought a Fender Mustang and did his first gig two weeks later. Influenced previously by jazz trumpeters, he was exposed by Slovak to Led Zeppelin, Rush, and Jimi Hendrix. Meanwhile, at school he saw somebody slapping a bass, and he began trying it.

At 19 Flea changed directions and joined the punk band Fear, bringing to his style punk's play-every-note-like-it's-your-last ethic. Drawn to funkier feels, however, he eventually left the group. He was living with

Slovak and another high school buddy, future Chili Peppers singer Anthony Kiedis, when a mutual friend needed an opening act. The three put a band together without rehearsing, billing it as Tony Flow & the Miraculously Majestic Masters of Mayhem. "When we got onstage," Flea recalls, "I started some funk-bass thing, Anthony read a poem, and we just played. At the next show, we were the Red Hot Chili Peppers. From then on, things went pretty well: we were together for only a few months and people were trying to give us record deals."

Flea

What's your opinion of the role of the bass?

It's difficult to generalize, but I like hearing the bass when it's really locking in with the drums. I like it simple. I like it when it makes you want to fuck—that warm, good feeling. Very seldom do I enjoy bass playing that takes center stage; even on a funk song where the bass is the focus, such as Funkadelic's "(Not Just) Knee Deep" [*Uncle Jam Wants You*], it's just a funky groove—it's not "look at me." Plenty of bass players have fancy chops, but they don't make you feel any emotions. You don't feel anger, fear, or love. That's what I call "all flash and no smash," a phrase I got from Lonnie Marshall of the band Weapon of Choice. Lonnie's one of the funkiest bass players alive today—I've *totally* copped stuff off him.

So what's your function as the Chili Peppers bassist?

My position goes beyond that of just a bass player; I also consider myself an entertainer. As a bassist, my job is to *kick ass*. When I pick up my bass and play with the band, it's time to get serious. It's my job to give my all every time I play, no matter how I feel. But I also buy into the show-biz aesthetic of giving a dazzling performance, and I'm into putting on a show.

Does the entertainer side of your job ever interfere with the bass-playing side?

No. Standing in one place and playing isn't what the Red Hot Chili Peppers are about—it's about being the wildest rock band on earth. I think as much about dancing and being bizarre as I do about playing well. I'm not saying that to do a good show you have to jump around and do an avant-garde dance while spinning on your head—but no one would have liked Charlie Chaplin if he hadn't fallen on his face every once in a while!

You've said your influences tend to be more emotional than technical. What experiences besides punk rock had a big impact on you?

Seeing my stepdad play upright bass in our living room when I was eight had a *huge* influence on me. I'd watch him and his friends play hardcore bebop, which to me is one of the highest forms of expression—intellectually, emotionally, spiritually, and technically; America has come up with nothing better than bebop. Seeing them play filled me with this incredible feeling of joy I'd never experienced before.

Meeting Anthony Kiedis in high school had a lot to do with how I ended up as a musician. He was the first kid I met who didn't give a shit about being like anybody else. The way he talked, the way he dressed, and the way he acted had a big influence on me. He was so *anti*; he thought anyone who tried to be like anyone else was lame.

Also, taking acid was a big thing for me as a youngster. I don't recommend drugs to anyone, but I can't deny that I did them. Anthony and I would sit and listen to Eric Dolphy play "God Bless the Child" [*Here & There*] on the bass clarinet over and over again—for about five hours. How could I not be deeply affected by that? I couldn't believe a human being was making that noise! There's nothing more amazing than a human creating that energy through an instrument; I've never reached that level, because I'm just not studied enough in music to do something as amazing as Eric Dolphy did.

The thing that's changed me is having realized the importance of becoming a loving person: someone who thinks, What can I give? rather than, What am I going to get?

What's your basic technique?

I'm sure I play all wrong, even though I can get around okay. For instance, I don't consciously try to use one finger per fret. Usually, I don't use my left-hand pinky, so I've been doing some exercises that put it to use. I pluck with my first two right-hand fingers, mostly alternating. As far as economy of movement is concerned, I don't have that down at all. When I slap, I slam the strings as hard as I can with my thumb; I use only my middle finger—never my index or ring fingers—to pop. If the part is very intricate, I use mostly a wrist motion, but usually it involves the whole arm. I've seen people slap and hardly move their hand at all, but anyone who's ever seen one of our shows knows that's not me! I believe if I get my whole body into it, I can play better.

Are you working on learning any theory?

No, but I need to. A friend of mine, a great upright bassist named Hilliard Green, was talking to me about theory. The way he explains it, there are certain things very easily within my grasp; I just need to spend some time to figure them out. My music is mostly based on intuition and instinct, but I could go further with a better understanding of theory.

Since you trust your instincts, are you afraid of being affected negatively by learning theory?

No—I'm a punk rocker, so it can't hurt me! I'd love to walk into a room and be able to play with Wayne Shorter and McCoy Tyner—that would be *beautiful*. I feel I could play well in any rock, reggae, funk, or African band in the world, but jazz . . . that's intense! I *feel* jazz, but I just don't know enough about theory to play it.

Compared to the full-bore thumbwork of early Chili Peppers records, Blood Sugar Sex Magik *showcased a more stripped-down, rudimentary approach. On* One Hot Minute *did you try to combine elements of both?*

Not on a conscious level. I was trying to play simply on *Blood Sugar* because I had been playing too much prior to that, so I thought, I've really got to chill out and play half as many notes. When you play less, it's more exciting—there's more room for everything. If I do play something busy, it stands out, instead of the bass being a constant onslaught of notes. Space is good.

I think my playing on *One Hot Minute* is even more simple; I just wanted to play shit that sounded good. I thrashed through the recording and didn't care about the parts being perfect. It's not that I don't love the bass passionately anymore—I just felt I'd been getting too many accolades for being "Joe Bass Player."

So the simpler approach is a reaction to all the recognition you've received?

That, plus the whole concept of being a jack-off musician and not thinking about the big picture. I do consider myself fortunate to have achieved popularity as a bassist, but I felt there was too much emphasis being placed on playing technique, as opposed to just playing music. So before we recorded this album, I spent more time strumming an acoustic guitar than I did playing bass. To me, my bass parts are more incidental to the song now, because I'm thinking less as a bass player and more as a songwriter.

Playing guitar has definitely helped me as a song-writer; instead of thinking in terms of bass lines and grooves, which is an amazing way to think, I now think about chord progressions and melodies. It's another musical dimension for me.

Do you think bass players make good songwriters because they think of the groove instead of just chords?

A good songwriter is someone who has something interesting to say, period. I've heard great songs from people who could barely string together a couple of chords, and I've heard shitty music come from world-renowned virtuosos. Obviously, more good music comes out of good musicians—but I think being a good songwriter requires being in touch with all the emotions and stuff that are flying through the air around you.

Overall, how do you think One Hot Minute *differs from* Blood Sugar Sex Magik?

 Red Hot Chili Pickers

Flea most frequently swats his Modulus Flea Signature Bass, in 4- and 5-string versions. He also plucks his Ernie Ball Music Man StingRay 4- and 5-strings, an Alembic Epic 4-string, and various Fender Jazz Basses, Wal axes, and Spectors. His strings are GHS medium-scale Boomers, gauged .045, .065, .080, .100, with a .126 *B* string, and he uses Monster cables.

Live, he plugs into three Gallien-Krueger 2001RB heads through three GK 410RBH cabs and three 115RBH cabs (which replaced his long-favored Mesa/Boogie cabinets). For effects he's been known to step on Electro-Harmonix Bass Balls and Q-Tron ped-als; an MXR M-133 Micro Amp; Boss Auto Wah, Dynamic Filter, and ODB-1 Bass Overdrive pedals; a Dunlop Cry Baby wah, and a DOD/FX25 Envelope Filter.

There are two big differences. First, I was in a different place emotionally for this record. I was coming out of a two-year period of misery, when I was down emotionally, physically, and spiritually. Second, Dave Navarro is intensely different from John Frusciante. When we recorded *Blood Sugar*, John played all his tracks once and maybe overdubbed a few solos, so the whole record was very spontaneous. Dave is really into the studio; he would spend *weeks* on every song, put something like 15 tracks of guitar on every tune, and weed through it in the mix. Dave's sound is more layered and "effecty" than John's, which was like, *boom*—play it dry and leave it alone.

There are a bunch of different styles mixed together in the bass line of "Aeroplane." How did you come up with the slap part in the verses?

I was sitting in my garage with a bass Louis Johnson gave me—a Treker Louis Johnson Signature 4-string—and I started playing that '70s funk line. The bass had light strings on it and had that *whacka-whackita* sound. It's kind of a "been done" groove, but it's nice and Anthony liked it. The chorus part was one of those things where we were stuck; sometimes when we're looking for another part, I'll have no idea what I'm going to do, but I'll say, "What about this?" I went [*mimics upwards glissando*]; it's all sliding on the *E* string.

"Coffee Shop" is chock full of bass stuff, including a solo.

It's funny—"Coffee Shop" would never have been a song if it weren't for this effect called the Bass Balls. I started playing with it one morning in Hawaii, and it had the most amazing underwater, Bootsy kind of sound—and it also had this siren effect going on. But when we got to L.A. to start recording, the box never made the sound again. I got so mad I crushed it! I almost didn't even want to record the song, because to me, it was all about that bass sound. I ended up using a Boss Dynamic Filter on the record.

In the solo it sounds as if you're ripping the strings off the fingerboard.

We didn't know what to do at the end, so I said, "I'll solo." I played the track once, and I wanted to fix it later because I thought it sucked, but I never did.

"Walkabout" is built around the bass, especially the verses.

I had gone to see the Spike Lee movie *Crooklyn*, which has this cool '70s funk soundtrack. I came home, picked up my bass, and started playing that verse line. I wrote the intro at rehearsal—it was another one of those "What about this?" things.

"Transcending" centers around a twisted ♭7 bass riff.

I play the root and the ♭7, which ring at the same time, and then I play the 4th and bend it up while I keep plucking. I wrote that part on my acoustic bass guitar while I was sitting on the beach in Hawaii, before I decided we should all write there.

How did you come up with that funky fingerstyle line on Alanis Morissette's "You Oughta Know" on Jagged Little Pill?

It was very instinctive—I showed up, rocked out, and split. When I first heard the track, it had a different bassist and guitarist on it; I listened to the bass line and thought, That's some weak shit! It was no flash *and* no smash! But the vocal was strong, so I just tried to play something good.

In August 2002, E.E. Bradman talked with Flea about his streamlined, functional approach to the Chili Peppers' ninth CD, By the Way. *Noted Flea, "The bass playing on this record is about helping Anthony and John express themselves, and the overall focus was on trying to write really good pop."*

Why did you start playing with a pick?

I was ready to do something different. I started playing with picks at our jams, and then I had to get my pick chops together with Jane's Addiction because the songs called for it. [Flea played on 1997's *Kettle Whistle*.] Eventually, I tried one on *Californication*'s "Parallel Universe," and when John brought in the chord structures for *By the Way* it just made sense for me to try a more melodic pick approach.

I always want to play melodically, even if I'm playing percussive funk—but when I'm playing with a pick, I'm more likely to strum chords or use double-stops. Bass lines take on a different type of melody with a pick. Playing a high pick part over simple chords gave songs like "Zephyr" a nice effect, and with Anthony singing his vocal melody, it makes for a really nice pop chorus.

Who do you consider the expert on melodic pop bass?

Paul McCartney. Most Chili Peppers songs have started with the bass, but for this album, John came in with complete song structures. Someone told me that the bass lines were often the last thing to go on Beatles records, so I decided to try another approach and re-record my bass line on "I Could Die for You," the one song I play fretless on. I played something first that sounded good, but after the vocals went on I heard something different. I'm not saying that's a better way to do it, but it made me play differently.

The album's tambourines, organs, and multi-tracked harmonies are also reminiscent of the psychedelic '60s.

John has been in a very focused, creative, ambitious place. When we were going in to make this record, he studied old pop music and doo-wop, and he overdubbed lots of vocals, guitar parts, and synthesizers—he went for it. I was like, Dude, go on and do it! I'm just happy to be there and do the right thing for the songs.

Were most of the songs born out of jams?

Every song is different, but most start that way. Sometimes I come in with a bass line or John brings in a guitar part. After we decide it's worth building a song around, we'll jam on it. Take "Universally Speaking," which began as a pretty bass line with a nice droning feel. As soon as we started jamming on it, Anthony came up with a vocal melody. We thought, Wow, we could do something with that—let's make it a real song by adding a chorus. Then John and I did a "face off": We looked at each other, went out to the rehearsal studio parking lot, and sat in different corners. We had five minutes to come in with parts.

What impact does producer Rick Rubin have on your bass lines?

We've come to trust him a lot. Rick thinks so differently than us—we'll play something and it'll mean so much to us, but to him everything's changeable. The Mexican-style "Cabron" is a good example. John wrote it on acoustic guitar. I played what I thought was an authentic Mexican bass line, but no one liked it; they liked my second idea better. When we recorded it, though, Rick didn't like my second idea. So I played every bass line I could think of—anything you could do over those changes, I did.

Later on, we came back to that tune. John and I jammed on it, and John suggested that I play his '60s Vox bass with a capo around the 7th fret. He figured that playing with a capo would make me see the neck differently, and he was right. By trying something different, I was able to come up with something we liked.

It's a treat to hear you stretch out on "Don't Forget Me."

I played a simple pick part all the way through, except for the fuzz solo in the chorus, which I improvised over several takes. On one take, I did a run that John liked, but when he asked me to do it again a week later, I couldn't remember it. The funny thing is, he could play it note for note. So there's one bitchin' bass fill on there that's John.

What gear did you use for the recording?

I used the Vox on "Cabron," and I'm playing a fretless, either a Music Man or a Fender Jazz, on "I Could Die for You." I played my pink matching-headstock '63 Fender Jazz Bass on some of the stuff, but I don't think any of it made it onto the album. Otherwise, it's pretty much all the Modulus Flea Bass. I didn't use any effects; I was going to borrow a distortion pedal for "I Could Die for You," but I got the best sound by playing my Modulus through a cranked-up Marshall.

You keep showing up in movies. Is there a relationship between acting and bass playing?

They're completely different! Acting is about being someone else; bass playing is about being me. People ask me to be in a movie once in a while, and if I like it, I do it. I'd love to produce and do film soundtracks, but I'd want to give my all to it. There are a few other things I want to do first. Right now, I'm working on upright bass and piano. For now, just being the bass player in the Chili Peppers is a big job—it's a whole lifestyle, and it's enough for now.

How would you evaluate your playing style?

Flea Selected Discography

With the Red Hot Chili Peppers: (on Warner Bros.) *By the Way*; *Californication*; *One Hot Minute*; *Blood Sugar Sex Magik*; (on EMI) *Mother's Milk*; *The Abbey Road EP*; *Uplift Mofo Party Plan*; *Freaky Styley*; *Red Hot Chili Peppers*. **With Action Figure Party:** *Action Figure Party*, Blue Thumb. **With Alanis Morissette:** (both on Maverick) *Under Rug Swept*; *Jagged Little Pill*. **With Jewel:** *Spirit*, Atlantic. **With Johnny Cash:** *Unchained*, Universal. **With Mike Watt:** *Ball-Hog or Tugboat*, Sony. **With Mick Jagger:** *Wandering Spirit*, Atlantic. **With Ziggy Marley:** *Dragonfly*, Private Music. **With Tricky:** *BlowBack*, Hollywood. **With Banyan:** *Anytime at All*, Virgin. **With Jane's Addiction:** *Kettle Whistle*, Warner Bros. **With Porno For Pyros:** *Good God's Urge*, Warner Bros. **With Gov't Mule:** *The Deep End, Vol. 1*, ATO. **With Warren Zevon:** *Sentimental Hygiene*, Virgin. **With Cheikha Remitti:** (both on Absolute) *Sidi Mansour*; *Cheikha*. **With Sir Mix-A-Lot:** *Chief Boot Knocka*, Sony. **With Young MC:** *Stone Cold Rhymin'*, Delicious Vinyl/Rhino. **With Michael Brook:** *Albino Alligator*, Warner Bros. **With Bone Thugs N Harmony, Henry Rollins & Tom Morello:** *War*, Dreamworks. **With Rambient:** *So Many Worlds*, Immergent. **With Pigface:** *Notes From Thee Underground*, Invisible. **With the Weirdos:** *Condor*, Frontier.

It's pretty simple, and it always has been. Providing support is what bass playing is all about—being there for the musicians who are playing the higher-frequency instruments. I try to do my own thing, but being supportive is my goal. So far I've relied on emotion and intuition to accomplish this, which has served me well, but there's a lot more to learn. Someday I want to be able to sit in with any jazz band and play standards. I know that to be able to play good jazz bass lines, I have to get into chord theory.

Overall, my life is my bass playing, and my art is who I am. It's been the most rewarding when I've done it purely for the sake of bringing something beautiful into other people's lives. The only way I'm going to keep growing and changing is to be vulnerable as a human being. People I admire—musicians who have remained relevant throughout their entire lifetimes—seem to be the ones who age with dignity and who have love in their hearts. That's my goal.

What general advice do you have for bassists?

Play all the time and practice all the time. Listen to what's going on, and be supportive of what you're hearing. Go beyond aesthetic and style and get into the substance of bass playing, because the right bass part can make or break a song. Don't be all flash and no smash. Plenty of bass players have fancy chops, but they don't make you feel any emotions—anger, fear, or love.

Web Sites

www.redhotchilipeppers.com
home.pacbell.net/dmramse/

Flea in Your Ear

THE FOLLOWING "FLEA BITES" from two Red Hot Chili Pepper eras show not only the stylistic range of one Michael Balzary, but also the development of his approach over the years, from psycho-slapper to song servant.

Example 1 shows a muscular thumbstyle riff typical of Flea's playing on *Blood Sugar Sex Magik*. Flea tuned down a step for this kind of sub-*E* line. "I like that loose, sloppy sound," he notes. Check out "Naked in the Rain" to capture the feel. **Example 2** shows the kind of outro Flea laid down for tunes like "Funky Monks." In bar 2, note the interweaving of open *D*'s and the chromatic walk-up. In **Example 3**, inspired by the Mu-Tron–hued line on "Sir Psycho Sexy," the influence of Bootsy Collins is apparent. Check the funky rests on the downbeat of beat *four* in bar 1, and the string-crosses in bar 4.

On 2002's *By the Way* Flea explored pick playing, fretless bass, and even a trad Mexican groove—all while still delivering his raw, unmistakable feel and energy. **Example 4** shows the style of his furious finger-funk chorus on the title track. Tune your *E* string down to *D* for a Flea-friendly sound. For **Example 5,** play the laid-back, soulful 16ths legato to cop the vibe of the main "Venice Queen" line. The feel is reminiscent of Flea's part on "Down and Out in New York City," from Gov't Mule's *The Deep End, Vol. 1.*

Example 6 recalls Flea's main "On Mercury" bass line. His edgy part, as well as the overall feel, merges medium ska with a cheesy wedding-band vibe. **Example 7** shows the style of Flea's opening fretless fills on "I Could Die for You," on which Flea played fretless. "I had never really played a fretless before. It was a challenge to keep it controlled and in tune, which was good because it probably stopped me from playing too much. I was trying to create melodies that went against the vocal, almost like harmonies or countermelodies that could be keyboard or horn parts. I waited until the vocal melody was down so I could play off it."

Ex. 1

♩ = 118

(tune down one step)

Ex. 2

♩ = 92

Ex. 3

♩ = 80

Ex. 4

♩ = 125

Funk rock

Ex. 5

♩ = 90

Mellow soul-rock

Example 8 uses 10ths going to octaves to add melodic tension, as Flea accomplishes with his picked line on "Warm Tape." **Example 9** approximates his killer opening and recurring line on "Throw Away Your Television." The *C*'s at the end of bar 2 throw the ear a tasty little curve.

Ex. 6

Ex. 7

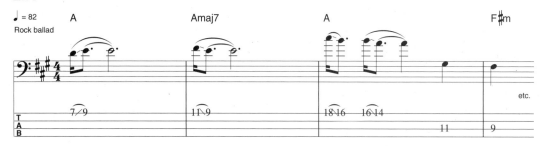

Ex. 8

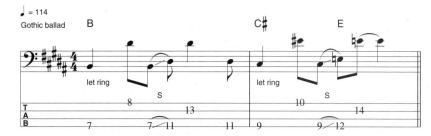

Ex. 9

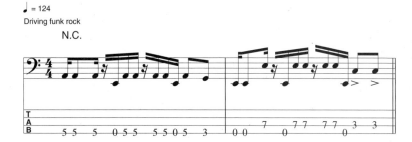

LES CLAYPOOL
Anti-Bass Hero

Interviewed by Karl Coryat, January/February 1993 and October 1999; and Chris Jisi, December 2001 and October 2002.

PROBABLY NO BASSIST in the last 15 years has prompted more baggy-shorts-wearing youngsters to pick up the instrument than Les Claypool. As leader of the enduringly popular, *way*-alternative band Primus (featuring guitarist Larry "Ler" Lalonde and drummer Brain), Claypool and his wacky slaps, taps, and strums—often on the most daunting type of bass: the fretless 6—proved a bass player can have fun, break all the rules, *and* be successful, innovative, and admired. Sure, his carefree attitude and blasphemous technique rankle purists. But there's no denying Les has stretched the instrument's boundaries while giving it considerable visibility onstage and on MTV. And his influence extends well beyond the masses. Says Flea: "What Les does is completely different, but it's great in its own way. It's not that one style is cooler than the other—it's just a different trip." Adds 311's P-Nut, "I put Les in my personal hall of fame because anyone who can make a unique piece of art deserves to be immortalized in some way."

Aside from his prolific Primus output—a slew of studio discs plus two collections of wacked-out covers—Claypool has led the spinoff band Sausage,

Les Claypool

whose *Riddles Are Abound Tonight* harkened back to the early Primus years. He also made two solo albums—*Purple Onion* and *Les Claypool & the Holy Mackerel Present Highball with the Devil*—two live CDs with his Fearless Flying Frog Brigade, and one with Oysterhead (a collaboration with Stewart Copeland and Trey Anastasio). In addition, he has logged time as a sideman—most notably Tom Waits's *Bone Machine* and Gov't Mule's *The Deep End, Vol. 2*. And of course there's his theme to the TV favorite *South Park*. Still, a Claypool high-water mark is the 1991 Primus disc *Sailing the Seas of Cheese*, on which he settled into his then-new fretless 6 and pulled out grooves, riffs, and melodies that brought the whole Primus package together.

Born in Richmond, California, in 1963, Claypool heard AM radio while growing up, but he didn't decide to take up an instrument until junior high, when he saw bands at school dances playing Led Zeppelin and Yes covers. Just as he was feeling an attraction to "the big, fat-sounding guitar with four strings," a guitar-playing friend asked him to join his band. With his dad's help Les bought a flatwound-strung Memphis P-Bass copy

Claytools

Best known for funking it up on his notorious Carl Thompson fretless 6-string, Les Claypool is most at home on his old Thompson 4-string (equipped with a Kahler vibrato/whammy bar). Other basses in his rotation included a newer Thompson 4, a fretless Thompson 4, a fretted Thompson 6, an NS Design electric upright 5, an old aluminum-neck Kramer 8-string, his Whamola one-string upright, and his white late-'70s Rickenbacker. His strings are Dean Markleys and Carl Thompsons.

Live Les plugs into an Ampeg SVT-3PRO head and two SVTPR-410H cabinets. His effects include a Korg Toneworks AX300B pedal (used mostly for the envelope filters), a SansAmp Bass Driver DI, and a Boomerang Phrase Sampler. He records his bass variously direct, miked-amp, and through his old ADA MP-1 guitar pre-amp (modified to accommodate low end).

and began playing progressive metal, influenced by Geddy Lee and Chris Squire. At school he started learning the upright and played in the concert, jazz, and dance bands. Funk would be the final ingredient of Les's developing style.

How did you discover funk?

One day a friend of mine said, "Geddy Lee is good, but he's nothing compared to Stanley Clarke and Larry Graham." I told him he was crazy, even though I didn't know who those guys were. Then I saw Stanley's *I Want to Play for Ya* in a record store. I bought it and it blew my mind. I also saw Louis Johnson on [the TV show] *Don Kirshner's Rock Concert*, saw him go *bang-bippety-bip-bang*, and thought, "Man, that's the coolest thing!" By my junior year, I was getting way into all the funk players. Guys would give me shit and call me "Disco Les" because I was playing all this funk stuff.

Around my senior year I bought an Ibanez Musician EQ bass. I had always wanted a Rickenbacker, but then I decided the Rickenbacker was no longer the cool bass to have. I hung around Leo's [music store] in Oakland all the time; they had tons of new and used stuff. One day, I saw a Carl Thompson piccolo bass sitting there. I had stared at the photo in *I Want to Play for Ya* where Stanley has all his basses lined up, and a couple of them were Carl Thompsons. I always thought, 'Man, that sure is an ugly bass.' I picked up the one in the store, though, and I couldn't believe it—it was *so* easy to play. Suddenly there were a lot of things I could play that I couldn't play on my Ibanez. I used to test basses by trying to play "Roundabout," and it was pretty easy on the Carl Thompson. I begged and pleaded with my mom for the rest of the money I needed to buy that bass. She lent me some, and I went back and bought it. It's still my main 4-string.

How did you develop your right-hand dexterity?

One of the big things I decided to do when I was starting out was to play with three fingers. A lot of guys play with two fingers, so I figured if I played with three, I could be faster. When you're young, that's the goal: to be fast. I still use three fingers most of the time—going ring, middle, index, ring, middle, index—depending on how sore my fingers are. Sometimes I'll mix it up and favor certain fingers over others.

Where did you pick up the strumming technique?

From Stanley Clarke, because of songs like "School Days." The first time I saw Stanley shoot the ol' chords—he'd start at the top and go *pow!* [*mimes strumming and sliding a chord down the fingerboard*]—I thought that was way cool, and I decided to do it. It hurt like hell when I first started.

Did Stanley also inspire you to start slapping?

Yeah, him and Louis Johnson. Louis's right arm would go way out away from the bass. Stanley, though, used minimal hand movement, and I was always into the minimal hand-movement thing. A friend of mine told me your thumb should just graze the string and rest against the next one, as opposed to whapping the string and bouncing off it. My thumb got pretty fast, since I was more into thumbing than plucking.

One thing that helped me a ton, probably more than anything in my career, was playing with a group called the Tommy Crank Band. The other guys were all in their 20s and 30s, and I was 19. I had been playing fusion, and when I played with them the first time I was like *bloobilla-bloobilla-bloobilla*. They said, "Cool," and I got the gig. I had to learn all these blues and R&B tunes; we played everything from James Brown to John Cougar, everywhere from biker bars to weddings. I had never learned any of these songs, so I just asked what key they were in and did my own interpretations. A lot of the time I overplayed, and everyone else in the band was always clamping down on me to mellow out. By playing these tunes four hours a night, three to five nights a week, my groove got really good, and I learned to improvise and pull off songs we hadn't even rehearsed.

In 1984 Claypool put together his own band, Primate, which quickly evolved to Primus and the release of Suck on This *in 1989,* Frizzle Fry *in '90, and* Sailing the Seas of Cheese *in '91. Though he favored the tightness of the trio format, Les strove for a denser sound by piling up his bass techniques. Thus the Claypool style was born.*

What made you decide to form your own band in 1984?

I was auditioning for every band I could find; I wanted to make it big, but every band around just *sucked*. At the time, I was getting into some pretty obscure stuff, like Fred Frith, King Crimson, and Public Image Limited. I had a LinnDrum [drum machine] and a 4-track, so I started writing songs in my bedroom. I couldn't sing for shit; not only did I not have a voice, I was scared to get up to the mike. But I wrote all these lyrics, and I didn't like the way anybody else sang them. This friend of mine, Todd Huth, called and said, "Hey, I hear you're looking for a guitar player." He was into Black Sabbath and Blue Öyster Cult, and I was looking for some weird, freaked-out guy like Fred Frith. But we jammed, and he was perfect. He played the most out-there stuff; he'd play a line in a weird time signature without even knowing it—just responding to the way his heart was beating at the time or something. It was consistent, but on the moon.

I decided to go into the studio, record a tape, send it to all these record-company names I had gotten from some magazine, and make it big. I sold my car, and we made the first Primate demo with a drummer friend of mine named Perm Parker. One of the songs was "Too Many Puppies"— back then it was a double-time, B-52's kind of tune. The tape got some airplay on local radio.

Were you influenced by other rock bass players at that time?

I always wanted to play bass parts *and* rhythm guitar parts. I never really listened to other bass players that much.

When did you get your Carl Thompson 6-string?

I was doing a demo at NAMM [music-instrument trade show] for ADA, and this guy came up to me and said, "Oh, you play a Carl Thompson bass? Look at this." He whipped out this amazing Carl Thompson 6-string fretless. After that I knew I had to have a 6-string, but I wasn't sure if I wanted a fretless.

I didn't actually get my 6 until just before we started *Sailing the Seas of Cheese*. We were on tour in New York, and I tracked down Carl Thompson. I told him I was interested in a 6-string; he was impressed that I had been playing his bass for years and loving it. A little while later he started hearing my name around, so he called me and said he'd start building me a bass if I sent a deposit.

I couldn't decide whether I wanted a fretted or a fretless. But I was getting to a point with my 4-string where it was like a stalemate; I was getting bored with it. I needed something that would just blow things wide open, so I decided to go for the fretless 6-string.

Carl told me he was going to make the best bass he'd ever built. He basically made a butcher block out of all these different pieces of wood, and then he cut the body shape out of it. He called it the Rainbow Bass. Apparently it almost killed him to make it; he had a bad sinus problem, and all the dust was making it worse. And I was saying, "Carl, I need the bass before we start our next record," so he had to rush—he even had to go to the hospital at one point. But he finished it on his birthday, and the serial number is his date of birth.

When I got the bass, I thought, "Ohmigod—what have I done?" It was *so* much more difficult to play. I was used to my 4-string's 32" scale, and all of a sudden I had this big hunk of wood with a 36" scale and no frets. When I tried to play chords they all sounded like shit, and I couldn't move around very well. But I kept playing it and playing it until I got to the point where I felt comfortable on it.

Do you ever have trouble playing and singing simultaneously?

Yeah, all the time—especially if I try to do other people's songs. Usually, I try to get the playing so solid that I can just sit in front of the TV and not think about it, and *then* I'll start laying the vocals down.

What do you have to say to a young player who wants to be just like you?

Anyone who wants to be just like me is in for a life of boredom! You should always play with as many people as you can. If they're terrible, you'll learn from their mistakes. But it's even better to play with people who are better than you. It's just like anything else—if you skate with people who are better than you, you'll become a better skater.

When Karl Coryat spoke to Claypool in October 1999, Les had followed his own advice, enlisting outside help for Primus's 1999 studio effort Anti-Pop—*possibly the band's final CD. Les discussed the maturation of his style and moving away from the fretless 6.*

Do you find yourself playing less as you get older?

I'm actually playing more than I did on the *Brown Album*. On that one I was trying to be more bare-bones. I watch players who start to "mature" and say they've been playing too much and want to get more basic—but sometimes they go too far in that direction, and it takes away the quality that made them an individual. For the past few albums I've been thinking things like, [*adopts analytical tone*] Well, James Jamerson would probably choose something more conservative here. I wasn't being myself as much as I probably should have been. But for that time period it's what I was into.

What was your bass approach for this project?

For one thing, there's no fretless at all on this record. Most of it is just straight-up 4-string. I was going to use my Jazz Bass, but I have this Carl Thompson I've always used as my backup; I just started playing it a lot, and it sounds and feels awesome. So I called Carl and told him I wanted to retire my main 4-string, the one with the whammy bar, because it's very midrangy. But it takes Carl a long time to make a bass—he builds the damn things in his apartment—so in the meantime I used my backup bass and my fretted 6-string.

You don't tap as much as you used to, either.

I haven't done much of that since *Pork Soda*. Tapping never really flew with me. I like the rhythmic concept, but some of it gets a little too noodly-sounding. For this record I wanted to be aggressive without being noodly.

There were periods when the band as a whole got too noodly. *Tales from the Punchbowl* is probably my least favorite Primus album; it's just us jamming in the studio trying to get the record done, because we weren't having that much fun. And when we made the *Brown Album* all I was listening to were Creedence

Clearwater and Led Zeppelin records—so Brain got the biggest drums he could find, and we stuck them in a room and put up one microphone. It was this big, bombastic sound—definitely an acquired taste. Tom Waits told me that's his favorite Primus record, because it has that ugliness—but for most people it was not an easy pill to swallow. *Frizzle Fry* is still the one for me, and for a lot of people it's *Sailing the Seas of Cheese*—but I never really liked *Seas of Cheese*. The songs are good, but I always thought the tones were kind of strange.

What was the songwriting process?

This time there was much more emphasis on scooping the cream off the top. We went into the rehearsal space and jammed, and when we came up with something we liked, we recorded it on a boom box. Larry [Lalonde] then took the tapes and put the best sections on a CD. We listened to the first ten seconds or so of each part and gave it a thumbs-up or thumbs-down. We just threw it away if it didn't immediately make us dance around and say, "That's awesome!" We didn't want anything that had to grow on us; it had to excite us right away.

This was the most work we've ever put into a record's music. We've put more work into recording other projects—the hands-on knob-turning and all that crap—but that was always a bit distracting. It helps a lot to leave certain things to the other guys.

Does listening heavily to other artists affect your bass playing?

You know, I don't listen to a lot of bass players or listen for a lot of bass parts. If I were a guitar player, I'd probably write the same lines I write on bass. It just happens to be the instrument I picked up.

When I interviewed Claypool in December 2001, he was making the most of his Primus hiatus via cool collaborations, including flexing his musical mussels . . . er, muscles, in Oysterhead—a trio with Phish guitarist Trey Anastasio and ex-Police drummer Stewart Copeland. The group's debut was a 13-track exercise in low-tide lunacy called The Grand Pecking Order.

How did Oysterhead come together?

I was approached by a New Orleans promoter to put something together for the annual Super Jam concert. The first person I thought of was Trey because of the jam aspect. He said he'd always wanted to do a project with me and Stewart, who had produced a song on *AntiPop*. Stewart said yes. We got together briefly in Vermont and again a few days before the show in New Orleans, where we wrote seven tunes in three days. As soon as we started playing I felt this amazing chemistry. I've been playing with a lot of people the past few years, but this was something I'd never experienced before. The flow of ideas was incredible—like we'd hit a gusher. The show turned out great, even if there were a few trainwrecks. Stewart wanted to release a live album, so he started editing tapes from the show—but I said, "Man, we need to make a *real* record." Eventually we found a time slot, so we went back to Trey's Vermont studio, The Barn, and started throwing spaghetti at the wall.

What gear did you use?

Mostly my original Carl Thompson 4-string with fairly old Thompson light-gauge strings. It's walnut with a maple neck and one pickup, and it has a distinctive sound I keep coming back to. There's not a lot of low end, but it's very punchy and cuts through like a foghorn. I recorded two direct tracks—one clean, the other through my effects pedals—and for the first time in a while I also recorded a miked-amp track, using my Ampeg SVT-3PRO head and a PR-410H cabinet. Then we blended the three tracks for each song. My effects were a Korg ToneWorks AX300B, SansAmp Bass Driver DI, and Boomerang Phrase Sampler, which you can hear at the beginning of "Polka Dot Rose." I also played my NS Design 5-string electric upright, recorded the same way.

It's interesting to hear your bass interaction with Trey's acoustic guitar on "Radon Balloon."

That's a total Trey track—his song with his vocals. I played a supportive upright part, and he said, "No—get your electric and give me the Les Claypool plunkity-plunkity stuff!" So I went back and approached it sort of like Bakithi Kumalo with Paul Simon, using arpeggios and fills. That was another cool thing about this project: We all pushed each other into directions we wanted to see each other go. I'd challenge Trey to go crazy and play Buckethead-style solos. And since Trey and I are huge Stewart fans, we'd ask him to play drums like he did with the Police and on his album *The Rhythmatist*. Or Stewart would ask me to do some of my Primus-character singing.

Much of the harmony throughout the album is ambiguous, with no one committing to major or minor 3rds.

Part of that comes from much of it being done on the fly, where we didn't know exactly what the others were doing; we'd just grab some pentatonic stuff and away we'd go. When I write, I try not to think about what key I'm in or what the chord change might be; instead, I look for tones that add tension and then release. I tend to bounce around and use a lot of ♭5's.

What's the story behind "Army's on Ecstasy"?

I read an article about ecstasy abuse in the military, and I thought the irony was incredible, so I wrote some lyrics. Stewart found the groove among our tapes, and we jammed and got the song together. Originally, we were going to have just one vocal line through the whole tune, like the Police's "Voices Inside My Head" [*Zenyatta Mondatta*]—but when we went to mix we thought, Damn, this is boring! So I put on more vocals.

What bass are you using on "Birthday Boys"?

That's another Trey track with his vocals and "rural" slide guitar, although I wrote the lyrics. I first recorded an upright part, but a week later the guys asked me to do the electric "Claypool" thing and fancy it up. But I didn't like how it was turning out, so we stopped halfway and I convinced them to use the original track. I ended up thinking it was cool to have both. I'm not sure where, but after one of the guitar breaks the bass switches from the Thompson to the NS.

How many bass tracks are on "Wield the Spade"?

I played only one track, using the upright. The other sort of muddled bass line is Trey's guitar slowed down and looped on the Boomerang. That's how the song started. I tried to get into my big, simple, Tony Levin groove bag, and I added some squirrelly Percy Jones–like fills. At the end I bowed some notes, too. [*Les uses a German bow with a French-style grip.*] Stewart did the spoken voices and I did the character singing.

Your Black Sabbath influence is evident in "Pseudo Suicide."

Totally. I came up with the Geezer Butler–like main riff with the ♭5, and I tried to get Trey to add a Tony Iommi vibe. Then the outro goes into a live-Zeppelin rock-out thing. My original bass line in that section sounded corny to me, so I cut another part where I lay off the downbeat and play on the "and" of *one*. We weren't thrilled with the finished version, so we let Toby Wright have a crack at it—he's the big rock producer. He mixed it the way he wanted, turning it into this amazing, huge-sounding rock song.

What's your bass approach on "Owner of the World"?

Years ago, in the R&B band I played with when I was 19, we opened for John Lee Hooker. He had a young guy on bass who played the bouncing, Chicago-blues shuffle style like no one I've ever seen—all over the neck. In only one night of hearing him, he had a major influence on my playing. I emulate that approach whenever I play a blues, and I've adapted it to other styles and feels as well, as I do here.

In December 2002 Claypool and I discussed Purple Onion, *billed as his first studio solo album. The 12-track disc features Frog Brigade members Jay Lane on drums, Eenor on guitar, Skerik on sax, and Mike Dillon on percussion, plus such notable guests as Allman Bros./Gov't Mule guitar god Warren Haynes and Fishbone's Norwood and Fish Fisher.*

What were your goals in recording Purple Onion?

Creatively, it's the result of a tremendous growth period for me, having worked with so many talented people over the last few years. When you play with folks the caliber of a Stewart Copeland or Trey Anastasio you come away with a great deal of knowledge, perspective, and inspiration. I wanted to write songs that were a bit more intricate; I was trying to come up with more parts and have those parts move into different sections. It was a return to the way I wrote in early Primus, where I sat down and wrote a song and lyric that supported each other and then brought it to the guys—as opposed to later Primus, where we jammed and then made songs out of the jams.

The disc opens with the short, mostly instrumental title track.

I came up with the concept before creating the track. I had just finished reading Bob Dylan's book *Down the Highway*; his first paying gig was at a pizza parlor called the Purple Onion. That rang with me, and it became the album title. I've always loved two words that have interesting contrast, like "Pork Soda" or "Oysterhead." I laid down some percussion first, and then I played my Carl Thompson 4-string through various effects—such as distortion from a Sans Amp Bass DI, envelope from a Korg Toneworks AX300B pedal, and a Boomerang sampler—to get the revving motorcycle sounds.

How do you play the galloping opening line of "Barrington Hall," and what is the song's orchestration?

I used my new fretless Thompson 4-string, which had flatwounds; I just plucked the notes with my index, middle, and ring fingers. I have violin and cello on the track, played by two local guys named Ben and Sam. I've always wanted to use strings, and this was my chance. I sang their parts to them for this song and for "Cosmic Highway."

How did you get the big, bass-in-your-face sounds on "David Makalaster" and "David Makalaster II"?

On "David Makalaster" I used the white late-'70s Rickenbacker that Alex Lifeson of Rush gave me, recorded direct. The DI I was using—which shall remain nameless—sucked, so I called a friend and he sent me a few, including this little old British solid-state unit he had in his closet. It sounded great, so I used that here and on most of the CD. "Makalaster II" is my NS Design 5-string electric upright played with a bow and recorded direct with slapback delay. I'm not a great arco guy. The cellist, Sam, offered me some tips, but then he said, "Screw it—you've got your own thing going that works for you." So I'm just squeaking, squealing, and cracking along and it's all part of the sound. I used a French bow I recently got at a pawnshop; I also have a German bow, but I hold it French-style.

What was the genesis of "Buzzards of Green Hill"?

It was kind of a throwaway tune I had since the Primus days; it was almost on *AntiPop*. We were done with the disc but there was some time left, so I started playing this riff and we got it down. I used my Thompson 4 recorded direct with some Korg Toneworks envelope, and Skerik doubled the main bass riff on baritone sax. Later, Warren Haynes, who I've become good friends with since working with him on Gov't Mule projects, was in town for a day, and I knew he'd be perfect for the tune's rural, country-blues vibe.

What instruments are you playing on "Long in the Tooth" and "Whamola"?

"Long in the Tooth" features a short-scale electric upright I got at a pawnshop for $200. I play it on a cymbal stand; it has a cool, odd sound. Everyone wants to know about "Whamola," which is named for the instrument I play on the tune. It was given to me a few years ago in Vermont at 3 AM by two guys who had waited at my hotel after a show. It's a weird washtub bass–type instrument with a single *D* string on a stick, a pickup, a peg on the bottom like an upright bass, and a big handle that you pull to change pitch. I play it by beating on it with a drumstick. One day I brought it to a soundcheck, and we started jamming on 8- and 16-bar cycles that I eventually fashioned into a song. For the track I sent the Whamola through the SansAmp distortion and the Korg envelope. As a rule, when we're playing somewhere and the crowd is kind of dead, we go into that song and everyone comes alive. The Whamola sounds good on tape, but when you hear it live it's incredible—it's like your face is melting.

What inspired the shuffle-feel "Ding Dang"?

I was thinking along the lines of an old John Lee Hooker groove; then in the middle we go into a sort of skiffle beat, like early Herman's Hermits/English Invasion. I used my Thompson 4 recorded direct, with some SansAmp distortion.

What led to the three-bass attack on "D's Diner"?

I had run into [Fishbone bassist] Norwood Fisher and told him we had to get together to record this song I had. Then [Fishbone drummer] Fish Fisher called me, and we flew him up here and he played on "Whamola." So I figured I might as well get [Weapon of Choice bassist] Lonnie Marshall involved, because they're all part of the same circle of friends. I had this structured song and I was trying to show them the arrangement, but it just wasn't going to happen [*laughs*]—everybody was partying and having a good time. So I said, "Let's just jam." I played a riff on my fretless Thompson 6-string and we all fell into it. Norwood played his Warwick 5-string and Lonnie had his Steinberger, and we all went direct to the console, with Fish in the drum room. I tried to get a second take, but I looked over and Norwood was asleep, so that was the only performance I got. I just edited it down a bit, put lyrics over the top, and panned the basses. I'm straight down the middle, Lonnie is on the left, and Norwood is on the right playing the funky Clavinet-like part through some pedal. It's the only track on the disc that was a straight-up jam, but I like it much better than the structured tune I had.

How do you play the rhythmic line on the "Lights in the Sky" rideout?

That's a tapping thing on my Thompson 4; with my left hand I play the pentatonic figure up on the *G* and *D* strings, and with my right hand I tap ghost-notes on the *A* and *E* strings around the 12th fret. That was the very first piece I recorded for the album. I laid down drums, percussion, and bass, and then I added instruments as the guys came in.

"Up on the Roof" is in three, which you seem to prefer.

I've always liked three; it feels good to me. The first song I learned how to read in high school, "Scarborough Fair," is in three. This is probably the most Primus-like song on the record. I played my Thompson 4 direct, with a little SansAmp distortion.

"Cosmic Highway" is a more extended, live Frog Brigade–worthy track.

That's the album's big prog-rock song. It started off with the droning bass part, which is something I've done on a few Primus songs, like "Fish On" and "Southbound Pachyderm"—I drone on a string and then play a melody line on the next string up [see Lesson]. I used my Thompson 4 with some Korg envelope, and halfway through I hit a MIDI pedal that triggers this Taurus-like patch on my Access Virus analog synth. [The Taurus was Moog's late-'70s/early-'80s bass-pedal synth.]

With the reissues of the early Primus CDs Suck on This *and* Frizzle Fry, *first-time listeners are hearing past and present Claypool all together. How is your playing different from what it was back then?*

I'm kind of coming around full circle by approaching writing like I used to on the old Primus stuff. Bass-wise, in those days I was consciously attempting to be completely different than anything I'd heard. I might try to play a bass part and a rhythm guitar part at the same time. I don't think I do so much of that anymore; nowadays I'm aware of trying to play a bit more melodically. That comes from listening to Paul McCartney and albums like the Beach Boys' *Pet Sounds* over the last few years. I'm concentrating more on the song, and the bass is following suit. Another key is the musicians I've been seeing and playing with in shows like the New Orleans Jazz & Heritage Festival or jam-band gatherings like Bonnaroo in Tennessee.

Have any of the bassists in those bands caught your ear?

Chris Wood is unbelievable—he's one of the best players out there. Also, you'll be hearing a lot about Reed Mathis from the Jacob Fred Jazz Odyssey, because he's doing innovative stuff. One of my favorite bassists of the last ten years is the late Mark Sandman [of Morphine]; he was going places with his 2-string bass that no one had gone before, making amazing sounds and writing great songs. And I still love Paul McCartney, who wrote and played the most incredible song bass lines ever.

What's that status of Primus and other projects?

With Primus we're still using the term "hiatus"; we haven't signed the divorce papers yet. I played in some spontaneous festival bands recently that were fun. In New Orleans I got to jam with [Headhunters drummer] Mike Clark, [Jacob Fred Jazz Odyssey keyboardist] Brian Haas, and [saxophonist] Casey Benjamin from DJ Logic's Project Logic. And at Bonnaroo I did a thing called Colonel Claypool's Bucket of Bernie Brains, with [P-Funk keyboardist] Bernie Worrell, Buckethead, and Brain. I'd like to resurrect that again at some point. I've been enjoying growing as a musician, and I'm going to continue on that path. I want to be remembered as more than just the guy who did "Jerry Was a Race Car Driver."

Web Sites

www.lesclaypool.com
www.primussucks.com

Fearless Flying Funk Lines

LES CLAYPOOL'S BOLD BASS LINES tend to use repeating one- or two-bar phrases, with small variations from measure to measure. His parts feature lots of muted, thumbed, popped, and strummed notes, and he favors barred 4ths and root-5th-octave chords.

From Primus's *Frizzle Fry*: **Example 1**, from "Pudding Time," is a fairly simple introduction to Claypooldom. Mute the *E* string with a left-hand finger or thumb, barre the top notes with your index finger, and strum the top two strings with your right-hand fingernails in a quick downward motion. For the slide, have your left hand moving as you slap the string so the slide begins on an indefinite pitch.

From Primus's *Sailing the Seas of Cheese*: In the 11/8 time "Eleven" the beats are grouped in an easy-to-grasp way: *one-two-three, one-two-three, one-two-three, one-two* (as the eighth-notes are grouped in the notation.) **Example 2** illustrates the repeating pattern. The strums should be strong to emphasize the beats they fall on (the *pa-pa* of the *oom-pa-pa* feel). The hammered notes should be merely embellishments. For the slides, fret the *D* string with your middle finger and the *G* string with your ring finger.

It's possible to play **Example 3**, from "Jerry was a Race Car Driver," on a fretted 4-string by moving all the notes down an octave, but it's harder to execute and doesn't sound as good. In this line, none of the notes is plucked—they're all either hammered or pulled off. The first *A♭*, for instance, is played simply by hammering the note onto the fretboard (as are the *B♭* on *two* and the *D♭* on the "and" of *four*). The ghost-notes are produced by slapping the left hand down on the strings without letting any of the actual notes sound.

Ex. 1

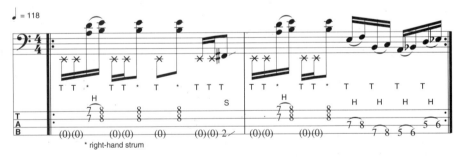

Ex. 2

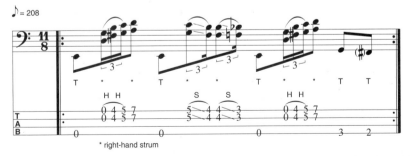

From Oysterhead's *The Grand Pecking Order*: **Example 4** shows the opening groove of "Army's on Ecstasy." For the double-stops in bar 2 Les uses "clawhammers." "It's a banjo-like technique where you shoot your fingers out and graze the strings with the back of your fingernails." **Example 5** contains the opening walking line of "Rubberneck Lions," a link to his teenage stint playing upright in a swing dance band. Here he uses his Thompson 4 and mutes the ghost-notes with his left hand. **Example 6** shows a cool variation of the main "Little Faces" bass line. Les slapped the line—on the Thompson with chorus and distortion—entirely on the *E* string.

Ex. 3

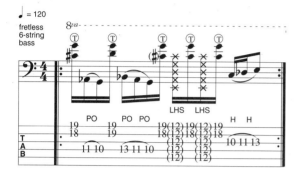

Ex. 4

Ex. 5

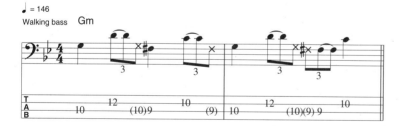

Ex. 6

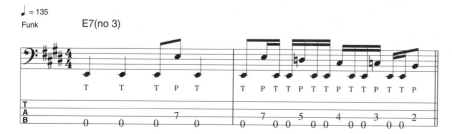

You can hear Claypool's Black Sabbath influence in **Example 7**, the main riff of "Pseudo Suicide." "That riff started as just a low *E* to a high *E,* and I gradually fleshed it out to include the hammer-on and the ♭5." He also added some envelope and chorus. **Example 8** shows the blues-bass-influenced "Owner of the World" opening, with its octave–root–♭7 shape. Melodic and rhythmic alterations occur in bar 4. **Example 9** contains the second incarnation of Les's electric upright line on "Wield the Spade." "On upright and fretless I love to move the notes around via slides and heavy vibrato. It adds tension."

Ex. 7

Ex. 8

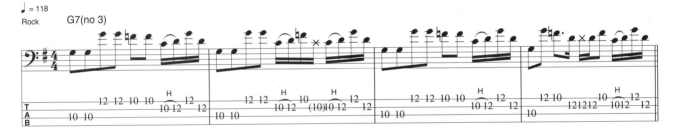

Ex. 9

Ex. 10

From *The Les Claypool Frog Brigade Presents Purple Onion*: Whether he's peeling off a sub-hook, doubling a vocal melody, or laying down a deep-fried support groove, Les Claypool's song-focused bass permeates *Purple Onion*. **Example 10** shows the main riff of "Buzzards of Green Hill," on which Skerik's baritone sax doubles Claypool's Thompson 4. Listen for the subtle changes that occur in the phrase's fourth bar. **Example 11a** contains the main shuffle ostinato from "Ding Dang." In **Example 11b**, Les—who slapped his Thompson 4—adds potent fills to the riff when the band "rocks out" on it, in the choruses following each "B" section.

Examples 12a and 12b are taken from "Lights in the Sky." During the breakdown interlude, Les—with Thompson 4 in hand—spins moody melodic lines. Note his note choices in bar 2 of both examples—they draw the ear away from the *E* minor tonality. **Example 13** features Claypool's Thompson 4–slapped groove on the "Up on the Roof" chorus. Check out how he negotiates the shuffle-in-three feel, working both the *E* and *A* strings to get those two *C*'s.

Examples 14a and 14b come from "Cosmic Highway." In Example 14a (at the start of Eenor's guitar solo) Claypool continues his drone approach, with his Thompson 4's open *D* ringing, while he punctuates the groove with interesting rhythmic and melodic colors on the *G* string. The intensity builds in Ex. 14b, with Les adding more rhythmic motion and pitches, including the boldly clashing *G* major tonality alluded to in the second ending. Listen also for Les's use of sitar-style hammers and pull-offs, which incorporate intervals like 2nds and 3rds throughout the track.

Ex. 11a

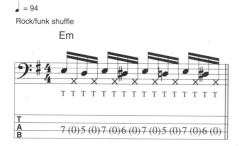

Ex. 11b

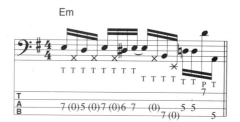

Ex. 12a

Ex. 12b

Ex. 13

Ex. 14a

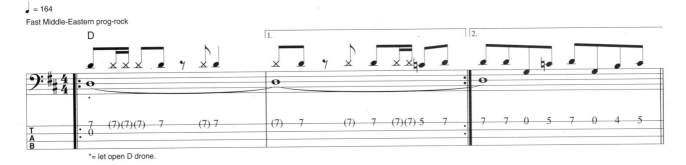

*= let open D drone.

Ex. 14b

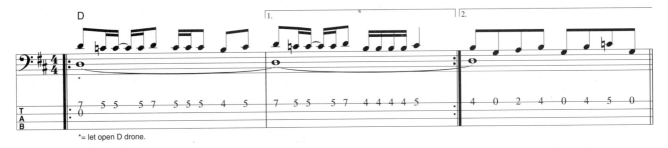

*= let open D drone.

MIKE GORDON
Deep Thoughts

Interviewed by Karl Coryat, December 1996, and Chris Jisi, February 2003.

MIKE GORDON HAS LONG BEEN A LOW-FREQUENCY PHILOSOPHER, having kept journals on his craft since the early Vermont days of Phish, the improvisational quartet in which Gordon weaves his bass magic. If you're a musician, you have to love Phish—even if you're not crazy about their music. Here's a highly accomplished band that can sell out Madison Square Garden in four hours with no hit single, very little mainstream press, and very minimal MTV exposure. Their excellent albums have been "hits" not through corporate wheeling and dealing but because of a grass-roots network of devoted fans. And since the death of Jerry Garcia, they've been adopted as the band of choice by several thousand former Dead-heads, who make the Phish-concert parking lot scene virtually indistinguishable from a Dead show's.

Is Phish merely the "Truckin'" band of the '90s? Not on your life. Hardcore Phish Heads know a Phish concert is more a musical event than a countercultural convention. While the Dead's jams could be great at times, Phish is consistently much tighter, more creative, more energetic, and more sophisticated. In fact, strip away all the tie-dyed, trippy-dancing, ticket-begging trappings, and you'll find four great musicians capable of reaching heights of spontaneous artistry surpassing that of most other rock 'n' roll outfits working today.

It's appropriate that Phish—which also includes guitarist Trey Anastasio, keyboardist Page McConnell, and drummer Jon "Fish" Fishman—hails from Vermont, land of maple syrup and Ben & Jerry's, the very antithesis of the dog-eat-dog L.A. music scene. Gordon (who was born in Boston on June 3, 1965, and grew up in nearby Sudbury, Massachusetts)

Mike Gordon

joined the group while an engineering student at the University of Vermont. Hundreds of local and college gigs followed, which led to a word-of-mouth following that spread from campus to campus across New England, then down the Eastern Seaboard, and finally across the country. Meanwhile, the boys were systematically honing their improvisational chops in rehearsals through an ingenious listening exercise. Standing in a circle, they would jam over a riff and take turns altering the riff while the others reacted and followed; this heightened each musician's improvisational sensitivity and fused the band into an extremely cohesive, communicative unit. After releasing two indie records, Phish was picked up by Elektra, which quickly learned to leave them to their own snowballing devices.

We spoke to Mike about how he got his sea legs with Phish, and how the foursome has been able to cast away so many of the musical and commercial clichés that permeate other bands like the odor of, well, rotting fish.

Can you trace your musical development from your childhood and adolescence?

I was a very strange kid. I never played any sports, ever, and I spent much of my time alone. I didn't want to be a kid—I wanted to be an adult. I spent a lot of time planning projects; when I was nine I planned a full-length feature film, and I put together these clubs that never existed, with a hierarchy of president, treasurer, and everything. Finally, in high school, I came out of my shell, and music started to become this thing I cared about more and more. I had always enjoyed music; I probably listened to *Abbey Road* a thousand times when I was a kid. Music started to slowly develop as my way of soul-searching. Certain songs would take over and represent the struggles I'd been going through. I had played piano since about age six, and I really liked to sit down and play things by ear—I didn't like taking lessons very much. Later I decided I wanted to play guitar, and I took a guitar course at the local music store when I was 12 or 13.

When did the bass enter the picture?

I was in the Bahamas with my family, and at the hotel there was this calypso band that played all day long at the poolside. It sounded *so* good—much better than any music I had heard, and I was completely into it. I was in the pool, I could feel the bass vibrating me, and I told my dad, "If I'm ever in a band, I want to play *that* instrument!" Shortly afterwards, I rented a Beatle Bass copy and an old tube amp and took some bass lessons at the music store.

In my last year of high school I joined the jazz band, and the guest conductor, Diego Poprokovich, hooked me up with Jim Stinnette, who later became my bass mentor. I went to college and studied electrical engineering, but I quickly learned my professors didn't want me to be a mad scientist—they basically wanted me to build a small, secret part of a missile that would kill Russians. So I eventually switched to filmmaking. When I was a freshman, I saw a sign that read BASS PLAYER NEEDED. The first Phish jam was in a dorm lounge, and there were actually 25 people dancing. When it was all over I asked, "So, do I get the job?" And I got the job.

How did you get so fluent at playing odd rhythms?

There was a four-year period when we were playing nothing but odd rhythms. Fish refused to hit the snare on the *two* and *four*; it was always a 16th-note off or something. He would practice doing these weird meters, like playing seven with one limb and five with another, breaking down the metronome pulse very scientifically. As a bass player, I had no idea what they meant, but I learned real fast.

Phish is one of the few bands that tackles such disparate styles as jazz and bluegrass. How did you learn to play them?

We spent one year playing jazz gigs every Monday night with local horn players. We did the same thing with bluegrass; we bought a bunch of bluegrass instruments while we were in Kentucky, and we learned how to play them on the bus. But understand that we don't pull it off the way a real jazz band, for instance, would; we're just trying to learn something from music that inspires us.

How do you see your role in the band?

Sometimes I play like a bassist, holding it down in the traditional way. Other times I don't play like a bassist; I might jump up the neck and harmonize a riff Trey is doing for two minutes. And then other times, I play like a bassist but don't play the chord progression that's been bestowed upon me. That way I can harmonically lead the band in different directions.

Taking the lead doesn't necessarily mean taking a solo.

Right. I'm not interested in playing solos. I love to see incredible bassists play solos, but even with a great soloist such as Oteil Burbridge, I prefer what he plays in the *middle* of a groove. He might go up the neck and play some wild, five-note chord and make it fit in. Weaving into the network of the motion—that's what I like about bass and music in general. By playing a high note, I can take the band higher, almost like a hang glider on an updraft. Rather than having to create a solo the music world will think is cool, I can be in the gears of the motion, in the engine room. The notes vibrate different parts of my body, and on the best nights it feels three-dimensional—where it's way inside but also way outside. I might see someone in the tenth row, and I'll weave the bass line past his head. At that point I'm not the introvert I was when I was younger; I'm completely opened up to the point where I'm not even the musician—God is the musician coming through. The bass seems to lend itself really well to that.

I keep wanting to come back to the analogy of flight. If you were actually flying, your inner ear would be giving you information about balance, there'd be wind rushing past your face, and there'd be pressure from the altitude. All of those senses come into your brain, which perceives that you're flying. My theory is that by standing completely still, you can create not only a feeling similar to flight but the *exact* feeling of flight. When music is great, that's how it is for me—and the bass is the vehicle for that to happen.

Phish is constantly being compared to the Grateful Dead. Was Phil Lesh a major influence on you?

I've never spent a lot of time studying any one bass player, so it's hard to say—but I definitely love his playing. To me, it feels as if he has a sense of the kinetics of sound. There's a sense the notes are resonating through your whole body, and he seems to know how to give a bass line a lot of gravity in its interaction with the other instruments. To achieve that, I think it takes a certain sensitivity to what's going on. You can pick up the bass and just start thrashing on it—which is fine if you're an aggressive person and that's what you want to get out of the instrument—but if you're sensitive to what the notes are doing to you, things can blossom unexpectedly.

How hard did you have to work to develop the band's cohesiveness?

It's funny, because the first time we jammed together 13 years ago, it didn't really click; there were other people I had jammed with where I felt it had clicked better. Now, in retrospect, I think that was a good thing, because it made us work at it. We still practice a lot when we're not on the road, but we used to do it all the time—after school, every day. For hours and hours we would jam, write music, and experiment; we tried to zero in on certain things and push them—rhythms we weren't good at, or grooves, or styles. The listening exercises were the culmination of all that.

Our favorite thing to do was just to throw all caution to the wind and jam without expectations. But we also realized how easy it is for the four of us to lapse into our own little worlds, playing up and down scales or whatever, not necessarily in the group mind. By getting together and just allowing

Phish Phood

On Phish tours Mike Gordon has been playing two basses: his older Modulus Quantum 5-string with a 34"-scale bolt-on neck, bubinga top, and EMG DC humbucking pickups; and his new Modulus TBX neck-through 5, which sports a walnut top, EMG DC humbuckers, 26 frets, and a 34" scale. Both are strung with Ken Smith Slick Rounds, gauged .044, .062, .084, .106, .130. Gordon plucks them using Dunlop 1.5 mm "stubby" nylon picks. Other basses in his collection include a custom National Reso-Phonic 4-string acoustic bass guitar (with a piezo pickup), and his Paul Languedoc custom basses: "Dragon," a koa-body, ebony-fingerboard 5-string; and "Fish," a 5 with a curly-maple body and an *f*-hole.

Live, Mike's bass signal flows through a Korg DTR2 rack tuner; Countryman DI; Custom Audio Electronics 4x4 Audio Controller, which has four loops for a Lexicon LXP-15 multi-effect, Eventide 4000 Harmonizer, Love Tone Meatball envelope filter, and EBS Octabass; a second CAE 4x4 Audio Controller with a Boss BF-2 Flanger, Ibanez TS10 Tube Screamer, Boss SYB-3 Bass Synth Pedal, and Akai SB-1 Deep Impact Bass Synth Pedal; an ADA MB-1 Preamp (which goes to the house); a Meyer Sound CP-10 digital sound processor; and a second Countryman DI split two ways to the amps: an Eden World Tour 800 head with two Eden D-410XLT cabinets, and a Meyer Sound P750PL powered 2x18 subwoofer. The two Eden cabs sit on the Meyer cabinet, which lies on its side; the rack lies alongside. In his monitors Mike hears all of the vocals, piano, some kick drum, a small amount of snare and hi-hat, and a bit of himself if he's situated far from his rig.

this group mind to exist, we grew together. Also, our relationships when we weren't playing developed the same way. When we're jamming we're communicating, but if we're just having a meeting we're also communicating, and it's sort of the same dynamic. We recently did this photo shoot that lasted for eight hours, and the whole time we were trying to make each other laugh by going in a circle and saying stupid things, which felt a little like jamming.

The other guys in the band would say music *is* communication; I'd rather say communication is the vehicle, and music is motion. Either way, communication is the first step, and if one person is thinking, How do I look? or, Is this a cool bass line? or, Are we having food on the bus later? it throws the whole thing off. What happens in that case is it feels as if we're mocking ourselves—pretending to be Phish.

Do you ever get lost?

All the time. These great journeys are the ideal, but there's another side. Sometimes we get off the stage and fight with each other about who wasn't concentrating. It always comes down to hooking up and communicating.

Jamming is definitely the most important thing for me. There are other important parts, like songwriting and arranging, but all I really care about is going on these journeys. It's impossible for people—let me rephrase that—it's impossible for *me* when I'm not on one of these journeys to remember how ecstatic it feels and how much of a celebration life becomes. On the other hand, it's the worst feeling to get together and play bad music, and we definitely do that sometimes. The good side, though, makes it all worth it.

Your hands look somewhat small. Does that ever present problems?

At one point I thought they'd keep me from becoming a great bassist. But Jim Stinnette had me doing these unnatural stretches up and down the neck, which felt like more stretching than I'd need—but after that, the size of my hands didn't matter. Plus, with my philosophy of playing as few as two notes, I can put those two notes right next to each other!

These days, I'm into stretching other limits; if there isn't a limit you're stretching, you can probably imagine one. It could be how fast you can play over a song, but it could also be how slowly, or how softly. You can always find new limits to stretch.

When I spoke to Mike in 2003, his career had stretched to include two non-Phish projects: Clone, *a duet album with acoustic guitar legend Leo Kottke, and* Rising Low, *his DVD/video documentary on the making of Gov't Mule's multi-bassist Allen Woody tribute* The Deep End, Volumes 1 & 2. *The film also examines Woody's life while expounding on bass in general. In addition, Phish had completed its 13th studio album,* Round Room.

What did you learn from making Rising Low?

Much of it had to do with themes I'd been contemplating all along, but what took me by surprise personally, while driving home a point I already knew, was the restraint shown by all of the great bass players involved. There was no display of egos or flashy, look-at-me overplaying. They all had the maturity and refinement to serve the song; they had learned in their careers that just doing what's necessary for the song results in a deeper experience. Being around those players was a period of growth for me, but it was more subtle and spiritual, as opposed to copping licks or techniques. I tried copping some things, though; I transcribed Oteil Burbridge's incredible version of "Amazing Grace," I wrote down the names of Larry Graham's vintage effects, and I was mesmerized by John Entwistle's three-finger technique.

One of the film's themes was the essence of bass playing. What did you discover?

I looked at what attracts people to bass, how it moves people—the effect of the vibrations on the body, mind, and spirit. I wanted to figure out how the mind and soul work while you're playing; can you make decisions for emotional and intellectual reasons simultaneously? But I arrived at a broader question that used bass playing as an example: As an artist, what does it take to achieve greatness? I posed the question to all the bassists, and I developed a three-level theory of the steps required. The first step is being inspired by what's already out there in a wide variety of musical styles. The second step is to transcend those influences, find your own voice, and express it through your instrument and craft. The third step is to transcend your own voice and tap into the moment—the sort of universal vibration—and let it flow through you in a deeper, almost spiritual way. You become a conduit, as so many great musicians speak about. I've since realized there are aspects of greatness I didn't get to cover in *Rising Low*, including confidence, passion, luck, talent, focus, timing, and attitude.

How did you play to the environment in the scene where you're standing with your bass in Manhattan traffic?

I tried to get to that third level by opening myself up and just playing; a little pattern came to me, and it felt right based on what I was tuned in to. I was trying to show a two-sided concept: At first, I'm playing to the mood and rhythm of what's going on around me, so the environment is playing me. Then the traffic slows down at the red light and my bass line gets slower, and the scene changes to a park. So the flipside is, I played something that caused the surroundings to

> ## Mike Gordon Selected Discography
> **Solo Album:** *Inside In*, Ropeadope. **With Phish:** (all on Elektra, except where noted) *Round Room*; *Live Phish, Volumes 1–16*, Dry Goods; *The Siket Disc*; *Farmhouse*; *Phish (The White Tape)*, Dry Goods; *The Story of the Ghost*; *Slip, Stitch & Pass*; *Billy Breathes*; *Stash*; *A Live One*; *Hoist*; *Rift*; *Lawn Boy*; *Picture of Nectar*, *Junta*. **With Leo Kottke:** *Clone*, Private Music. **With Gov't Mule:** *Deep End, Vol. 1*, ATO. **With Fiji Mariners (featuring Col. Bruce Hampton):** *Fiji Mariners*, Polygram. **With Gordon Stone:** *Touch & Go*, Alcazar. **With El Bu'ho:** *The Wham Bam Boodle 2000*, Ecotone. **With New Orleans Musicians Clinic:** *Get You a Healin'*, Orchard. **With the Dude of Life:** *Crimes of the Mind*, Elektra. **Video/DVDs with Phish:** *Phish: Live in Las Vegas*, Dry Goods; *Bittersweet Motel*, Dry Goods. **Films:** *Rising Low*, ATO; *Outside Out*, Dry Goods.

react and change. The point is once you learn to get in tune with the environment you're in, the environment will react to you as well. An example is when you're jamming and you play a note that introduces a new tonality; suddenly everyone else shifts to a new space and color because of that note. My theory is that if your playing conjures up a mood or place for you, the best thing you can do for that bass line is to bask in it and think only about that place—not the actual notes.

After you finished Rising Low *you entered a fertile writing period.*

I wanted to *make* music rather than talk about it, so I got a little office in downtown Manhattan's Woolworth Building. I brought my Languedoc semi-acoustic 5-string, a chair, a hard-disk recorder with built-in drum pads, a microphone, a pile of lyrics from my friend Joe Lintz, and some of my own ideas. My goal was to go in each day for an hour or two and write. I came up with about 50 songs or song ideas that I developed for the upcoming soundtrack to my film *Outside Out*, for the Phish album, and for the Leo Kottke album.

How did you get together with Leo?

I had been a fan since 1983, and I felt I could get along with him. In '99 I bought one of his albums [1971's *6- and 12-String Guitar*], and for fun I recorded a bass line—actually more of a duet part—to "The Driving of the Year Nail," and I gave it to him. He called me and said he liked it, we made plans to get together, and about a year later we went to Trey's barn to play. It took us a while to click, but we finally hit on this one little polyrhythm that became the intro riff on the track "June." From that point everything jelled. We each got a half-dozen tunes together and worked them up, along with two covers. We recorded *Clone* over three sessions in Burbank.

What is it like playing in a duo with him?

Eye-opening. At first I found that if I played a standard-type bass line, it could make what he was doing sound cliché because it defined it too much. Leo comes up with his amazing parts on the spot, and he doesn't have the technical training to tell you what he's playing, so it was even more challenging. I found that acceptance and not thinking saved the day. As soon as I stopped worrying about what I should be playing and accepted what I *was* playing, we'd get into a flow of notes and scales. We developed a sort of counterpoint. Not having drums and keyboards enabled me to let loose and fill more space, but at the same time I'd take on the timekeeping duties when needed.

What's the state of your technique these days?

I've been playing almost exclusively with a pick for a few years now, except for a bit of slapping. When I took away the fingerstyle side I realized there are certain kinds of grooves, ghost-notes, and string-crossing moves that I could only approximate with a pick, but I'm always working on getting better at it. I like the pick's sound and attack, and I wanted to focus on one tone so our soundman can always dial me in. I also like that it's uncool to the jazz and funk people—I always go against the grain, ever the outsider.

Who are your pick influences, and what's your approach?

I'm influenced by the great bluegrass-guitar flatpickers, like Tony Rice, Doc Watson, and Clarence White, and I'm hip to the great pick bassists, like Paul McCartney, Phil Lesh, Joe Osborn, Bobby Vega, Steve Swallow, and Anthony Jackson. I use a heavy nylon pick and strike the strings in between my pickups using up-and-down wrist strokes. I don't care for the glassy, grungy, top-end sound some players get. I prefer a round, almost upright sound, so I do a lot of muting with my right palm and left fingers. I've been a long-note guy in the past, but my style is constantly morphing. Right now I'm into shorter notes.

Was there a concept for Round Room?

We didn't even really know we were making the disc. We spent nine days learning 22 songs and then four days recording demos with the idea of re-recording the songs later. But we ended up liking the demo versions, so we did two more days of overdubbing, and that was the album. The concept—and it almost sounds cliché—was to learn how to play with live energy in the studio. We recorded at Trey's barn with everyone in the same room with the API sound board, so it sounds very raw—I played my Modulus 5 and just plugged into whatever amp was there. We realized there's nothing like the chemistry of 17 years of playing together, and we were able to catch that jubilant, relaxed, easy feeling right at the moment of conception. At one point Trey said that it would be a good album if we didn't ruin it by spending too much time on it.

Did you do any overdubbing?

Very little. I fixed a few wrong notes and downbeats that flammed with the kick drum, but I didn't change any bass lines. That's quite a contrast to early Phish albums, where I would go in and replace most of the bass parts. We overdubbed some of the vocals and added some acoustic guitar and percussion, but sparingly—it's very much how it sounded in the barn.

How did you put together "Round Room"?

I wrote it in my Woolworth office. The bass line is in nine but the melody is in four, so the vocals sort of wait for the bass line to catch up. The guys had some trouble figuring out how to sing it at first. We also found there were too many rhythms going and we needed an anchor to make it more danceable, so we added a King Sunny Adé–like pounding kick-drum beat to match the vocals in four, while the percussion stays in nine. The whole piece is inspired by West African music and musicians like Adé and [guitarist] Diblo Dibala and his band, Loketo.

"Seven Below" showcases a new focus on groove between you and Fish.

That has some funkiness—a little Medeski Martin & Wood vibe. In addition to my own current groove-awareness phase, Fish has come a long way, compared to the non-traditional way we both approached our instruments 17 years ago. There was the period when the band was playing so much odd-time stuff that we realized we couldn't play a simple shuffle, so we spent all our soundchecks playing straight blues. But really, the groove focus for Fish and I began six or seven years ago. We had this video of James Brown performing on an old TV show, and we would watch it every day on the bus. Gradually we got much better at locking the bass and kick drum, and it's so much more powerful to have that aspect, even if you don't always use it. Fish has big ears and he can tune into and follow anyone, but now he has the firm grounding, too.

My ultimate goal as a bass player is to be both solid and melodic. The best bassists do that, like Phil Lesh—he has this perfect synthesis of groove and melody going at the same time.

During the closing jam section of "Seven Below" the key moves from C, where it had been all along, to F, and then you introduce D from out of nowhere.

[*Laughs.*] That's typical. Trey recently told me that while listening to old tapes he realized many of our unexpected peak moments could be traced to a change in the bass line a few minutes before the peak happened. For me, a cool thing about the band is our ability to not just improvise but to go places together by coming up with chord progressions on the spot or changing the tonal center. Even on the groove side, I like to know where the *one* is because it gives me confidence—but it's also cool to be unsure and disoriented for a moment, because it makes me feel like I'm on an adventure. I like anything that can get me into that dream state of being untethered. It's amazing what there is outside the box when you are willing to discover it.

"46 Days" casts you in a new bass light.

That's our rock song; I don't think we have anything quite like it on any previous album. Everybody was taking a break or eating, and Fish sat down and started whacking out this beat for one of Trey's tunes. I picked up my bass and thought to myself, I'm going to lean back and play a deeper, grittier, looser bass line than I normally would—I'm just going to be a different character for a minute. Everyone dug what we were doing, and they came back to their instruments and rolled tape. The track has a thrashing rawness to it. I had Trey's demo bass part in mind, but you can definitely hear the *Rising Low* influence. There's some John Entwistle and Allen Woody in there.

How do you relate your filmmaking skills to bass playing?

For me it has always been about visualization. I think visually when I play; I'm either imagining fretboard patterns or scenes that the music is conjuring up. So capturing visions on film made perfect sense for me. When I'm shooting or editing a film and working with visualizations, it's the same kind of riffing that happens on bass, where I visualize sections of a song and edit my part accordingly. The merging of the two is fascinating. In *Outside Out* I had all these jammed cues that I'd try with a scene, and I found that if the music was slower it made the scene seem to go slower, and vice versa. It's pretty broadly accepted in the film world that sound, and music in particular, is 99 percent of a scene's emotion. What you see is more like the intellectual information that the brain takes in, but the *sound* is the emotion. That's a connection I want to continue to pursue in all mediums.

Web Site
www.phish.com

The 6th Element

MIKE GORDON'S POST–*RISING LOW* STYLE combines his concept of bass playing, his technical knowledge and experience, and his ability to free his mind and play instinctually. The results are some of Gordon's most profound bass lines to date on *Clone*, his collaboration with Leo Kottke, and on Phish's *Round Room*. Helping ground Gordon's improvisational flights is his preference for the interval of the 6th. On the fingerboard he employs it most frequently in the shape of an inverted major triad—for example, *G*, *C*, *E* in the key of *C* major (10th fret on the *A* string, 10th fret on the *D* string, and 9th fret on the *G* string). In that inversion the major 6th—the *G* to the *E*—represents the chord's 5 and 3, which also helps account for Mike's penchant for non-root tones.

Example 1 shows the main bass/melody line of "Whip," named for the whipping slide into the high *C* on bar 4's downbeat. Says Mike, "It's sort of a bluegrass lick, so a key is to let the other notes and strings ring throughout, the way bluegrass players do." **Example 2a** shows the opening and verse bass line of "With," which Gordon played on his National Reso-Phonic bass. Note his trademark use of the inverted triad with the major 6th shape in beats *one* and *three*. "Try not to rush the slides," he advises. **Example 2b** has the chorus part, which is made up of descending major and minor 6ths. Kottke's arpeggio fingerpicking style inspired both parts.

Ex. 1

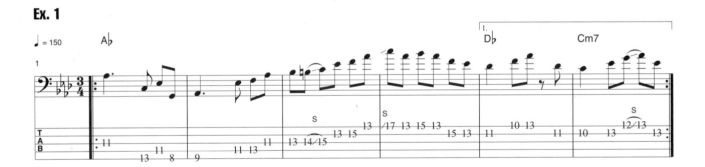

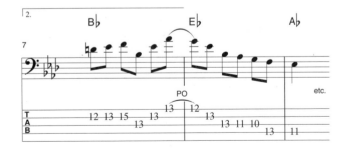

Example 3 shows the main "Clone" bass line, which boasts interesting color tones like the 2nd, 4th, and—no surprise—the 6th. "The hardest part was singing while playing it. Try to make it flow." **Example 4** shows the main bass part of "The Collins Missile." The 5/4 line, though odd-metered, flows smoothly and naturally, and it's rife with 6ths. "Let the top notes ring a little longer than the others." says Mike.

Moving to Phish's *Round Room*, **Ex. 5** shows the main odd-time bass line of the West African–inspired title track. Mike feels each measure in three groups of three, further dividing the polyrhythm of the 9/8 bass against the 4/4 drums. "I played up high on the *B* string to get a rounder sound. The notes shouldn't ring like an arpeggio, and the last note of each grouping is especially short." Need we mention the 6th-heavy inverted triads? **Example 6** shows the main "Mock Song" bass line/sub-hook. Mike takes it down an octave at times and rarely plays the line the same way twice, especially bar 2. And yes, the 6th is a dominant color.

Example 7a contains the funky main "Seven Below" groove, which continues in the jam section. (Note how he slips in a 6th from beat *three* to *four*.) "I came up with that to go along with Trey's guitar part. Except for the ghost-note, all the notes are legato." **Example 7b**, a variation of the original groove, occurs later in the jam section and continues for a while. "It's just supposed to drive the jam along." **Example 8** shows a cool fill in "46 Days." "Actually, Trey had a similar fill on his demo; he likes using the flatted 5th on the downbeat. This was my Allen Woody–ized interpretation."

Ex. 2a

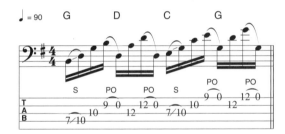

Ex. 2b

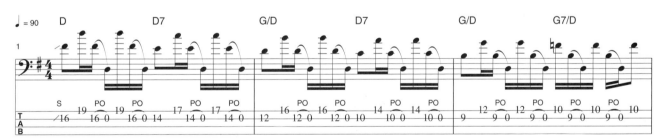

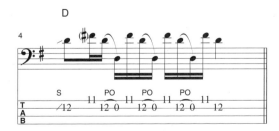

Ex. 3

Ex. 4

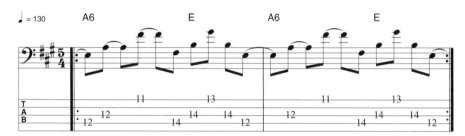

Ex. 5

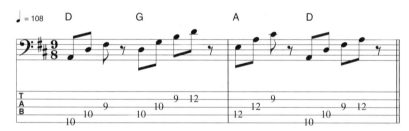

Ex. 6

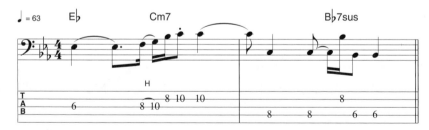

Ex. 7a

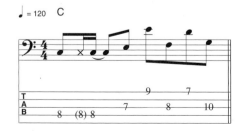

Ex. 7b

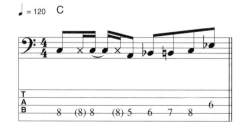

Ex. 8

CHAPTER 7

R&B Visionaries
ME'SHELL NDEGÉOCELLO • RAPHAEL SAADIQ
JONATHAN MARON

R&B's hip-hop incarnation mixed man and machine, rapper and musician, remix and original vinyl, club DJ and concert hall. On bass a group of groovers embraced all of those sensibilities to chart new sub terrain. They have seen the future, and it is funky.

ME'SHELL NDEGÉOCELLO
Peace, Passion & Bass

Interviewed by Chuck Crisafulli, April 1995, and Bill Leigh, March 2002.

FEW BASSISTS REACHED AS WIDE A VARIETY OF LISTENERS over the past decade as Me'Shell NdegéOcello. The breakthrough success of her 1993 debut, *Plantation Lullabies*, led to high-profile gigs with artists from John Mellencamp to Herbie Hancock. But Me'Shell's influence on the bass world far exceeds that of a versatile session player. Both *Lullabies* and 1996's *Peace Beyond Passion* made it clear the accomplished multi-instrumentalist, singer, and composer is first and foremost a bass player—and as such a role model for bass-toting songwriters everywhere. Not since Sting has the voice of an adept pop songsmith been so sympathetically aligned with the low end. "I think my bass playing ties in with my mother fetish," she told *Bass Player*. "I want to hold you, cradle you, and let you do whatever you do." Such thinking explains Me'Shell's supportive tendencies—but what of her spare, bass-centric writing style? "I write on other instruments, mostly piano and guitar, and then I write the bass line to kind of sing along. The biggest thing with bass is to get away from clutter. Just voice the chord and keep it simple. Why do I need these five extra notes?" Live, however, she does require a second bassist. "I cannot sing and play—it's just not one of my skills. When I play the bass, I have no interest in anything but the bass part, so it never really works for me to sing, too."

Slinky, soulful, sensual, with more than enough power to lull and caress before snapping you rudely to attention—NdegéOcello's bass playing, singing voice, and knife-edged lyrics share the same qualities. And whether she's opening tunes with snappy funk figures, weaving upper-register licks in and out of vocal lines, or just laying it down like a savvy soul vet, NdegéOcello wrings delicious tones out of her flatwound-strung Fender Jazz. Even as she leads song after song with supremely singable bass lines, though, Me'Shell the songwriter is always close at hand. "I don't own any bass player albums. Forty minutes of bass solos just ain't gonna work for me."

Born Michelle Johnson in Berlin, Germany, in 1969, NdegéOcello grew up in the Washington, D.C., area in a house full of music. Her father and brother are accomplished jazz musicians. Playing bass wasn't part of NdegéOcello's original plan; at first she wanted to be a drummer. "That was my big hope. I had this album of Max Roach and Buddy Rich playing with a big band, and that was just amazing to listen to—I thought the drums were the *shit*. Plus, I think I had figured out that the drummer always gets to be the asshole of the band, and I liked that."

Me'Shell's drum dreams were put aside when one of her brother's friends happened to leave his bass at the house. "It was a copy of a Precision—a really nice one, come to think of it. It seemed huge to me, because of that long-scale neck, but I fell in love with it. I started playing it right away, and I kept playing the bass line to a Herb Alpert tune, 'Rise.' It just felt so cool, and I knew I had to learn the instrument." Before long, Me'Shell acquired a more manageable Fender Mustang. "That's the bass I went to work on. I had a little 4-track, and I'd make up bass songs—me playing bass against four more tracks of bass."

Me'Shell NdegéOcello

At 16 she began to get serious about her bass chops. Her training ground was D.C.'s vibrant go-go scene, where she played with local stalwarts Little Benny & the Masters, Chuck Brown & the Soul Searchers, and Rare Essence. NdegéOcello credits her discipline as a musician to both her father's training and her work with the D.C. go-go bands. "My father had a jazz group, and he had me sit in when his bass player didn't show up. Even though I had been playing for less than a year, he was like, 'You're going to learn to read charts now.' He told me the more basic I was, the better I'd be. I remember going off on some tangent on one of the standards, and he just looked at me like, 'Oh, you've lost your mind!' But it was great training to work through stuff like 'My Funny Valentine' and stay in a groove. And playing in the go-go bands really teaches you to hold back; you're always running into these breaks—84 bars of *nothing*—and you just have to tell your hands, 'I'm not going to play a note.'"

NdegéOcello's father gave her another important lesson. "On his horn he showed me how you could play the same note harsh and ragged or smooth and beautiful, so I became a stickler for tone from the beginning. Some of that came from listening to Police records, too—I've heard people say Sting's not the greatest bass player, but he has such a nice, warm tone. That stuck in my mind as important."

After a brief stint studying music at Howard University in the late '80s, Me'Shell headed to New York City to work with Vernon Reid's Black Rock Coalition. In New York NdegéOcello—whose adopted Swahili surname means 'free like a bird'—began to set some of her extensive journal entries to music. The resulting demo tapes found their way into the hands of pop luminary Madonna, who was looking for talent to sign to her fledgling Maverick label. For Madonna, NdegéOcello was an irresistible package—a five-foot-tall, bass-toting, bisexual single mother with a shaved head full of heavyweight music. Me'Shell was signed to a multi-album deal and teamed up with producers David Gamson, Andre Betts, and Bob Power to bring her solo debut *Plantation Lullabies* to fruition.

By the time Bill Leigh interviewed Me'Shell in March 2002, the 60-inch-tall bassist had blossomed into a larger-than-life musical presence. A perennial favorite among top bass players, she was hailed by Bass Player *as one of the ten most influential bassists of the '90s. With Leigh she discussed her art, her album,* Cookie: The Anthropological Mixtape, *and her veteran band—guitarist Allen Cato (who produced* Cookie*), keyboardist Federico Peña, drummer Gene Lake, and bassist David Dyson.*

Do you consider yourself first a songwriter or a bass player?

I love the bass—and the way I play is very much my personality. I'm all right standing way behind who-ever's up front, just holding down a groove. I like to make everything lock, gel, and be funky. Compositions move me more than anything, though—the construction of the song, the lyric, and everything. My goal is to be a great writer, not a great bass player.

Most of my favorite bass players are writers. Jaco's my hero because of his virtuosity and craft in composing and arranging. Of course his bass playing is way up there, but the songs are beautiful. *Jaco Pastorius* is the greatest bass record ever made, but *Word of Mouth* was a big part of me wanting to hear strings and orchestral sounds in my music. Probably my favorite bass player when I was growing up was Prince. His bass lines, like "Let's Work," [*Controversy*] are like songs within themselves. Then there's Paul McCartney—an incredible songwriter and bass player, and Sting, who writes the lines you remember.

Are there bassists you admire just for their playing?

Rodney "Skeet" Curtis from P-Funk—put him way up on the list; everybody slept on him. Paul Jackson with the Headhunters—he sounds like a bass player. I also had a great mentor: Mike Neil, who played in a go-go band when I was growing up in D.C. Our playing is very similar. He played on the first Maxwell record. He's been my teacher as far as developing my bass personality and just holding it down. He always said, "You've got to know what *not* to play. Just hold it down—it's a waste of time if nobody can dance to it." I definitely got that slide stuff I do from him. It's the period, the end of the sentence.

What does writing bring to your bass playing?

Simplicity and flow. Bass is the harmonic and rhythmic foundation, and I like that. I like to make it feel good and give it a personality. I'm okay not being a solo bass artist; I don't want to be so alone. I'm never going to be Victor Wooten. That's not my gift; I didn't get virtuosity in bass playing.

What is your gift?

I have virtuosity in creativity. You can sit me onstage with a drummer and I'll come up with a bass line. You can put me in any setting and I'll make it work. I can play with anybody: I could play with Incubus, with Lynyrd Skynyrd, or with Joshua Redman if he didn't mind me playing electric.

Is there a reason Cookie *has much more bass than your previous record,* Bitter, *yet you're not playing as much bass live as you did on the Bitter tour?*

People say there's not a lot of bass on *Bitter*, and that it's not funky. I'm like, *whatever*. I like the bass on *Bitter*; it's beautifully legato, it's cool, and it sounds good. As a bass player, when someone calls me for a gig, I am there to implement their needs, not my ego. The music I wrote for *Bitter* called for that bass style. Live, though, the Bitter tour was the first time I ever tried singing and playing. As it evolved, I realized I could play a little more while singing. I noticed Jimi Hendrix had a tendency to play along with the phrases he was singing, so I tried that, and the bass lines got a little fuller. With the new material, sometimes the bass lines are so contrapuntal I can't sing with them. And it's rapping more than singing, and rapping while playing bass is too difficult. Plus, I have to front a show. I have to tell the band what to do and interact with the audience.

When I'm playing bass, I disappear—I become part of the band, and I don't think about the people out in that audience. When I take the bass off, I can interact with them again.

You give the band a lot of stage direction.

I see all the songs as groups of phrases, and sometimes I want the band to go to a different phrase. I learned this from Gene, who played with saxophonist Steve Coleman. Steve would play a certain lick that would be a signal for the band to go somewhere else. So I'm keeping the band together and trying to see where it should go. If something Gene plays inspires something else, I'll say, "Break it down—let's see what can happen." I'm just directing.

So your show is very improvisational.

There are structures, but if we feel something, we'll go with it. We're all huge Prince fans, but we also have records by Allan Holdsworth, Weather Report, Pat Metheny, and Lyle Mays. We come from that mental place where music is supposed to grow and evolve and be expansive, so there are some songs in the set where we leave room for that. I think of it as improvisational, hip-hop–based R&B.

The hardest gig is probably David's, because he has much less room for improvisation. It's a challenge for him, because he can play a whole lot of bass, but the new compositions require more of a foundation. That's just where I come from. If I die tomorrow, I want people to say, "Well, it was funky. It was definitely groovin.'" David doesn't try to play like me. I like the members of my band for who they are as people. We sound like we sound as a band because everyone plays like they are. Our common ground is the song I wrote; it's the topic we're going to discuss. Every night we take that topic and see what we can do with it—what we can find in ourselves. Like when we play the beginning of "Better by the Pound," sometimes I wish it could go on forever.

When you play that intro live, you can really hear the difference between your style and David's.

Even more on "God.Fear.Money." I play *super* behind [the beat]. It's a very D.C. go-go feel; everything has this lope in it. David, on the other hand, tends to play on top of the beat. It's still funky but it's totally different. David has the percolating style, but mine is to just let it go, let it breathe. Space is where it *is*. I can take my hands off the bass for a good bar and be fine. Here's how I see it: If you were doing this all the time [*breathes really fast*], you'd think, I can't breathe! I'm hyperventilating! Instead, it's all about [*takes slow, easy breaths*]. That's what I'm trying to get to. To me, music is like sex—you've got to relax and take it slow. You can't be just on it all the time. A lot of musicians think they've got to be at the bat—pow! pow!—hitting home runs all the time. I'm fine just taking it easy.

In addition to electric bass, you also play keyboard bass on Cookie.

I love playing keyboard bass. Give me a keyboard and a pitch bend and it's *on*. Keyboard bass and regu-

Cookie Cutters

On all four solo albums, Me'Shell has recorded primarily with her pre-CBS Fender Jazz Bass, which has been strung with the same flatwounds ten-plus years. For other sessions she selects from her collection of 4-strings, which includes a Modulus VJ, Celinder, Ernie Ball/Music Man StingRay, a Gibson Les Paul Bass, and a Surine. Though she used a SansAmp PSA-1 for *Cookie*, she usually takes an Aguilar DB680 preamp or an Avalon U5 DI to recording sessions. Her tech, Mauro Tatini, strings her basses with Thomastik-Infeld flatwounds and Dean Markley roundwounds.

Onstage, her Celinder and Modulus VJ basses are run through a Whirlwind Selector A/B box and Behringer Ultra DI DI-100 to an Ampeg SVT-4PRO head powering Ampeg 4x10 cabinets. "I don't like 'pankiness' or bite," she says. "So I often roll off the highs. But sometimes the engineer says, 'Look, you've got to have *some* highs.'" NdegéOcello has used various effects, including a Zoom 506 bass multi-effects pedal for distortion, envelope filter, and chorus, and a Boss AW-2 AutoWah.

Me'Shell NdegéOcello Selected Discography

Solo albums: (all on Maverick) *Cookie: The Anthropological Mixtape*; *Bitter*; *Peace Beyond Passion*; *Plantation Lullabies*. **With Madonna:** *Bedtime Stories*, Maverick. **With Alanis Morrisette:** (both on Maverick) *Feast on Scraps*; *Under Rug Swept*. **With Gov't Mule:** *The Deep End, Volume 2*, ATO. **With John Mellencamp:** *Dance Naked*, Mercury. **With the Rolling Stones:** *Bridges to Babylon*, Virgin. **With Santana:** *Shaman*, Arista. **With Joan Osborne:** *How Sweet It Is*, Compendia. **With Roy Hargrove Presents the RH Factor:** Hard Groove, Verve. **With Chaka Khan:** *Epiphany: The Best of Chaka Khan*, Warner Bros. **With Scritti Politti:** *Anomie & Bonhomie*, Virgin. **With Citizen Cope:** *Citizen Cope*, Dreamworks. **With Holly Palmer:** *Holly Palmer*, Warner Bros. **With Joe Henry:** *Scar*, Hollywood. **With Eric Benet:** *A Day in the Life*, Warner Bros. **With Boney James:** *Seduction*, Warner Bros. **With Marcus Miller:** *Tales*, PRA. **With Vanessa Williams:** *Greatest Hits: The First Ten Years*, Polygram. **With Tina & the B-Sides:** *It's All Just the Same*, Sire. **With Harvey Mason:** *Ratamacue*, Atlantic. **With Ledisi:** *Soulsinger*, Tommy Boy. **With Guru:** *Jazzmatazz, Vol. 2: The New Reality*, Capitol. **With Get Set V.O.P.:** *Voice of the Projects*, Polygram. **With the Indigo Girls:** *Come on Now Social*, Epic. **With various artists:** *Ain't Nuthin' but a She Thing*, Polygram; *Inner City Blues: The Music of Marvin Gaye*, Motown; *Stolen Moments: Red Hot + Cool*, GRP. **Soundtracks**: *Standing in the Shadows of Motown*, Hip-O; *Living Single: Music from and Inspired by the Hit TV Show*, Warner Bros.; *Batman & Robin*, Warner Bros.; *White Man's Burden*, Atlantic.

lar bass are both a part of me. Cato wrote the bass line for "Dead Nigga Blvd. (Pt. 1)"—it's me playing the Fender; I'm also playing a Moog synth bass line behind it. I love keyboard bass and regular bass interacting. Supa Dave West, who produced De La Soul, came up with the hip-hop line on "Hot Night" using sampled bass notes on an Akai MPC60. I replaced his line with the Fender. Hip-hop is really grounded in how it feels. Gene and I like to dance; when we go to a club, we like to get our freak on. When I played "Hot Night," I tried to tap into that feeling. I rolled off all the tone on the bass and locked on it. "Priorities 1–6" is all keyboard. To me, the other greatest bass player of all time is Stevie Wonder. The way his keyboard bass percolates on "Boogie on Reggae Woman"—oh my God, you don't want to play after that! I just wanted to tap into that Stevie energy.

The moods on Bitter *and* Cookie *are totally different. Are there some moods that make you want to pick up the bass more?*

Oh, no. There's three years between each of my records, and in between I change and grow and hear new things I like. Before *Cookie*, I was getting into Outkast, some Master P, and Incubus, but I also was listening to a lot of "out" stuff—*Weather Report*, *Miles Live at the Fillmore*, and the Miles Davis *Bitches Brew* box set. It all sort of permeated my consciousness along with the lyrical content of what I wanted to talk about, and they just sort of morphed themselves together. With *Bitter*, I had just come off the Lilith tour. I started thinking, I could do that—strumming guitar chords and writing songs. So I got a metal guitar—a National—and I started messing around with it, and those tunes came out. Maybe I'll make the next record using only a Rhythm King, a Moog, and a string machine. That's it. I just get in these moods.

That's how I am about basses, too. Sometimes my Fender doesn't sound good on a gig, so I have an array of basses. I'm a painter, and I'm going to have a lot of brushes. I don't believe you have to stick with one sound—I have a bunch of different sounds. In fact, I'd be afraid if somebody said I had a sound. I'd rather they say, "She has a certain feel."

What was it like meeting the surviving Motown studio musicians in the documentary film Standing in the Shadows of Motown?

First of all, if you're playing R&B there's no way you could believe that you're not influenced by James Jamerson. For me and many others, it's on a blood level. Your momma played it, you know it, you feel it, it *is*.

What's so interesting about the Motown cats is that this was their 9-to-5. They weren't going to eat if they weren't playing on top of their craft. Yet they are still the paradigm for artistic integrity. They were blue-collar, but at the same time they set the bar higher. Look at the arrangements that came out of their minds! I definitely have to respect them, pay homage, and let everybody know, because that kind of thing still goes on to this day. There's some little genius cat somewhere coming out with brilliant stuff and struggling. There are probably thousands of bass players who are more incredible than Marcus or Victor, and we'll never hear them. I'm very aware of that. I'm not that great a bass player; I'm probably not that great a songwriter. But I have the one thing: I have faith. I have an extremely strong belief in life and goodness, and I believe that whatever you put into it is what you get out of it. I just want to do good, be a positive person, and learn as much as I can.

Web Site
www.meshell.com

Cookie Crumbs

ME'SHELL NDEGÉOCELLO'S BASS LINES ARE ALWAYS ABOUT THE GROOVE, thick and deep. On "Hot Night," from *Cookie*, she underscores a salsa horn line with an understated hip-hop bass part. **Example 1a** shows the style. In a tried-and-true funk fashion she uses syncopated rhythms to anticipate strong beats—like beat *three* of bar 1 and beat *two* of bar 2—while never failing to play on the *one*. The line's spaciousness makes room for the busy 16th-note fill like the one at the end of **Ex. 1b**.

Ex. 1a

Ex. 1b

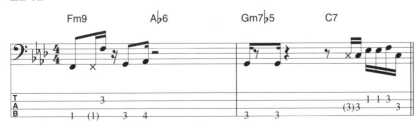

The "Barry Farms" groove is a slow, sexy variant of the loping, shuffle-16th funk style known in Washington, D.C., as go-go. Though there's little harmonic variation throughout the song's gradual build, Me'Shell's bass line brings in the quirky chord progression that becomes the tune's instrumental outro. In **Ex. 2** on beat *four* of the first bar and beat *two* of bar 2 she punctuates the phrases with downward *E*-string slides.

Example 3a shows one version of the much-varied line of "Better by the Pound," which Me'Shell ornaments with syncopated ghost-notes. While she acknowledges that percussive funk technique is a key part of her style, in her private practice time Me'Shell has been aiming for a cleaner approach (**Ex. 3b**) inspired by the sound of keyboard bass. "Putting all the spaces and hiccups in there—I've got that down. Now I'm trying something different, getting simpler, and letting the notes ring out." **Example 4** is inspired by Me'Shell's part from "Criterion." Playing a rented upright, she looped a few different takes of the syncopated, two-bar line; it features a simple four-note statement that she rhythmically varies in the second bar.

Ex. 2

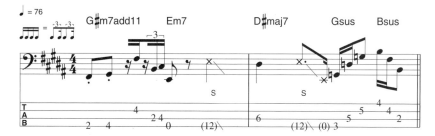

Ex. 3a

Ex. 3b

Ex. 4

Example 5a recalls Me'Shell's bass line on "God.Fear.Money," though the example is written rhythmically straight. While David Dyson plays the line on top of the beat, a straight reading is far from Me'Shell's behind-the-beat interpretation. "Make sure the musical direction says, 'Supa laid-back, like you smoked a blunt.'" She develops this skill by specifically practicing feel. "At home I take one of my lines, turn on a drum machine, and just play it over and over, messing with the pockets, cutting up the phrases, and trying to see how many different ways I can make the line sit around the beat." **Example 5b** is an excerpt of Me'Shell's demonstration of this practice routine. "I try not to listen to the drums to play *with* them, but just to feel them and groove with them."

Ex. 5a

Ex. 5b

RAPHAEL SAADIQ
Gospeldelic Vision

Interviewed by Chris Jisi, December 2000 and July 2002.

AS HIP-HOP CONTINUES TO INFLUENCE STYLES ranging from R&B to heavy metal and beyond, the musician-meets-machine concept is being played out in various ways. Few have a more cutting-edge approach than Raphael Saadiq, who has merged hip-hop's programmed approach with his Old School R&B roots to create a new rhythm-section style. Explains Glenn Standridge, one half of Saadiq's production team, Jake & the Phatman: "When we're creating tracks, everyone sort of plays to their own beat, with everything revolving around Raphael's bass—so it has that loose, hip-hop quality of samples layered together. The result is a best-of-both-worlds scenario that creates a feel all its own. It's deeper than hip-hop because it's all played or sampled on the spot, mostly on real instruments. It's inspired by great old records, yet it's contemporary. It doesn't sound like just a bunch of people mimicking classic grooves on vintage gear."

The best-known examples of Saadiq's post-modern potion are his groove-breaking collaborations with neo-soul crooner D'Angelo, and Lucy Pearl, his short-lived trio with ex–En Vogue vocalist Dawn Robinson and A Tribe Called Quest's Ali Shaheed Muhammad. But Saadiq has been applying his concept since his frontman days with gold-selling neo-soul trailblazers Tony Toni Toné, and as an in-demand bassist/producer with everyone from Snoop Dogg to John Mellencamp.

After Pearl rolled off the table, Raphael at last recorded his solo debut, the aptly titled *Instant Vintage*. Spanning more than 76 minutes and comprising 21 tracks (two hidden), *Instant Vintage* is a masterstroke. Its rich R&B landscape is tinged with everything from country and rock to jazz and pop, over which Saadiq delivers his musical and social messages and tells his own story. Helping out are hip-hop heroes D'Angelo, Angie Stone, and TLC's T-Boz, ex-Tony Timothy Riley, the Tower of Power Horns, Charles Veal & the South Central Chamber Orchestra, and an old tuba played by Saadiq and Kelvin Wooten. At the core are Raphael's singular vocal and guitar work and his unmistakable, penetrating bass.

Guitar was actually the first instrument played by Saadiq (born in 1966 as Raphael Wiggins) in his native Oakland, California. After hearing James Jamerson's upright on Marvin Gaye's "How Sweet It Is (To Be Loved by You)," and being visually attracted to the electric bass in his church's band, he asked for and received an Orlando Jazz Bass knockoff at age seven. "The first bass line I learned was Rufus's 'You Got the Love' [from 1974's *Rags to Rufus*, with Dennis Belfield on bass]. My brother taught it to me, and he played the guitar part." With a quick ear in a musically fertile neighborhood, Saadiq soon graduated from jamming with family and friends to having his pals ask their dads if he could sit in with them at clubs. Paying gigs followed, with days spent playing trombone in the junior high school jazz band and bass in UC Berkeley's Youth Music Program. "I was constantly playing in all kinds of settings, from quartets to solo. I'd go into coffeehouses alone and just improvise grooves behind rappers or poetry readings."

In 1987, while the 18-year-old was putting together demos with his brother D'wayne Wiggins and cousin Timothy Christian Riley (for what would eventually become Tony Toni Toné), a friend told him Sheila E. was coming to the Bay Area to audition singing bassists for her touring band. Raphael beat out 40 other hopefuls, and a month later he was opening for Prince in huge Japanese arenas. Prince soon enlisted Sheila's band for his notorious after-concert club gigs. Upon Saadiq's return Stateside in 1988, the "Tonys" were signed, and he began his musical quest.

One of your trademarks is a super-laid-back feel, as on "Excuse Me" and "Make My Day" from Instant Vintage.

I don't have a name for it; it's sort of like ghosting or shadowing the snare drum. I'm locking with the drums but a step behind, kind of sneaking up on them. You hear the snare hit and then I ghost or echo

Raphael Saadiq

that. But for it to work, the drummer has to be aware of what I'm doing, and stay right in the middle of the beat, to keep that rubber-band-like tension. It's hard to learn, especially for people who always play on top, so it's best to listen to it being done; eventually you'll feel it. It's not something I've tried, but I suppose you could also practice it by setting up a basic drum loop with a *two* and *four* snare. First play a simple quarter-note or eighth-note pattern that locks with the loop, and then gradually pull back until you're ghosting the snare by playing a split-second after it hits.

Does this approach have hip-hop roots?

It came about when D'Angelo and I first played together on keyboard and bass. We just started doing it, and the more we laid back, the more we'd laugh. We could go so far back that people around us would be like, "No, stop it!" That's the way D sings and plays, but it's something we both felt naturally; I don't think he ever did it with anyone else. When he got his road band together, he found players in Pino Palladino and Ahmir Thompson who could do it well—but so far they're some of the very few who can. I would say it has roots in hip-hop's sloppily synced samples, but there's also a link to Old School gospel, blues, and R&B, with bands like Sly & the Family Stone. Spanky [guitarist Eddie Alford], who plays on my album and who is in D's road band, comes from that background, and he totally gets it.

Has it ever elicited a negative reaction?

Oh, sure. D and I were doing a session for a well-known rock/R&B artist who shall remain nameless, and when he heard our track, he said, "What's with the time lag?" He thought it was a technical glitch. Needless to say, he didn't like or use what we did.

Talk about how you merge hip-hop and R&B.

My whole thing is, if I want to sample something, I'll play it myself, sample it, and EQ it—rather than sample some old track. People sample stuff because they can't play. I can play. The hip-hop side is the repetition—simple, funky, and tasteful, but banging hard. My measuring stick is that the groove has to make an MC want to rhyme to it—to make him want to bust freestyle to my bass line. I grew up on R&B, but I was right in the middle of hip-hop, too. I dug artists like Mobb Deep, NWA, Wu-Tang Clan, and A Tribe Called Quest. When I heard the sampling, though, I felt I could do it better through real playing. Some people call my stuff progressive hip-hop or creative hip-hop, but it's not about that. It's just my music.

The Deader the Better

Raphael Saadiq's prized '62 Fender Precision puts the vintage in *Instant Vintage*. Marvels Glenn Standridge, who with partner Bobby Ozuna makes up Saadiq's production team of Jake & the Phatman (TLC, Angie Stone, Ginuwine): "I've never heard another bass like it. Between the foam under the bridge cover and the old Rotosound flatwounds, it's so dead you can't even play it live. We tried at one soundcheck—you couldn't even hear a tone, and there was no pop at all. But in the studio, with Raphael's touch, it's a killer." In addition to Saadiq's P-Bass on nine tracks, Preston "P-Groover" Crump and Kelvin Wooten play their own P-Basses on a track each. Elsewhere, Raphael played his '90s reissue Fender Jazz on a pair of tracks, an '80s Ibanez Musician on "Charlie Ray," and his Ransom 5-string "flag bass" on "Be Here" (seen in the song's video). All of Raphael basses have old medium-gauge flats or roundwounds. On several tracks keyboard bass appears in the form of a Korg MS2000 Analog Waveform synth or MS2000-triggered Akai MPC samples of Raphael's flag bass.

Credit Saadiq's hands and an assortment of studio gear for the variety of tones coming from his P-Bass. According to Standridge, the usual signal path was direct box or mic preamp, followed by a compressor, into Pro Tools. The favored gear was an Avalon U5 DI/preamp (which has a passive tone selector and variable-gain preamp and filter) to a Teletronix LA-2A limiter. "The Avalon really allows us to feel and hear his thumb and fingers, and once we found out Motown used the LA-2A, that became our first choice." Other processors included a Countryman Type 85 DI, Urei 1176 compressor, Avalon VT737SP tube mic pre/compressor, mid-'70s Neve 1073 mic pre/EQ, Vox AC30 and "Big Cabinet" Line 6 Amp Farm settings on Pro Tools (for the second hidden track), and on "Body Parts" and "Charlie Ray," an old B72 Telefunken mic pre—the kind the Beatles used.

Onstage Raphael plugs into an Ampeg SVT rig or an SWR SM-900 head with SWR Goliath 4x10 and Big Ben 1x18 cabinets. His studio amp is an SWR Silverado Special combo. His outboard effects include a Big Briar MF-101 Moogerfooger Lowpass Filter, a ProCo Rat distortion pedal, and a Dunlop Cry Baby bass wah.

What was your concept for Instant Vintage?

I wanted to have a record that thoroughly entertains, with something that would appeal to a wide array of listeners without losing the integrity of what I learned as a musician. I tried to make every song a bit different from the next, and I wanted each one to feel like a single—along the lines of what Michael Jackson and Quincy Jones did with *Off the Wall*, where every song had an impact. Rod Temperton, one of that album's writers, had a theory that each song should have a strong introduction, develop as it went along, and end with an even stronger outro. I tried to take a cue from him.

Throughout the CD your bass is the main voice.

It's the centerpiece. Jake & the Phatman tease me that I play lead bass. When I record, I almost always put down the drums and guitar first, and then the bass. I like doing the bass and vocals together because they feed off each other; I get my vocal part from the bass and vice versa. I'll give the bass its own space and then sing around that, like on "Body Parts," so each one stands out as a melody or they call and answer with each other.

Jake & the Phatman say your "independent parts" approach is a key to your hybrid sound.

I play a lot of everything on the record—bass, some guitar, a bit of keyboards, plus the vocals—so as a kind of one-man band I have to do it that way. As I play each part I try to be loose with it, and I tend to sit back in the pocket. When we put it all together, it can sound like everything is sampled because my parts aren't in perfect time or live-band-sounding time. There are many points where I want it to sound like a dropped-in sample from another record, like the opening bass line of "Be Here." But on "You're the One that I Like," where I'm playing bass, guitar, and organ, it's more of a general looseness between parts. I also enjoy playing in a different pocket space than the drums, like on "Skyy, Can You Feel Me." Raymon Murray came up with a drum groove, and then I added a bass part that's completely counter to it.

On "Charlie Ray" you apply what you call "the grease." What is that?

I get it with my thumb plucks. It's when I don't play any real pitches—just dead notes with a lot of percolating between rhythms. I use it on other tracks, but it's hard to hear at times. It's sort of like what Larry Graham and Prince do on bass. People think Larry used left-hand pats, but he pretty much did everything with his thumb, using up- and downstrokes.

Sonically, you tend to EQ and place the bass differently from track to track.

How it sounds and where it sits is a big part of the feel, aside from notes and phrasing. Sometimes I pan the bass front and center, and sometimes it's to the left. Likewise, at times I'll go for rumbling, earthy lows, or if I'm doing a lot of muting we'll have less lows and more mids. It's always different. I'll use onboard EQ and I'll have Jake & the Phatman set the Avalon U5 and Teletronix LA-2A, or whatever mic pre and limiter we're using, so I'm getting the tone I want when I dig in. Then I'll play half as hard so I can shade it further with my hands.

Raphael Saadiq Selected Discography

Solo album: *Instant Vintage*, Pookie/Universal. **With Lucy Pearl:** *Lucy Pearl*, Pookie/Beyond. **With Tony Toni Toné:** *House of Music*, Mercury; *Sons of Soul*, Polygram; *The Revival*, Wing; *Who?*, Wing. **With D'Angelo:** *Voodoo*, Virgin; *Brown Sugar*, Capitol. **With Angie Stone:** *Mahogany Soul*, J-Records. **With Marcus Miller:** *M2*, Telarc. **With the Isley Brothers:** *Eternal*, DreamWorks. **With the Bee Gees:** *Still Waters*, Polydor. **With John Mellencamp:** *Mr. Happy Go Lucky*, Mercury. **With Snoop Doggy Dogg:** *Top Dogg*, Priority; *The Doggfather*, Interscope. **With A Tribe Called Quest:** *Beats, Rhymes & Life*, Jive. **With TLC:** *3D*, La Face. **With Kenny Latimore:** *Weekend*, Arista. **With the Roots:** *Illadelph Halflife*, Geffen. **With Bilal:** *1st Born Second*, Interscope. **With Mica Paris:** *Black Angel*, Import. **With Joi:** *Star Kitty's Revenge*, Universal. **With Truth Hurts:** *Truthfully Speaking*, Interscope. **With Total:** *Total*, Bad Boy. **Soundtracks:** *Brown Sugar*, MCA; *Baby Boy*, Uptown/Universal; *Love & Basketball*, New Line; *Soul Food*, La Face; *Poetic Justice*, Sony; *Boyz N the Hood*, Qwest.

Who were your early bass influences?

Aside from Jamerson on the radio, it was a pair of great local players who are still two of my favorites: Joel Smith, who was with the Hawkins Family, and Robert Ball. My godfather, James Levi, played drums in Herbie Hancock's Headhunters; one day, when I was maybe eight, he asked this bassist to drive me home, and he pulled out his bass and gave me some pointers. Years later I found out it was Jaco! Eventually I got into Verdine White, Bootsy Collins, Bobby Watson, and Louis Johnson—but my two main guys were Bernard Edwards and Larry Graham. I saw both Chic and Sly & the Family Stone at the Oakland Coliseum.

Can you describe your techniques?

I learned to slap first, because as a kid I didn't have the forearm strength to finger-pluck. I don't slap much anymore because it's not the thing right now. I alternate my two fingers, and I do a lot of what I call thumb-plucking: Holding my thumb parallel to the strings, I use the meat of my thumb on the downstroke and top side of my nail on the upstroke. I can mute to varying degrees with my fingers or palm.

What did you learn while playing live with Prince?

Mainly, how to play all night long, and also the power of simplicity. One night we were playing funk in *E*, and he went over and picked up my bass—but it was tuned to *E♭*, so he just found one note that worked, and he stayed on it the entire song and drove the groove home.

What was it like singing on "Hurricane" on Marcus Miller's M2?

That was cool. I told him I got a "D" in one of my classes in school because I was always reading magazine articles about this young bass player with Miles Davis instead of paying attention. I did an okay job on the track, but I could have done better—I was a little nervous and intimidated being around him. I'm thrilled that he won a Grammy, though.

Who are your vocal influences?

Stevie Wonder, Donny Hathaway, Al Green, Marvin Gaye, Aretha Franklin, and James Brown, who are all big musical influences as well.

Who are some of your favorite bassists, and who are some hip-hop bassists to watch?

I like the meat-and-potatoes guys, like Pino, Marcus, Will Lee, Nathan Watts with Stevie Wonder, and Derek "DOA" Allen, who works with Bobby Brown, Brandy, and Wayman Tisdale. When it comes to creative hip-hop bassists, Preston "P Groover" Crump is *the* man. He's got a feel and a melodic thing happening that's all his own. On my CD he plays his P-Bass on "Different Times."

The first of your disc's two hidden tracks, "Gospeldelic," is also how you refer to your music in the opening tune. Can you explain the term?

When I was a kid our church was about two blocks from the Oakland Coliseum. With the windows open we would hear the soundchecks and concerts going on, so I'd be sitting there listening to P-Funk playing "We Got the Funk." "Gospeldelic" is the truth of expression. The gospel, or truth, is the part of my music that came from all the great older musicians I look up to, and the records they made. The delic, or funkadelic, is the fun part that gives me the freedom to be wild and funky.

Web site

www.raphaelsaadiq.com

Instant Groovage

WHETHER IT'S MIXED IN THE BOTTOM OR THE MIDDLE, panned front-and-center or to the left, or played fingerstyle or thumbstyle, Raphael Saadiq's bass carries the songs throughout *Instant Vintage*. **Example 1** shows the main two-bar groove of the disc-opening "Doin' What I Can." "I wanted to have a surging bass line that drives the track," explains Raphael, who played his '62 P-Bass. **Example 2** contains the main four-bar "Body Parts" groove, which Saadiq played on his reissue Jazz Bass. Notice how he leaves the downbeats open for his vocals, and check out bar 3's cool major-7 double-stop. "I got that from Michael Henderson and Preston Crump—they use that a lot." **Example 3** shows the opening bass melody/groove of "Be Here," which Raphael played on his Ransom 5-string. "I wanted it to stand out, as if someone had sampled it and dropped it into the track." Hip-hop also inspired the "A"-section groove of "Excuse Me" (**Ex. 4**). Says Raphael, who applies some of his "snare ghosting" feel to the P-Bass line, "I wanted it to have a hypnotic Wu-Tang sort of vibe." Listen also for his Jamerson-like "B"-section line: The track is a prime example of his new and old influences working together.

Example 5 contains the one-bar "Charlie Ray" P-Bass groove, with its nasty sliding fill on beat *four*. Saadiq leaves space for guitar accents but adds some grease courtesy of percussive thumb plucks. **Example 6** shows his opening line on "Tick Tock." Instead of a guitar arpeggio leading into the Sly Stone/"Sing a Simple Song"–like climb, Raphael played it all on his P-Bass.

Ex. 1

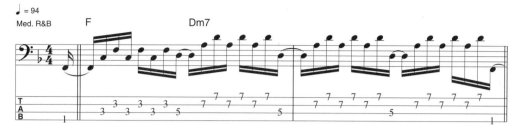

Ex. 2

Ex. 3

Ex. 4

Ex. 5

*Slide back and forth

"Body Parts," "Charlie Ray," and "Doing What I Can" by Raphael Saadiq, Glenn Standridge, and Bobby Ozuna, © 2002 Ugmoe Music and Jake & the Phatman Music. "Be Here" by Raphael Saadiq, D'Angelo, Glenn Standridge, and Bobby Ozuna, © 2002 Ugmoe Music, Universal-PolyGram International Publishing, Inc., Ah Choo Music Publishing, and Jake & the Phatman Music. "Excuse Me" by Raphael Saadiq, Glenn Standridge, Bobby Ozuna, Angela Stone, and Calvin Richardson, © 2002 Ugmoe Music, Jake & the Phatman Music, Angela Stone, and Calvin Richardson. "Tick Tock" by Raphael Saadiq, Raymon Murray, and Olivia Ewing, © 2002 Ugmoe Music, Murray Media Music, and Olivia Ewing. All rights for Ugmoe Music controlled and administered by Universal-PolyGram International Publishing, Inc. All rights reserved. Used by permission. Warner Bros. Publications U.S. Inc., Miami, FL 33014.

More gunk funk can be heard on the debut *Lucy Pearl*. **Example 7** contains the main riff from "Trippin'." Raphael used his Ransom 5-string "flag bass," strung with old flatwounds and recorded through a miked Ampeg B-15. "That bass's low notes have a great growl—they sound just like a Minimoog." **Example 8** shows the melodic main riff from "Without You," on which Saadiq used his flag bass sent direct to Pro Tools. "That's my Bernard Edwards/Chic side— the way the line is kind of flipped around and doesn't start on the root." Listen how he subtly varies bar 2's last two beats throughout the track. Lastly, an Earth, Wind & Fire flavor is evident in **Ex. 9**, the tasty root-5-octave groove from "Everyday." "Verdine White is another one of my idols," says Saadiq, who sent the flag bass direct to a Pro Tools Fender Bassman amp patch.

Ex. 6

Ex. 7

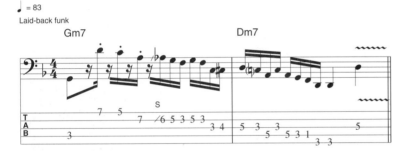

Ex. 8

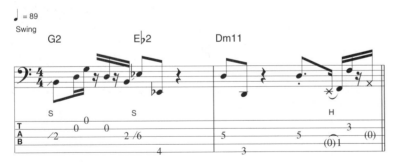

Ex. 9

JONATHAN MARON
Playing Like a Listener

Interviewed by Bill Leigh, March 1999, and Chris Jisi, April 2001.

Jonathan Maron

APACKED NIGHTCLUB buzzes with anticipation as a DJ barely contains a crowd that's ready to get down. Groove Collective is set to hit the stage, and fans in this West Coast hot spot are eager to catch the ten-member New York ensemble at a rare club date.

The band gradually fills the stage—horns, vibes, keys, flute, drums, percussion—and on bass Jonathan Maron looks prepared to lead the musical charge. Jonathan thinks he knows what the first song will be, but it's no big surprise when drummer Genji Siraisi starts off in a completely different rhythmic direction. A keyboard pad provides a splash of tonal color, and Jonathan perfectly completes the backdrop, his boyish mien giving way to a more serious funk face as he settles into a bass line few would guess he was constructing on the fly. Groove Collective is off on one of its colossal jams, and the sea of heads nods in approval.

"Sometimes Genji will surprise me," confirms Jonathan. "I'll try to think long enough before coming in so I don't sound like I'm searching." Business as usual for the eclectic band, with whom Jonathan has played since the group formed out of early-'90s jams with New York DJs. His muscular funk tone and inventive rhythms have anchored the Collective's studio albums, which contain a powerful blend of jazz, funk, and Latin rhythms. Normally packing in crowds at larger venues, GC thrives on blending well-arranged parts with on-the-spot creations.

Jonathan grew up in Englewood, New Jersey, which he calls an R&B town. A self-described teenage "bass geek" whose high school band teacher was jazz tubist Joe Daley, Jonathan looked to New York as a musical mecca. Eventually he settled in downtown Brooklyn; his New York work outside Groove Collective has since included the now-defunct R&B group Repercussions, various remix sessions, and album tracks with R&B singers Maxwell and D'Angelo.

Jonathan's distinctive bass voice is way up front on GC's *Dance of the Drunken Master*—aim your laser at the first track and take off on a deep bass vibe with a hypnotic bass solo. The rest of the album shows Jonathan's strengths as a versatile, high-impact player, comfortable with blistering slap-funk, Latin feels, effects-rich

Gear Collective

Let other people drool over $4,000 hi-tech basses—Jonathan Maron does just fine with his array of inexpensive instruments. "I always get better sounds out of passive instruments. Active circuits always sound too sculpted—I want the natural sound." Two of the more recent axes in his collection are a $100 semi-hollow Aria Diamond and a $150 semi-hollow Univox. "The Univox is a copy of a Gibson EB-2 but smaller, and it has a cool mute by the bridge and black plastic strings I can't find anywhere." His groove collection also includes a blond Guild B302 solidbody (favored on *It's All in Your Mind* simply because he left it at Genji Siraisi's studio); black-and-white Yamaha BB3000s; a mid-'60s red Guild Starfire; a late-'80s Guild Pilot 5; and a Hagstrom Swede originally made for a synth-bass system. He strings with DR Hi-Beams, .045–.105, or similar-gauge La Bella flats.

Still undecided on the ultimate rig, Jonathan favors the Aguilar DB680 tube preamp and likes to mic his Ampeg B-12 in the studio. On the road he usually rents SVT cabinets. His new and vintage effects include a Roland Space Echo, Maestro Phase, Mu-Tron Micro V envelope filter, Electro-Harmonix BassBalls and Big Muff, MXR Distortion +, DigiTech Whammy Pedal, Ross Phase Distortion, Ibanez Envelope Filter, and Boss Dynamic Filter and OC-2 Octave pedals.

Bootsy-isms, and innovative fingerstyle R&B lines. At record stores Groove Collective's discs are often filed under acid jazz, but Jonathan hates the term. "We prefer to call it 'groove jazz' or 'jazz funk.' Acid jazz encompasses too much; it's meaningless. It makes me think of organ-funk records with mediocre playing or programming that's not very exciting, but since it's kind of funky they'll have it on in a clothing store. It starts to sound really generic." A fear of slipping into the generic motivates Jonathan to keep his playing inventive. "Certain rhythms just feel corny to me," he says, describing corny as "the opposite of sincere." "I want to stay away from things that don't make a clear statement. I try to avoid playing throwaway funk lines; they're still pretty cool, but if I go there it means I don't have anything. Certain lines I play might make my friends say, 'Oh, there's a Jonathan line.'

"I always want the sound of forward motion in my playing. I like playing that bubbles: The bassist holds things down but incorporates accents—little blips and bleeps that keep the track moving without being super hack. And I love good bass fills," he says, citing Anthony Jackson as his bass-fill hero. "It's like taking on two parts instead of one. Once you get comfortable with a line, you come to know where the holes are so you can go away from it for a second and come back in a way that's satisfying, without sacrificing the flow. It gives you a chance to be expressive in the context of a solid part—not trying to be the star of the show but a really present character. It's important not to play throwaway fills. Someone I used to play with told me his approach to fills was to keep saying 'no' to yourself until you *have* to play something. Then you know it will be something worth playing."

Occasionally Maron takes an extended solo during the band's longer sets. "I'm not the kind of player who can blow over any set of changes. But I try to hint at enough colors and really open things up with notes you wouldn't expect. The bigger the tension you create, the bigger the release."

Despite Groove Collective's melting-pot style, Jonathan has a short list of bass influences: Anthony Jackson, Paul McCartney, Paul Jackson, Bootsy Collins, Verdine White, and the Gap Band's Robert Wilson. Still, he's cautious about copping other players' styles. "It can be dangerous; you can find yourself mouthing other people's words. When I first started playing professionally, people always told me I had a Paul Jackson thing going on. I hadn't heard him much, so I started checking out the Headhunters. He's so *bad*—but as much as I've learned listening to him I almost wish I hadn't, because I started thinking too much about the way he plays. When I was a kid I thought I had drawn a perfect Mr. Magoo—I was sure that I nailed it. But when I compared it to the real Mr. Magoo I realized I was completely wrong. All my creativity is like that; it comes from having a vague concept of the spirit of something."

What does Jonathan think about onstage? "I'm trying to give everything I can to making it feel good. I want to lose myself, play like a listener, and make it feel like music. When I scrutinize records that I think have incredible playing on them, I realize there are all these imperfections—particularly on old records. But you don't notice them; the music is coming from such a clear place. I'm trying to play more with my ears and spirit than with my nerdy scrutinizing self that wants things to be perfect. Because if you can nail the vibe on something, you're all the way there."

When I spoke with Jonathan two years later, in 2001, he was on his way to becoming a new millennium groove hero—able to find the pocket in any of the myriad shadings of funk and R&B, not to mention the dance sides of Latin and jazz. We discussed Groove Collective's concept and their fifth studio CD, It's All in Your Mind.

What's your vision for Groove Collective?

Our goal has always been to emulate the range of music a DJ plays during the course of a night at a packed club. A great DJ knows the songs that can ignite the room and fill the dance floor—whether it's a classic Donald Byrd & the Blackbyrds side, a recent Masters at Work track, or something completely new. Some of my favorite musical experiences have been in clubs, where you listen and realize how well all of these different styles blend together into one big idiom of its own.

What was your goal on It's All in Your Mind?

We wanted to create music that was more textural and atmospheric, with a kind of sparse, mellow, trippy vibe, as well as include some tracks with our usual funk/jazz/Latin blowing and jamming sides. A lot of the material evolved during a four-and-a-half-month tour that debuted our smaller 7-piece lineup. Following the tour, we had a couple of rehearsals to solidify the material and break in a few new tunes. From there, all but two songs were cut in Genji Siraisi's home studio, starting with basic rhythm tracks by Genji, myself, and [keyboardist] Barney McCall. When a take felt good we kept it, rather than overdubbing individual parts to go with a good drum take. It was all pretty low-tech. I recorded my basses direct to a Mackie 1604VLZ board and into the ADAT machine.

The opener, "Time Pilot," establishes the CD's trippy flavor.

That was the first song we recorded, as a demo—but we liked its open sound so much we kept it, and it set the tone for the rest of the tracks. The song took shape on the road; it was a vamp from another tune, and eventually we made an entire song out of it. I used my Guild B302 solidbody, and I tried to play big, round McCartney-like notes.

What's the groove influence on "Ransome"?

Ransome was the original middle name of the late Fela Kuti, who has been called the African James Brown. We were listening to a lot of his music on the tour bus, which inspired this track. We've attempted some of his feels and other Afrobeat grooves in the past. I used my Guild Starfire with La Bella flatwounds, and I also played a few guitar parts trying to emulate the Fela style—though I ended up sounding more like Don Ho!

How did you get the Baby Bass sound on "Stargazer"?

I used my black Yamaha BB3000 with La Bella flatwounds, recorded through a miked Acoustic 360. I plucked the strings up over the base of the neck. We cut that track live as a full band to accommodate a guest appearance by pianist Chucho Valdés. Jay Rodriguez, who plays sax in Chucho's quartet, wrote the song and

Jonathan Maron
Selected Discography

With Groove Collective: *It's All in Your Mind*, Shanachie; *Live . . . and Hard to Find*, www.groove-collective.com; *Declassified*, Shanachie; *Dance of the Drunken Master*, Shanachie; *We the People*, Giant Step/Impulse; *Groove Collective*, Reprise. **With Maxwell:** *Maxwell's Urban Hang Suite*, Columbia. **With Erykah Badu & D'Angelo:** *High School High Original Motion Picture Soundtrack*, Big Beat/Atlantic. **With Repercussions:** *Earth and Heaven*, Warner Bros.; *Charmed Life*, Pony Canyon; *Promise*, MoWax. **With Satoshi Tomiie:** *Full Lick*, Sony. **With Big Muff:** *Music from the Aural Exciter*, Maxi. **With Richard Worth:** *Stone Monkey*, Replay. **With Joe Claussell:** *Mix the Vibe*, Night Grooves. **With Slide Five:** *People, Places and Things*, Ubiquity. **With the Last Poets featuring Pharoah Sanders:** "This Is Madness," *Stolen Moments/Red Hot + Cool*, GRP. **With Raw Stylus:** *Pushing Against the Flow*, Geffen. **12" singles:** (all on Giant Step) "Rise," Richard Worth/Ron Trent; "No More Excuses," Atlantis/Ron Trent/Jonathan Maron; "Holiday," Donnie/Ron Trent; "Lamentations (You, Son)," Carl Hancock Rux/Ron Trent.

the A-section bass line, which I elaborated on. Chucho had us change a few arrangement things he felt were fighting the clave, and he gave me some suggestions that worked with certain montunos he wanted to play.

Why did you play keyboard bass on "Winner"?

Bill Ware wrote the tune and gave me a basic line to work from. I originally played my B302 on the "A" and "B" sections, but it wasn't sitting right in the "A" section. Genji and I both play so far back, and I genuinely have trouble playing on top of the beat. The keyboard bass let me be edgy and jerky enough to be more on top. I used my Roland XP50 with some bass sounds a friend downloaded off the Internet. My inspiration was Herbie Hancock's synth-bass work on his album *Man-Child*, though I also love Bernie Worrell and Walter "Junie" Morrison with P-Funk—and, of course, Stevie Wonder.

There's a strong ethnic feel on "Priye," "Earth to Earth," and "Comparsa Tunina."

That's the composers' influences coming through. "Priye" is a Dominican folklore melody; the main drum we used is an *atabal*, which is a huge, hollowed-out tree trunk with a skin over it. The start of "Earth to Earth" has Jay Rodriguez playing a Native American–like folk melody on flute and on a rice stalk called the *flauta de millo*. My intention in writing the song that way was to feature Jay and [flutist/singer] Richard Worth and their collection of world instruments when we play live, now that they're the only horn players. As for Bill Ware's "Comparsa Tunina," there was so much heavy percussion on the track I just had a blast bubbling along with it—and probably playing too much! I love listening to conga rhythms and melodies for inspiration. You can always hear a bass line happening in there.

"Skye" and "Demon Chaser" bring the album to a trippy close.

"Skye" has a '60s-rock, "Riders on the Storm" vibe. Richard insists there's a genuine meeting place between Led Zeppelin and Pharoah Sanders, and he pursues it here. "Demon Chaser" is probably my favorite song on the album, because it has a really accessible vibe yet it's harmonically interesting to play over—sort of a backbeat song with depth. On the "Hey Jude"–ish outro I take a solo that sounds like heavily effected lead guitar. I used my Yamaha through a DigiTech Whammy, Electro-Harmonix Big Muff, and Ross Phase Distortion.

How did downsizing from ten to seven pieces affect Groove Collective?

In addition to losing our rapper, Nappy G, we no longer have a four-piece horn section. Having trombone and trumpet gave us a bright sheen and the ability to really clobber a crowd if we wanted. Instead, we have a darker sound with a different kind of intensity, and we feature the rhythm section more. In some ways it's better than ever. The communication between fewer people has enabled us to make some really sharp turns onstage.

You've been heavily involved in the 12" vinyl dance-remix and house music scene.

A lot of good house music has been coming out because it's stylish and in vogue—not only in the underground club scene but in trendy clothing stores, coffeehouses, and restaurants. I've been collaborating with DJ/producer/keyboardist Ron Trent. He, Genji, and I jam along with his programmed tracks, and then he mixes it all together. Aguilar's Dave Boonshoft has a label called Naked Music; they do cool, stripped-down, trippy house music. Dave plays bass, and he and DJ/producer Jay Denes have hired me to play guitar and keyboard bass on some of their sessions.

How do you see your various musical sides developing?

I plan on doing much more writing and production when Groove Collective isn't on the road. I want to release some dance sides under my name. Also, I'd love to be a sideman for a great artist/leader. I played behind Jewel on David Letterman's show in 2000, which I enjoyed because I rarely get a chance to just be the bass player, performing someone else's music. I'd like to balance those three areas into a sort of career collective.

Web Site

www.groovecollective.com

Maronated Grooves

WHETHER JONATHAN MARON IS IMPROVISING OSTINATOS onstage with Groove Collective or cutting next week's hottest dance-remix track, his lines are sure to be soaked in '70s funk. "That's my all-time favorite music," he says. "Even my favorite new music has strong elements of that era—from D'Angelo to Medeski Martin & Wood. They have their own fresh take on it, and I'd like to think Groove Collective does as well."

Example 1 shows the "Ransome" groove idea. "I based this on a similarly shaped bass line on Fela Kuti's 1977 album *Zombie*. I usually play up the *E* string so I can easily reach upper-register melodic and chordal fills." **Example 2** shows Maron's bubbling bass part during the instrumental "B" section of "Dance with You." Bars 1 and 3 state the line, while bars 2 and 4 are open for responding fills. "I just tried to play a push-it-along line, in the style of Chic's Bernard Edwards or Brick's Ray Ransom."

Example 3's slapped phrase, recalling the "Ocean Floor" "B" section, continues in a similar disco/funk vein. "I was thinking of Slave's Mark Adams and Nathaniel Phillips of Pleasure," says Jonathan, who used his Guild Pilot 5; he then doubled the part by slapping it up an octave. **Example 4** takes its cue from the bass-and-horns soli on "Earth to Earth." Though it's not notated, he also keeps the bass line going between the soli line. "I've always liked GC to have unison passages or solis between different instruments, because they bring the band together during what is usually

Ex. 1

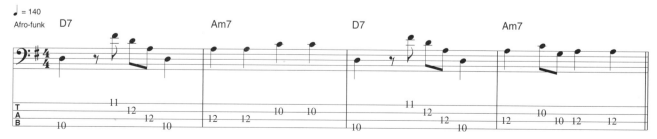

full-blown jamming. In this case, the way the line moves in 4ths is inspired by Eddie Harris's jazz composing and a group called Stone Alliance."

Example 5 shows the groove style of "Calling All Monsters," from the sold-online disc *Live . . . and Hard to Find*. The snippet finds Maron—using his Yamaha and an Ibanez Envelope Filter—improvising a nasty groove behind Jay Rodriguez's tenor solo. "That's a nod to Bootsy Collins—in particular, 'Night of the Thumpasorus Peoples,' which is on Parliament's *Live: P-Funk Earth Tour*." **Example 6** shows the main bass groove idea of "Rise," a 12"-vinyl dance single released by Richard Worth. Jonathan recorded his semi-hollow Aria Diamond direct and through a miked SVT. "I've been working with adding little breaks or pauses in phrases, such as those created by sitting on the quarter-notes at the ends of bars 1 and 3."

Ex. 2

Ex. 3

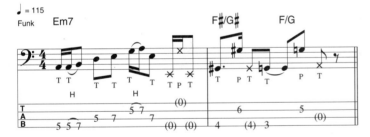

Ex. 4

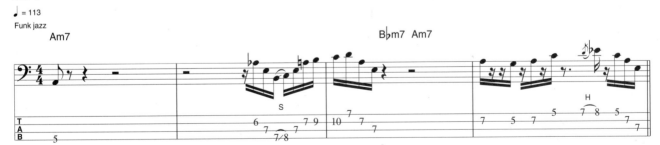

Ex. 5

♩ = 114
Funk

Ex. 6

♩ = 124
Dance-funk

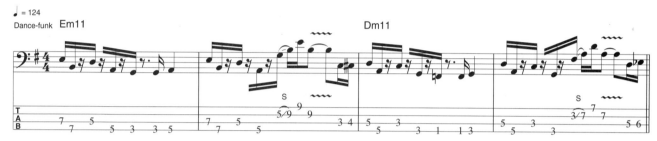

CHAPTER 8

Raising the Bar

OTEIL BURBRIDGE • MATT GARRISON • RICHARD BONA

As we marvel at the advances in the art of bass playing in the past three decades, it can seem as if we've reached the peak. Then someone comes along and shows us that there are still more heights to explore.

OTEIL BURBRIDGE

Beltway Breakout

Interviewed by Chris Jisi, June 1997, November 1998, and June 2003.

ACKNOWLEDGING THE JOURNEY that took him from Florida through the remaining 49 states and on to worldwide acclaim, Jaco Pastorius named his second solo album *Word of Mouth*. Some 20 years later a similar path was followed from the South by a bassist whose over-the-top musical abilities and high-energy stage presence created a buzz of Pastorius-sized proportions. After initially making a splash in the cult alternative band Aquarium Rescue Unit, Oteil Burbridge broke out big time by joining the Allman Brothers Band (as well as satellite groups such as Allman drummer Butch Trucks's Frogwings and Oteil's own Peacemakers). Says session bassist/record exec/*American Idol* judge Randy Jackson: "Oteil is an amazing talent as a player and a writer; he and Victor Wooten are the two most original bass voices in today's clone-dominated scene. They remind me of when I first heard Stanley and Jaco." Responds Oteil—whose friendly, enthusiastic demeanor is surpassed only by his humility (he remains too awestruck by many of his fellow musicians to approach them at trade shows): "I've just been blessed to be in the right place at the right time."

Oteil's timeline began on August 24, 1964, in Washington, D.C., where he was born and raised just down the block from the White House. Music was an essential part of the Burbridge household in the '60s and '70s. "My parents were both audiophiles, and they knew music would keep me, my brother, and my two sisters off the street—so there were plenty of instruments and records in all musical styles around the house." Living up to his Egyptian first name, which means "explorer" and "wanderer," Oteil tried trumpet, piano, and violin, and at age eight settled on drums, inspired by his father's love of jazz. He also followed his older brother Kofi, a flute prodigy, into acting and dancing. These pursuits began to overshadow Oteil's musical interests until a growth spurt put an end to his dancing days at age 14. To fill the void, he started fooling around with a Beatle Bass copy Kofi had left behind on a visit home from music school. "In no time I was totally hooked," Oteil recalls. "I started learning songs and watching how people played the instrument. I would call Kofi, and he'd help me to tune the bass over the phone!"

Recognizing his passion for the instrument, Kofi and Oteil's father turned the teen on to jazz and fusion music anchored by such bass greats as Jaco, Stanley Clarke, Alphonso Johnson, Paul Jackson, Ron Carter, Milt

Hinton, and Paul Chambers. In addition, Oteil immersed himself in the funk of Larry Graham, Verdine White, Louis Johnson, Bernard Edwards, and—especially—Bootsy Collins. After receiving a '79 Jazz Bass for his 17th birthday, Oteil found himself playing everywhere—from jazz clubs with much older musicians to heavy-metal halls with schoolmates. His decision to become a full-time musician was cemented by a Weather Report concert. "Seeing that show changed my life; it gave me faith in my decision and made me realize I didn't care about the risk; it would be worth it if I could end up

Oteil Burbridge

where they were. Fortunately, my parents were very supportive of my choice; they let me live at home and bypass college while I continued to study on my own."

Eager to land a paying gig to help support himself, on Kofi's recommendation an 18-year-old Oteil successfully auditioned for a Virginia Beach Top 40 cover band, and he immediately settled in the seaside town. Although the band's nightly sets consisted mostly of bland '80s synth-pop, Burbridge discovered musical advantages. To capture the lower range and busy lines of the sequenced synth-bass parts he had to learn, Oteil switched to a Yamaha BB-5000 5-string and raised his chops to new levels of precision and endurance. In addition, he got to meet and play with a host of great musicians on the local scene, including jazz drummer Billy Drummond, Dave Matthews Band stickman Carter Beauford, saxophonist Steve Wilson, and fellow bassists Victor Wooten, Keith Horne, and James Genus. Three years later, after leaving the cover band and heeding a friend's advice to move to Atlanta, Oteil found himself in dire economic and spiritual straits. That was when the future Aquarium Rescue Unit bassist was himself rescued by an unlikely character known as Col. Bruce Hampton.

How did you meet Bruce Hampton?

I had reached a really low point, and I was about to give up music. Every original project I'd tried in Atlanta had failed, and the cover gigs—which I had grown to hate—weren't even paying enough to live on. Jeff Sipe [the drummer also known as Apt. Q258] told me the one guy who could save me was Bruce Hampton. Though I'd never heard of him, Bruce had a big underground following as a philosopher, poet, composer, and vocalist along the lines of Captain Beefheart, Tom Waits, and Leonard Cohen. He had recorded with Frank Zappa and released several critically acclaimed albums featuring prominent musicians. Best of all, he had zero tolerance for bullshit music; if it wasn't real, he couldn't deal! We met at a local bar called the Little Five Points Pub, and it was mystical from the start. He guessed my birthday within a few minutes—before he even knew my name—and gave me copies of some of his records. I listened to them—he was saying exactly what I wanted to say about everything I was feeling. For the next three years I spent all of my time with him. He basically saved my life, spiritually and musically.

What did you learn from him?

One of the main lessons he taught me, by taking me back to the Delta blues musicians, is that there is no such thing as "in" or "out" music. Those early artists didn't tune up or follow a steady meter or song structure—yet they sound totally natural and in harmony because they're playing *themselves.* To Bruce, most modern-day musicians who've attended conservatories have been taught to lie, because the school took all of the nature out of their playing. Consequently, when I went back and listened to Sun Ra and Ornette Coleman, I was floored; suddenly their music made perfect sense.

Soon after, Bruce started a Monday night jam at the Little Five Points Pub, and all kinds of frustrated musicians—from classical to bluegrass—would come down to blow off steam and get "Hampnotized." He would create a totally improvisational atmosphere with the goal of expressing the core of who you are through your playing. Sometimes we would even put our instruments down and do impromptu skits and monologues. It was constant performance art.

How did the Aquarium Rescue Unit evolve out of this?

A set band gradually fleshed itself out around Bruce. Jeff Sipe and I became the steady rhythm section; Matt Mundy, an incredible progressive bluegrass mandolinist, and guitarist Jimmy Herring, with whom I had played in an Atlanta fusion band, came onboard to complete the lineup. The chemistry was magical. We weren't trying to get a record deal or anything—we were just enjoying the process of making honest music. Eventually, though, we started getting popular. Bruce and I wrote some material, and we all came up with arrangements of other songs and put together sets. We also opened for Widespread Panic, and when they signed to Capricorn Records they helped us to get a deal, too. Their producer, Johnny Sandlin, flipped for A.R.U; he convinced Capricorn to let us record our first album [*Col. Bruce Hampton & the Aquarium Rescue Unit*] live, which is extremely rare. When *Rolling Stone* gave the album a great review and the rest of the print media followed suit, we were off and running. We started opening for Blues Traveler, Phish, the Dave Matthews Band and Béla Fleck & the Flecktones, who were friends of ours. That really put us on the map, and we owe all of them a great deal of thanks.

How did you start scat singing with your bass solos?

Through Bruce back in the Little Five Points Pub days. In one of his routines to inspire our creativity, he'd call out the name of a famous musician, and whoever was soloing had to imitate that person's style. One night he called out "George Benson" to the guitarist, who wasn't game, so I stepped up and took a shot at it. After that, Bruce started asking me to take a scat solo every night. I had a tendency to repeat the same old patterns when soloing, but singing along opened things up; it forced me to listen and to be more melodic. I figured if everyone from Benson to Slam Stewart and Major Holley could do it, there had to be room in there for me to find my own little voice. The more I did it, the more I liked it and the better I became at it. Now it's a signature of mine.

What's your approach to singing while soloing?

For the most part, there's a stream-of-consciousness flow between the two—although I still think in terms of shapes on the neck at times. My vocals are much more limited than my hands, which always want to run ahead. But that's actually good, because it keeps me in check and forces me to play more melodically and from the heart.

Can you explain your approach to playing chords?

I most frequently use three-note chords on the top three strings. They're all built off a basic root/5/major-7 shape, within which I usually move the middle voice around. For example, if I were playing in the key of *E* minor on a 4-string, I would finger a root/5/major-7 shape by grabbing the *G* on the 10th fret of the *A* string with my 1st finger, the *D* on the 12th fret of the *D* string with my 3rd or 4th finger, and the *F#* on the *G* string with my 2nd finger. If I let the open *E* string ring against that, I have an *Em9* chord. From there, by moving the

D note on the second string up to *D♯*, down to *C♯*, or down to *C*, I can play and *Em9maj7*, *Em6/9*, or an implied *Cmaj7♯11*, respectively. And I'll take it even further than that, because I've found that as long as the note on the top string is in the scale of the chord you're playing over, the whole shape usually works.

Your right- and left-hand techniques seem pretty straightforward.

They are. I pluck with two alternating fingers on my right hand. I use the standard thumb-and-index slap-and-pop approach, although I incorporate a hammer-on with the 3rd finger of my left hand to get another hit in three-note figures. I also do some basic tapping I learned from Regi Wooten [Victor Wooten's guitarist brother]; it involves the index and middle fingers on my right hand and the first three fingers on my left hand. When playing chords, I strum with my fingers or fingerpick them using my thumb and first three fingers. For muted notes I mute the strings with my right-hand palm and pluck the notes with my thumb, *à la* Anthony Jackson. And occasionally I use a pick.

Vibrations, metaphysics, and ancient Egyptian beliefs also figure into your music.

I'm a Virgo and therefore very analytical by nature. I've always been curious about why things are the way they are. The different philosophies I learned from Bruce Hampton and the Wooten brothers, along with my own studies of ancient Egyptian teachings, brought to light the way various musical frequencies vibrate our body centers, or *chakras*. Vibration is the key to everything, including the correlation between the 12 tones in our modern harmonic system, the 12 numbers on a clock, and the 12 months on the calendar. Understanding these concepts has greatly enhanced my spiritual awareness, and I've always been very spiritual about music, because it saves me from the veil of tears that is life.

Who are some of your favorite musicians and current bass players?

My all-time, desert-island-disc favorites are Sun Ra, Howlin' Wolf, John Lee Hooker, Charlie Christian, Jo Jones, and especially Elvin Jones; that's my spiritual food. On bass these days I love Marcus Miller, Victor Wooten, Gary Willis, Matt Garrison, Me'Shell NdegéOcello, and Fima Ephron.

How did you get into the Allman Brothers Band?

When Allen Woody and [guitarist] Warren Haynes left, Butch Trucks recommended me for the bass chair, for which I'm most grateful. After getting the call to come and play with them, I immediately went out and bought all of their records and I began 'shedding. The first thing that struck me, having not been completely familiar with [original Allman bassist] Berry Oakley's playing, is what a phenomenal player he was—without

 Oteil's Orchestra

Oteil Burbridge's main bass is his 2003 custom Fodera Monarch 6-string. It features a walnut back, sugarleaf maple top, Madagascar kingwood neck, "extended B headstock" (to go along with its 35" scale), Seymour Duncan single-coil/humbucking J/J pickups, and a Fodera/Pope preamp. Remaining in his rotation are his signature semi-hollow Modulus Quantum 6, his Kydd Carry-On electric upright (which he likes because of its short 30" scale length), his '64 Jazz Bass (used with the Allman Brothers, along with a Steve Clayton acetal/polymer 80mm rounded-triangle guitar pick), a custom J-style 5 built by Alabama luthier Billy Gallant, a Modulus Quantum 5 and fretless Quantum 6, and an Alvarez Wildwood 4070 4-string acoustic bass guitar. For his 5- and 6-strings he uses D'Addario XL170s (gauged .032, .045, .065, .085, .100, .130), and flatwound D'Addario Chromes for his Kydd, Fender, and Alvarez (gauged .032, .045, .065, .080, .100, .130).

Live with the Peacemakers and the Allmans, he plugs into two Ampeg SVT-4PRO heads, with two Ampeg SVT410HLF and two SVTPR-15H cabinets. He rarely uses effects, but he does have a Boss OC-2 Octave pedal and a Morley PBA wah. For recording he prefers to go direct and through a miked vintage Ampeg B-15.Dunlop Cry Baby wah, and a DOD/FX25 Envelope Filter.

a doubt, one of the greats. Some of those tunes have ridiculously funky, swinging bass lines, and in the jam sections Berry played these amazing sort of countermelody lines that wove around the guitar. I'm trying to honor Berry by playing more of his original parts, and I'm mainly using a Jazz Bass with flatwounds and a pick. I play my Modulus 6 on my featured solo and I've been working it in on some of the tunes.

What is it like playing with two drummers at once?

Actually, they play so tightly together that most of the time I'm not aware there are two of them. I tend to listen to them as one drummer, focusing on the whole rather than the individual parts. Butch Trucks has more of a heavy, rock approach, and Jaimoe plays jazz on top of that. That's why they complement each other so well; they're like the yin and yang.

How do you develop your bass lines during the band's extended jams?

The bass takes on a very guitaristic role, filling a lot and interplaying with the guitars. Basically I listen to the melody or the soloist—including Greg Allman on keyboards—and play variations on a theme, using little turn-arounds and phrases within the song's harmonic structure. The guitarists like me to gradually inch up the neck with them as they build to a solo's climax. And sometimes they'll play a lick at me and wait for me to answer.

> When I spoke to Oteil six years later he was firmly entrenched with the Allmans and working with side bands such as Frogwings, Vida Blue, and Gov't Mule. His main focus, however, was his solo project, the Peacemakers, with whom he had just released an impressive CD/DVD package, The Family Secret.

The Family Secret *is half vocal and half instrumental. Was that balance intentional?*

I would have liked more vocals, because as Col. Bruce taught me, the instrument people relate to the most is the voice—but I didn't have enough vocal tunes for the album. That said, we'll always have a prominent instrumental side where we can stretch and blow, even within vocal tunes. This is a band-oriented disc, with everyone's writing and input. And unlike most projects, where you write, record, and then tour, we were able to play most of these tunes on the road for a year and work them into shape before tracking them.

All of your funk grooves have a swing element.

That's deliberate, but only in the sense that I hear them that way. It comes from being raised on jazz—hearing Elvin Jones when I was in the womb—and from playing in an African drum group when I was eight. Plus, the sound of go-go—which has that swung funk feel—was everywhere in D.C. when I was growing up. In fact, the drum groove on "Thank You" is my nod to go-go. To me, funk and swing are really the same thing: Swing is normally on the *two* and funk is on the *one*, but both have that pulse, that bounce. Drummers like Bernard Purdie, Jabo Starks, and Zig Modeliste do both together.

The instrumentals "Honk If You," "Rewind It and Play It Again," and "My Dog Sassy" all have catchy hooks.

We try to give the instrumentals a groove so people can dance to them, and a good hook takes them even further. Mark wrote "Honk" and "Rewind," and Chris wrote "Sassy"—which is actually about Mark's dog. "Sassy" is the loosest, most fun tune to play. It captures the band's sense of humor, which connects with people, but it also has a straightahead jazz solo section. I've always believed there's a way to deliver material that's over average people's heads without alienating them. It's been done before in pop by Stevie Wonder, Steely Dan, and Earth, Wind & Fire. For me, that sense developed in the Aquarium Rescue Unit, because Col. Bruce would get lost harmonically if he wasn't hearing I–IV–V. So Jimmy Herring and I figured out all the chord substitutions we could get away with playing while still giving Bruce the I–IV–V. Actually, that's where I got a lot of my tritone subs and pedal tones.

What shaped your chordal approach?

Well, the reason I went to 6-string in 1990 was to explore chords. Regi Wooten showed me chord-melody basics on the 6, and then I figured out I could change all the variables underneath—and as long as the top melody note was in the scale of the chord I was playing over, it worked. At that point it became like painting—trying different colors from the palette. I usually play three-note chords on the top three strings and I move around the middle note, or I play four-note chords and move the middle two. And I think in terms of triads or four-note chords on top of a pedal, so instead of *E13sus*, I'll look at it as *D* over *E* or *Dmaj7* over *E*.

Do you sing when you solo, whether you're on the mike or not?

I try to; I sing in my head. Like I say on the DVD, I'm looking for that weird note. That all comes from Miles and Wayne Shorter. They can play one note and change the band's whole tonality; it's because they're composing, not soloing. When you learn to solo you go through three stages: You learn a few licks and moves, then you build on that to where you're improvising fluidly, and then you get to composing on the spot, which to me is the truest form of improvising and what separates the men from the boys. A good example is Wayne's recent CD, *Footprints Live!*, with John Patitucci, Danilo Perez, and Brian Blade. They'll play a head and then all of a sudden it's four different songs, because they're each rewriting the original melody.

Do you use the same singing-in-your-head approach when you're playing a groove and improvising the bass line?

No; in groove mode I'm coming totally from the rhythmic, African, Elvin Jones side. I hear rhythms and rhythmic phrases in my head the way I hear melodies when I solo. It's like I have six conga drums—one for each string; that's how I think. But it all ties together. Great drummers play melodies like keyboard players—their drums are the keys.

On the DVD you allude to a certain Southern sound you like having. Can you describe what that is?

I'm not sure I can put my finger on it. After living down South for 15 years, I just feel it. When you step off a plane down there, the air is immediately different from Boston's or New York's. That feeling is in all Southern music, from James Brown to the Meters to bluegrass to jazz; there's a thickness to it, and it's looser and more swampy. I love wearin' that—it feels like silk or velvet on the body. [Vocalist] Paul Henson, [guitarist] Mark Kimbrell, [drummer] Chris Fryar, and [saxophonist] Kebbi Williams are all from the South, which gives us that strong flavor. [Keyboardist/violinist] Jason Crosby and I are the only Yankees in the band!

What inspired The Family Secret *opener, "Too Many Times"?*

That was one of four songs I wrote for the Allman Brothers that they didn't end up using—which worked out well for me, since I needed songs for my album. I played the drum groove to "Whipping Post" [from *The Allman Brothers Band*] in my home studio, jammed along with it on bass, and came up with the tune. I did

Oteil Burbridge Selected Discography

Solo albums (with the Peacemakers): *The Family Secret*, Artists House; *Love of a Lifetime*, Nile Records. **With the Allman Brothers Band:** *Hittin' the Note*, Peach Records. *Peakin' at the Beacon*, Epic. **With Aquarium Rescue Unit:** *In a Perfect World*, Intersound; *Mirrors of Embarrassment*, Capricorn; *Col. Bruce Hampton & the Aquarium Rescue Unit*, Capricorn. **With Stranger's Hand:** *Stranger's Hand*, Tone Center. **With Frogwings:** *Croakin' at Toad's*, Flying Frogs. **With T Lavitz:** *Gossip*, Wildcat. **With Gov't Mule:** *The Deep End*, Vol. 1, ATO. **With Vida Blue:** *Vida Blue*, Elektra. **With Soulive:** *Turn It Out*, Orchard. **With Count M'Butu Orchestra:** *See the Sun*, Terminus. **With Trey Anastasio and John Fishman:** *Surrender to the Air*, Elektra. **With Victor Wooten:** *What Did He Say?*, Compass. **With Bass Extremes:** (both on Tone Center) *Just Add Water*; *Bass Extremes, Vol. 2*. **With CeDell Davis:** *The Best of CeDell Davis*, Capricorn.

the same thing with "Check Yourself," which is from the "Black Hearted Woman" drum groove [same album]. I even had twin guitar lines, which are covered by guitar and violin on our version. The only other change was taking an eighth-note out of my original bridge to give it an odd-time 15/8 feel.

What's the groove inspiration on "Get Ready"?

That's based on a great Jimmy McGriff soul-jazz disc from 1969 called *Electric Funk*—specifically, the second cut, "Chris Cross." The rhythm section is unlisted, but I confirmed with both Bernard Purdie and Chuck Rainey that it's them. It has a Medeski Martin & Wood quality; John Medeski has said the album is one of his favorites.

"Get Ready" also serves as your main scat-and-solo feature.

I started soloing regularly on "Get Ready" during the course of our live gigs. I like the feel, and I found a cool chord substitution against the *G7–F7* changes. I play *G* major pentatonic against the *G7*, but when it goes to the *F7* I think *B7#9*, and I use a sort of diminished whole-tone scale that has become a favorite of mine. The notes are *B, C, D, D#, F, G, A, B*, so the first half is diminished and the last five notes are whole-tone. Against the *F7* it kind of cocks your head to the side a little [*laughs*].

What inspired the instrumental "Full Circle"?

People think it's coming from Indian music and the Mahavishnu Orchestra, because of the violin lead and mellow, trippy feel, but I actually wrote it a long time ago on steel-string guitar with a Ralph Towner/Oregon/ECM vibe in mind. The bent melody notes that I play along with Jason's violin and Kebbi's sax were in my original steel-string melody. Then the contrasting heavy "B" section is a flat-out Jaco tribute.

"Hard to Find" sonically brings to mind Marcus Miller.

The two influences are Marcus in the verse and Stevie Wonder in the choruses. But the whole piece is inspired by Miles Davis's *Tutu*, which is one of my favorite albums; Marcus is a genius bassist and composer. The open sound of the keyboard chords, which are reminiscent of *Tutu*, actually are chords I played on my bass when I was writing the tune.

How about the flavor of the scat-and-solo that ends the track?

That's over the chorus harmony, which is pretty much #9 chords in a cycle of 5ths. I had been working on a chord melody created by harmonizing the diminished whole-tone scale I always use, and I knew I could apply it over this chord movement. I do everything by ear and by chord and pattern shapes on the neck, so I made a graph of the fingerboard and wrote the scale in *A* on the top three strings, and then I grouped them together and learned the shapes. So for example, with an open *A* pedal ringing, the first chord is *C#* [11th fret, *D* string], *G* [12th fret, *G* string], and *C* [12th fret, *C* string]. The next is *Eb* [13th fret, *D* string], *A* [14th fret, *G* string], and *C#* [13th fret, *C* string]. The next is *F, Bb,* and *Eb* [15th fret *D, G,* and *C* strings], and so on.

You use dissonance as a statement in your solo cover of "America the Beautiful."

That was my post-9/11 version. Part of the dark harmony is the sadness of what I was seeing, and part of it is a protest song. I don't agree with our government's recent war policy, but to me that's the essence of being an American—having the freedom to say this is wrong and to encourage change. I end the song in the original's major tonality, and that represents the hope and faith I have in our country. We're not perfect, but we have so much more potential than almost anywhere else.

What can you offer about the CD package of The Family Secret?

It's all the concept of John Snyder, who is a visionary genius. He's a legendary jazz and rock producer who pioneered the use of artist-friendly, extensive liner notes featuring transcriptions, discographies, and other extras when he first had the Artists House label back in the mid '70s. I met him through Derek Trucks, and when he revived the label this year he contacted me about doing an album. It was his idea to include the DVD with the bass lesson, the documentary, the commentary—over four hours of material all for the price of a CD.

Best of all for the artist, the label is nonprofit and grant-funded, which means I still own my masters.

How has your role with the Allman Brothers evolved as you approach seven years in the band?

I started out playing a Jazz Bass with a pick, in the spirit of Berry Oakley—which I still do at times—but since the departure of guitarist Dickey Betts [in 2000], I can play as much 6-string as I want. In fact, I use it exclusively on *Hittin' the Note*, which is the band's first album of new material since the mid '90s. I still play my '64 Jazz with a pick on old hits like "Stand Back," "Don't Keep Me Wondering," and "Midnight Rider," but if it's a bluesy shuffle, like "Statesboro Blues," I use my fingers.

Overall, I feel real comfortable right now; with Derek and Warren Haynes the gig has taken on a new shape. A potential problem is that the three of us can easily get too modern and step out of classic Allman mode, but I think we've found this enormous middle ground where we can stretch further forward, yet still be tied to the tradition. And I think Warren really bridges that gap between me and Derek and the rest of the band.

Your version of "Amazing Grace" is a fitting end to Mike Gordon's film/DVD Rising Low.

That was Mike's idea. I had wanted to do it on Gov't Mule's *Deep End* CDs, but there was no room. I've done the piece live with the Allmans and the Peacemakers. It came to me one morning; I was trying to work out "Precious Lord Take My Hand," which has similar chords, but it wasn't happening. So I tried "Amazing Grace" instead, and a flood of ideas and harmonies came pouring out.

In Rising Low *as well as your DVD lesson, you address Col. Bruce Hampton's concept of letting go of preconceptions so your true self can come through. How has that applied to you?*

The perfect example is how I spontaneously started scatting with my solo. It happened on a dare from Bruce to imitate George Benson at an ARU gig one night, and now it's a signature of mine. All I did in that moment was try to get my preconceptions of myself out of the way and be open to whatever happens. Before that, in my mind I was going to be an amalgamation of Jaco, Stanley, Alphonso, and Bootsy—which *is* a part of me—but there's this whole other side of myself that I never would have thought to develop. Ultimately, it's all about opening yourself up musically and tuning into what God put you here to do.

Web Site

oteil.hittintheweb.com
www.allmanbrothersband.com

Rhythmic & Harmonic Convergence

WITH THE EFFORTLESSNESS OF MARINE LIFE CHANGING DIRECTION IN A FISH TANK, Oteil Burbridge moves from style to style, buoyed by his drum-rooted rhythmic approach and his jazz harmony–drenched chordal and solo side. (We've tabbed following examples for 5-string bass.)

In the slapped **Example 1** line, note how the upbeat placement of the *G* on the last 16th of every bar gives the groove its turned-around, off-center feel. The kind of groove, notes Oteil, comes from his experimenting with independence training on drums against a metronome beat. "My musical inspiration was Tower of Power–style funk." To capture the feel, check out ARU's "No Ego's Underwater," from *Mirrors of Embarrassment.*

Examples 2–6 are inspired by Oteil's solo debut, *Love of a Lifetime.* **Example 2** recalls the basic two-bar *A* Dorian groove from the beginning of "Subterranea." "I haven't slapped much since Victor Wooten has been on the scene," Oteil laughs, "but slapping in three was just different enough to make me feel comfortable about doing it."

Example 3a reflects the verse groove of "Butter Biscuit," which Oteil dirties up throughout with ghost notes. "It's my homage to James Brown and the Meters. Meters tunes are essentially a bunch of rhythm tracks—but they always sound like complete songs because of their simplicity." **Example 3b** shows a bridge groove that goes to the IV chord in classic James Brown fashion. For that kind of the staccato feel, says Oteil, "I shortened the notes with my left hand, *à la* Rocco Prestia." On the bridge Oteil might play a boppish lick like the one in bar 4.

Example 4 shows the kind of gorgeous melodic scat solo Oteil performed on "Ankh." Note the use of E♮ in bars 2 and 3. "One of my favorite sounds is the minor 6 chord." **Example 5** recalls Oteil's incredible tumbling 16th-note line from "Listen Bart." He was inspired by Jaco's "Crisis" from *Word of Mouth*. "He tears through random-sounding 16th-notes beneath free-form blowing from the rest of the band. I came up with a sort of two-bar, *E* Mixolydian pattern built in groups of five against four, which repeats through a descending chord progression."

Example 6 shows the kind of chords Oteil strums, arpeggiates, and sings over in the rubato "Hymn to the Nile." "In most cases, my three-note chords consist of a major or minor 2nd between the two bottom strings and a major or minor 6th between the two top strings. The first four chords descend diatonically in *A* major and then repeat down a whole-step to *G* major, creating an *A* minor tonality against the *A* pedal. Try to use light left-hand fingertip pressure. You can really squash the chords with a heavy touch."

Ex. 1

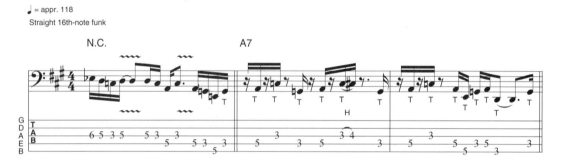

Ex. 2

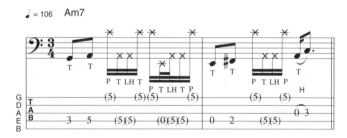

Ex. 3a

Ex. 3b

*LH = left hand hammer

Ex. 4

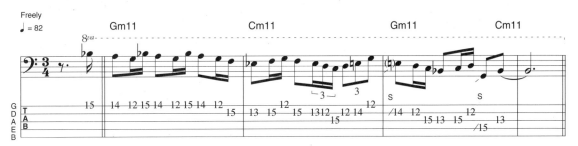

Ex. 5

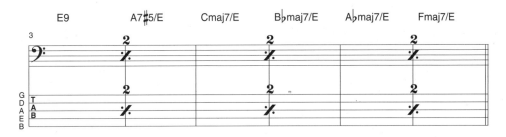

Ex. 6

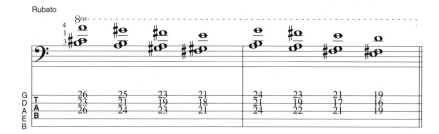

MATT GARRISON
Deep and Wide

Interviewed by Chris Jisi, February 2001.

WHEN IT COMES TO ELECTRIC-BASS SOLO DEBUTS, Stanley and Jaco had it. John Patitucci and Victor Wooten had it. And if you don't count his pair of pop-geared '80s platters, Marcus Miller had it, too. "It" is that rare blend of vision, skill, timing, and luck to create an album that raises the bar. Matt Garrison nudged "it" up a bit, too, with his compelling self-titled debut.

The ten tracks of *Matthew Garrison* go deep, expanding on the sheer technical prowess of Matt's groove, solo, and chordal sideman work with Joe Zawinul and John McLaughlin. He mixes in whirling Third World rhythms with his Marcus-like gift for rich, multi-layered compositions. Over a dozen guests rise to the occasion, including guitarist David Gilmore, keyboardist Scott Kinsey, and ex-Zawinul percussionist Arto Tuncboyacian—but this is Garrison's baby all the way. Unwilling to label-chase, Matt recorded the entire disc at "Underbed Studios," the bedroom of his Brooklyn brownstone apartment. Fittingly, Matt dedicated the album to his parents: his mother Roberta and his late father Jimmy, the legendary John Coltrane bassist.

Born in New York on June 2, 1970, Matthew never got to know his father well. His parents separated when Matt was only two, and Jimmy died of lung cancer four years later, one day after the couple had remarried. Soon after, Matt moved with his family to Rome, where at age 15—inspired by Level 42's Mark King—he got his first electric bass. Soccer and breakdancing replaced his interest in music, but not his desire to return to the U.S. In 1987 he accepted an open invitation to live with Jack DeJohnette's family and finish high school in upstate New York. There, while watching one of the drummer's perennial star-studded jam sessions, Matt's musical desires re-ignited. "Something clicked. I felt like I'd left my body and was watching, from above, this incredible level of communication going on." Lessons with Dave Holland and a full scholarship to Berklee followed.

While in school in Boston, Garrison toured with Gary Burton and recorded with Bob Moses, leading him to meet trumpeter Miles Evans, son of famed arranger Gil Evans. Evans invited him to New York to play with the Gil Evans Orchestra, leading to countless connections. Upon moving to Brooklyn in 1993, Matt began fielding a steady stream of gigs with everyone from Gil Goldstein and John Scofield to Dave Liebman and Betty Carter. Interspersed were extended stints with M-Base saxophonist Steve Coleman, Zawinul, and McLaughlin. After the guitarist's spring 2000 tour, Matt at last began work on what might be the millennium's first great electric bass album.

What led you to record your solo debut?

The combination of playing great material with amazing musicians filled my head with ideas and inspiration. It reached a point where I needed to let them out. Plus, I was constantly asked by people at shows if I had a CD of my own, which made me realize what an opportunity I was missing. In 1998 I made my first attempt to put together a band and record live to 2" analog tape at a local studio, but the technical difficulties and logistics eventually led me to halt the project. Instead, I bought a hard-disk recording system, and it completely changed my life. It enabled me to do everything right at home at my own pace, from rewriting and arranging the song structures to bringing in the sidemen I wanted, or sending them tracks to play on.

Matt Garrison

How did you record?

I used my Macintosh G3, a Korg 1212-I/O sound card, Logic Audio software, a Mackie 1604VLZ 16-track analog board, and Mackie HR824 powered studio monitors. I also used an Alesis XT20 ADAT to bounce onto my Mac the tracks Gene Lake, Ben Perowsky, and Adam Rogers cut at outside studios. Scott Kinsey sent me his keyboard parts by CD-ROM. Other than that, I recorded drums, percussion, vocals, sax, accordion, sitar, and upright bass live here with just one mic, a Shure KSM32. I did my keyboard parts and programming and sampling on my Nord Lead 2 Virtual Analog synth and the Mac. I recorded David Gilmore's guitars and my Godin 12-string guitar direct to hard disk. And I sent my electric basses through an Aguilar DB680 preamp straight to hard disk, bypassing the board's preamps. I added effects and compression in the mix via software plug-ins, and I also used my Axon AX100 MIDI controller bass pickup to play a couple of melodies.

How did you compose and organize the material?

When I write I use an approach I learned from Coleman and Zawinul: They prepare a series of rhythmic structures and harmonic structures, which they put side by side and then mix and match to create compositions; it gives you countless possibilities. Part of my practice routine has always been to come up with melodies, progressions, and bass lines, and put them on tape. For the album I went through a stack of tapes, picked out what I liked, and began mixing and matching the material. It was a long, difficult task, but I enjoyed every minute of it.

The opening track, "Family," introduces harmonic colors and themes that recur throughout the album.

That was my intent. Part of the title refers to the family of music I introduce on the track—elements that keep reappearing through the final tune, so it's like a whole story unfolding.

Much of your writing seems to feature a simple melody on top, with brooding harmonies and dense rhythms underneath.

Most of my melodies are like hummable little children's rhymes, but what goes on underneath makes the

Matt's Garrison

Matt Garrison's Fodera 5-strings lie at the heart of his extended-range pursuits. His main newer signature model is an Imperial with a scaled-down walnut body and chestnut top, a 33"-scale ash neck with a 26-fret ebony board, and custom JJ/JJ Duncan dual-coil pickups with a Pope/Fodera preamp. His older signature model is a full-sized 34"-scale Imperial with identical pickups and electronics. Both are tuned *EADGC*; a Hipshot Xtender can drop the *E* string all the way down to *B*, giving him 6-string range. His strings are signature Fodera nickel roundwounds, .028, .040, .060, .080, .100. Also appearing on *Matthew Garrison* are a fretless Fodera NYC 4-string; the first Jazz Bass–style prototype Roger Sadowsky built for Marcus Miller (which ended up in Garrison's hands via Chaka Khan's brother, Mark Stevens, with Miller's blessing); a Vektor Electric Bassette electric upright; and Jimmy Garrison's 1920s Czech flatback acoustic bass. Matt uses an Italian-made French-style bow.

Garrison's live rig features an Aguilar DB680 preamp and Aguilar 728 power amp run through Epifani T-115, T-310, or T-112 cabinets. Effects include an Ernie Ball volume pedal and a DigiTech Vocalist VHM5 vocoder.

piece happen. That's the direct influence of my favorite composers, who often use this device—Zawinul, Wayne Shorter, Herbie Hancock, Marcus Miller, and on the pop side, Stevie Wonder, Donny Hathaway, Sting, and Peter Gabriel.

How about the disc's distinct harmonic flavor?

I got attracted to a scale a Yugoslavian guitarist friend showed me, the symmetric augmented scale. It works well with major chords and pentatonic-type melodies yet adds a subtle "out" quality. In the key of *C*—which I used often so I could have an open high *C* string droning—I used the *B* symmetric augmented scale, which is *B, C, D♯, E, G,* and *G♯*. So it's basically two whole-tone scales or two augmented triads right next to each other, or a *C* major triad moving in major 3rds to *E* and *G♯*. The way I play it on the fingerboard opens up other possibilities solo-wise. [*Plays the scale descending: 10th, 9th, and 6th frets on the* D *string, and 10th, 7th, and 6th fret on the* A *string.*]

"Shapeless" showcases your chordal side as you trade ideas with David Gilmore. Who influenced that aspect of your playing?

That goes back to what attracted me to music initially, which was hearing pianists like Art Tatum and McCoy Tyner. My goal was to be able to cover that same expanded range on bass. By the time I got to Berklee, I knew the instrument's technical possibilities from listening to Stanley and Jaco, and I picked up three more important influences: John Patitucci, Dominique Di Piazza—who is the all-time chord monster—and Skuli Sverrisson, a classmate I heard in a club one night. More recently it's been Oteil Burbridge, whose singing and chordal work resonate so powerfully in me, and Victor Wooten, for his simultaneous comping and soloing. When I'm soloing there may be a certain harmony I'd like to hear that bandmates aren't aware of, so I've developed a way to make a chordal statement and then follow it with a phrase from that chord. That enables me to accompany myself and keep the groove going, and it gives me multiple directions to take my solo in.

How did you create the drones on "Manifest Destiny"?

I'm bowing my Vektor Electric Bassette and fingerpicking arpeggios on my newer Fodera. The chords, which move up in major 3rds, are all from the *B* symmetric augmented scale. So is the theme that enters midway, which is a restatement of a "Family" melody.

Both "Dark Matter" and "Duet" are departures tonally.

"Dark Matter" is based on more of a diminished sound—although the symmetric augmented flavor returns in the closing section. I used my Nord Lead synth for the strange keyboard bass sounds. We cut "Duet" live with Arto on percussion; it's based on a Spanish Phrygian sound that has both a minor and major 3rd.

Also, I was getting tired of my top string being tuned to *C*, so I used a capo at the 2nd fret to bring everything up a whole-step.

What's the interesting meter and feel in "Lullaby"?

The time is 5/8, but it feels like Afro-Cuban 6/8. The beat is based on a Gnawan feel, from Northern Africa/Morocco. Playing with Zawinul had a big impact on me that way. Between the international flavor of his bands and music, and the people we met and jammed with, it was like taking an advanced degree in world music. With regard to odd times, I got incredible on-the-job training from two masters: Coleman and McLaughlin.

What's going on in "Say What?"?

I wanted to play my dad's acoustic bass on the album. It's a 1920s Czech flatback; Jack DeJohnette and I traced it from being wrapped in newspaper in

the Village Vanguard basement to Curtis Lundy to Richard Davis's house in Wisconsin. We brought it back to New York, where David Gage restored it. For "Say What?" John Arnold came over; I put the KSM32 between the bass and his drums, and I counted off—no key, no chords. We just went for it. Then I overdubbed a solo with my newer Fodera, randomly detuning the strings as I played.

How big an impact did your father's style have on you?

I learned about him mostly when I lived at the DeJohnettes'. Jack played me all the essential recordings and explained how my father was part of one of the key rhythm sections in jazz. Plus, people like Dave Holland and Stanley Clarke would tell me he was a bridge to the modern upright approach because of the way he broke up the pulse to play with Elvin Jones. I know his style intellectually, but his influence on me is more spiritual. When I play, I feel his inner drive and energy in a deep, connected-to-the-earth way.

How do you simulate the sitar-like sound during your "Time" solo?

It involves three notes per attack, all played on the same string: I fret the target note and the next highest note with my left-hand index and middle fingers, and I position my right index or middle finger above another note in the scale higher up the fingerboard. Then I tap that high note and pull off to the target note from the fret above in one quick motion. It has both an Indian flavor and a vibrato that reminds me of the Bulgarian Women's Choir. I also get a bit of harmonic in the tapped notes, and I incorporate a lot of slides to approximate the microtonal pitches sitar players get when they bend a string. Of course, listening to Amitava Chatterjee, who plays sitar on the track, is what really got the sound in my ears.

Another one of your techniques produces a rapid flurry of notes.

I use a four-finger plucking technique based on Gary Willis's three-finger approach; I developed it during my Zawinul stint to play a few of his up tunes. It really came in handy with McLaughlin—without it, I couldn't have played those fast unison passages. On one string I play a downward thumb pluck and upward plucks with my index, middle, and ring finger, which are curled underneath; I can start with the thumb or the ring finger, and sometimes I alternate fingers. Also, I'll spread it over four strings for chords, arpeggios, and runs. I'm still working on it, so I'm quick to admit that sometimes my left hand gets ahead of my brain [*laughs*]—but my musical intent is either an Art Tatum–like run, or when I stay on one note, a sort of New

Orleans–style drum roll. As for my standard techniques, I pluck with two fingers; I have a fairly light slap-and-pop touch with my thumb and index finger; and I use my palm to mute notes while plucking with my thumb, index, and middle fingers.

What insight did you gain making the CD?

It's been very rewarding to experience the entire process, from writing music, hiring sidemen, gathering equipment, recording, mixing, mastering, packaging, and finally marketing the album, which is a whole other challenge. For anyone in a similar position, I've found the best path is to combine selling direct to audiences and CD retailers, along with securing a distribution deal, which I'm working on. But while the solo approach can work on the business side, I've learned that on the creative side, collaborating with other musicians is the key to making your music come alive.

Web Site

www.garrisonjazz.com

Major Moves

BASS ABOUNDS ON MATT GARRISON'S EPONYMOUS DEBUT, anchoring world beat grooves, dishing out defiant chord clusters, rendering singsong melodies, and improvising through hairpin major-chord twists and turns. **Example 1** is from the opener, "Family." As Garrison doubles the repeated two-bar melody on the top line, he alters the harmony every two beats with an ear-captivating line of ascending 10ths on the bottom. The bracketed *C*'s represent Matt's open *C*, which he plucks with each 10th. (The tab is written for 4-string.)

Example 2a reflects the basic "Groove Tune" slap groove. Matt's right hand position, with his index finger curled under his thumb, lets him alternate slaps and pops on the same note. **Example 2b** shows his solo's first eight bars. Note the rich bebop flavor throughout: chromatic approach notes and passing tones, and implied upper-structure

Ex. 1

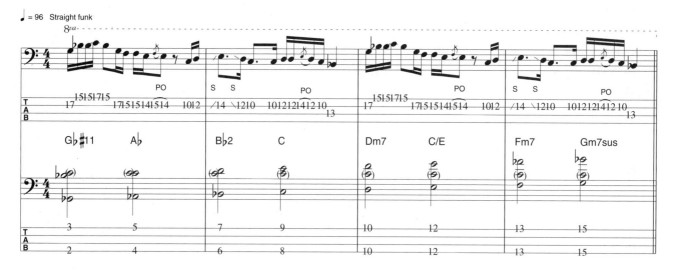

Ex. 2a

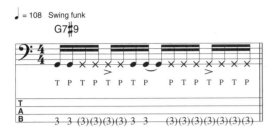

Ex. 2b

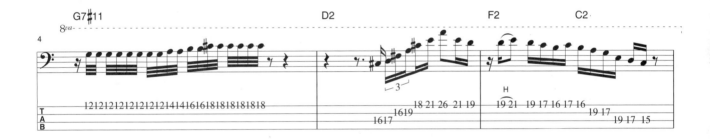

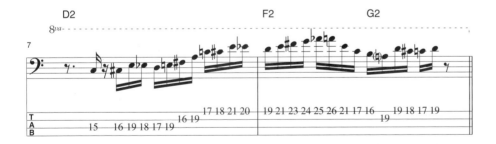

Ex. 3

Ex. 4

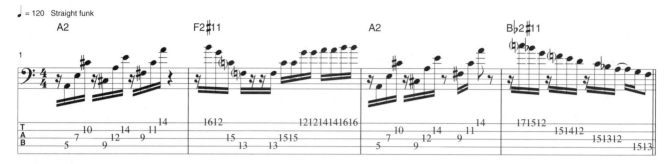

chord tones over basic major chords. He suspends this briefly with 32nd-note bursts in bars 3 and 4. (The 4-string tab puts some of Garrison's top notes on the *G* string, out of the range of many basses.)

Bar 1 of **Ex. 3** shows the style of the main 5/8 Gnawan-flavored "Lullaby" groove (written in 5/4). Bars 2 and 3 contain Matt's Afro-Cuban 6/8-style embellishments during David Gilmore's guitar solo later in the track. Garrison explains, "As in jazz and Latin music, Gnawan musicians tend to lay back on the last note of triplet figures, which I emulate here."

Example 4 shows the second four bars of the neck-eating bass line/melody from the "Solitude" "B" section. The repetitive rhythmic pattern, arpeggio-like spacing, and range of the lowest notes in bars 1 through 3 allow the part to retain just enough of a bass line feel, while still blending smoothly with bar 4's more linear line.

RICHARD BONA
Making the Bass Sing

Interviewed by Bill Milkowski, Fall 1999, and Chris Jisi, January 2002. In the first section below, Milkowski recounts his experience with Bona.

N NEW ORLEANS IN 1995, AN OLD PAL AND BASS-PLAYING COLLEAGUE alerted me to this new cat on the scene who was sitting in after hours here and there and blowing everybody away. "This is the most awesome bassist I've seen in ten years," he said. "He's like the African Jaco."

Two years later I finally got to hear Richard Bona when the Zawinul Syndicate played a week-long engagement at New York's Blue Note. Bona's facility on fretted and fretless electrics was indeed awesome. His sheer speed, fluidity, and crisp 16th-note articulation were astounding, his soloing conviction heroic. He was definitely coming out of the Jaco school, with a funky muting technique, unerring time, a melodic fretless approach, attention to the groove, and uncanny endurance on ridiculously uptempo burners. Bona's daredevil approach strongly recalled Jaco, but there was something extra—something uniquely his own.

Watching Bona play I was first struck by the instinctive and unpredictable nature of his right-hand technique. Rather than staying anchored in a conventional pivot position, his hand seemed to fly wildly from tune to tune. He was plucking with his index and middle fingers down by the bridge, strumming in furious four-finger flamenco fashion up by the neck, chording with his thumb and two fingers, slapping percussively, strumming downstrokes with his thumb while palm-muting—whatever suited the tune. Richard's hands created myriad tones and textures as the mood struck him. He seemed particularly in sync with his bass when he sang: Putting his hands into automatic pilot, he would close his eyes and in an angelic falsetto deliver lyrical and poignant melodies that harkened back to his native Cameroon.

It's this artistic side that Bona presents on his solo debut, *Scenes from My Life*. Although he does play electric bass on all 12 tracks (most notably his fretted Fodera 5-string and his fretless Pensa-Suhr 4), it's all

Richard Bona

largely in the service of his expressive singing voice. Throughout this appealing African world fusion project Bona holds his formidable chops in check, letting the melodies and his songwriting skills take centerstage. "I wanted to start off exactly where I came from," says Bona, who lives in Manhattan. "This is the kind of music I grew up with. I come from a singing and dancing culture, so I wanted to start from there and surprise people. It's a good idea to do songs; it's easy to reach the public that way. I want to share this music. I want to speak to the people with these melodies." Sung in his native language of Douala, Bona's songs reflect incidents from his life ("New Bell," "Te Dikalo"), more universal concerns such as having faith ("Dipita"), a plea for communication ("Eyala"), and a reminder to slow down and experience life more fully ("Eyando").

Born in 1967 in the eastern Cameroon village of Minta, Bona began to perform in public at age five, playing the marimba-like balafon and singing in the village church with his mother and four sisters. By age 11 he was starting to develop a facility on acoustic guitar. In 1980 Bona began a steady house-band gig at a local jazz club. "I didn't know anything about jazz, but the gig paid really well, so I took it." The club owner made available to the band his collection of nearly 500 vintage jazz LPs. Purely by chance, the first one Richard pulled out of the stack was Jaco's self-titled 1976 Epic debut. Talk about serendipity.

"I never hear about Pastorius before. Never. And then I put it on and was amazed. 'Come On, Come Over' and 'Portrait of Tracy'—boy, that changed my life. I took two strings out of my acoustic guitar. So my guitar become a bass, and then I start learning those songs just playing by heart." Richard had no teacher or mentor—only Jaco's recording to guide him. "That thing Jaco had was so deep that when you really feel it and work it, you don't need a teacher. What Jaco was doing touched me so deep."

Bona kept his club gig for nearly ten more years. "We played from nine o'clock at night to six in the morning, every day—I cannot do this anymore. But we loved music so much, we just couldn't get enough. Sometimes we used to walk miles and miles just to go and play." In 1990, after his father's death, Richard relocated to Paris. Within two months he was working with such renowned French musicians as guitarist Marc Ducret, violinist Didier Lockwood, and Paris-based African stars such as Manu Dibango and Salif Keita. To refine his writing skills Bona enrolled in music school and immersed himself in the work of Miles Davis, Chet Baker, and Ben Webster. He finally moved to New York in late '95 and began hanging out on the late-night

Bona Basses

Richard Bona has one singing voice, but he prefers to perform his bass songs on a selection of instruments. His main fretted bass is custom-made Fodera Imperial 5-string, his main fretless a Pensa-Suhr 4. Other key colors include his Fodera Beezelite fretless 5, í70 and í72 Jazz Basses, a Fender Telecaster bass, a fretless Zon 5 with piezo pickups, a fretted Zon piccolo bass tuned *ADGC*, a fretless Yamaha 5, a '70 fretted Music Man, an Atelier Z fretless 4, an Athlete fretless 5-string acoustic bass guitar, and an old German upright. He strings his electrics with DR Hi-Beams and Lo-Riders or Fodera Diamond roundwounds. For amplification he favors an EBS HD350 head or an EBS 1 Classic preamp with an EBS EXT power amp. He sends those into two Epifani T-112 cabinets. Bona's effects include a T.C. Electronic chorus pedal, a Lexicon LXP-1511 (for reverb), an EBS Octabass, MXR chorus and phase shifter, and a Korg volume pedal.

jamming scene. He immediately contacted Joe Zawinul, whom he had met earlier in Paris, and was recruited to play on one track ("Orient Express") on Zawinul's *My People*. Bona subsequently went on a world tour with the Zawinul Syndicate and in 1997 toured with Harry Belafonte. In '98 Richard began a series of regular Tuesday night Jaco tributes at an intimate downtown club called the Izzy Bar, where he would interweave Jaco classics like "Liberty City," "Portrait of Tracy," "Continuum," and "Opus Pocus" with his own roots-oriented African-flavored originals. He would also blaze his way through Jaco's arrangement of the jazz standard "Invitation."

Since moving to New York, Bona has played with a long list of jazz greats including Mike Stern, Michael and Randy Brecker, Steve Gadd, Dave Liebman, Bob James, David Sanborn, Joe Sample, Gil Goldstein, and Pat Metheny, with whom he recorded *Speaking of Now* and embarked on a subsequent world tour in support of the disc. "That's the great thing about living in New York—you run into people all the time. I try to play with as many musicians as I can, because it enriches my own music. My tune 'Te Dikalo' came from hanging out with New York salsa musicians. I always learn something from each encounter."

Making the transition from bassist to singing bassist has helped Bona reach out to more people, which he says is his ultimate goal. "You can really bring joy to people by sharing your music. It's a great power. I had to find this power in myself, and that's not easy. It's difficult to find the right place to be. And now I think I've found my place—singing and playing my bass."

In January 2002 I engaged Richard in a track-by-track discussion of his second solo effort, Reverence. *As on his previous album, he delivered personal parables via his striking falsetto voice—sung in his native Doula language—on top of an exotic tapestry of jazz, funk, reggae, Latin, and West African sounds:*

"Bisso Baba," "Ngad'a Ndutu," and "Ekwa Mwato" seem to combine African feels with your New York–influenced grooves.

That's true. "Biso Baba" is a traditional *makossa* slowed down, with some reggae and funk accents. "Ngad'a Ndutu" is a mix of *essewe* and *mazurka*, with some of my own left hooks [see Lesson]. And "Ekwa Mwato" has a salsa touch, with Luis Quintero on percussion and the horn shouts. I've grown to love Afro-Cuban music through playing with Latin musicians in New York. The amazing thing is the link to traditional African music. You can take any clave and put it into a *makossa* or *ambassey bey*, and it fits perfectly—you don't have to alter anything!

Your Jaco influence is evident on "Suninga," "Reverence," and "Mbanga Kumba."

Yes. And I was fortunate to have Gil Goldstein orchestrate all three for real strings, and to have Pat Metheny play acoustic guitar on "Reverence." That song is about how God blessed Moses to part the Red Sea. I just wanted to write a nice ballad and play expressive fretless like Jaco. Some say it brings to mind "Three Views of a Secret." "Suninga" tells the story of a man who falls in love with a woman but doesn't get a chance to tell her his feelings before she vanishes. "Mbanga Kumba" is about the only train that ran between those two cities. It starts with Gil's orchestral section and then Vinnie Colaiuta kicks off a fast *makossa* groove and I take a solo on my fretless Yamaha five.

Do you recommend playing and singing?

Absolutely! Playing and singing changed my sound and my entire bass concept. My advice is to sing and play melodies on bass; try to make the bass sing your vocal melodies as opposed to just playing them. When you're doing both together you develop a different approach to bass tone. Your attack changes, because you're playing the bass like you sing and striving to get each part to compliment the other.

RICHARD BONA
Selected Discography
Solo albums: (both on Sony) *Reverence*; *Scenes from My Life*. **With Joe Zawinul:** (all on ESC) *Faces & Places*; *World Tour*; *My People*. **With the Jaco Pastorius Big Band:** *Word of Mouth Revisited,* Heads Up. **With Mike Stern:** *Voices*, Atlantic. **With Pat Metheny:** *Speaking of Now,* Warner Bros. **With Randy Brecker:** *Hanging in the City*, ESC. **With Bobby McFerrin:** *Beyond Words*, Blue Note. **With Mino Cinelu:** *Mino Cinelu*, Blue Thumb. **With Danilo Perez:** *Motherland*, Polygram. **With Lee Ritenour:** *A Twist of Marley: A Tribute*, GRP. **With Larry Coryell:** *Spaces Revisted*, Shanachie. **With Jane Monheit:** *Come Dream with Me*, N-Coded/Warlock. **With Bob James:** *Joyride*, Warner Bros. **With Regina Carter:** *Rhythms of the Heart*, Verve. **With Jacky Terrasson:** *What It Is*, Blue Note. **With Robert Dick:** *Jazz Standards on Mars*, Enja.

Are U.S. musicians rhythmically underdeveloped compared to Africans?

We're all born the same, with the same blood; it's a matter of where and how you are raised. The musicians here are as brilliant as anywhere else, and they're quick learners—they just aren't culturally exposed to polyrhythmic music. When the slaves were brought over here their hand drums were banned, because that's how they communicated. So in effect, society killed the rhythm. I want to do my best to help bring it back.

Web Site
www.richardbona.net

Bona Parts

"THE RIGHT HAND IS *SO* IMPORTANT—it's really everything when it comes to feel," insists Richard Bona, echoing the sentiments of his chief musical inspiration, Jaco Pastorius. And what a nimble northpaw Bona displays on *Scenes from My Life* and *Reverence*. A key to Richard's percussive, polyrhythmic approach is his penchant for hitting the strings on the upbeats with the tips of his plucking fingers. "That's my way of playing the drums or percussion at the same time as my bass part." Here are examples of Richard's right- *and* left-hand groovework as heard in his two solo discs.

Examples 1a through **1d** get their triplet feel from a traditional West African rhythm called *bolobo* (bo-lo-BO)—you can hear the groove in "Konda Djanea" for *Scenes from My Life*. Example 1a is the basic rhythmic figure. Examples

1b and 1c show one-bar locking bass parts like the ones Bona laid down in the song's "A" and "B" sections. He played the descending and ascending 10ths on his Fodera 5 "guitar-style"—using his right thumb and index finger—with his left hand muting the ghost-notes. "The origin of music is how we speak. In Cameroon what makes music different is the dialects, and we speak 277 different dialects. The musical dialect on this song is called *douala* (doo-AH-la), which is also the name of a Cameroon city and the language I grew up speaking and sing on the album."

Example 1d simplifies Bona's jaw-dropping repeated one-bar phrase from the end of "Konda Djanea." Bona has spent his whole career mastering this fingerstyle technique—which is rooted in his early-teen years playing traditional music on guitar—but it's become his trademark. (It also appears 1:29 into "Eyando.") So don't expect to conquer its two-dimensional feel and hair-raising tempo in a day! With Fodera 5 in hand, Richard used his thumb to play the four *B*'s and the *D♯* and *C♯* on the downbeats, all on the *A* string. The upbeat notes and chords (all on the *G* and *D* strings)

Ex. 1a

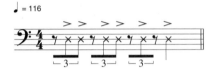

Ex. 1b

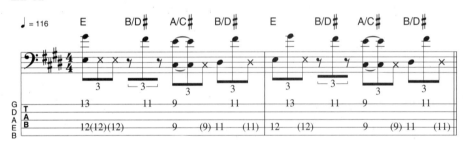

Ex. 1c

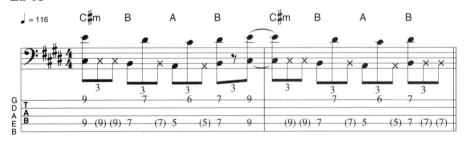

Ex. 1d

are plucked or strummed with his index, middle, and ring fingers. "Listen to the passage and get into the vibe, and then start slowly. I also recommend singing it. I sing everything I play, whether it's a bass part or a solo. It creates a natural balance."

Example 2 shows eight bars of a bouncing 6/8 two-finger groove in the style of "Eyando" from *Scenes from My Life.* (It's written here in 3/4.) Bona describes the feel as a combination of a rhythm called *bikutse* (bih-KUT-zee), from southern Cameroon, and traditional African 6/8. Style points: Richard's aforementioned drum-like attack on the second eighth of many beats, the way he often accents a beat's last 16th, and his staccato articulation throughout.

Example 3 recalls the Fodera 5–played groove of the second section of "Te Misea," from *Reverence*. It combines and African *makossa*-like feel in 3/4 with some Afro-Cuban-like anticipations (at the end of bars 1 and 3). **Example 4** is inspired by Bona's lyrical opening bass figure from "Muntula Moto." He played his Pensa fretless.

Bona refers to the repeated four-bar phrase in **Ex. 5** as being in "13"—the sum of three bars of three and one bar of four. To capture the style, listen the main groove of "Ngad'a Ndutu," from *Reverence*. On that tune Bona played his Fodera 5, dampening and muting most of the notes with his left-hand 3rd and 4th fingers as well as his right 3rd finger.

Ex. 2

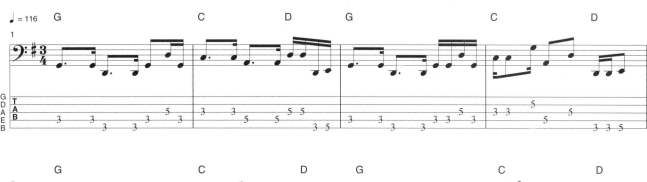

Ex. 3

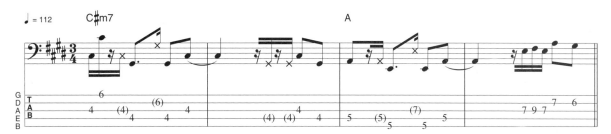

Ex. 4

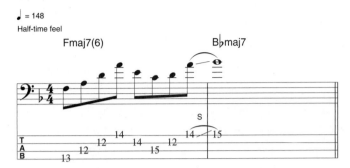

Ex. 5

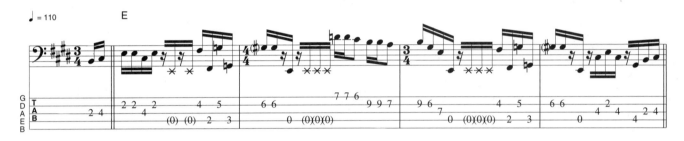

Acknowledgments

T HIS BOOK took 12 months to put together, but it was really written over the course of 12 years of conducting interviews with my bass heroes. Therefore, both the book and my music journalism career would not have been possible without several giants of the written word: Former *Bass Player* editor and current Backbeat Books Executive Editor Richard Johnston, the finest idea man in the game and a treasured friend. He came up with the concept for this project, guided me through it—and even helped with the tab! Longtime *Guitar Player* Editor and original *Bass Player* Editorial Director Tom Wheeler, who took the time to give style tips over the phone to a budding young writer in New York. Jim Roberts, *Bass Player*'s founding editor, whose vision for the magazine was championship caliber from Day One, and whose friendship and support have been unyielding. Former *Bass Player* Senior Editor Karl Coryat edited my stories so well for so long he can even do a wicked imitation of my "Noo Yawk" accent. Current Editor Bill Leigh, whose poise, savvy, knowledge, and passion ensures a bright future for *BP*. Greg Olwell, the glue that holds *BP* together. Paul Haggard and his *BP* art team, simply the best in the business. Printed-music mavens Liz Ledgerwood and Jesse Gress, plus Amy Miller and the rest of the great production staff at Backbeat. Ed Friedland (a teacher's teacher) and the other contributors to this book, who toil at their computers daily to bring the best of bass to readers worldwide. And Anthony Jackson for his foreword and his musical genius. Thanks to the players in this book for sharing their art. Special thanks to the loyal readers of *Bass Player*—we do it all for you. Many thanks to Danette Albetta, Allan Slutsky, Matt Resnicoff, Vinnie Fodera and Joey Lauricella, and Bibi Green. Additional thanks to Dave Lavender, Neal Rosen, Tom Bowes, Jim Vallis, Mark Falchook, and the Uptown Mix band for 20 years of invaluable friendships and musical lessons learned. And most of all, sincere thanks to my family; my parents, Bud and Connie; and *especially* my wife, Joan Walker.

Contributors

Jim Roberts is the founding editor and former publisher of *Bass Player*, and the author of Backbeat Books' *How the Fender Bass Changed the World* and *American Basses: An Illustrated History & Player's Guide*.

Richard Johnston is a former editor of *Bass Player* and the executive editor of Backbeat Books, and the editor of Backbeat's *How to Play Blues Guitar* and *How to Play Metal Guitar*.

Karl Coryat is *Bass Player*'s senior editor and the editor of *The Bass Player Book* (Backbeat Books).

Bill Leigh is *Bass Player*'s editor in chief.

Ed Friedland is a *Bass Player* contributing editor and the author of *The Working Bassist's Tool Kit* (Backbeat Books).

Greg Isola is a former *Bass Player* managing editor.

Scott Malandrone is a former *Bass Player* technical editor.

E.E. Bradman is a former *Bass Player* assistant editor.

Bill Milkowski is a freelance contributor to *Bass Player* and the author of *Jaco: The Extraordinary and Tragic Life of Jaco Pastorius* (Backbeat).

Alexis Sklarevski is freelance contributor to *Bass Player* and the creator of *The Slap Bass Program* and *Fingerstyle Funk* instructional videos (Video Progressions).

Chuck Crisafulli is a freelance contributor to *Bass Player* and the author of several books, including *Teen Spirit: The Stories Behind Every Nirvana Song* (Fireside).

Sources

In addition to dozens of issues of *Bass Player* magazine from 1990 to 2003, numerous players' and equipment manufacturers' web sites, and allmusic.com, I consulted Jim Roberts's *How the Fender Bass Changed the World* (Backbeat Books, 2000), my interview "Doug Wimbish: Bass in Your Face" (*Guitar Player*, October 1987), and the *2003 Guitar & Bass Buyer's Guide* (Music Player Network, 2003).

Photo Credits

Bob Barry: pages 17 & 85. **Jay Blakesberg:** page 193. **Jack Frisch ©2003:** pages 62 & 99. **Angie Gray:** page 180. **Paul Haggard:** pages 149, 235 & 241. **Andrew Lepley:** pages 1, 33, 43, 53, 62, 69, 75, 107, 115, 123, 131, 139, 157, 187, 249, 259 & 265. © **Jeffrey Mayer / Star File:** page 164. **Ken Settle:** pages 172, 201, 215 & 227. **Neil Zlozower:** page 90.

Index

WHEN IT COMES TO THE BASS, WE WROTE THE BOOK.

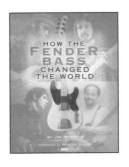